New Masters of Fla

TOMASZ JANKOWSKI
TODD PURGASON
IVO VAN DE GRIFT
LUKE TURNER, thevoid new media°
ANDRIES ODENDAAL
ERIC JORDAN
MANUEL CLEMENT
BRENDAN DAWES
TONY KE

friendsof

DESIGNER TO DESIGNER™

New Masters of Flash

friendsof

DESIGNER TO DESIGNER™

Published by friends of ED Ltd. 30 Lincoln Road, Olton, Birmingham. B27 6PA
Printed in Canada
ISBN 1-903450-03-9

Credits

Authors

Tomasz Jankowski
Todd Purgason
Ivo van de Grift
Luke Turner, the**void** new media°
Andries Odendaal
Eric Jordan
Manuel Clement
Brendan Dawes
Tony Ke
Irene Chan
Yugo Nakamura
Jayson Singe
cut-and-paste.com
Olivier Besson
James Paterson
Vince Suriani
Joel Baumann, Tomato
Yasuto Suga
Joshua Davis

Flash Consultant

Sham Bhangal

Copyright Research

Louise Carr

Translators

Dominic Lowe
Rachel Earnshaw
Bill Sharp

Editors

Mel Orgee
Eleanor Baylis

Graphic Editor

Deborah Murray

Technical Reviewers

Brian Donnelly
Leon Cych
Dan Maharry
Jake Smith
Thomas Wang
Kristian Besley
Kevin Sutherland

Proof Readers

Joel Rushton
Carmen Orgee
Marianna Plater
Elley Reinhart
Matthew Knight

Index

Martin Brooks
Andrew Criddle
Alessandro Ansa
Adrian Axinte

CONTENTS

CONTENTS

This book was conceived in February 2000. The plan from the start has been to provide two books in one — a book of highly individual essays about design, and alongside it a compendium of well-paced, advanced tutorials in the art of Flash design pushed to the edge. These two books we've interpolated, chapter by chapter, so that the author of each essay, after talking about their influences and design vision, their inspirations and intentions ("all the arty bollox" as Brendan Dawes so succinctly described it when we first called him) then moves directly into professor mode and shows exactly how you can create the effects they've pioneered and refined.

So is it a book to read from cover-to-cover or a volume of reference and inspiration for dipping in and out of? Well naturally it's both. But there's also a third way you can juice the material within these covers.

Enter Sham Bhangal, household god at friends of ED, and consultant throughout this project. He's written a topic map (see opposite) of the New Masters of Flash, grouping chapters thematically and explaining how you can carry on with a particular subject thread by jumping across to related chapters. It could almost be a case-study in how hypertext can't be made to work in print but Deborah has also laid the book out so that the tutorial sections follow a uniform pattern and color-scheme, making it easier to move from one technical section to another.

One last thing. Extending and souping up Flash design to yet higher realms of fantasy and wild interactivity seems to be accelerating by the day. If you want to nominate yourself or someone else for consideration as a writer/contributor on the next volume of New Masters of Flash, please get in touch with us through the website. We'd also like to say here that for reasons of space and time (i.e. pagecount and deadlines) some of our favourite New Masters had to be iced at unforeseen stages in the edit process.

We're looking forward to them flashing brighter still in the next edition.

Topic Map

Zen and the Art of Flash

Words of wisdom from the masters are always a good start to any journey. Jayson Singe (12), Tomasz Jankowski (1) and Yugo Nakamura (11) are amongst our first batch of Flash philosophers. You may not find yourself, but perhaps you will find their thoughts sending your creativity down new paths.

Use of Basic Flash Tools

the**void** (4) provide an introduction to the creative use of tweening and timeline animation. Tomasz Jankowski (1) shows how Flash's drawing tools can be used to create subtle colors and hues, as well as touching on other effects such as masking. Tony Ke (9) teaches how to handle bitmaps and vectors, and shows their relative advantages via practical examples. The cut-and-paste (13) chapter gives a good introduction to basic ActionScripting, and its integration within the overall website design. Brendan Dawes (8) explains how to use the new ActionScripting window in 'Normal mode' to build up scripting commands.

Animation

Compare and contrast the**void**'s offering (4) above with Irene Chan's 'rainfall' text effect (10). Additionally, Irene's use of alpha and colour animation tweens is used to create some slick cinematic style transition effects. Yasuto Suga (18) shows how simple animation techniques can produce eye-catching effects. Just add creativity. For those of you who already know tween based animation and want to start looking to using ActionScript to free you from the fixed linearity of the timeline, Jayson Singe (12) is a good starting point.

Sound

Todd Purgason (2) of Juxt Design shows how to create, import and use sound to spice up your web presence.

Advanced ActionScripting

For simulating real world physics via ActionScripting, try Olivier Besson (14). Andries Odendaal (5) is your man for real time script-driven 3D. Many cutting edge Flash interfaces require ActionScripting as a major ingredient. Ivo van der Grift (3) and Brendan Dawes (8) provide a good transition towards the more complex ActionScript-driven visual effects, and Yugo Nakamura (11) shows how to create effects using ActionScripting alone.

Advanced Flash Movie Structures

Eric Jordan's chapter (6) provides a good introduction to load/unload technique, showing how it can be used to reduce initial download time, and also how it can be integrated into a website's design. Once you have digested this technique, move on to Jayson Singe (12), who expands it to show how multiple .swf files can begin to communicate with each other. The advanced use of multiple movies and timelines, all talking to each other, is introduced gently by Manuel Clement (7) (taking a break from his usual role as 3D guru), and driven to its ultimate, ActionScript-laden conclusion by James Paterson (15).

Flash Integration

Irene Chan's use of Photoshop (10) in her Flash-based art is a good first port of call, showing how Flash can be used with external graphic design tools to ease the creative flow. Joel Baumann (17) showers us with the more technical side of integration, as his use of Director and Flash take multimedia presentation onto the next level. Why squabble over which of these two applications is the better when you can have them both?

3D

Simple can look deceptively complex when used creatively, and Tony Ke (9) shows how you can create the illusion of 3D animation using uncomplicated 2D timeline based transitions. Andries Odendaal (5) is the Flash master of Cartesian geometry, the system that is at the heart of real-time 3D. Vince Suriani (16) shows how pre-rendered Swift3D graphics can be integrated with Flash to produce the illusion of solid 3D shapes. Finally for truly inspirational 3D, Manuel Clement (7) has it all.

Finally, Joshua Davis is Joshua Davis (Outro) and the world would be a sad old place without him.

Tomasz Jankowski

Tomasz Jankowski, best known for Mondo.com and BlueMondo.com, spent seven years working as a graphic designer and art director in advertising before turning to the web three years ago. In his work, Tomasz specializes in sound and script, exploring the relationship between sound and animation on the web.

Todd Purgason

Todd Purgason is the Creative Director for Juxt Interactive, a Web design shop specializing in Internet strategy and Flash-centric interactive websites. Todd has led the Juxt design team in creating work that has been cited in several web and print publications, and his own work has received numerous awards. Todd was also recently nominated among the top six web designers selected by El Pais, Spain's leading news publication, and speaks regularly on interactive web design.

Ivo van de Grift

Since he was a small boy Ivo has spent a lot of his time drawing and painting cartoon-figures. He got his first home computer when he was twelve and went on to be classically trained at the School of the Arts in Arnhem. There he discovered a new medium: the Internet. He bought a PC and started work, and then he discovered Flash 3. He was so taken with Flash he incorporated it into his final year exams. Fortunately one or two of his teachers were suitably encouraging, and on the back of this Ivo started his own web design business. Now, a few years and a lot of Flash design later, he feels his work is better described as interactive design or digital illustration.

Luke Turner, thevoid new media°

Luke Turner is the Founder and Creative Director of the**void** new media°. He has been a pioneer of innovative Flash animation and Flash 3D since his early experiments back in 1998, and has been featured in numerous publications from Computer Arts and Shift magazine, to the BAFTA (British Academy of Film and Television Arts) journal. the**void**'s fresh and design-oriented approach has attracted a number of high profile clients, including MTV Europe, Excite, Macromedia and UPS. Their success was highlighted at the Cool Site of the Year Awards in April 2000 where the**void**.co.uk received the Best Design site award.

Andries Odendaal

I completed a national fine arts diploma in printmaking and sculpture in the early 1990s, and went on to lecture in this area, specializing in sculpture and drawing. Then I went freelance, began dabbling in computer design, got interested in 3D animation and the multimedia industry, and eventually joined Wireframe Studio in 1998, where I could freely indulge my fascination with multimedia and get to grips with the applications I needed, like Flash. Today I work in studio production, specializing in Flash development.

About the Authors

Eric Jordan

I aim to manipulate technology in new and novel ways, to stimulate and engage the viewer's imagination, to shape the ultimate user experience. I currently work and extend my skillset at Design Insites in Laguna Beach, Ca. On my own site, 2advanced.com, I explore the possibilities of web experience. I try to push the envelope of current technology and develop and shape online experience – and have been enormously encouraged by the site's nomination for the Best Interface award at the FlashForward2000 conference in San Francisco.

Manuel Clement

Manuel Clement is the man behind mano1.com. At 21, his clients range from GOOEY to Data Project, Florida's Department of Health to Jacques Chirac. His seven years of classical piano and music theory training have stood him in good stead for his music industry site OnlineDJ.com. Winner of two Macromedia SSOD awards in 1999, Manuel is passionate about design, technology and the future.

Brendan Dawes

Brendan is a freelance interactive designer and creator of the acclaimed Saul Bass website. His portfolio includes work for Disney, Kelloggs, Fox Kids and Coca-Cola. Winner of three Macromedia SSOD awards, Brendan has been featured in many industry publications and has spoken at new media seminars around the world, including FlashForward2000 in New York.

Tony Ke

A traditional artist as well as a new media designer, Tony Ke's work is unique on the web and has won numerous awards, including a Flash Kit award, Webmasters Design award and a Superior Graphic Award. Currently Tony works at Form Media, as well as being art director at KEICON (www.keicon.com) an online publication about new media exploration. When he's not immersed in media design, Tony spends his time training for kickboxing and submission fighting with world rank professional NHB fighters.

Irene Chan

After graduating in 1997 with a graphic design degree at Savannah College of Art and Design (US), Irene Chan started out as a web designer in Atlanta, Georgia. Eneri.net was launched in the summer of 1999, an award winning, experimental website that accentuates its primary themes of the personal and the feminine with rich Flash design.

Yugo Nakamura

Yugo Nakamura studied engineering, architecture and landscape design at university in Japan. After graduating he worked as an engineer specialising in bridge design. The global success of his MONO*crafts web project means he now works in interface design with Business Architects Inc in Tokyo. In July 2000 he presented his work to huge acclaim at FlashForward2000 in NYC.

Jayson Singe

Jayson Singe is a photojournalist and multimedia producer living in North Carolina. He started out as a photojournalist after graduating from the University of North Carolina in Chapel Hill in 1994 with degrees in psychology and photojournalism. He then began experimenting with Flash in order to create multimedia documentaries for the Web.

cut-and-paste.com

The cut-and-paste team is based in Dublin and is made up of Teri MCSherry, Aiden Grennell, Richard Assaf, Joanne Conlon, Paul Craig and Mark Hooper. Cut-and-paste.com is an independent lifestyle magazine which is in its first year of pushing the creative boundaries in both print and web design.

Olivier Besson

Olivier Besson originally trained as an engineer, although he harboured a passion for graphics and 2D and 3D animation. He joined a multimedia agency in 1995, where he learnt how to take a multimedia project from the point of initiation to completion. He left to go it alone as an independent designer, specializing in creating games and interactive animations using Flash. His Flashy Dancer (1998) took the web world by storm, and continues to amuse thousands of Internet users to date. Today, he co-directs a content production company (GlobZ.com) based in Paris.

James Paterson

James Paterson studied Fine Art at a few different schools, did a lot of life drawing, and was spurred to learn Flash thanks to the influence of one Martin Spellerberg, (www.empty.com, www.0003.org). Over the past three years James has done so much fiddling with Flash that he has a big red callous on his right wrist that hurts when he puts his hand on tables, and looks really sore. In return for this horrid red callous he has developed a style unlike anyone else's. Along with Robbie Cameron and Eric Jensen (Cheetah head and Beard Head), James works on Presstube.com every spare minute he has. Presstube is the best website in the universe and just because it didn't win anything at FlashForward doesn't mean that it is not far cooler than Praystation, Volume One or ExtraLucky. James' number one wish in life is to go back in time and steal everyone else's cool Flash ideas (maybe a few AC/DC songs too), and do them first. James Paterson is a British born Canadian, and currently lives in NYC. Please send him money for his dream computer. He will mention you on television when he is famous if you do.

About the Authors

Vince Suriani

Vince is responsible for all of WackedUSA.com, some of BeyondMedia.com, co-moderating the 3D forum on FlashKit.com and several articles on 3D at Flashzone.com. He was nominated for best 3D site at the 2000 Flash Film Festival, and spoke at the FlashForward2000 NYC show. Having exhausted himself flitting from job to job and client to client, Vince has finally settled down at BeyondMedia.com, beta testing, reviewing and writing in his out of office hours. On a more personal note, Vince doesn't have any peeves. He tells us that he doesn't think peeves should be kept as pets. He says they should be allowed to roam free on the rolling planes of Montana. His interests include apathy - he says he's turned it into an Art Form - and his favorite Chinese dish is General Tsao's chicken, because he likes to say General Tsao.

Joel Baumann

I was born in the year a man walked on the moon, allegedly, and about which Serge Gainsbourg wrote that song, "69 Année Érotique". This happened in Bogota, Colombia although, as we left when I was two, I don't have any recollection about that either. The only thing I do know is that my passport is checked every time I go through customs. Funny that. I got my first computer when I was 14. It was an Apple IIe. Unlike many, I have absolutely no nostalgia about my first computer. It was grey. I learned to communicate with it, and then it took up residence in the corner of my room.... Ten years later I came across another computer, at University, and boom!!!! It's been a ball.

Yasuto Suga

Yasuto Suga was born in Japan, but was raised in the United States for most of his life, and currently lives in Los Angeles. He has always enjoyed art and visual stimulation, and began drawing and sketching very early on. Although he went to the University of Southern California with the intention of becoming an architect he quickly changed direction and studied fine art instead. In his work, Yasuto aims to capture and portray feelings, emotions, and experiences through a number of different mediums and he now employs his fine art skills on the web, creating famously rich and elaborate sites. He has high hopes for new and developing technologies, believing that they will enable designers to express their creativity more freely.

Joshua Davis

Joshua Davis runs www.praystation.com as a one-man research and development web site. Its objective is to apply design and technology in a collection of small, sometimes daily, modules where the common rule is to deviate from the common rule, to produce something that's not easily classified in a world that is in constant flux. He is also the sole creator of www.once-upon-a-forest.com, which is the nemesis of what we perceive the web to be. No easy, short domain name. No easy to use navigation. No instructions. No FAQs. No Ads, No Links, No Tech Support. No Help. No Answers. A good amount of time is spent trying to unite, communicate and explore on www.dreamless.org. but, when the sun rises, clients come to him at Kioken, (www.kioken.com) because they want an 'out of the box' experience.

" ... I like to think of my Flash designs
as sort of digital happenings, hovering in the
space between browser and real world."

TOMASZ JANKOWSKI
www.mondo.com.pl

Shadow

Salvador Dali, *Hallucinogenic Toreador*, 1969 - 70

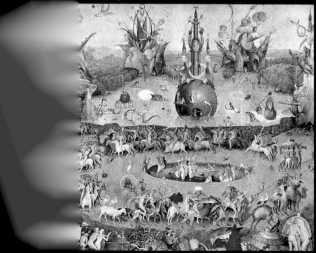

Garden of Earthly Delights, Hieronymous Bosch

I do miss the scent of oil paint and varnish. I made my first impressions as an artist on canvas, in charcoal and paints; abstract memories from my childhood depicted in vast, surrealist landscapes.

Modern day visionary Salvador Dali and the old master Hieronymus Bosch have both been strong influences on my work as it has evolved around the theme of the elements: wind, water, fire and earth, and predominantly the harmony of light and shadow that these elements create together.

Tomasz Jankowski

My turn towards digital art has been a long and gradual one. I began by scanning in and adapting my existing drawings, graduated to using a tablet and spent hours in front of the monitor, developing ways to express myself graphically. I took on work with an ad agency, which brought about my first encounter with new media.

As my medium changed, the fascination I have with the elements of light and shadow stayed the same and was given a new perspective when I discovered 3D imaging packages. My views on art and design entwined and evolved, taking new direction.

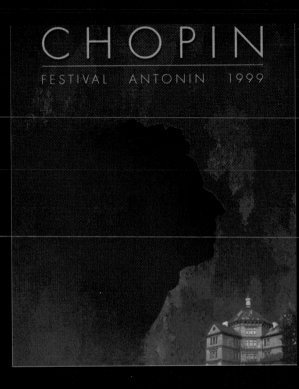

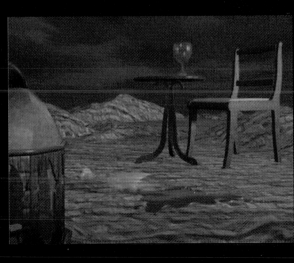

Shadow

I quit the ad agency to give myself the freedom to delve deeper into my abstract visions. I was driven by the need to search out and develop my own artwork style, my own approach to digital media. Freelance work allowed me the space to build surrealistic virtual worlds from scratch and to redefine my approach to the way light and shadow work together.

New dimensions were added to the elements that form the overriding definition of my work, dimensions that shaped the pictures in my head coming from Tolkien, Herbert, Asimov, Williams, and movie visionaries Lang, Kubrick, Scott, Lynch, Gilliam and Oshii.

© Bettmann/CORBIS

Tomasz Jankowski

Then came photography, and particularly portraiture. I had always shot lots of film, but seemingly without proper direction. I was simply documenting the reality around me. Merging my graphic design skills and knowledge together with real world pictures created by camera, I could add another flavor to my artwork. I always tried, and still do, to open up the lines of communication with my models, and to make sure that they feel natural within their environment. Once they are settled, I have a playground in which to explore variations of harmony between light and shadow, and the impact they have on the subject of the piece. At that time, photography began to occupy more and more space in my design work and I started experimenting with complex collages using all sorts of digital graphic forms and photos.

At last I felt I had found my equilibrium – pure creation, without boundaries. I began to live and breathe design. Everything that had ever happened to me found reflection in my digital artwork, and every influence left its mark: literature – the vast, dangerous and beautiful world of Tad Williams' *Otherland* network; art – the twisted biomechanical forms of H.R. Giger and rough lines drawn by Moebius; music – the jazz/electronica soundscapes of Jimpster and Kosma, ambient, drum-n-bass worlds of Audio Lotion, surrealistic sound passages of ProjeKct Two. Every medium was merging together.

Shadow

As ever, the same two basic elements of light and shadow formed a theme for all the art I produced with every tool I picked up. Still, though, I was lacking a proper outlet for my work. Then I had a stroke of fortune. I began working as a reporter for one of the Polish photo/press agencies. During some research I opened a browser for the very first time and discovered surfing the Web. Gradually the memories of oil and varnish began to fade.

I found myself exposed to the Internet all day, every day. This was about two years ago when having an e-mail address was a sign of highlife in my country. I set up a company/design studio called MONDO. I don't remember where the name comes from – I just liked the sound of it: I felt that it had a global feel. MONDO Design is still a freelance project and I'm owner, graphic designer, painter and photographer.

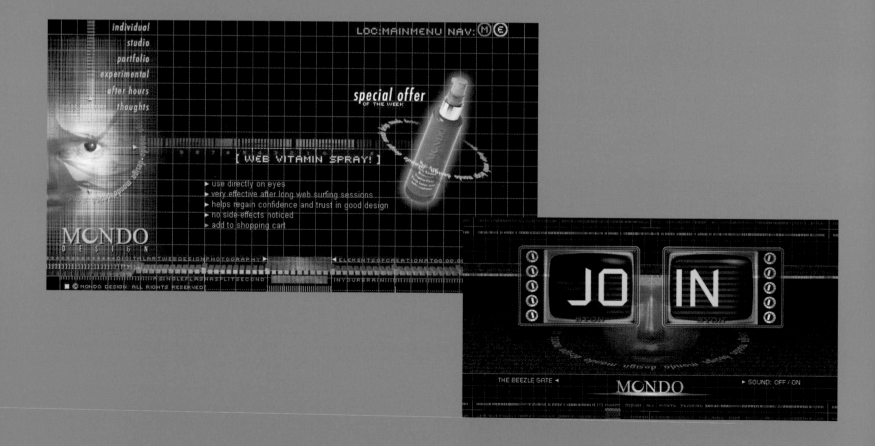

Tomasz Jankowski

In the early stages of MONDO, I designed simple self-promotion projects; simple web pages that looked more like print layouts than fully functional web sites. I worked on it in my spare time and put together an online portfolio called Bizarre Illumination Pages, later renamed Mondo Bizarre. I put it together for fun. It wasn't intended as a serious company portfolio – at that time I hadn't really noticed the power of the Internet. Slowly, however, it began to attract people's attention and some job offers arrived. I stopped working on conventional print design in favor of developing new forms of web graphics. I'd finally found the proper medium and outlet for my artwork. I dedicated myself totally to the Web and focused on creating my online portfolio in earnest.

The design of the web site itself was, at that time, changing every week. I was very excited by the new possibilities of graphic expression, especially animation (no more than simple .gifs at that time) and interactivity. I simply don't know how many design reincarnations MONDO has gone through, but from the very beginning it was permeated with black. I've always liked its mysterious characteristic, and a black void provides a great backdrop for experimenting with light and shadow. There was one exception: one day I designed a white, mirror-like MONDO web site, and the response was instant – an awful lot of people wanted to know why I had created such un-MONDO-like design.

Shadow

The look and feel of today's MONDO (www.mondo.com.pl or www.mondo.pl) is the result of about a year's experience and experimentation, but, like all my web projects, it's in a state of constant change. At the time of writing it has a kind of industrial/technical/biomechanical style. Of course, the same influences and inspirations stand firm. Literature, art, music and film are part of the virtual worlds that I create on the net. Sometimes it's even enough to walk through the streets of my own town, observe the architecture, nature, the looks on people's faces – then Flash gets in on it and I know exactly what the next design will look like.

A lot of people find MONDO very personal and don't recognize it as a corporate design studio web site. I'm happy with that. My web site is the mirror of myself - everything I see and feel finds its way into the design, which is the main reason I create. To mix information from the outside world and convert it into 0-1 data stream. To mix different kinds of media and create new hybrid, graphic forms of expression.

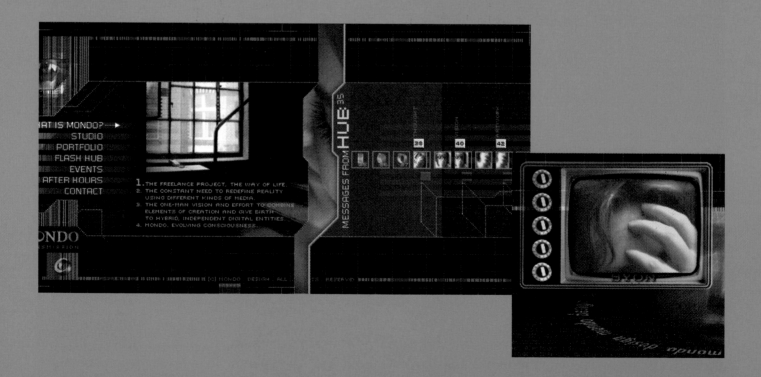

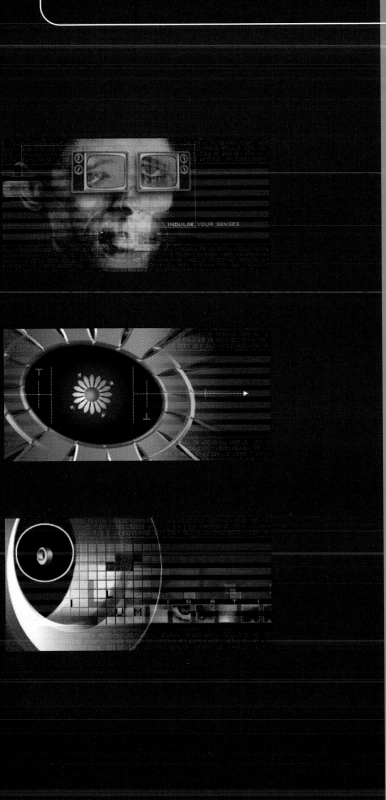

Tomasz Jankowski

On the other hand, some people recognize MONDO Design as a new media agency, so I receive resumes, CVs and requests for positions in my company. While I can't accommodate people there, because MONDO has always been and will remain a freelance project, my other site has an entirely different role to play in web design. I've called it blueMONDO Project (www.bluemondo.com or www.mondo.v.pl) and it's a kind of open happening. Every designer is welcomed.

The main objective of this project is to bring together different styles from different people, mix them together and bring out some freestyle, hybrid, animated form. Animated? Yes. The entire web site is designed using Flash, and will continue to be so. Which reminds me, I've finally got to the point - Flash!

One day I was browsing the net and accidentally popped in on a movie promotion web site, which offered me the choice between the html version and the Flash version. I had no idea what it was all about, so I entered the Flash version and my jaw dropped! Things were moving as if they belonged to a regular movie trailer. I watched the same animation over and over again. It was science fiction in action to me.

Shadow

Flash looked like everything I needed. Until that moment, all my visions and creative ideas materialized statically, although the ideas themselves were constantly moving and changing. The power of Flash allowed me to express myself through moving pictures, mimicking my own creative processes.

After a long battle with local software dealers, I finally managed to purchase Flash, version 3. Flash was virtually unheard of in my country at that time. When I asked about it in local software stores, people looked at me as if I was speaking a different language. I studied hard at tutorials for a week of sleepless nights, and then began work.

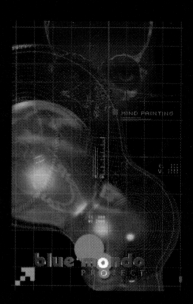

Tomasz Jankowski

My first animations were very simple vector objects, moving around the screen in a single timeline. Then I began to adapt static elements of my existing web site to the Flash environment. The results were quite satisfying, although my .swf files weren't optimized to run smoothly online. I realized that I wasn't ready to introduce my animations to the World Wide Web.

It took weeks of testing: adjusting frame parameters, optimizing bitmap elements and vector elements' curves, and combining all these aspects in the timeline. I started replacing parts of my web site with Flash substitutes. Again, the response was instant. Since Flash was pretty unknown in my country at that time,

my animations were a little bit of a sensation in the Polish web design community. Although they were very simple Flash solutions, I tried to use approaches other than the standard ones. Since my first encounter with Flash 3, I've tried to use the tools differently. I tried to approach the lessons I found in tutorials with my own ideas about building that certain effect. Maybe that's why viewers found my Flash presentations interesting. They were even plagiarized!

I've always tried to imitate the basic elements of nature in my animations, and I've found Flash to be the perfect tool for creating the things I'd always worked with: light and shadow in movement.

Shadow

My Flash animations are probably best described as streams of consciousness. Although I get some really heartwarming feedback from site visitors, saying that wandering through my site feels like an escape from everyday, from reality, I also get a myriad of questions that I simply can't answer. How did I put together that flare? Why did I use this color? What's the significance of that group of pixels? And so on. I don't have any answers because my Flash designs seem to come together of their own volition, like entities in their own right. I like to think of them as sort of digital happenings, hovering in the space between browser and real world.

Flash 4 brought with it a plethora of new possibilities, especially in terms of sound and script. When I was looking for design tools, it was simply the most flexible and platform-independent tool for creating interactive web animations that I could find. I began playing with the new sound compression capabilities (especially mp3 compression), coordinating the timelines of my animations and movie clips with sound effects and background music. The new expression this brought to my animations opened up a whole new design dimension to me. Six to eight months of animation and sound experimentation later, I found the flavor of my two primary Flash projects: MONDO Design and blueMONDO Project.

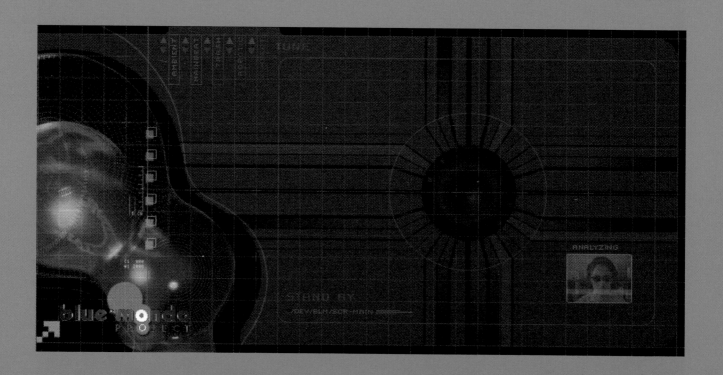

Tomasz Jankowski

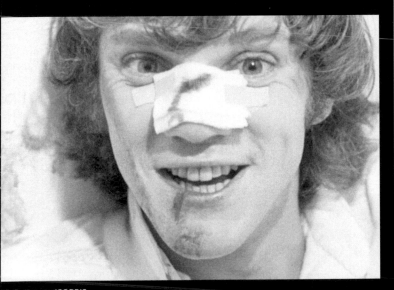

© Bettmann/CORBIS

Animation and sound have equal significance in my current work - I can't imagine creating Flash animations without sound now. When I was working on the introduction for blueMONDO Project I was inspired by Stanley Kubrick's film *A Clockwork Orange* to use fragments of classical music (if you've seen the film, recall Alex's visions brought about by Beethoven's *Ninth*). The dramatic impact was incredible! I promptly got a lot of feedback from viewers asking 'why?' again. It's experiences like these that keep me designing in Flash: people think, ask questions and learn something about themselves, while I learn about myself. As my Flash designs become more complex I've begun to use storyboards to help orientate me within the animation loops. Because I like to have complete control over all of it, I create everything myself: graphic 2D and 3D elements, sound loops and music. So far, I'm happy with the results that this produces.

So what is MONDO? Well, I think it's a state of mind, an evolving consciousness. A freelance project and a way of life. It's my effort to combine the elements of creation to give birth to hybrid, independent digital entities.

Shadow

In this section of my chapter, I'm going to focus on two of the effects I used on blueMONDO Project. They are both looped animations that play while the user chooses a topic from the menu: a glass sphere containing interactive elements and a background of circuit wires with a hollowed center, which doubles as the background for other menu items.

My idea for the glass sphere was that it should contain interactive elements that respond to user mouseovers. I wanted the contents to behave as if they were submerged in a glowing liquid, casting lights and shadows.

I'll start by creating the inner piece. This is a kind of blue flower made up of three petals with radial gradients and dots of light around the edges.

First, create a single petal and fill it with a radial gradient that is transparent from the inside.

Make three copies of it and rotate each petal until you get the look that you want. You should end up with a small flower that looks a little 3D because of the inside transparency of the petals.

Add the small dots of light around the edges of the flower by creating another radial gradient, going from white, through dark blue (similar to the single petal's gradient) to transparent black. The result should look like a small glowing star.

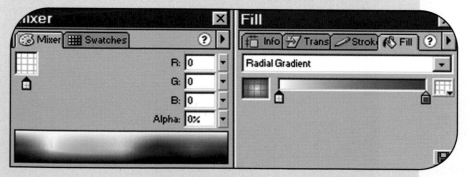

Now we're ready for some animation. I kept the flower invisible to begin with, then faded it onto the screen while enlarging and rotating it, and finally made it disappear again. Before you begin, make sure you've defined it as a graphic symbol. Then create a new movie clip and place the flower on the timeline.

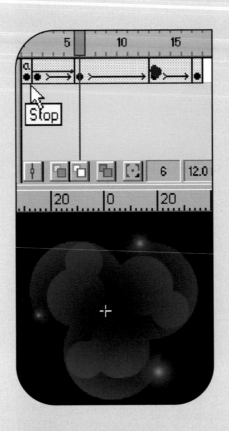

The movie clip depends upon a condition being set that will trigger the flower's movement. I used an invisible button for this, by first putting a simple graphic symbol in place. Set up a simple gray square, 25 by 25 pixels, go to Insert>New Symbol and select Button. Edit the button, putting the gray square graphic symbol in the Up action. Right-click on the square symbol. to go to Properties>Color Effect Set the Alpha effect to 0%, and you're done.

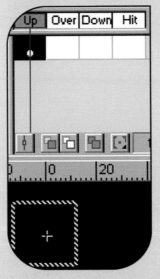

Shadow

Now go back to the movie clip you created earlier and put a button on frame 1. You need to assign an action to this button that will check whether the user has moved their mouse over it. I used the Stop action on frame 1 to prevent the clip from running by itself without the proper command. To place the Stop action, bring up the Frame Actions panel (you can do this easily by double-clicking any frame), select the frame and choose a Stop action from the left hand list (third one down in Basic Actions).

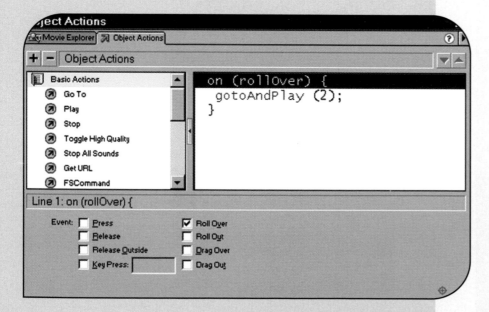

Right-click on the button on frame 1, choose Properties and click on the Actions tab. You need to set up a condition to stipulate that the timeline will jump to frame 2 and the flower animation should begin when the mouse moves over the button. The mouse cursor rolling off the button should bring the animation to a halt.

The flower animation will begin at frame 2. Insert keyframes at frames 2, 6, 13 and 17 using F6. Then create a motion tween between frames 2 and 6.

Go to the Frame Panel and choose Motion with Automatic rotation. Set the Easing parameter to 100% Out, to smooth the rotation of the flower. Set the same tweening properties between frames 6 and 13, and 13 and 17.

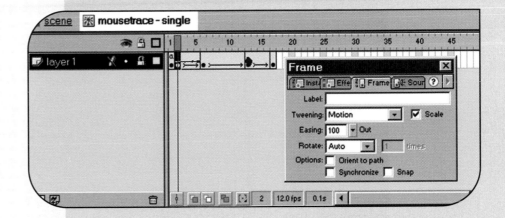

Go back to frame 2, click on the flower symbol on the stage and make it invisible. Right-click on the flower, choose Alpha on the Effect tab, and set the Alpha effect to 0%.

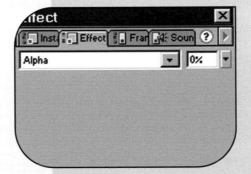

While you're there, decrease the size of the symbol to about 10% of the original. Now go to frame 6, click on the flower and rotate it about 45 degrees to the right. Go to frame 13 and rotate the symbol about 270 degrees to the left, while decreasing its size by about 10%. Finally in frame 17 increase the size of the symbol about 50% and set its Alpha to 0% again. The animation is ready. The flower will rotate while changing in size and visibility.

Shadow

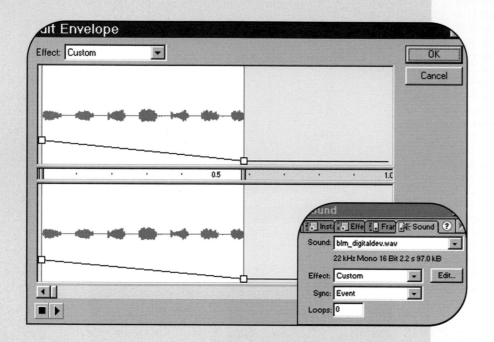

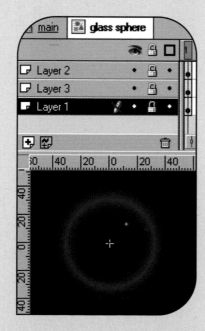

The next thing to add is some sound. I used the same layer for graphics and sound. (Although it's commonly accepted that everything should be put on different layers, I find that using as few layers as possible makes my animation smoother. I always try to put sound on an existing layer.) The first sound plays while the flower becomes visible, and the second as it fades away again. To import sound files (.wav or .aiff) into the Flash environment choose File/Import and select the sound file you have pre-prepared. To add the sound, right-click on frame 2, choose Properties and click on the Sound tab. Adjust the sliders to get the volume and length of the sound you want. In this case, the sound is fading away while the flower is growing. Experiment with sound lengths and volumes to suit your needs.

So we're finished with the basic element. Now we need to create the environment for the flower. We'll put this interactive flower into a glass sphere. In fact, we'll put a lot of them inside, but first let's create the sphere itself. The best way is to render/raytrace the glass sphere in some good 3D software - you'll be able to define the colors later in the Flash environment. I made my sphere up of three different radial gradients, adding a bit of glow to the edge. You will need to experiment with different gradients and setups until you're happy with it.

Now we have all the components we need to create a fully functional interactive sphere with animated content. Let's start by creating the movie clip that will contain all these components (Insert>New Symbol>Movie Clip). The movie clip consists of four layers and four distinct symbols defined on them. The first layer, **glass sphere** contains the glass sphere that we created a moment ago.

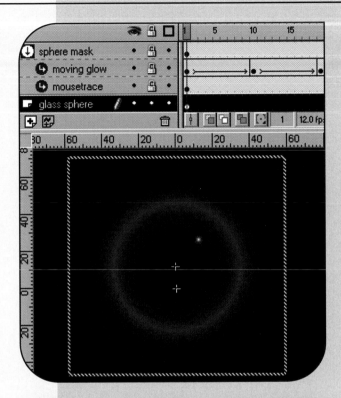

The second layer, **mousetrace**, is the most important one: it contains several of the copied movie clips that we created earlier. As you remember, these movie clips contain a condition check to ascertain whether the user is moving the mouse over them. I put a lot of these clips in a small sphere shaped space so that it would look like the flower entities were melting together in some liquid. You'll need to vary these clips in size in order to add depth and shadow and to create the sense of perspective inside the sphere environment (smaller on the outside, bigger at the center).

Once you're happy with the positions of all clips, group them (Modify>Group) and define as a new object (Insert>Convert to Symbol). As you'll see, this becomes important as we finish creating the clip.

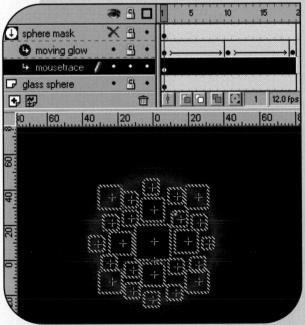

Shadow

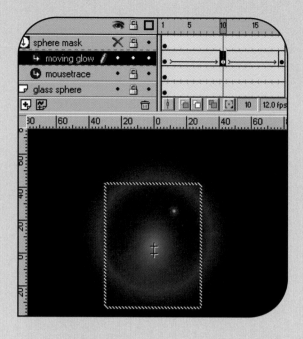

The next layer is a sort of **moving glow** that adds some light source to the whole animation. It might appear as a reflection on the glass sphere or as a glowing fluid inside it. The layer contains a simple radial gradient that is stretched a little bit vertically to fit better to the shape of the sphere. Next, it is animated through nineteen frames, using three basic keyframes. Frame 10 in the middle shows the 'light' gradient fully visible, while the two keyframes at the start and end of the timeline are transparent (using the Alpha effect). To animate this gradient, recall the tweening motion and color from what we did earlier.

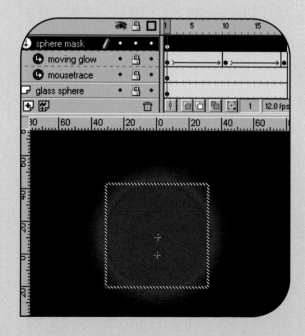

The last, topmost layer, is the **sphere mask** - a simple oval symbol but of great importance. This symbol is used as a mask for the two lower layers, moving glow and mousetrace. The reason for using the mask is simple: you don't want the elements placed inside the sphere to be visible outside it. To create the mask, first put the oval symbol on the first frame of the timeline. Make it a little smaller than the glass sphere on the first layer. Then right-click on the layer name and check the option Mask.

To make the two lower layers respond to the mask you've just created, you have to change their properties. Right-click on the layer's name and choose the option Properties. In the Layer Properties window check the option Masked. Do the same with the second layer. And that's it!

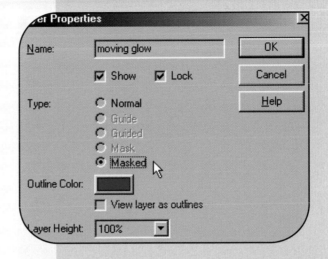

The interactive sphere with its animated content is ready. You can test it by using Control>Test Movie. You should see a reflective, glowing glass sphere, containing digital entities that melt together in some fluid and make noises when the viewer's mouse moves over it. Experiment with colors, the timeline settings (speed, time of reaction) and sound effects.

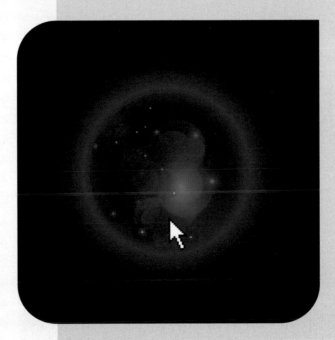

Shadow

Now, we can create a background for the 'full of life' sphere. The background to my blueMONDO Project also plays the role of menu screen. The main design element of the background is a basic gray circuit-like surface with a node at the center.

First I created the basic vector element using some other vector software. I sometimes find Flash graphic tools very inconvenient, particularly when I'm working with complex vector elements, something that I hope is going to improve with later Flash releases. I saved the vector element in .ai (Adobe Illustrator) format and imported it into Flash. To do this, create a new symbol (Insert>New Symbol>Graphic). Then, from the File menu choose Import.

As you may have noticed, this basic surface has different colors and gradients. To create this effect you have to separate the parts of the surface and assign the relevant color settings to them. Choose Modify>Break Apart and repeat until you can select a single part of the surface. Then use the Paint Bucket tool to set up the colors and gradients that you like. In this case I created different shades of gray and a gradient coming from gray and fading into transparent black. The circuit background is ready. Now, we have to prepare some elements which will simulate the electricity/electron movement inside the circuit.

Let's start by creating the basic light source. It's another radial gradient, which has some white and some light blue rings. Experiment with color settings to obtain the effect you want. In this case, the color of the gradient matches the other elements in the scene. Every symbol has different tints of blue, from very light to very dark, with different saturation. The gradient we've just created will spread the light behind the circuit surface.

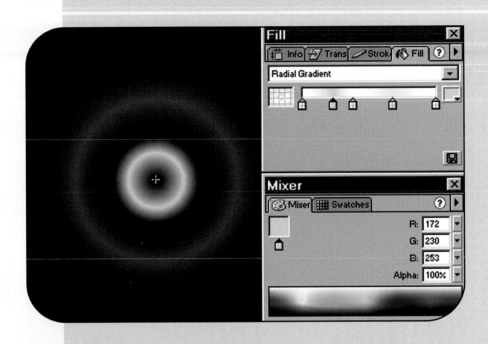

But the light should only be visible in the thin lines between the circuit's elements.

To build that effect we have to create another mask to control the spreading of the light. The important thing is that the mask must fit exactly the space between the circuit's elements. No more, no less. The best way to do that is to go back to the vector software where you created the basic gray surface (I used Macromedia Freehand) and invert the surface itself. You can also perform the Boolean operation with two elements: gray surface and some rectangles, and save the intersection of these two elements as the result. Save it in .ai format, import it into Flash and convert into a symbol. You should have something like what you see on the right as a result.

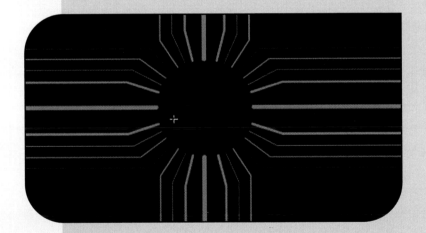

Shadow

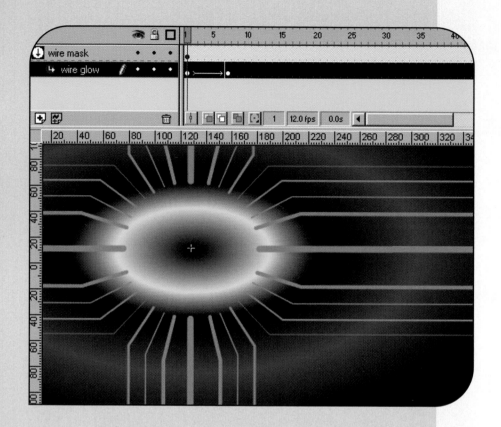

Now we have to create a movie clip that will combine the two elements we've just created: the light glow and the circuit wires. The movie clip will contain two layers. The first layer, **wire glow**, is occupied by the gradient. The second layer, **wire mask**, is the mask for this gradient. The layer with mask is static. No action or movement takes place there, it simply covers the whole timeline in the movie clip. The wire glow layer with the gradient, however, must be animated to simulate an electricity/electron flow. Put the gradient on the first frame of the layer, then go to frame 7 and press F6 (Insert Keyframe). Right-click between frames 1 and 7, choose Properties, and select the Tweening tab. Choose Motion without rotation. Set the Easing parameter to 100% Out. Now go to frame 1 again and increase the size of the gradient until it almost reaches the boundaries of the mask above. I also squashed mine a bit vertically.

When the movie clip starts to play, the oversized, squashed gradient will pop up into scene instantly, and, in about half a second, decrease in size and disappear behind the mask. The movement will be quick and it will simulate some light/electron flow. Now, we have to put the mask above the gradient. Put the symbol with the circuit wires on the timeline. Right click on the layer name and choose Mask. Go to the wire glow layer and right-click on the layer name. Choose Properties and, within this window, choose the Masked option.

The end result should look something like the picture you see here. There is one more important thing - the glow animation in this movie clip should be very quick in order to imitate the light behavior as accurately as possible (in this case, seven frames), but the timeline of the movie clip should be long enough to prevent the glow animation being repeated too frequently. It should, in fact, be long enough to be unobtrusive and not distract the viewer's sight too much - don't forget, this is only the background animation which plays in the movie while the system is waiting for the user's reaction. In this case, I used 127 frames, which means that after reaching this frame, the movie clip goes to the beginning and plays it again: a short 7-frame glow and then nothing until the 127th frame, then glow again.

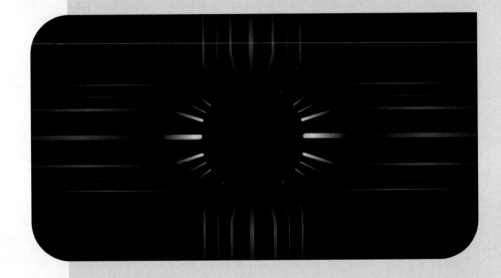

Shadow

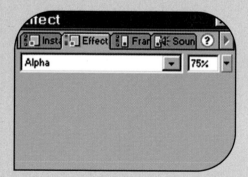

We have all three elements for our animation in the Flash movie: a glass sphere with the interactive content, an electronic circuit background and a light/electron animation for the background. The whole animation is placed in the last scene of the movie. The main goal was to create some movement and impression that the machinery works by itself. Of course, there are a lot of other graphic elements and movie clips which contribute to the mood. I'd like to show some techniques that can be used to imitate light and shadow behavior. The work is not, of course, finished. We have to combine all three elements in the scene and add some final touches and flavors.

As with the first layer of the movie, you can add some background images to make the overall scene look better. Remember, though, that it should cohere with the animated elements on the next layers. In my movie I used a background that I often use in my projects, a kind of grid with trace symbols. On the second layer you should place the circuit background symbol. The symbol is mostly opaque and it should merge with the basic background, so make it a little bit transparent by right-clicking on it, choosing Properties>Color Effect, and set the Alpha to 75%. The next layer should be the light/electron flow movie clip. Since it's masked and perfectly fits into the background circuit effect, it doesn't matter if it's above or below the background in terms of layer order.

The last layer contains the glass sphere. This will be placed in the node of the circuit background (the big circular hole in the middle of the circuit background symbol). Now, everything's set up and we can test the movie. The result should look something like these pictures.

You can experiment with size and intensity of colors to create more dramatic effects. When you're creating vector elements of the movie always remember to optimize them as much as possible, by choosing the Modify>Curves>Optimize option. Unless you want to deform the element totally, don't sacrifice the elements' shape over the smallest possible amount of the curves.

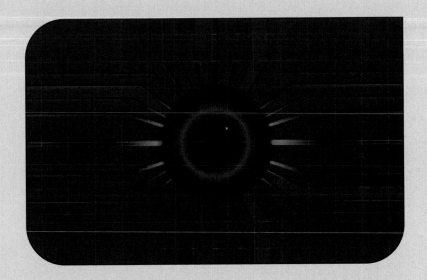

Well, that's it. I hope you've found my chapter interesting and now you know more about MONDO and the Flash techniques I use. When I look back at the MONDO Design and blueMONDO Project designs, I feel I should have changed a lot in them. I probably will someday. I think that's probably my obsession – the constant urge to improve and redefine existing project parts. At the same time, I'm thinking about new projects, new Flash experiments, new forms of redefining reality around me. It seems like since my childhood I've been wanting to express myself through different kinds of graphic forms. And I think this urge, this search for new forms of expression will accompany me 'till the very end...whatever that means.

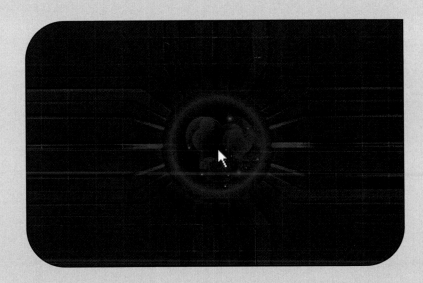

" We are surrounded with layers of visual drama in nature, in erosion, in progress or even in the Net. Capturing these things at just the right moment when I'm driving down the road or walking into a store provides the roots of my inspiration."

TODD PURGASON
www.juxtinteractive.com

Effect

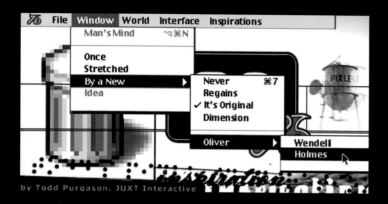

by Todd Purgason, JUXT Interactive

by Todd Purgason, JUXT Interactive

I am the creative director of Juxt Interactive, a web design firm based in Southern California. Although I'm not a trained musician, my main responsibility is developing the sound for the majority of the projects developed at Juxt. In my five years of web design experience, I have led JUXT Interactive's creative team in building intelligent and engaging experiential web projects. Given this background, I'm going to write here about the relationship between sound and design. This is a partnership that is becoming increasingly important with the advent of Flash 5 and the more involved design goals that the community is striving towards.

For me, inspiration is less a thing to point a finger at and more a process of looking at the world. I did an entire project on this concept of looking at things around me for www.bornmag.com, called OS76, www.juxtinteractive.com/os76.

I'm inspired by things that I see; things that might at first appear ordinary, but which trigger off different ideas, depending on my state of mind when I see them. I look for humor, irony, irrationality and joy in the way the world presents itself to me. I may be looking at a billboard showing dirty laundry, and be struck by the juxtaposition of a well-tanned woman in a BMW convertible pulling up to wait at a stop sign directly beneath it. I'll see an old steel barn that has rusted and collapsed and been overtaken by the growth that it originally crushed seventy years ago. Or it may simply be the way a shadow is cast from a fire escape onto the brick wall beyond. We are surrounded with layers of visual drama in nature, in erosion, in progress or even on the Net. Seeing these things at just the right moment when I'm driving down the road or walking into a store, for me, provides the roots of my inspiration.

Todd Purgason

I also love seeing and experiencing other people's creativity, just for the sheer joy and beauty of what creative thought and different perspectives can produce. Like everyone, I learn the names of those who do this well and seek out their work for more joy. In architecture, I love the work of Frank Ghery, Zaha Hadid, Morphisis, and in art David Hockney, Henry Matisse, Pablo Picasso and Keith Harring. Saul Bass and Kyle Cooper inspire me with their films, and designers David Carson, Carlos Suegra, and Stephen Segmister continually produce works that amaze me.

Of course, my work is always affected by the designs that I see around me within the web community, particularly from M.A.D., my good friend Hillman Curtis, Brad Johnson, Josh Ulm and all the designers within this book. But, most of all, the creativity that blows my mind is that of God. I look around at the world I live in and see the vast gap between the crudeness of the most extravagant thing that man has ventured to create and the amazing balance of complexity and simplicity that exists in even the smallest thing in nature. A simple flower like the one I used in the JUXT identity is an achievement in both visual and functional design that all humankind will never surpass. This inspires me, but also keeps my perspective: I know that everything I create can and eventually will be thrown away, so I shouldn't take myself as seriously as, sometimes, I'm tempted to.

Arlington Road
© Kyle Cooper, Imaginary Forces

Mission Impossible
© Kyle Cooper, Imaginary Forces

Effect

The Relationship between Sound and Design

What I'd like to do in this chapter is to share some knowledge and strategies that might help you to develop and implement effective sound design within your Flash projects. I personally couldn't carry a note and have absolutely zero rhythm. However, I do know how to cast a mood with design, and how to use various sound tools to create and employ sound that reinforces the design intent of the experiences we create. To me, sound is one of the most crucial elements of an interactive experience.

The principle challenge to creating effective sound for the Web comes from the limited bandwidth environment and not necessarily Flash itself. Although Flash offers numerous compression methods for audio, there is no changing the fact that sound files are large. The complexity of sound and duration both increase file size.

There are two basic sound types in Flash: **Event sounds** and **Stream sounds**. The event method involves importing a handful of sounds that you loop or use in conjunction with certain events in the Flash movie that trigger that sound to play. The event can be a frame or a user interaction, for instance a mouseover. The streaming method basically allows you to have a long continuous soundtrack that streams into the files as it plays.

Now that we have established the importance of sound and types of sound, let's get to the heart of the matter: where do you get the right sound or sounds for the job? There are four options: you buy it, build it, download it or steal it. I strongly discourage you from stealing your sound source, particularly as I've had artwork stolen and re-used on the Web. So, that really leaves us with three options.

The easiest way to get sound is to download it from free sound resource sites on the Web. This is great for learning, but, you might find that your clients aren't too happy if they find the sound on their site also on several other online projects, they might feel it cheapens or marrs their reputation. The next option is to buy your sound either through a stock resource or from a professional. Stock sound is sometimes very useful and of decent quality for sound effects and certain event sounds. However, it does put you in a similar situation as the free download sound. You have no guarantee that some really cheesy site won't be using that same sound, thus undermining your client's brand, and what happens if their biggest competitor uses the same sound?

If you can't make your own sound, the best option for you and your client is to go to a professional who will build the sound that your project needs to match the quality and originality of the experience you are creating visually. There are a vast number of very talented sound composers out there doing custom sound for multimedia and Flash projects. A good professional can look at your storyboard or prototype along with a creative brief and come up with sound source that matches the mood you're trying to generate. One guy I recommend is Joshua Jancourtz (jjancourtz@earthlink.net). You could also take a look at www.endekks.com.

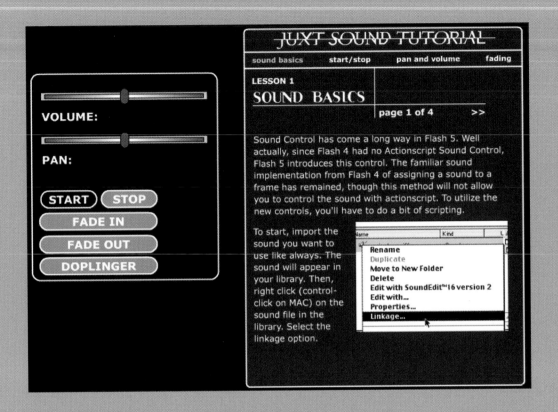

JUXT SOUND TUTORIAL

sound basics　　　start/stop　　　pan and volume　　　fading

VOLUME:

PAN:

START   STOP
FADE IN
FADE OUT
DOPLINGER

LESSON 1

SOUND BASICS

page 1 of 4　　　>>

Sound Control has come a long way in Flash 5. Well actually, since Flash 4 had no Actionscript Sound Control, Flash 5 introduces this control. The familiar sound implementation from Flash 4 of assigning a sound to a frame has remained, though this method will not allow you to control the sound with actionscript. To utilize the new controls, you'll have to do a bit of scripting.

To start, import the sound you want to use like always. The sound will appear in your library. Then, right click (control-click on MAC) on the sound file in the library. Select the linkage option.

Name	Kind	L

Rename
Duplicate
Move to New Folder
Delete
Edit with SoundEdit™16 version 2
Edit with...
Properties...
Linkage...

Sound Mixing Applications

If you can't afford a professional, hate cheesy stock sound and don't have a background in music, fear not. It's for you that I'm writing this chapter. That's the category that I fell into when I started with Flash. Since the beginning, I've found a handful of applications and techniques that have allowed me as a Flash designer on a project to score sound tracks efficiently and effectively, and still enjoy every second in the process. In this role, I see myself as a kind of film director: he may not know exactly what score a piece needs but he knows the mood that it needs to carry and can come up with starting points to get that mood expressed. He works with the composer and, when the sound is right, they know it.

I'm going to briefly show you four sound generation tools: Rebirth, from Propellerheads in Sweden; Sonic Foundry's Acid; Mix Man and Groovemaker. After these, I'll show you one editing app, Sound Edit 16 (which is very similar to Sound Forge if you're a PC user). As a whole book could be devoted to this one topic, it's not my intent to show you how to use these apps. Rather, I'll discuss what they're each capable of and add a little information that can guide you to choose the best for your work. For my demo, I will generate some quick sounds in Groovemaker and edit them for optimized performance in Sound Edit 16.

Effect

Rebirth

Rebirth is a software synthesizer that emulates a hardware platform, including two synths and a drum machine. Musicians, movie composers, DJs and multimedia sound-smiths have used this tool across the world for several years. It has developed a reputation as one of the best tools in its class.

Just as in the world of traditional synthesizers, you build your composition by programming several tracks a single note at a time. Each track is made up of sixteen measures and you have eight tracks per synthesizer. It also has a drum machine that you can use just like standard drums, to customize your own sounds.

Mix Man

This fun little application lets you interactively build your sound files by attaching sound samples to up to sixteen keys that you play or lock on to create your piece. It comes with a number of samples from a range of genres and has made a lot of headway in the music industry. A demo version comes bundled with many music CDs and many artists have assembled some of their own songs into the Mix Man format for users to download and remix. It's a lot of fun and you can use it to create some interesting loops.

Todd Purgason

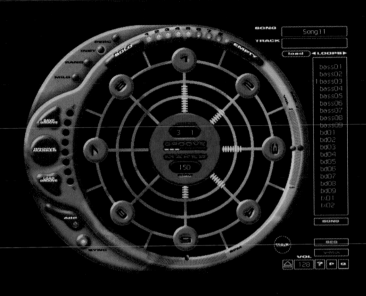

Groovemaker

Groovemaker is one of my favorites, if not for its freaky UI alone. It comes from Italy and has several disks of songs in the Groovemaker format for you to remix. Basically, Groovemaker breaks songs down to bass beats, drums, percussion, pads, etc. giving you sixty or so sounds that can be remixed into an eight-track environment. You can build several loops and mix them together with the sequencer to create an entire song. It also has this freaky player - I still don't know what it does, but it sure looks cool.

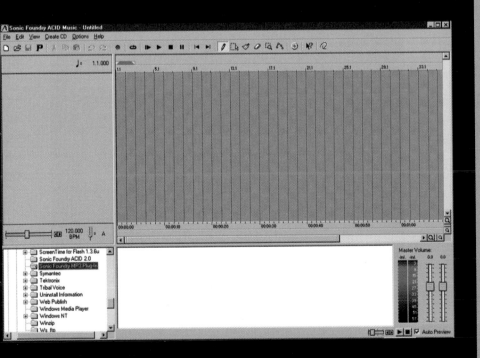

Acid

This is by far the most popular of all these tools and has become a kind of a de facto standard. It allows you to build a score by laying out samples in layers on a timeline. The sounds can blend and match the master time of the score automatically, and you can also apply a number of effects to the sounds. This is a very powerful tool and offers a lot, but it does come with a little learning curve and it takes time to build a loop that is just so. If you suck as a musician, it may be too much freedom

Acoustic

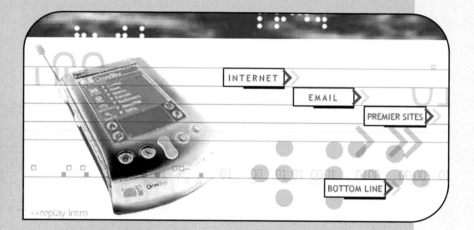

Building the Sound Loops

To show how to use loops and accent sounds in Flash, I'll use one of our recent projects, www.omniskywireless.com. For this, we created the sounds in GrooveMaker, optimized them in SoundEdit 16, then imported material into Flash and used the movie timeline to score the piece. As my intent is not to teach you every sound application inside and out, I'll walk you through the important steps of making the tight loops from the raw source and the Flash implementation.

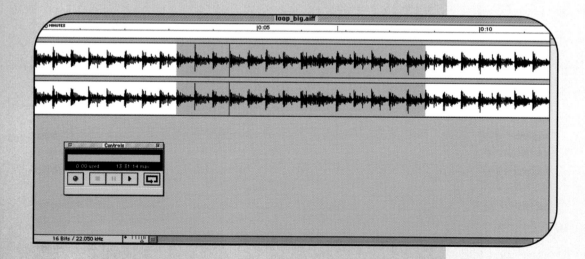

The loops I get out of GrooveMaker are great, except that they're each 12-16 seconds long, which is just too big. So, I open these loops in Sound Edit 16 and crop the sound down as small as I can get it. I usually try making one main loop around 2 - 6 seconds long.

First, open the large loop in SoundEdit 16 and select a shorter section within that loop that will loop fluidly.

Todd Purgason

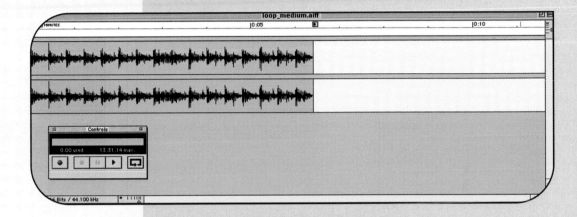

Now copy that section to the clipboard, create a new file, and paste the loop into the new file.

Now Select All and go the Xtras menu in option Loop Tuner. This allows you to step from the beginning of the loop to the end of the loop until you get the point where the sound wave connects perfectly. This will allow the sound to loop fluidly with no nasty cracks or pops.

Save the file in .aiff format, as a .a .wav file or as .mp3. Flash 5 imports them all.

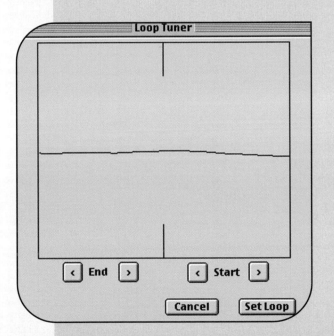

Acoustic

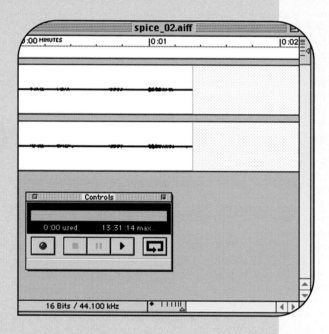

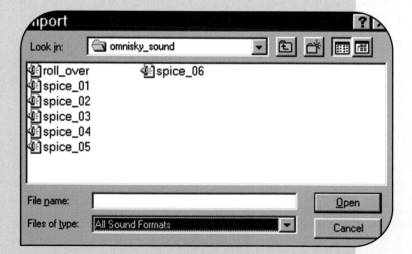

Now that you have a main loop, use the same method to create a handful of accent loops that should be simple effects, as small as you can make them. They can be percussion, drum and bass FX, or whatever. The idea is to add these sounds on top of the main loop to add depth to the sound experience and accent certain events within the Flash motion graphics. I try to make several sounds that are about one second in length and import them all. In the end, I'll experiment within Flash and narrow it down to just a few.

Creating the Score in Flash

Now that we have created our sound source files in Sound Edit 16, or another similar application, we can go into our Flash file and get to work. First we need to import all of our sound files into Flash.

You'll see here that I have exported as .aiff files. These are uncompressed because Flash will not load compressed .aiffs

Once I've imported the sounds into Flash, I go through and set the compression on each file individually. Typically, one format will work across the board but for some, accent sounds can be compressed to a higher degree and not be noticeable when the score is built. To do this, open the Library window and double-click on the sound. This will open the Sound Properties window, in which you can set the compression format on the sound, as I've done here.

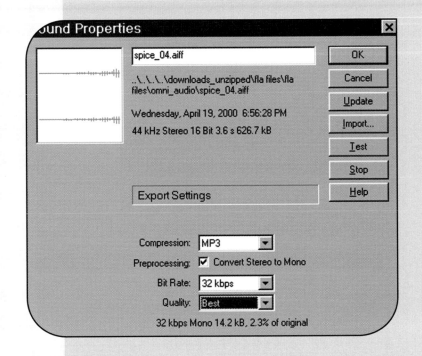

You can try different formats and test them, which allows you to hear the impact of the compression and see the resulting reduction in file size. I prefer to use MP3 compression to try and stay in the 24-32kbps range. But, for voice over and some effects, I'll go all the way down to 16kbps.

Before we build the score, let me first explain the four sync methods available in Flash: **Event**, **Start**, **Stop** and **Stream**. You select any of these from the sound panel Sync drop-down menu.

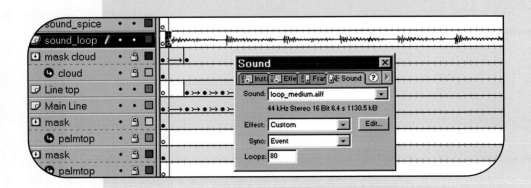

Acoustic

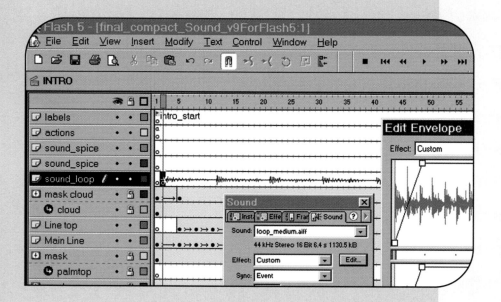

Event and Start

Event and Start are very similar. They basically call a sound to play on a frame. The difference is that, for the Start sync, the player will check to see whether this sound is already playing from a previous frame action. If it is, it won't play, thus preventing sound overlap. This is useful for long button sound effects, for which an overlap will sound like a mistake. Both Event and Start can be looped. The Stop sync will basically stop the playback of the selected sound. The Stream sync will stream in a sound and is the only method that you can use to sync frames to sound. This is great for voiceovers and very long sound files. If you use this method, you must be careful because the player will drop frames in order to keep the sound in sync with the playback. So, if your motion is complex and CPU intensive, on weaker CPUs the playback will be very choppy.

Now we're ready to build our score in Flash. Select the frame in which you wish the main loop to start playing, double-click and select the Sound tab in the Frame Properties window.

From the Sound pull-down menu, select your main loop and set the sync method to Event. Next, you need to set it to loop enough times to cover the full playback time of the Flash movie. Lastly, to prevent the sound from coming in too abruptly and sounding unnatural, you may want to have it fade in. Flash allows you to set any number of ease in and out points. For this, you just need to add a sound envelope. Click on the Edit button next to the Effect menu to bring up the Edit Envelope window. Simply click the sound volume line on either track, near the beginning of the sound loop. This will set a point in both tracks. Now pull down the point at the very beginning of the loop all the way to the bottom. Repeat this in the other track and we're all set.

Now that we have our main background loop running the length of the movie, we'll move through the movie and add accent sounds to key visual events that we want to emphasize with sound. We'll want to add a few more layers for sounds and then move down the timeline to the first event. We will add a keyframe in one of our sound layers and add one of our accent sounds as an Event sound.

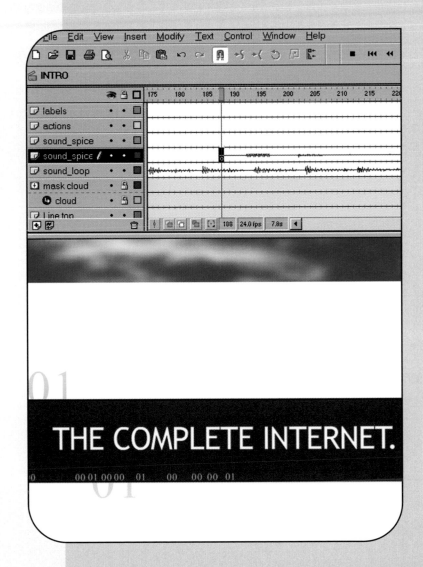

Acoustic

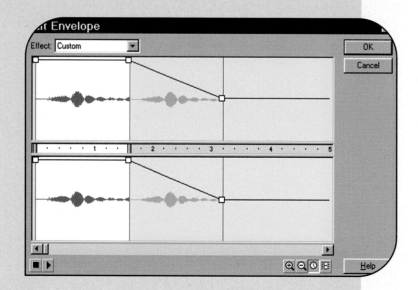

Move through the timeline of your file and look for opportunities to add impact to the key visual events in your movie. Once you have emphasized all the visual events in the project, you can test the movie and listen to the flow of the score. You should be testing to make sure the accent sounds work with the score and are effective in emphasizing the visual events of the movie. Going through this process will help you narrow down the sounds that are effective and add the right amount of depth. Next, listen to the project and note dull areas in which the loop seems to become redundant, or the visual attention wavers. Go into these weak spots and add some accents just to give depth to the piece. You can creatively fade in or loop and fade out accents that will add depth and keep the energy level at the right tempo for the piece.

Now, all we need to do is add sounds to user events, like buttons for example.

To add sound to a button, simply edit a button and add a keyframe to the over state, as I've done here with my Do It Now button. Then add a sound event to that frame. If you want a sound to play on a mouse click, add another keyframe to the down state and add a different sound there.

And that sums it up. We now have a beautifully scored Flash motion graphics piece that wraps our user into the experience that we've created. The real art of this process is building small loops that engage the user without becoming annoying throughout the duration of the piece. Creative use of accent sounds allows us to add depth to the main loop so that it remains fresh and engaging.

Acoustic

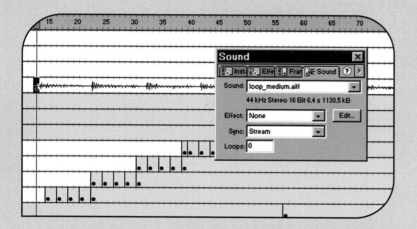

The other method of adding sound to a project is to add a Stream sound. This allows you to precisely sync the sound to the frames in the movie, which brings with it an upside and a downside. The advantages are that you can compose a dynamic sound score that has great depth and never gets old, as weak loops will. You can use the Stream option to precisely align visual events to sound events, making it a seamless experience. The disadvantages are that the files will command a large and continuous chunk of the bandwidth of your download. This will force you to be much lighter with the visuals you're using in the piece. Even more drastically, that Stream will force weaker CPUs to drop frames from a movie to keep the sound in sync with the visuals. The result is a movie that plays back with fluid audio but with visuals that may to jump and jitter. If you're creative about it, you can effectively employ streaming to create a rich and fluid project, but you'll have to approach it with a lot of self-control over what you'll try to acheive with the motion graphics.

Controlling Sound with ActionScripting

Next up to bat are the exciting advancements in sound control provided by Flash 5 actionScripting. Here, I hand the keyboard over to our lead ActionScripter at JUXT, Brian Drake. Brian is our senior Flash developer and an experienced musician with formal training in classical guitar. He has developed and scripted many of the projects developed by Juxt in the past year. He'll walk you through some simple but powerful techniques in Flash 5.

Sound control has come a long way in Flash 5. Actually, since Flash 4 had no ActionScript sound control at all, I guess we can say Flash 5 has made a quantum leap. The sound implementation that you'll be familiar with from Flash 4, i.e. assigning a sound to a frame, has remained, but, to utilize the new controls, you'll have to do a bit of scripting.

To start, import the sound you want to use. The sound will appear in your Library. Then, right-click/ctrl-click on the sound file in the Library. Select the Linkage option.

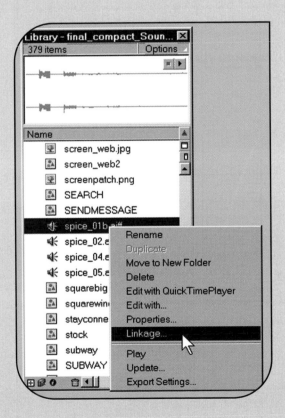

Acoustic

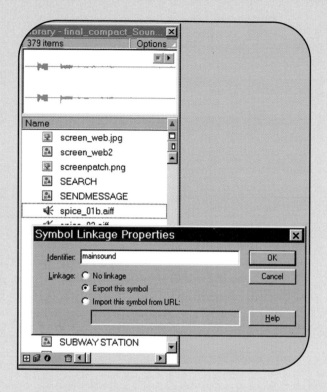

Now select Export this Symbol. This will cause the sound to be exported even though it's not 'used' in the file. Then give the sound an identifier name of **id** in the identifier field. This will be the instance name of the sound.

The next step is to create a variable to contain the sound. This can be anywhere in the movie depending on your need. We'll make it the first frame of the movie.

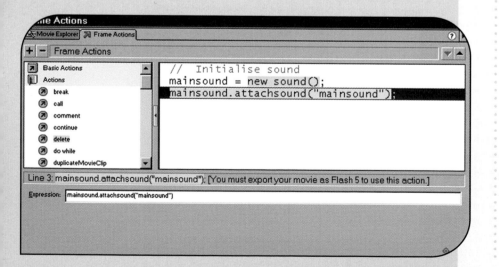

Click on the frame and open the ActionScript Editor. Start with a Set Variable action. The name you give the variable will be the name that's used to refer to the sound. Enter the value new Sound(). Flash will highlight the command in yellow to remind you this is a Flash 5 only command. Next, activate Expert mode in the ActionScript editor. Start a new line and type variable.attachSound(id). For the variable, enter the name of the variable that you've just created. id is the name you gave the sound in the linkage properties. It's a good idea to go back to Normal mode once you have done this to let Flash check your code.

This will attach the sound file to your variable. Now when you need to manipulate the sound, you will use the variable to reference the sound.

Start and Stop

Now we're going to control our sound by scripting it to start and stop. We'll start by assigning the action to a button. You can, of course, use these actions anywhere, but it will be easier to demonstrate on a button.Once you've created a button and have it selected, open the ActionScript editor and add an On action. Set this action to release. Then switch to Expert mode and type inbetween the curly braces of the On action:

variable.start(offset,loop);

variable is your sound name, offset is the number of seconds into the sound you want to start playing, and loop is the number of times it should loop.

WARNING: if you set an offset number, i.e. 10, the sound will start playing 10 seconds into the sound. If you have a loop, it will loop from that offset point.

To stop the sound, simply type variable.stop(), where again, variable is your sound name.

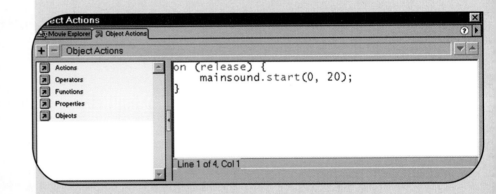

Acoustic

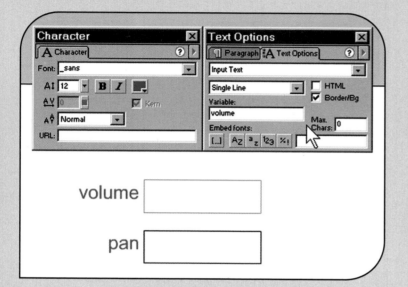

volume

pan

Pan and Volume

The two new controls that you will probably use the most are those for setting the pan and volume.

To demonstrate these controls, we'll control the pan and volume with text fields, although they can be controlled by anything you like. The usual choices are slider bars, buttons, or following the mouse cursor.

Create two new text input fields. Call one **volume** and the other **pan**.

Now, create a blank movie clip and call it **sound controller**. Edit the movie clip and add a blank keyframe so that the clip has two blank frames. On one of the frames, click on it and then open the ActionScript editor in Expert Mode. Now type /:variable.setPan(/:pan) where again variable is your sound name. Note the /: in front of variable. This is here because the variable for your sound is treated just like any other variable and since it's on the main timeline, it must be targeted as such. You can replace /:pan with a number, but we're controlling the pan with our pan variable.

Now, on a new line, type

/:variable.setVolume(/:volume)

Again, we'll use our volume variable to control the volume.

Finally, add a gotoAndPlay (,); in the second frame.

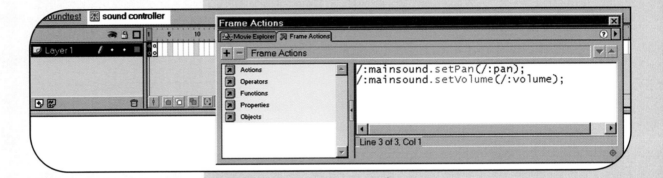

You now have a movie clip that continually loops and sets the volume and pan of your sound to the values in the text input fields. Drop the movie onto the stage on the same keyframe as the input text fields. Test your movie. If you left your text input fields blank, you shouldn't hear anything. Type 100 into your volume text field. You should hear the sound. Play around with different volume settings. The volume is supposed to respond to numbers 0-100, but the sound will actually respond and get still louder if you put in values over 100.

Pan is set with -100 equaling full left pan and 100 equaling full right pan. 0 is evenly balanced.

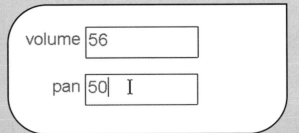

Acoustic

Fading

Using this approach to volume setting, we'll create a script to gradually fade the sound in and out. Create a new blank movie clip. Give it the instance name **fader**. Edit the movie clip. Create an additional layer and call it **Labels**, call the first layer **Actions**. Whenever you create a frame action, create it on the Actions layer and likewise, place your frame labels on the Labels layer.

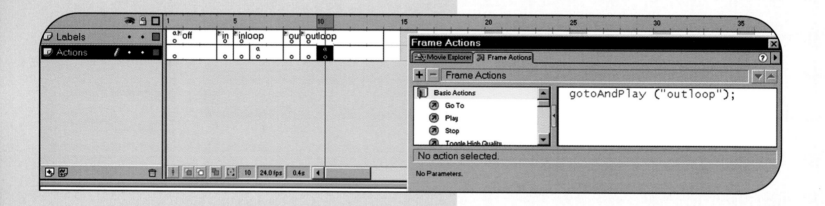

Label the first frame **off** and give it a Stop action. Then create three consecutive keyframes with the first two labeled **in** and **inloop**. Leave the third keyframe unlabeled. On the unlabeled frame, add a gotoAndPlay action to go to frame, inloop.

By setting up our frames like this, when we go to frame in, we can set up initial conditions and then cause a loop between the third frame and the frame, inloop, without disturbing the initial conditions.

Create three new keyframes and set them up like you did for the loop in, with a frame called **out**, **outloop** and **unlabeled**. Again, set the third frame to loop between the outloop frame.

Now let's script the fade in. On the frame, in, add an action and open the ActionScript Editor in Expert Mode. First, set the /:volume to 0 by typing /:volume = 0.

Since your sound controller movie clip is setting the sound volume to whatever the value of /:volume is, this should 'kill' the sound by turning off the volume.

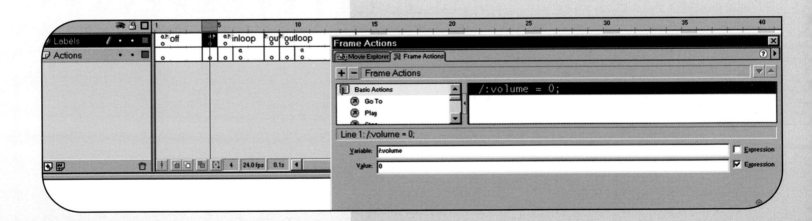

Acoustic

Now, on the inloop frame, create an action and edit it in the ActionScript Editor. Enter this script:

```
if (/:volume < 100) {/:volume2 = /:volume + ((100 - /:volume)/20);
/:volume = int(/:volume2) + 1;
} else {
gotoAndStop ("off");
}
```

This script will check whether the volume is less than 100. If it is, it takes the difference between the current volume and 100, divides it by 20 to make the number smaller, then adds it to the current volume. Using this value, the volume is set with an integer value. Once the volume has reached 100, the loop stops and the clip resets itself.

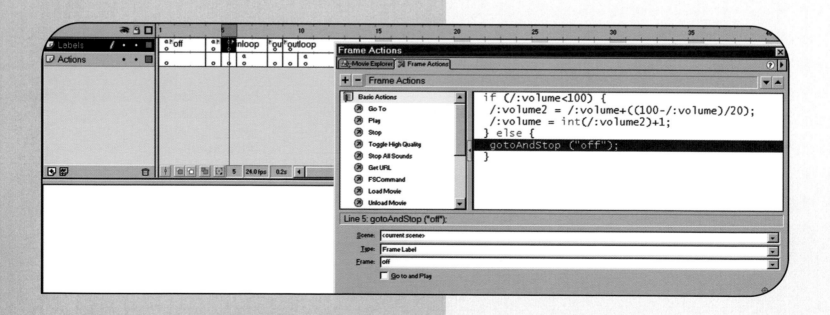

The fade out is similar. There aren't any initial conditions to set up, so add an action on the outloop frame. Create this script:

```
if (/:volume > 0) {/:volume = int(/:volume – (/:volume / 20));
} else {
gotoAndStop ("off");
}
```

This script will check whether the volume is greater than 0. If it is, it sets the volume to the integer value of the current volume divided by 20 subtracted by the current volume. When the volume has reached 0, the loop will stop and reset the clip.

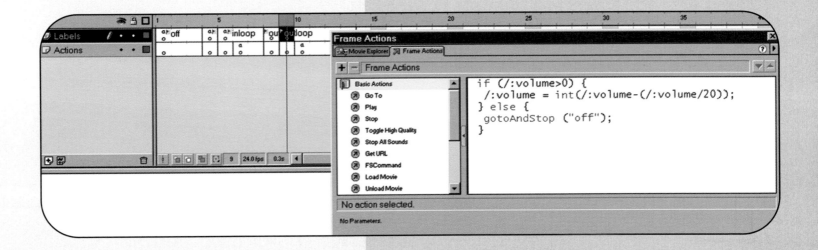

The last step is to make two buttons in the main timeline to fade in and fade out the sound. The actions for these buttons should telltarget the fader clip to gotoAndPlay either the in, or the out, label.

I hope that this has given you a basic understanding of sound control. Now it's over to you. I leave you with this challenge: try to create a Doppler effect (i.e. the sound of a car driving by). Good luck!

IVO van de GRIFT

"I like the idea of a web site being
a short story, bringing its users into
a short adventure."

IVO van de GRIFT
www.grootlicht.com

Flashlight

I don't think of what I do as web design, it's more like digital illustration. Most of the work I produce for the Web revolves around the techniques and ideas I developed when I was working with paint, and many of my influences come from fine art and graphic design, primarily 17th century painters like Vermeer and Frans Hals.

I love the way that these artists sculpt a person or an object with color and light. There's a lot to be learned from these Old Masters in the way they gave the illusion of a three dimensional space in their paintings - much more than any 3D program alone can give you.

The Allegory Of Painting, Jan Vermeer

Too much 3D animation and imaging is put together without enough thought for the mass of an object and its lighting environment, or a genuine understanding of how the third dimension works. You have to study the real world before you can create an accurate virtual one. A 17th century painter had to observe each little detail of an object before painting it, with time to decide which details to keep or leave out for the sake of the overall balance of the completed composition.

The Laughing Cavalier, Frans Hal

Ivo van de Grift

Bruce Nauman, *Window*, 1967
© ARS, NY and DACS, London 2000

Besides these Old Masters, I admire the work of 20th century artists like Andy Warhol, Gilbert and George, Bruce Nauman, Gerhard Richter, Bill Viola and many more. I like the way these works can change your perspective on the world, making you see it from another angle. I believe that art should surprise you and arouse your curiosity.

For similar reasons, I have to admit that the primary influence on my work has been comic books and motion pictures. Again, it's the balance in the work of my favorite comic book artists that I admire, as well as the striking colors and drawing techniques. Daring colorful compositions, together with rib tickling humor, have a wonderful impact on me.

I really enjoy artists who don't take themselves too seriously, artists like Simon Bisley (Lobo, Slain), Martin & Hewlett (Tankgirl), Boucq (Jerome Moucherot), Jean Giraud/Moebius, Geof Darrow & Frank Miller (Hard Boiled).

Flashlight

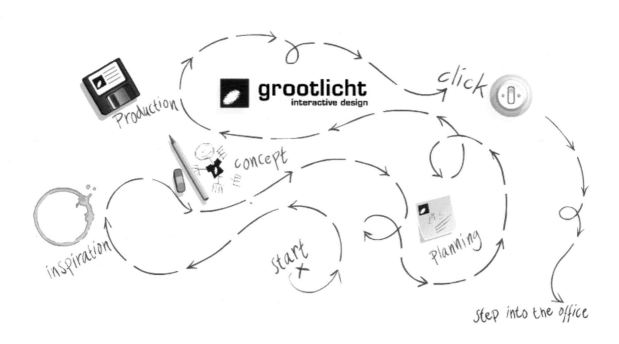

Production

grootlicht
interactive design

click

concept

inspiration

start

planning

step into the office

So, unsurprisingly, graphics and animation are the largest part of my work. When I start on a new project assignment, I begin by collecting word associations with the company name or product I'm working with. They might come from anywhere: personal interests, the evening-paper, or the movie I saw yesterday. Once I have a collection of words and associations, I look for the connections, which usually produce a sort of short story. I like the idea of a web site being a short story, bringing its users into a short adventure. Later in this chapter I'm going to talk about some of the techniques I've used to put one of my own projects together and which I built using this short adventure idea.

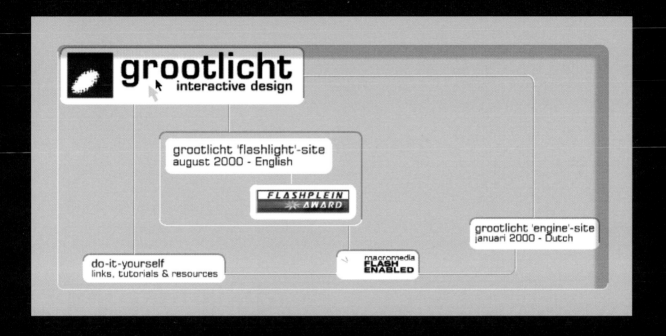

Before I begin, though, there's one final thing I feel I should say. It's the most important rule about working in Flash that I learnt the hard way, and it's simply this: every graphic, every button, every movie clip is part of a greater concept. It's very tempting to put every trick in the book into one Flash movie - Lord knows I did. You might pull it off once or twice, but, most of the time you'll end up with chaotic interfaces and useless streams of data. So my rule for working with Flash is this: don't let technique determine your concepts and designs. Finally, I'd also recommend using a graphic tablet. I always use one in preference to a mouse. The tablet allows me to more control over the lines, curves and shapes. I can produce vector-based graphics without the usual geometric shapes, and what's more, it reduces the risk of RSI. What more could you want?

Flashlight

I began working on the Grootlicht Flashlight site with the idea of an old detective movie. I like the contrast of light and darkness they used. I was also intrigued by the idea of investigation. I thought it would be more interesting to let users explore the site in their own time and find out what it's about, than to simply offer them a statement of intent.

I really wanted to create a web site that would stand out from all the techno-cyber designs that were about at the time ... and still are.

Ivo van de Grift

The detective movie concept lent itself almost immediately to the flashlight effect. I used a similar effect in a Flash animation before, but without user interactivity. This time around I had to work out how to let visitors drag the flashlight around the screen, while still making the light fall realistically. The shape of the flashlight had to be dependent on the angle and position of the light within the movie. Read on, and I'll show you how I produced this final effect.

Flashlight

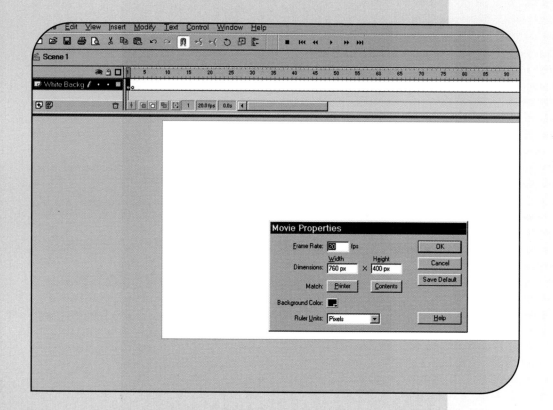

Before you begin, set your Flash movie's dimensions to 760 pixels wide and 400 pixels high. All the variables and expressions in this tutorial are based on these dimensions. To smooth the effect, set the movie to run at a frame rate of 20 fps.

Although you can set the background to your movie to black in the Movie Properties menu, I prefer to put a rectangle the size of the movie in the first keyframe. This prevents the HTML-page coming up with a confusion of black white in the background while the page is preloading. So, go ahead and put in your background layer.

You can use any number of layers on top of this layer to hold the graphics, as the number of layers has little bearing on the final size of the Flash movie. I use separate layers for all my graphics and shadow-effects. In general, I try to give every graphic, movie clip, sound and action its own layer. To keep my .fla files orderly, I usually put most ActionScript in the top layer

The Flashlight

So, let's create the flashlight itself. I used a gradient, set it to Radial, and selected three colors on the color-slide. I used black Alpha 0%, a dark yellow Alpha 30%, and another black Alpha 100%.

Draw a round circle, 131 pixels by 131, and use the Shift key with the gradient to fill it. Use the Transform Fill-tool to center the fill in the circle.

 I use this tool a lot to make various color effects.

Select the circle and turn it into a movie clip symbol called **flashlightl** Select flashlightl from the Library, or double-click on it, to get into edit mode, and group the circle .

I used a huge black rectangle with a circle cut out of the center to mask all the objects outside the flashlight range. So, draw a rectangle with no outlines and a black fill. Select the rectangle by clicking on it and use the Info Panel to set the width and height of the rectangle to 2200 x 1800 pixels.

Flashlight

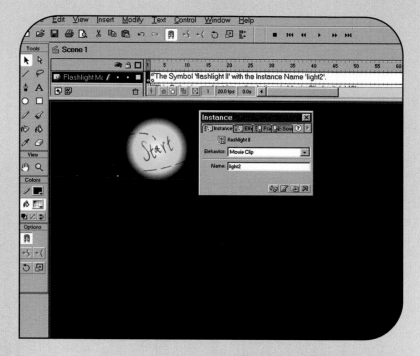

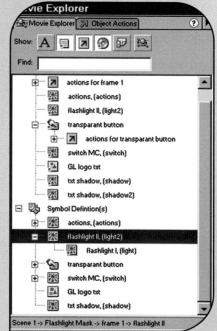

Align both the rectangle and the circle to the center of the edit-field and cut out the circle using the Break Apart command on the grouped circle. It will merge into the mask-field

Merge will only work if you group the circle before you draw the black rectangle. Don't group the rectangle, as your circle will end up behind the rectangle. If things are going awry, try adding a new layer below the existing layer in flashlightI. Draw the rectangle in the lower layer, setting the dimensions as before using the Info Panel Then align the rectangle to the center of the edit field and select the circle from the upper layer. Cut it, select the first keyframe of the lower layer and Paste-in-Place. The grouped circle is placed on top of the rectangle. Then simply break up the grouped circle, and the two shapes should merge into one. Finally, delete the upper (empty) layer.

Don't worry about the amount of data the huge mask-field produces. All together, the flashlightI movie clip is about 161 bytes. It's now ready, leave the edit field and return to the stage.

As the flashlightI movie clip is nothing more than a black rectangle with a gradient filled hole in the middle, we need to add in some dynamic movement. We'll use a combination of ActionScripts to make the shape and angle of the light appear to come from a flashlight moving over the rest of the movie.

Dragging the movie clip flashlightI around the movie isn't hard. We simply use the Drag Movie Clip action. The tricky part is to drag the movie clip around while simultaneously altering its shape. We'll work around this by placing flashlightI inside another movie clip, flashlightII, to separate the Drag action from all the other actions that alter flashlightI.

So, place flashlightI on the stage in its own layer, making sure that this layer is above the background layer (if you're using one), insert a new movie clip and call it flashlightII. You need to give each symbol its own instance name, so give flashlightI the instance name **light**, and flashlightII the instance name **light2**.

We'll assign the Drag Movie Clip action to flashlightII. Create a new layer above the other layers and call it **Drag Action**. Select the first keyframe and in the Frame Actions tab, select Actions. Pull the Drag Movie Clip action from the pop-up menu. Select the Target /light2 and constrain the Drag action to the following dimensions (or dimensions appropriate to the size of the flashlight area in the flashlightI).

Left:	100
Top:	100
Right:	650
Bottom:	310

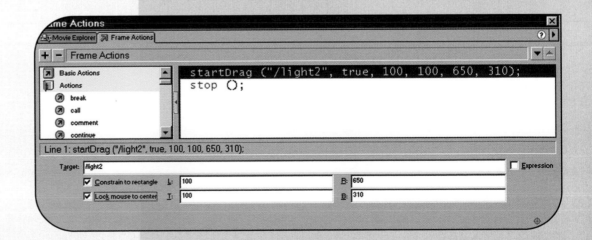

Flashlight

Be sure to select Lock mouse to center, otherwise the flashlight effect won't synchronize with the place and movement in the movie. Also, use the Stop action to prevent the movie playing any other frames. Click OK, and the Drag action is ready.

Now you can move the flashlight around the movie. Test the movie using Publish Preview.

The next thing we need to do is alter the shape of the flashlight while it's moving, according to the position of the flashlight in the movie. We'll retrieve the x and y position of the flashlight using the GetProperty action, and then use these values to set the angle and scale of the flashlight.

To check the flashlight position I made a movie clip called **actions**, consisting of two keyframes that work in a continuous loop at 20fps. The position of the flashlight is checked and the values assigned to variables in the first keyframe. The second keyframe contains the action, Go and Play Frame 1, so the actions are constantly refreshed.

Put a movie clip in scene 1 on a separate layer, called **actions**, so that the movie clip functions like a little sub-routine running independently behind the scenes. The GetProperty action will set two variables, x1 and y1, to check the center-position of the light2 instance, of the movie clip, flashlightll.

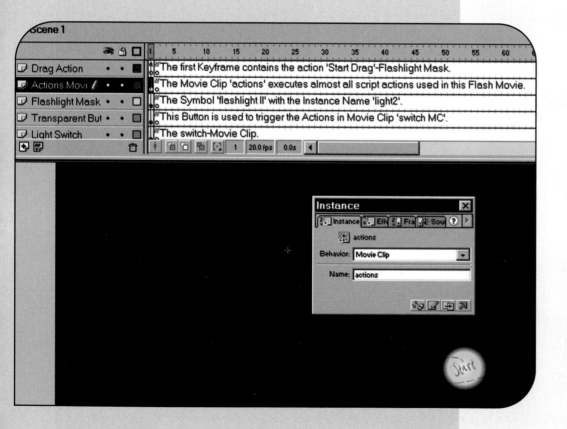

Ivo van de Grift

These actions in keyframe 1 check the position of the flashlight:

x1 = getProperty("/light2", _x);
y1 = getProperty("/light2", _y);

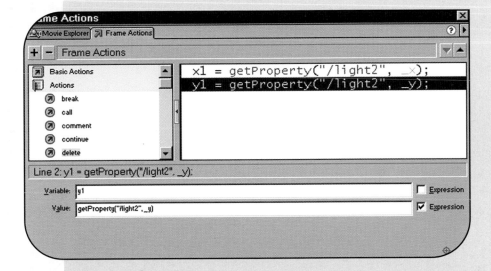

The x and y positions are calculated using the distance between the center of the clip and the upper left corner of the movie. We'll set the x and y values so that the beam of the flashlight appears to come from the middle of the lower edge. Do this by adding in two new variables, x2 and y2, that will use the values x1 and y1 to set the new center point:

x1 = getProperty("/light2", _x);
y1 = getProperty("/light2", _y);
x2 =int((x1-380)/4.22);
y2 = int((y1-300)*-0.8);

Don't worry if it doesn't make a lot of sense at first glance, I'm going to walk through each line of the calculations over the next pages.

Flashlight

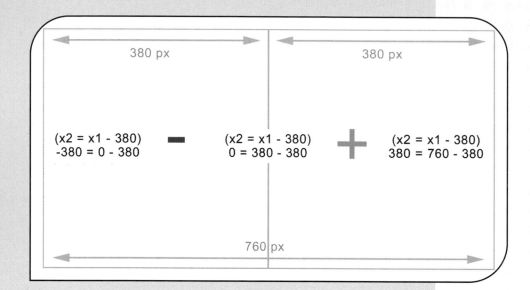

(x2 = x1 - 380)
-380 = 0 - 380

(x2 = x1 - 380)
0 = 380 - 380

(x2 = x1 - 380)
380 = 760 - 380

380 px   380 px

760 px

Both variable x2 and y2 are set as integers (Int), and x2 holds the calculation that will set the angle of the flashlight while it's being dragged around the movie. As the movie is 760 pixels wide, half this value (380) is subtracted from variable x1.

$x2 = int((x1-380)/4.22);$

This sets the horizontal center, splitting the movie between negative and positive sides, and the value of x2 lies between −380 and 380:

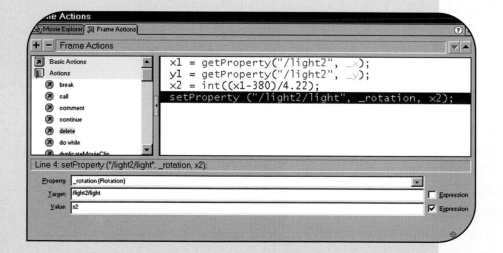

Dividing (x1-380) by 4.22 prevents the flashlight from spinning round, (because 380 pixels divided by 90 degrees = 4.22):

$x2 = int((x1-380)/4.22);$

Finally, we need to set the value of x2 between −90 and 90, using the setProperty action. The target of the setProperty action will be flashlightl, (instance, light), with the rotation property, and a value set by variable x2:

setProperty ("/light2/light", _rotation, x2);

Variable y2 stretches the shape of the flashlight vertically by a quantity dependent on the vertical position of the flashlight, so that the rotation effect can be seen:

$y2 = int((y1-300)*-0.8);$

This equation sets the flashlight illusion to appear at the bottom of the movie, so the beam points upwards, by setting the vertical center at 300 pixels down from the top of the movie:

The _yscale value of the flashlight is set, by variable y2, to between −300 and 0. If the value becomes negative, the flashlight would flip upside down. To stop that happening, the (y1-300)-value is multiplied by -0.8 (I used −0.8 because multiplying the value with −1 made the flashlight stretch out of the movie.)

```
x1 = getProperty("/light2", _x);
y1 = getProperty("/light2", _y);
x2 = int((x1-380)/4.22);
y2 = int((y1-300)*-0.8);
setProperty ("/light2/light", _rotation, x2);
```

Line 4: y2 = int((y1-300)*-0.8);

Variable: y2   ☐ Expression

Value: int((y1-300)*-0.8)   ☑ Expression

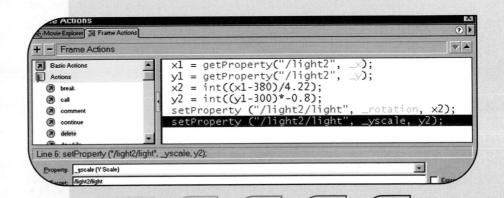

Int((y1-300)*-0.8)
240 = 0 - 300 * -0.8

Int((y1-300)*-0.8)
120 = 150 - 300 * -0.8

300 px

Int((y1-300)*-0.8)
0 = 300 - 300 * -0.8

Int((y1-300)*-0.8)
320 = -100 - 300 * -0.8

Apply this value using the Set Property action like this:

$setProperty ("/light2/light", _yscale, y2);$

```
x1 = getProperty("/light2", _x);
y1 = getProperty("/light2", _y);
x2 = int((x1-380)/4.22);
y2 = int((y1-300)*-0.8);
setProperty ("/light2/light", _rotation, x2);
setProperty ("/light2/light", _yscale, y2);
```

Line 6: setProperty ("/light2/light", _yscale, y2);

Property: _yscale (Y Scale)

Target: /light2/light

Flashlight

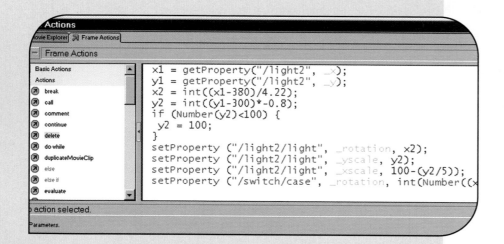

Unfortunately, the flashlight is still liable to flip upside down should the variable y2 have a value of less than 0. I also wanted to prevent the _yscale value dropping to under 100, because the scale property uses a percentage. I've used a simple If action to take care of everything:

```
if (y2<100)  {
    y2 = 100;
}
```

If you've made these changes, the flashlight effect is now almost ready. But, if you try it out you'll find that it's moving rigidly, so use the y2 variable to set the _xscale, to give it a more natural behavior:

```
setProperty ("/light2/light", _xscale, 100-(y2/5));
```

This works by setting the _xscale to 100 %, then subtracting the sum of y2 divided by 5.

So, the complete ActionScript that you are using to move and morph the shape of the flashlight is now:

```
x1 = getProperty("/light2", _x);
y1 = getProperty("/light2", _y);
x2 = int((x1-380)/4.22);
y2 = int((y1-300)*-0.8);
if (y2<100)  {
    y2 = 100;
}
setProperty ("/light2/light", _rotation, x2);
setProperty ("/light2/light", _yscale y2);
setProperty ("/light2/light", _xscale, 100-(y2/5));
setProperty ("/switch/case", _rotation, int((x2*-0.7))=67);
```

To improve the illusion, I put shadows behind some of the objects in my movie. I used the variables again, so that the shadows move with the flashlight.

We'll create the shadow-graphics. The easiest way to do this is to make a new symbol and drag the symbol you're creating a shadow for into the new symbol's edit-field. Break apart the original, and if there are any lines used in the original, use Lines to Fills (Modify> Curves>Lines to Fills). Create a half-transparent (30%) solid black color in the color menu and use this color as a fill.

I used a graphics symbol, called **txt shadow**, with the instance name **shadow** behind the Grootlicht text and logo. To make it look realistic, I needed to move the shadow both horizontally and vertically along with the flashlight, and stretch it vertically if the flashlight was near the logo. I put all these actions in the movie clip actions.

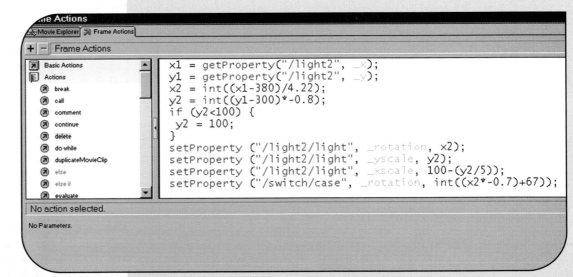

```
x1 = getProperty("/light2", _x);
y1 = getProperty("/light2", _y);
x2 = int((x1-380)/4.22);
y2 = int((y1-300)*-0.8);
if (y2<100) {
  y2 = 100;
}
setProperty ("/light2/light", _rotation, x2);
setProperty ("/light2/light", _yscale, y2);
setProperty ("/light2/light", _xscale, 100-(y2/5));
setProperty ("/switch/case", _rotation, int((x2*-0.7)+67));
```

So, the horizontal movement is set by variable x2. Use the setProperty action, setting the base X value at 406 pixels (from the left) and the sum of x2 divided by 2. This way, the shadow will move twice as slowly as the flashlight:

setProperty ("/shadow",_xposition) = 406+(x2/2);

Flashlight

```
x2 = int((x1-380)/4.22);
y2 = int((y1-300)*-0.8);
if (y2<100) {
  y2 = 100;
}
setProperty ("/light2/light", _rotation, x2);
setProperty ("/light2/light", _yscale, y2);
setProperty ("/light2/light", _xscale, 100-(y2/5));
setProperty ("/shadow", _x, 406+(x2/2));
```

```
 = int((y1-300)*-0.8);
if (y2<100) {
  y2 = 100;
}
setProperty ("/light2/light", _rotation, x2);
setProperty ("/light2/light", _yscale, y2);
setProperty ("/light2/light", _xscale, 100-(y2/5));
setProperty ("/shadow", _x, 406+(x2/2));
setProperty ("/shadow", _y, 35-(y1*-0.3));
```

Setting the vertical position is a bit more difficult because the shadow slides up and down while simultaneously stretching larger and smaller. First, set the base Y position at 35 pixels (from the top) and subtract the sum of y1 multiplied by –0.3.

setProperty ("/shadow", _yposition) = 35-(y1*-0.3);

This calculation won't give you the absolutely correct values, so you'll need to play about with them a bit. In fact, every new symbol will have a set of values for you to find.Now we'll add in the stretching part. Set the percentage of the Y-Scale to 180% and subtract the sum of y1 divided by 3. Again, you'll have to use trial and error until you're completely happy with it.

setProperty ("/shadow", _yscale, 180-(y1/3);

Now we'll work on the light switch, on the left, which has a different sort of shadow. This is easier because we're working with a round object that will have an oval-shaped shadow. I constructed the symbol **switch mc** in different layers, so that the **switch case** symbol turns around using a Set Property action, while the other graphics stay in place.

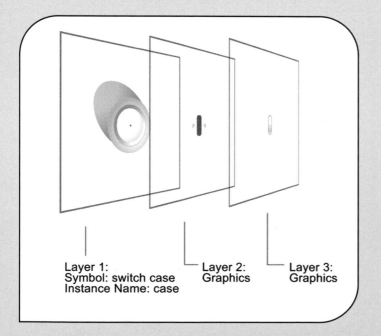

Layer 1:
Symbol: switch case
Instance Name: case

Layer 2:
Graphics

Layer 3:
Graphics

Put a graphic symbol, switch case, in layer 1. The switch case symbol is constructed with several oval shapes and gradient fills.

You must have switch case in the center of the edit field, so that the shadows, spinning around the case, off center, will look realistic.

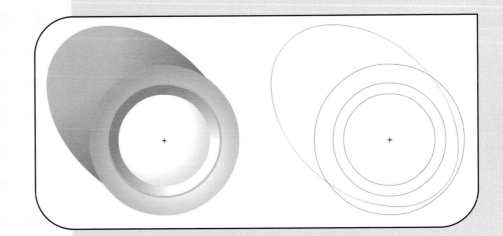

You can set the properties of the graphic symbol so it behaves like a movie clip. Just, set its behavior and set an instance name on the Instance Panel.

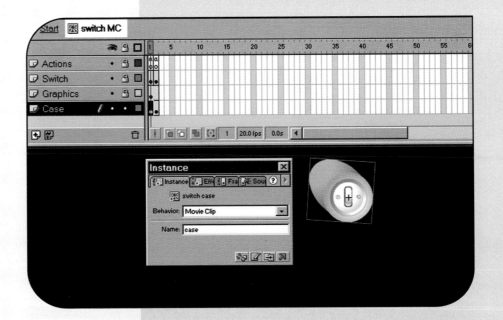

85

Flashlight

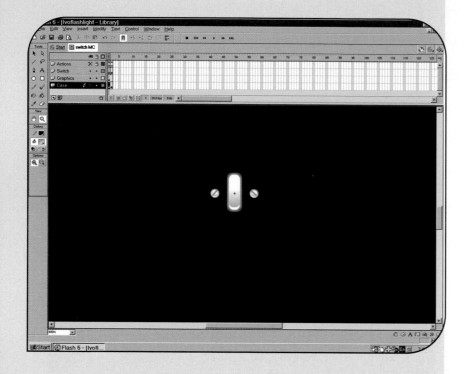

I placed some graphics in layers 2 and 3 to represent the button and screws of the light switch. These graphics will stay in their place and won't be affected by the angle of the switch case symbol.

Switch MC is now ready. I put it on the stage in its own layer and give the movie clip the instance name **switch**. I added another Set Property action to set the angle of the switch case symbol again.

SetProperty ("/switch/case", _rotation) = int((x2*-0.7)+67);

This works pretty much like tellTarget; set the target as the instance case placed in the movie clip switch: "/switch/case". Set the Rotation property, and the value as the sum of Int((x2*-0.7)+67).

Important: As a precaution, I set this as an Integer. Otherwise the Rotation property may also alter the size of the target.

The calculation (x2*-0.7)+67) is made up like this: the value of variable x2 decreases and is made positive by multiplying the result by -0.7. I used the value +67 because it set the angle correctly This, again, is a process of trial and error.

So, now your complete ActionScript looks like this:

```
x1 =getProperty("/light2", _x );
y1 = getProperty ("/light2", _y );
x2 = int ((x1-380) /4.22);
y2 = int((y1-300)*-0.8);
if (Number(y2)<100){
    y2 = 100;
}
setProperty ("/light2/light", _rotation, x2);
setProperty ("/light2/light", _yscale, y2);
setProperty ("/light2/light", _xscale, 100-(y2/5));
setProperty ("/shadow", _x, 406+Number((x2/2)));
setProperty ("/shadow", _y 35-(y1*-0.3));
setProperty ("/shadow", _yscale, 180-(y1/3));
setProperty ("/switch/case", _rotation, int(Number((x2*-0.7))+67));
```

To make the effect complete I wanted the light switch to work like the real thing, so users could switch it on and off again. For this I needed two major actions. The stopDrag action makes the flashlight mask and all shadows invisible. I also needed to switch on new 'daylight-shadows' to make the effect more realistic.

Flashlight

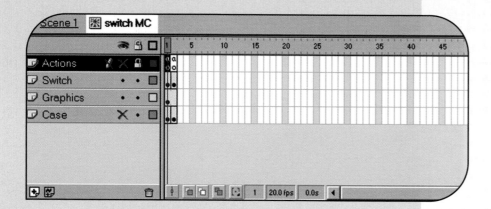

To switch off the mask and shadows, I made the **switch** movie clip behave like a real switch. I created a new layer called **Actions** in the switchMC. There, I placed all the actions to start the flashlight effect in the first keyframe and all the actions to stop it in the secondI found that the simplest way to stop and start the flashlight effect was to use the Visibility property, using Boolean values, so the movie clip should be visible with 1 and invisible with 0.

First, set all the movie clips to the visible 1, in the first keyframe,

```
setProperty("/light2/light",_visible"1");
setProperty ("/light2", _visible "1");
setProperty ("/shadow", _visibile "1");
```

Then move the startDrag action into this keyframe, (it was in the first keyframe of the the actions layer).

```
startDrag ("/light2", L=100, T=100, R=690, B=310, lockcenter)
```

Finish this script with the Stop action to prevent the movie clip from playing on to the next frame. NB: To follow the tutorial steps, the startDrag action in the accompanying flashlight.fla on the CD is still set in the first keyframe of the movie. Feel free to move it.

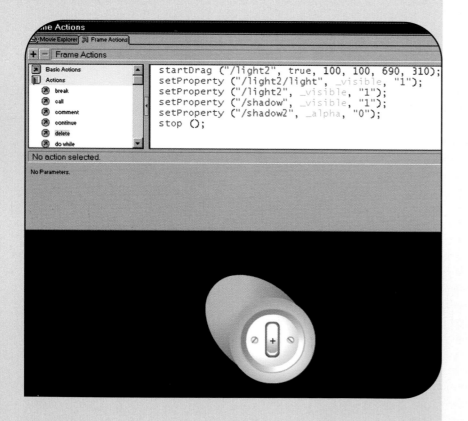

Now for the second keyframe of switchMC. End all the flashlight effects using property visibile=0 and stop the Drag action:

```
stopDrag ();
setProperty ("/light2/light", _visible "0");
setProperty ("/light2", _visible "0");
setProperty ("/shadow", _visible) "0");
setProperty ("/shadow2", _alpha, "75");
stop ();
```

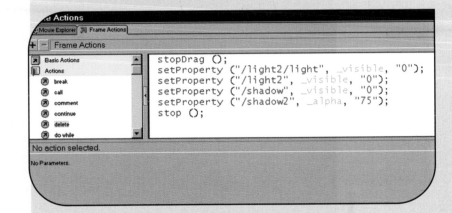

Daylight shadows are much easier to make. We'll be looking at the shadow of the light switch and the GL-logo. The light switch shadow is simple. We'll just make a new graphic, with a new shadow, and put it in the second keyframe of switchMC. We can also reuse the txt shadow symbol for the Grootlicht shadow. We'll put the symbol in a separate layer, call the instance **shadow2**, and make it into a movie clip. The properties of the symbol are set just like the others were.

Instead of using the visibility property I used Alpha to turn shadow2 on and off, because the txt shadow graphic has a color of Black 30% Alpha. This percentage is perfect for the flashlight effect, but too dark for the daylight shadow effect. Like the other actions, I added these properties in switchMC.

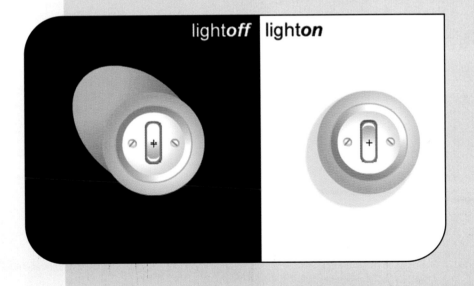

lightoff lighton

Flashlight

```
startDrag ("/light2", true, 100, 100, 690, 310);
setProperty ("/light2/light", _visible, "1");
setProperty ("/light2", _visible, "1");
setProperty ("/shadow", _visible, "1");
setProperty ("/shadow2", _alpha, "0");
stop ();
```

Line 1 of 7, Col 1

```
stopDrag ();
setProperty ("/light2/light", _visible, "0");
setProperty ("/light2", _visible, "0");
setProperty ("/shadow", _visible, "0");
setProperty ("/shadow2", _alpha, "75");
stop ();
```

Line 1 of 7, Col 1

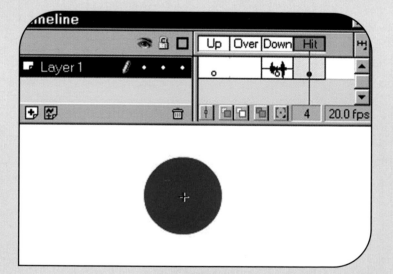

In the first keyframe:

startDrag ("/light2", true, 100, 100, 690, 310);
setProperty ("/light2/light", _visible, "1")'
setProperty ("/light2", _visible) "1");
setProperty ("/shadow", _visible "1");
setProperty ("/shadow2", _alpha "0");
stop ();

And in the second keyframe:

stopDrag
setProperty ("/light2/light", _visible, "0");
setProperty ("/light2", _visible "0");
setProperty ("/shadow", _visible "0");
setProperty ("/shadow2", _alpha "75");
stop ();

So, now all conditions are set, all we need is a button to trigger everything. We'll just make a transparent button for this. Make a new button, leave the keyframes Up and Over empty, set a keyframe Down and select a click sound, using the frame properties menu. Define the hit frame using a circle of similar dimensions to switchMC.

Place this button above switchMC on the stage in its own separate layer. Double-click the button to open the Instance Properties menu and set the following action:

```
on (release) {
   tellTarget ("/switch");
   play ();
      }
}
```

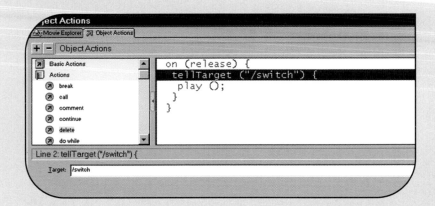

The only thing that this button does is play the next Keyframe in switchMC. All actions set in that keyframe are then executed. If the button is pushed again, switchMC will loop and stop in the first keyframe.

And Voila... an everyday flashlight effect with a light switch!

There's one more point you might need to take into consideration. The startDrag action takes a very short time to become active, so if visitors enter the movie when the flashlight is in the original x and y positions, the light will jump over the screen as it snaps to the cursor. To prevent this happening, I used a new scene, called **Start**. All that happens in this scene is that the movie stops and the visitor has to click a button in order to play the next scene.

Flashlight

This is how it works.

Select the first keyframe of the Start scene, and put in the Stop action. This will prevent the movie playing further.

Place the center of flashlightll in the flashlight scene, above the start graphic, so that this becomes the starting point. Then copy the start graphic into the start scene, positioning it using Paste in Place. Select the Start graphic again and use F8 to set it as a button. Once you've edited the button's hit frame, set the action:

```
On (release) {
    GotoAnd Play (flashlight, 1)
}
```

So now, when the visitor pushes the button, the cursor is in the same position as flashlightll in the scene flashlight.

And that's all there is to it. I built this flashlight effect a few months ago, and while I was putting this tutorial together I noticed that almost half the original scripting could be deleted or optimized. It's good to find that my scripting knowledge has improved in just a few months. Although it's definitely worth the effort to look at old projects now and again, most of the time I'm too busy with other stuff. It's the web designers' conundrum, familiar all over the world: I'm just too busy to build a proper site for myself.

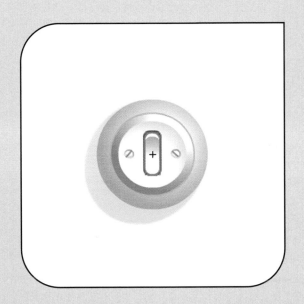

Ripple

thevoid's well-known motto is **content without clutter**; a phrase that sums up our aesthetic values and acts as a byline for the type of designs that we produce. We base that philosophy on our belief that everything within a design should be well thought out and serve a useful purpose with minimal distractions; content displayed clearly without needless clutter.

There are so many so-called 'design' sites out there that simply do nothing to move me. They seem to be design for design's sake; random typographic collages with no real function or substance at all. While they do often incorporate some sort of interface, this usually just consists of a number of discrete buttons along one side of the display with no real relationship to the graphics above them.

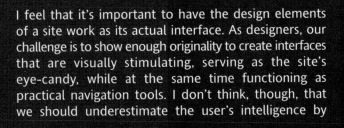

I feel that it's important to have the design elements of a site work as its actual interface. As designers, our challenge is to show enough originality to create interfaces that are visually stimulating, serving as the site's eye-candy, while at the same time functioning as practical navigation tools. I don't think, though, that we should underestimate the user's intelligence by designing extremely obvious interfaces and spelling out exactly how the site should be navigated. Our design ideas should leave room for the viewer to become immersed in the site, to use their imagination as motivation to explore and discover the site's inner workings themselves, making the experience a truly interactive one.

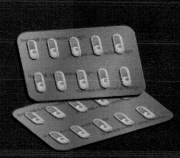

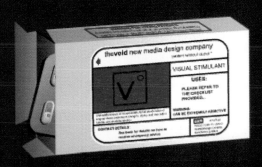

Ripple

I believe that it's the extent to which the user can become involved with the interface that makes the whole process of visiting a site for them much more effective and, importantly, more memorable. And, surely, that has to be our ultimate aim? An air of sophistication and individuality will make our sites stand out from the barrage of irritating, techno-pumping, trendy day-glo Flash sites that now flood the Internet and are beginning to look well past their sell-by dates. It's only against this simple background that we can design the interactivity that will motivate the user to invest some long-term mindspace into our work - and remember where they saw it.

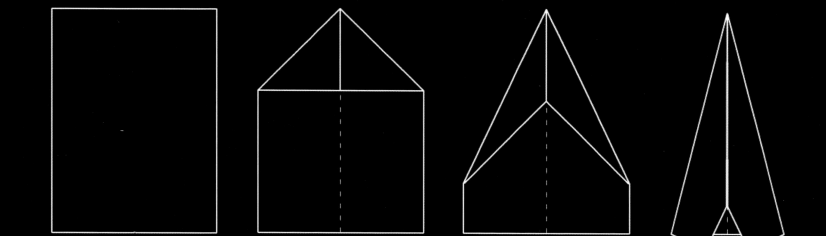

For us at the**void**, building a site is usually a process more of evolution than of design and construction. Before I begin working on a site I rarely sit at my desk with pencil and paper and draw out exactly what I'm about to create. I usually have a good idea in my head of what the finished site should look like, but this changes as the site begins to take form. I find that time spent at a drawing board is often time that I could spend much more productively putting ideas into practice on the screen. Having said this, I do always have a pad close at hand which rapidly fills up with my often meaningless but sometimes design-provoking doodles. Sometimes my ideas turn out not to be feasible, or beyond the capabilities of Flash, but, from that start, it's easy to go through iterations that improve on the initial draft idea and tackle design problems on the way. That's what good web site design is all about: the evolution of an original concept.

Ripple

Rene Magritte, *Mysteries of the Horizon*
© ADAGP, Paris and DACS, London 2000

As I look at the designs that I've created as a member of the**void** team, I can trace my ideas back to different inspirational sources.

Modern artists such as Roy Lichtenstein and Andy Warhol have fed me with their use of strong graphic images. René Magrite, with his vivid imagination, perverse wit and his meticulous technique, has been a long standing source.

Andy Warhol, *Double Elvis*, 1964
© The Andy Warhol Foundation for the Visual Arts, Inc./
ARS<NY and DACS, London 2000

More recently, though, I have drawn from Damien Hirst. I love his originality and boldness, constantly (and often controversially) pushing the boundaries of art. My particular favorite is his Cigarettes are Perfect Until You Light Them.

Andy Warhol said that he felt he was "very much a part of my times, of my culture, as much a part of it as rockets and television". I share his sentiment.

Other influences on my work include the vividly graphic images of the Russian revolutionary artist, Alexander Rodchenko, the stunning geometric abstraction of Ben Nicholson and the harmony and balance of Barbara Hepworth's art.

Alexander Rodchenko, *Chauffeur*, 1933
© DACS 2000

Although I have the greatest respect for all the artists and their work that I've shown here, I think it's important that such art doesn't take itself too seriously.

That's something that we try to keep in mind at the**void**. We try to keep a sense of perspective about all the design aspects of each project - and even show that we have a sense of humor!

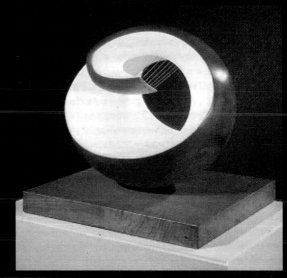

Barbara Hepworth, *Pelagos*, 1946
© Alan Bowness/ Hepworth Estate/ Tate Gallery London, 2000

Ripple

An illustration of the tongue-in-cheek nature of our work can be seen in part of our design for www.thevoid.co.uk. After the initial splash pages we present the viewer with a blister pack of medication to consume. He clicks on a capsule which launches a 2001-style monolith, as if to signify that a momentous event is about to take place. However, as the monolith eases closer into view and out of the darkness, it reveals that it's only there to introduce the next section of the site: the portfolio.

Spend a little time here and take a look at some of the designs which, I hope, will illlustrate what I've said here about the**void** design philosophy.

Stepping back from the portfolio, I'm going to spend the rest of my time taking you through an effect that appears earlier in our site.

The name of the**void** has become synonymous with the use and innovation of one Flash technique in particular: the ripple effect. This is a text effect, so called because it gives the impression that each of the letters in a particular word 'ripple' into and out of the stage. We have pushed this effect to its limit during the intro movie at www.thevoid.co.uk, where we apply it to the text within our motto, *content without **clutter***.

We first used the effect in our site back in 1998. The initial versions were very simplistic and jerky compared to how things look now, but were seen at the time as state of the art! Since then, through continuous tweaking and improving, we feel that we've learned to take the ripple effect to its limits. We've made things run as smoothly as they do by making sure that the file size isn't too overblown. The

content** without **clutter sequence appears towards the end of the initial intro movie to our site, so, for the movie to stream as soon as the file begins to load, we had to build the animation to load quickly. Text animations like this, which feature so many symbols and multiple layered animations, can consume a fair amount of file size. This is especially important in a situation where every last kilobyte makes a difference. We've found that around 60k for the entire intro movie is about the limit, so we've had to keep the ripple animation well within this constraint. If we say that 10 seconds is the longest you can reasonably expect the user to wait for things to happen, you could average out your file size to 30-50k. Of course, when you're creating Flash animations like this for use on CD-ROM, you have much more freedom when it comes to file size, so you can put much more complex effects to use.

Ripple

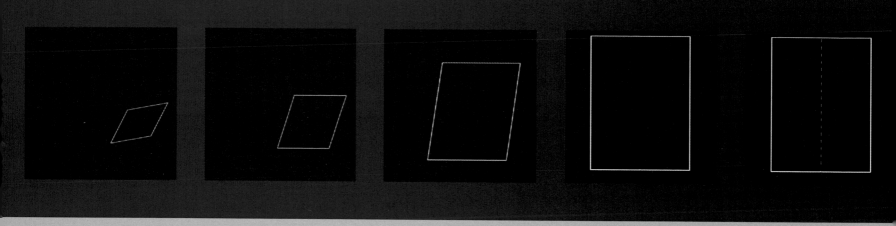

From a visual standpoint, the 'smoothness' of the movie is also very important. You can control this by changing the frame rate at which your Flash movie should run. While setting an extremely high frame rate would make for a very slick animation on a fast computer, it would mean a very long run through on a slow machine. It's always important to produce animations that will run smoothly on pretty much any machine and across different Internet connections. This means finding an optimum frame rate that doesn't look jerky on a fast computer, but doesn't take a long time to run through on a slower machine.

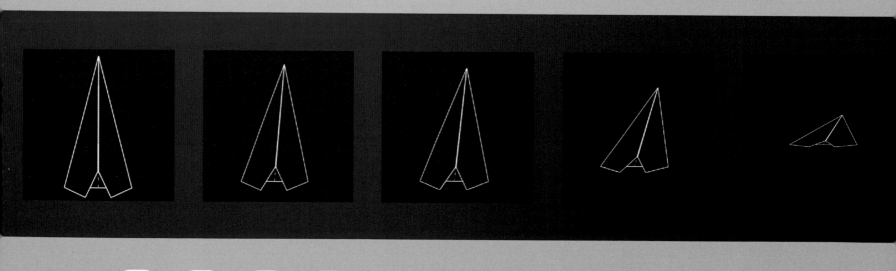

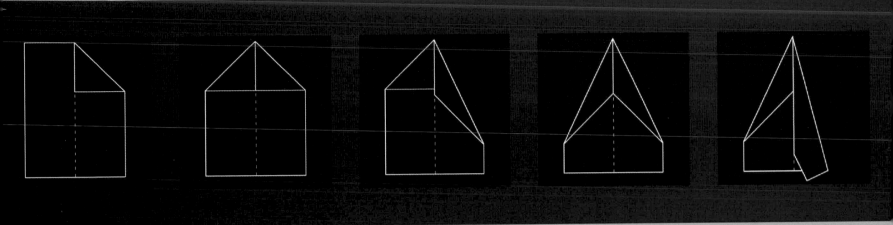

We've found that frame rate tends to be around twenty to twenty-four frames per second with our movies, but this varies depending on the scale and complexity of text being animated. You may find that a frame rate of twelve to eighteen frames per second cuts the download time of your animation to practically nothing. Remember, the higher your frame rate, the larger your file size; the longer the waiting time, the lower the user tolerance. You'll need to be very patient to produce a full Ripple animation, but the results can be well worth the effort. I'll show you how over the next few pages.

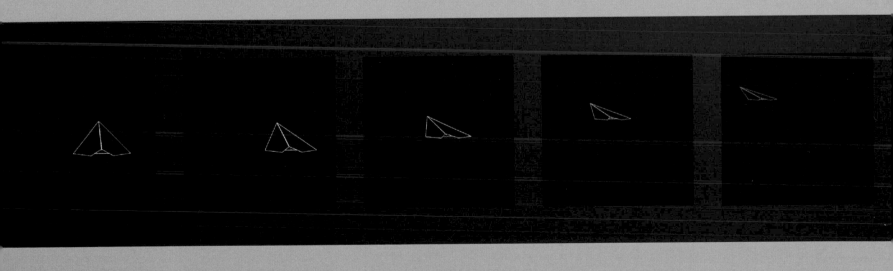

Ripple

Before I start, I always find it best to open a fresh window to create the text effect. It may be worth trying this because it stops the Library getting crammed with symbols as you're working on it. Incorporating the Ripple animation into your main movie later on is simply a matter of copying and pasting the relevant frames. As you add more and more frames and layers, you may also find it useful later on to switch to a shorter frame view within the Frame View pop-up menu.

The Ripple effect is split into two parts: the fade-in and the fade-out sequences. This is because, in this example, the text appears, pauses, then disappears a few seconds later as a part of an intro movie. You can use the sequence effectively on its own, say as part of an interface animation where you just want the text to appear, but not to fade out.

contentwithoutclutter

contentwithoutclutter

First, create the text that you want to animate. Do this using the Text tool, making sure that the typeface, style, spacing and color are exactly as you want them in the finished piece. This is important as they may become difficult to change later on in the process. In this example, I've used the fonts Arial and Arial Black.

Next, you must convert the type to its component lines and fills.

Select the type block using the Arrow tool. Choose Modify>Break Apart. The individual characters will be converted to shapes on the stage.

You now need to convert each letter into a graphic symbol so that each one can be animated individually.

Select the first letter using the Arrow tool. When the letter has two separate pieces, as in j or i, make sure that you select the entire letter. Choose Insert>Convert to Symbol.

In the Symbol Properties dialog box, choose Graphic as the behaviour and name the symbol after the text that it contains. For c as the first letter in **content** *without* **clutter** we called the first symbol -c. There's a dash before all the letters so that they will appear at the top of the Library's symbol list in alphabetical order when the animation is placed into the main movie. This makes them more accessible and is useful should you need to change the color or style of a particular letter later on. That's just our choice though. You may find that naming the symbols as numbers relating to their position within the phrase suits you better.

Once you've converted the first letter into a graphic symbol, you'll need to repeat this process for each letter in the word or phrase. When you have a letter appear more than once, simply name the letter -?2, -?3, etc. This is quicker and simpler than re-using the first -? symbol. See how I've done that here with the second letter t.

Ripple

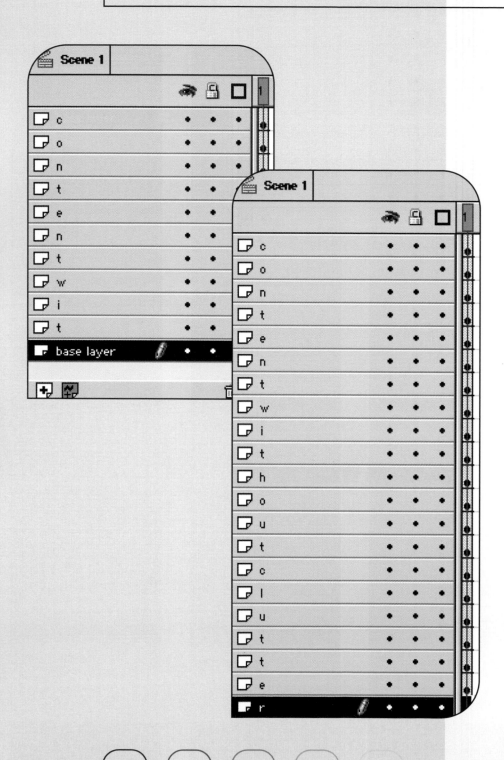

Once you've done this you'll need to give each of the symbols' instances their own layer so that they can be individually tweened. It's important to do this in the right order so that the first letter is on the top layer and the last letter in the word or phrase occupies the bottom one.

Select the first instance and cut it (Edit>Cut).

Insert a new layer above your base layer. Paste the instance into the new layer in its original position (Edit>Paste in Place). Label the layer after the letter that occupies it.

Repeat this for each of the letters in order, making sure that you insert each new layer immediately above the base layer. This will ensure that the letters are layered in order from top to bottom. You may delete the base layer, or simply keep the last letter within it and label it accordingly.

Now you need to insert a set of keyframes (Insert>Keyframe) in every layer somewhere further along the timeline – I've used frame 15 in this example. These keyframes will be where the fade-in animation ends.

The next step is to modify each of the instances in the start position, frame 1. For the *content* without *clutter* animation, each letter starts off at 500%, the eventual text size and at 0% Alpha.

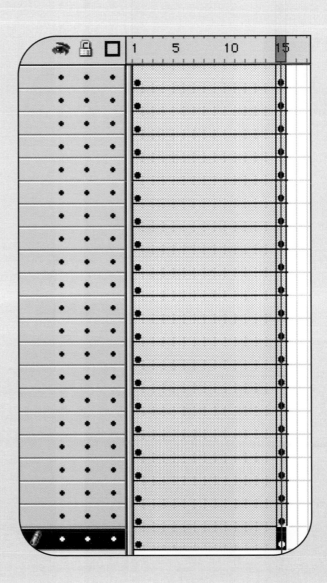

Ripple

Select the letter instance on the top layer in the first frame. Choose Window>Inspectors> Transform or use a keyboard shortcut to bring up the Inspector window and just click on the Transform tab.

Enter a scale value (500% in this case) and click OK.

Repeat this for each of the letters within the first frame, working your way down the layers from top to bottom.

To change the transparency of the letters, first select the letter instance on the top layer in the first frame. On the Effect Panel, select Alpha from the pop-up menu. Adjust the Alpha to 0%.

You can now animate the fade-in sequence.

Select the keyframes in frame 1 throughout all the layers. On the Frame Panel click the Tweening drop-down menu and make sure that the Motion Tween option is selected. Move the Easing slider to the fully Out, or 100 position. This will ensure that the letters gently ease into their final positions, making a smoother animation.

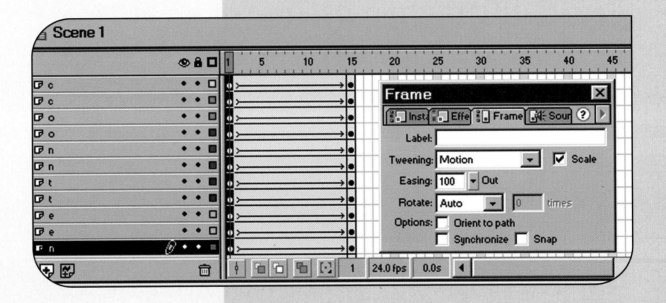

Now you need to create the blurring effect by duplicating each of the layers so that each letter has two layers of animation.

Ripple

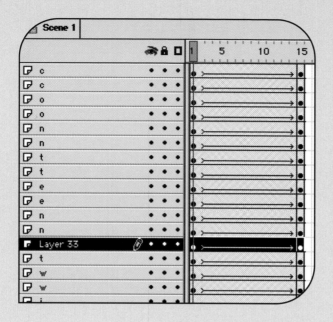

Select all the frames in the top layer and copy them (Edit>Copy Frames).

Create a new layer directly above the layer you've just copied from.

Paste the frames into the new layer in the same position as the originals; frames 1 to 15. (Edit>Paste Frames).

Repeat this for each of the layers, working your way down the layers from top to bottom. The layers' names should change automatically to the name of the layers the frames were copied from.

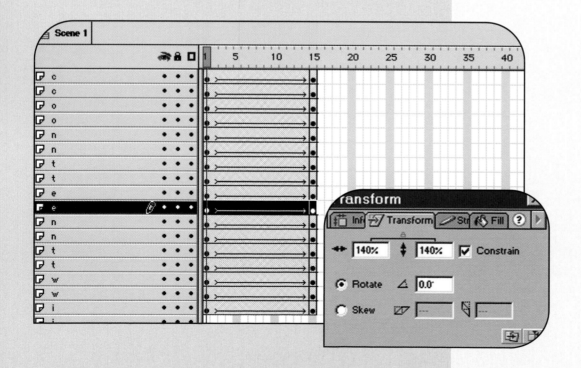

To create the blur effect, in frame 1, you need to give each letter in the series instances of two different sizes, one slightly bigger than the other. Select the letter instance on the top layer in the first frame.

In the Transform Panel enter a scale value (140% in this case), with Constrain ticked and click OK.

Repeat this for the letters within the first frame in every other layer, working your way down the layers from top to bottom, missing a layer each time.

Now that you're done with the animation work on the fade-in sequence, you can move on to the fade-out. This is just a matter of re-using the frames from the fade in animation in a different order.

You'll need to insert a set of keyframes somewhere along the timeline after the last keyframes. I've used frame 70 in this example. The number of frames between the end of the fade-in sequence and the beginning of the fade-out will determine the length of time the text is displayed (stationary) on the screen. Select the frames in each layer from top to bottom at frame 70. Choose Insert>Keyframe. These keyframes will be where the fade-out animation begins.

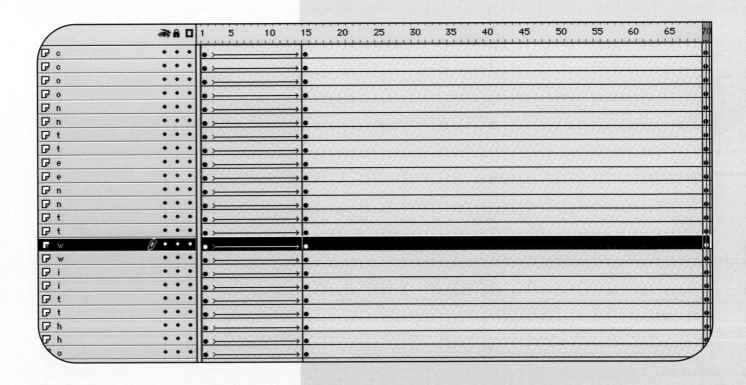

Ripple

You can now animate the fade-out sequence.

Select the keyframes at frame 70 throughout all the layers. In the Frame Panel click the Tweening tab and make sure that the Motion Tween option is selected. Move the Easing slider to the fully In, or -100 position. This will ensure that the letters gently ease out.

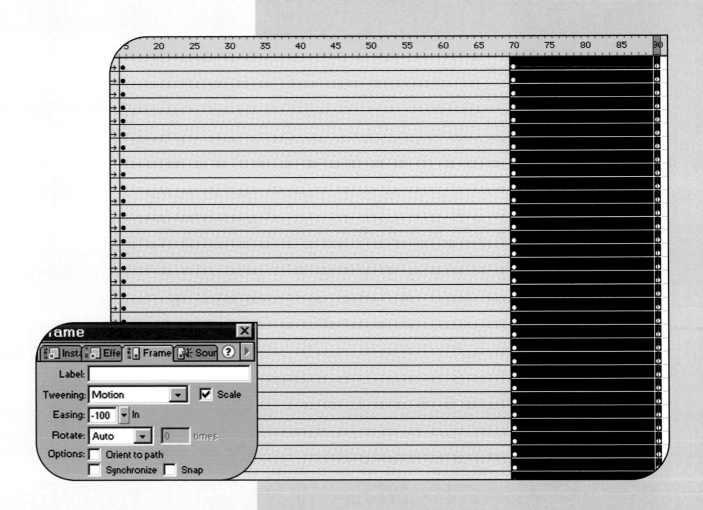

Ripple

The animation is almost complete. The last stage is to stagger the layers so that each letter appears in sequence, creating the ripple effect. In this example we'll stagger them by just two frames, as there are a lot of letters and we want the effect to be fast paced.

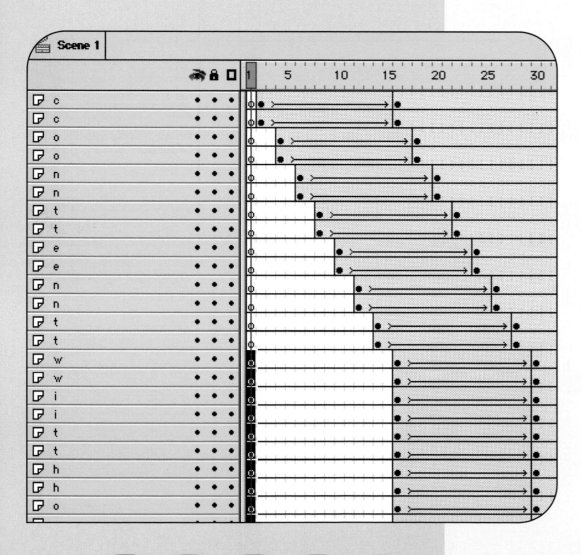

For the Insert Frame function to work properly you'll need to move the first keyframes in all the layers into frame 2 (otherwise it will simply add frames to the fade in frames). Just drag them across.

Next select all the first (now blank) keyframes at frame 1 in all the layers from the third layer to the bottom layer.

Insert>Frame, or F5 twice, to move these frames onwards two frames.

Now select all the first frames at frame 1 in all the layers from the fifth layer to the bottom layer and insert two frames, as in step three.

Repeat this for the 7th, 9th, 11th, 13th, etc. layers downwards until all the start keyframes are staggered.

The Ripple animation is now complete.

You may now want to create a movie symbol containing this entire animation. This can be useful if you want to move it within the rest of the movie as it becomes just a matter of copying and pasting. You can also scale, rotate or even tween the whole animation to create some spectacular effects.

What I've gone through here is just the basis of the Ripple effect. You can add countless variations of your own. Try to create something a little different by changing the letters' start positions, or skewing them. Increase the number of layers of animation used for each letter to see how that can make the blurring effect seem more seamless. My advice is to experiment yourself, and maybe you'll find a variation of the ripple effect that suits your particular style.

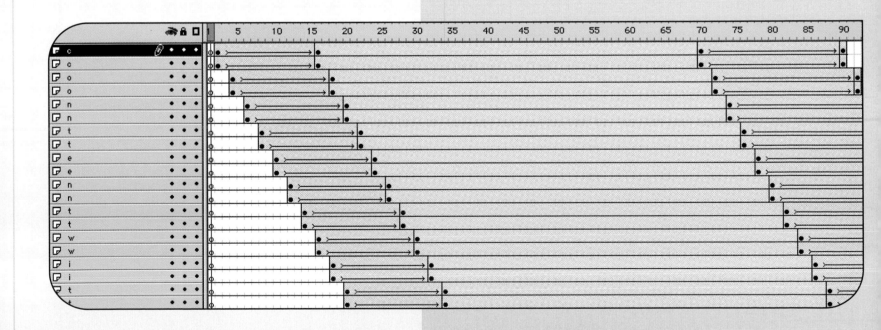

"This ability to seamlessly maneuver between the left and right side of the brain seems to be a key characterstic of a new brand of media artist and can be compared with Leonardo da Vinci's artist-, scientist- inventor profile."

ANDRIES ODENDAAL
www.wireframe.co.za

Dimensions

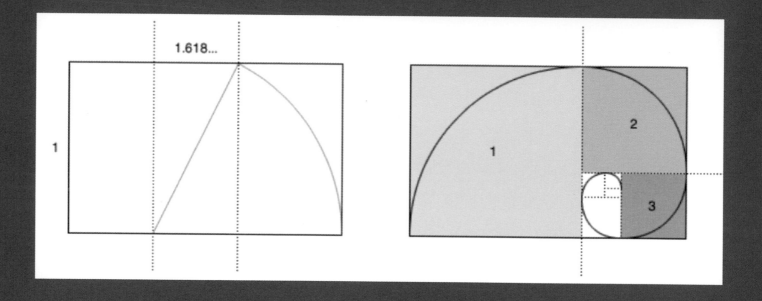

The idea of using maths to aid to the design process is certainly not a new one. Since early times, maths has been explored as a means of explaining the world we live in, so it's no surprise that artists would also have had an interest in exploring the use of mathematics in their creations. After all, most works of art have, in some form or another, been about exploring and experimenting with the ways in which we experience and view our surroundings and our relationship with them.

The application of mathematics in the visual arts has ranged from finding very practical solutions to problems as basic as perspective (how do I represent the three dimensional world on a two dimensional surface like a wall or canvas?), to more complex issues relating to aesthetics and our emotional response to compositions (what is the most 'pleasing' division of a line segment into two parts?).

In a very basic, yet fundamental, example of how mathematics can be used to solve aesthetic problems, artists often referred to the Golden or Divine Section. This is basically a means of dividing or sectioning a given line at the point where the shorter section has the same ratio or relationship to the longer section as the longer section has to the whole.

Using these measurements as its sides, a golden rectangle can be sectioned in such a way that the one section forms a square and the remaining section will form another golden rectangle, which can be divided again and again. In the diagram you see here, square 1 has the same relationship to 2 as 2 has to 3.

Andries Odendaal

These ratios can be seen in the growth patterns of ferns and shells, where the compartments in the shell share the same ratio.

Since it defined some form of underlying structure to nature and was almost be looked at as some form of 'blue print' for the natural world, it's not difficult to see why this ratio was considered to have 'divine' proportions.

My point here is that math forms the basis of everything. Artists and architects, not being ignorant about such matters, have always tried to incorporate this by using concepts such as the Golden Ratio in their compositions and, as a simple example, have often used the Golden Rectangle as a format for their canvases.

Dimensions

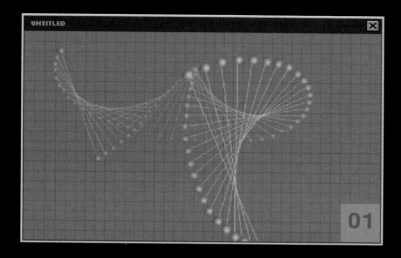

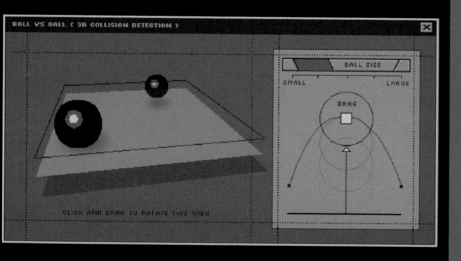

Today, with computers offering an alternative to canvases and brushes, the role of mathematics in the creative disciplines becomes even more prominent. After all, a computer's power lies in the ability to do calculations. Every time you apply a filter in Photoshop, for instance, math is being used to calculate the manipulation of the digital image, which, in itself, is simply information stored in the form of numbers. Beyond manipulating images, computers enable us to calculate these manipulations in real time, creating motion, and doing so on the user's command - adding interactivity.

We can now apply mathematical formulae to create real-time simulations of growth patterns and virtual 3D worlds, where objects collide and move, obeying laws of physics.

None of these concepts are, of course, particularly new. Computers have been around for some time now, but I can fairly confidently say that never before have designers been so actively drawn into these areas, traditionally reserved for math masterminds and programmers. Applications such as Director and, especially, Flash are sitting right behind all this activity.

Andries Odendaal

Flash has changed the way we look at web design, and I think, for a lot of designers, has changed the way they look at themselves. Not surprising, given the fact that it served as a point of convergence for a vast array of disciplines ranging from traditional artists to programmers.

This ability to seamlessly maneuver between the left and right side of the brain seems to be a key characteristic of a new breed of media artist, and can, to a large extent, be compared with Leonardo da Vinci's artist-, scientist-, inventor-profile.

So, at the moment, there seems to be a trend of Flash designers digging up their old trigonometry textbooks as sources of inspiration. This non-intimidating package ends up holding more power than anyone ever imagined and, on top of that, has turned out to be a lot of fun too. I guess that it's this fun element of Flash, combined with its simple but powerful scripting language that has opened the way for designers to freely experiment with new possibilities. Hence the wave of experimental works that we see both within this book and appearing each day on the Web.

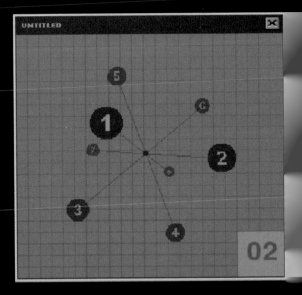

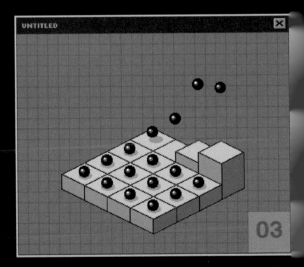

Dimensions

Sol Le Witt, *Arcs in Four Directions*, 1999
© ARS, NY and DACS, London 2000

As a direct contrast to these very high, artistic thoughts, I can start my inspirational trail at the time when, as a kid, I was spending countless amount of pocket money on arcade games at the corner café. These served as both a friendly introduction to technology and later as source of inspiration for my own attempts at creating games and interfaces.

I think that there's a lot to be learned from these old classic games, especially in the way they managed to captivate their audience despite their obvious techno-logical limitations. To me, there are still very few games that can claim to have matched the same level of playability of some of the old arcade classics, like Pac-Man and Q*Bert. I feel that while we're, to some extent, still dealing with similar limitations on the Web, these games serve me as a great resource for inspiration.

As an enthusiastic young Commodore 64 owner I spend countless nights coding and generating graphics for 'big game titles' that I had planned. Needless to say

that none of them were ever completed, but the idea was there, as well as plenty of pixel evidence in my graph pad, which was supposed to be reserved for more 'serious' work. I had no clue that I was actually going to draw on these experiences in the future, to me it simply was a lot more interesting than homework ...

I eventually went on to study Fine Art. My education was quite traditional (drawing, sculpture and printmaking) but later I, became more interested in industrial methods of manufacturing pieces. I felt an affiliation with a lot of the minimalist's work, such Sol LeWitt and to the sculpture of artists such as Richard Deacon. Taking inspiration from these works and also having developed an interest in kinetic sculpture (moving sculpture) and machines I later turned to the aid of the computer again, this time in the form of 3d modeling and animation. I enjoyed the structural clarity of the 3d wireframe models as they were presented on screen, something that I think is also a quality of both Sol LeWitt and Richard Deacon's work.

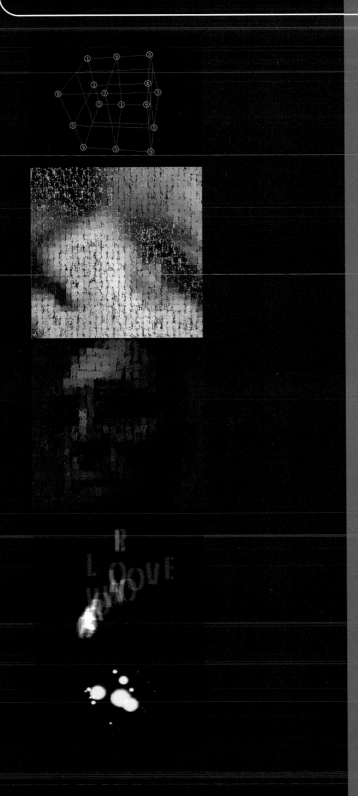

Andries Odendaal

I was intrigued by the new medium and its creative possibilities, but was facing a paradox. I felt that these moving images on the computer screen just simply didn't have the same impact as coming face to face with a sculpture and sharing its physical space, leaving me rather frustrated.

Inspiration came in form of a CD that shipped with an edition of Creative Review magazine. It contained a showcase CD from Ekidna Multimedia (www.ekidna.it).

The showcase, produced in Macromedia Director, consisted of a series of small experimental works that explored the use of maths to control motion and sound through interaction. When I saw the Ekidna CD-Rom, I realised that part of my frustration with the Web and computer related design/art, came from my using the computer as a *tool* and not as the *medium*. Its power lay in being able to do calculations based on a user's input and its networking capabilities, areas that traditionally lay in the domain of the programmer. I felt that if I wanted to explore this medium to its fullest creative potential, I would have no choice but to explore programming and the use of math.

Dimensions

To this end I picked up Director and started to dabble with Lingo. I took inspiration from Shockwave-based sites like www.ekidna.it Noodlebox up at www.amaze.co.uk and www.turux.org to name a few. It felt like being back on the Commodore 64 again and I immediately adopted a much more playful and experimental stance. At this stage I was already working as a designer at a multimedia agency (I've been supporting myself as a designer since I graduated from Fine Art School). So I was finding myself in a situation where I was doing commercial design during the day and exploring more personal experimental work in my spare-time and that still pretty much where I find myself now.

Flash 4 and 5, and the ActionScripting developments that they have brought with them respectively, have turned out to be the perfect environment to put to use some of what I've learned. Sites like www.praystation.com and www.yugop.com have been a great source of inspiration.

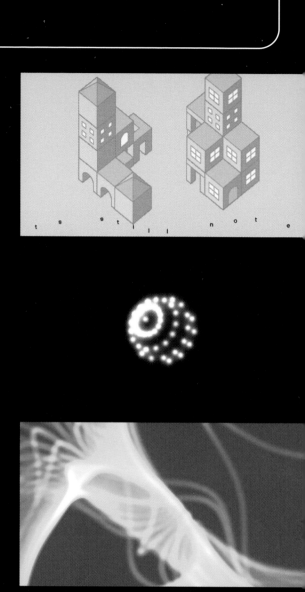

Andries Odendaal

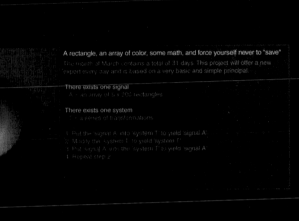

A rectangle, an array of color, some math, and force yourself never to "save"

The month of March contains a total of 31 days. This project will offer a new export every day and is based on a very basic and simple principal.

There exists one signal
A = an array of 5 x 200 rectangles

There exists one system
T = a series of transformations

1. Put the signal A into system T to yield signal A'
2. Modify the system T to yield system T'
3. Put signal A into the system T' to yield signal A'
4. Repeat step 2

WELCOME TO MONO: crafts

In both, the use of the technology is truly inspiring, but what has struck me most is the slick work around the limitations of the medium, something that I think has always been a characteristic of some of the best web design that I've seen. As with most applications that deal with moving objects around in real time, getting the best performance from Flash involves optimisation. The minimalist approach of both Joshua Davis and Yugo Nakamura, their use of simple rectangular shapes forms both an aesthetic and practical answer to this problem.

Through the use of scripting and basic trigonometry, the programmatic movement and interactivity can carry a large part of the concept of an interface or design, without unnecessary graphical execution. This just seems like a much more efficient way of designing, while still maintaining maximum user experiences.

Emphasis is then being placed on designing motion and interactivity rather than graphical execution, or rather, a harmonic fusion between the three. By using scripting and mathematics to design motion and interaction, user interfaces can be given much more tangible qualities.

In the tutorial that follows, I will be taking a more detailed look at 3D ActionScripting, which is just one of a countless ways of applying math to recreate certain effects or motion that we find in the natural world. You can use it to create very interactive and tangible interfaces, but it's important to remember is that it can also be used less literal ways since it is simply dealing with motion.

Dimensions

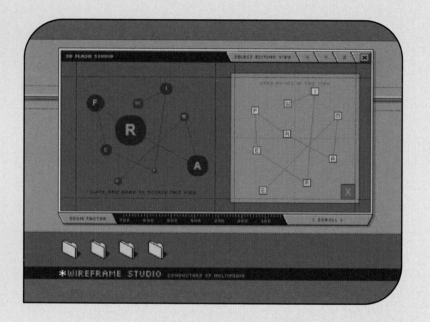

The following technique creates a simple 3D application that allows the user to interact and create their own simple 3D forms by manipulating vertices along the X, Y and Z axis. Although I don't suppose you would want to duplicate this very same application as is, I am hoping that this section will provide some insight into 3D ActionScripting, and clear away some of the mystique that surrounds the issue. It still remains quite a complicated subject, and the fact that ActionScripts in Flash are often scattered within buttons and other movieclips, makes compiling a logical, step-by-step tutorial something of a challenge.

To this end I have created a simplified version of the movie that you can find at www.wireframe.co.za (based on experiment 4, called 3D Flash Studio). I've taken out the perspective slider, and the movie load and unloading actions.

Let's have a look at the stage, which contains the following symbols:

/Mouseloc:

This empty movieclip is used to track the mouse movement when dragging in the 3D View

/TrailerObj:

This is another empty movie clip that follows Mouseloc to create the delay effect when /Mouseloc is dragged. The Rotation of the 3D view is set relative to the X and Y coordinates of /TrailerObj

Invisible Button

This button contains the following actions:

```
on (press) {
  startDrag ("mouseloc");
}
on (release, releaseOutside) {
  stopDrag ();
}
```

The script tells simply sets /Mouseloc to be dragged when the user presses the button, and to stop on a Release or Release Outside action.

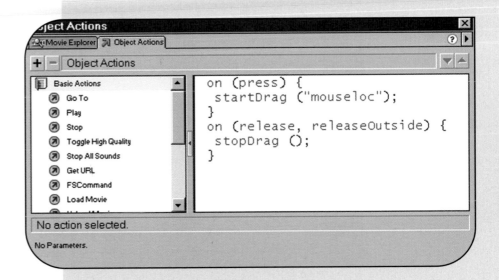

/Vertex:

This movie clip has nine frames, each of which contains the graphics for the different links or vertices in the 3D model. This movie is simply duplicated for each point and each of its duplicates are then told to stop at the appropriate frame, displaying the appropriate graphic. In this case, I wanted each link to represent a letter in the name W-I-R-E-F-R-A-M-E, so the first frame contains the letter W, the second the letter I, the third the letter R etc. Each frame also contains a grey circular button with a rollover state.

Dimensions

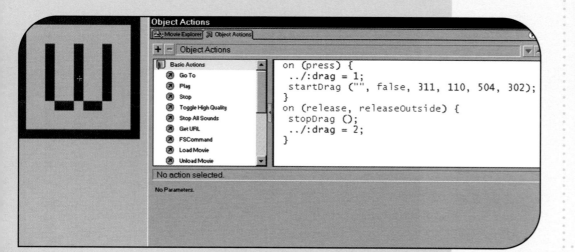

/DragVertex

Instance/DragVertex is similar to Instance:/Vertex; it also contains nine frames and will be duplicated nine times for each of the draggable links in the editing area. Each frame contains a button consisting of a small square with a letter from the name W-I-R-E-F-R-A-M-E. Each button has the following action:

```
on (press) {
  ../:drag/: = 1
 startDrag ("", false, 311. 110. 504 302);
}
on (release, releaseOutside) {
  stopDrag ();
  ../:drag" = 2;
{
```

The script tells the movie clip that receives the Press action to be dragged within a constrained rectangle and to be stopped from being dragged on release. Note that the constraining coordinates are very specific to my movie and are set to represent the edge of the grey editing window. Essentially, you could set these co-ordinates with the help of an expression which checks to see where the center of the editing window is and then deriving constraining coordinates from its _Width and _Height properties. But since I didn't need such dynamic features, I just set these manually, steering clear from making unnecessary calculations in the movie. The script also sets the value of variable :drag in the main movie to 1. Later on, this value will be used to tell the main movie to execute a script that will update the points in the 3D view.

/Line

This movieclip will be duplicated eight times to connect the links or vertices in the 3D object. It's important to note how this line is drawn. Because it's not possible to set the individual vertex coordinates for a line with ActionScripting, we have to find another way around the problem of connecting the individual vertices. The solution is to use a movie clip that contains a single diagonal hair-line and to scale this movieclip horizontally and vertically between the points that need to be connected. It's important that this movieclip must have the same width, height and scale values if the endpoints were to correspond with the vertices. In other words, we need a movie clip that is 100 units high and wide when it is scaled at 100%. To create this line, simply draw a diagonal line running down from left to right at 45 degrees and, in the Object Inspector, set its X and Y coordinates to 0 and its width and height to 100 with the Use Center Point box left unchecked

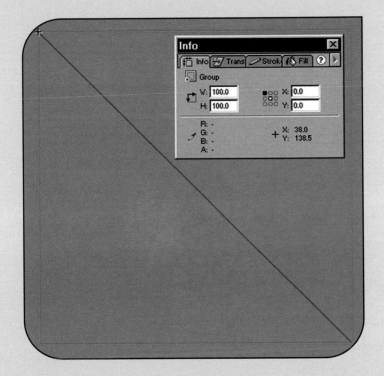

/dragline

This movieclip is the same as /line and will be used to connect the draggable vertices in the editing window. The only difference is that this line is more transparent, so it appears to be lighter in colour.

Dimensions

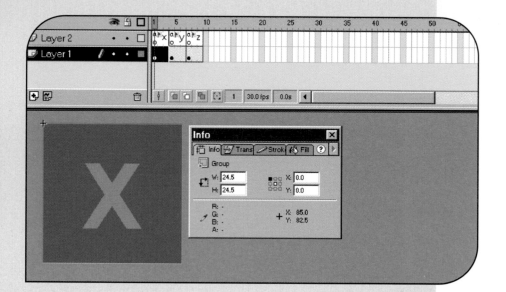

X, Y and Z Buttons

These three buttons tell the main movie which rotation angles to use for the 3D view. They also call a script that resets the positions of the draggable vertices in the editing window to the relative axis. I'll look at that in more detail later.

/XYZ

This movie clip has three frames, labelled X, Y and Z, and containing the corresponding letter. For instance, when the user presses the X button, /XYZ is told to go to and stop at frame X and displays the letter X. This simply serves to label the axis view that you are currently in.

/Window

This forms the background for all the actions. This is a transparent .gif that has been imported into Flash and was originally created in Photoshop. The image is set not to allow smoothing in the image property box. This helps to keep the crispness of the aliased pixel-feel. Because Flash sometimes distorts bitmaps (.gifs, bmps, pngs) around the edge on import, I've included a transparent border of one pixel around the window so that when this happens it won't be visible.

Flash also seems to have another problem with bitmaps. Sometimes, pixels are offset around the centre of the bitmap, causing a smudge effect. I've tracked this down to having something to do with the centre of the symbol (the crosshair in the centre or the 0,0 coordinate). When this happens, I've found that the simples solution is to simply offset the bitmap so that none of it overlaps the centre of symbol. Even if you trace the bitmap, this still applies.

/EditingBackground

This is also a transparent .gif and was treated in the same way as /Window. I made this graphic into a movie clip so that it can have an instance name that I can refer to in the Actionscript. The centre of the editing view is aligned with the centre of the movie clip.

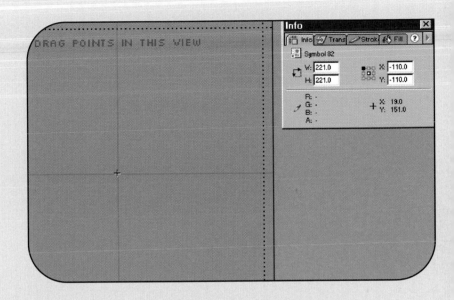

Now that the different elements are on the stage, let's have a look at the timeline. Since all the animation is controlled through the use of ActionScripting, I didn't need to create a separate layer for each individual element. I roughly divided these symbols into the static elements (the "/Window" and the XYZ buttons), which I placed in the background layer, and the symbols which will be controlled using scripting, placed in a layer above that. Rather than having them scattered all over the place, I keep all the ActionScripts in one layer named **ActionScripts** This simply makes it easier to manage them.

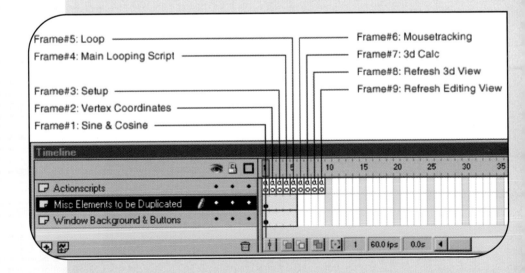

Dimensions

In the movie, I used a total of nine frames with actions. I can divide them into two categories. The first group is the set-up frames that I use to set variables and properties that will be used in the movie. All of this could be contained within one frame, but I have separated it into three clear steps for the purpose of explaining it here. The second group contains the main looping script that adds the interactivity or functionality and is responsible for the animations etc. Again, I could contain this within a single frame but have separated it for simplicity.

Let's have a look at the scripts in the individual frames. This is basically where everything happens. If you've looked at the diagram of the main timeline you'll see that there are no tweened frames or linear animations. All the motion is done through scripting which is contained within the frames that we'll look at next. For convenience, I have broken down the main functions and placed them in separate frames so that each frame deals with a specific task.

The Set-up Frames

The three set-up frames deal with the Sine and Cosine functions in Flash4, the setting of coordinates for our 3D model, and generally the setting of variables that is needed before the user can interact with the movie. Here we'll cover some issues around the Sine and Cosine functions in Flash4 and also look at a more general introduction to the concept of 3D.

Frame 1: (label Sine & Cosine) Sine & Cosine Functions in Flash

Given a particular angle, Sine and Cosine gives you the coordinate at which the angle intersects a circle. The points in the 3D model travel on a circular path around the center point (0,0,0), so Sine and Cosine are used to calculate the position of each point as the angle of rotation around the center point for each axis is increased or decreased. On a two-dimensional plane, Cosine represents the Horizontal (X) value and Sine is the vertical (Y) value for the coordinate.

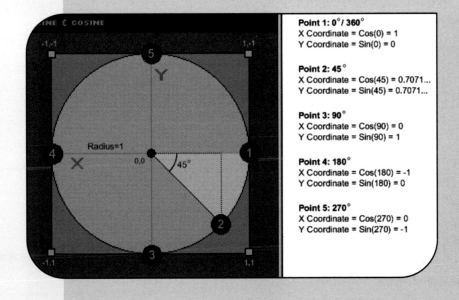

Point 1: 0°/ 360°
X Coordinate = Cos(0) = 1
Y Coordinate = Sin(0) = 0

Point 2: 45°
X Coordinate = Cos(45) = 0.7071...
Y Coordinate = Sin(45) = 0.7071...

Point 3: 90°
X Coordinate = Cos(90) = 0
Y Coordinate = Sin(90) = 1

Point 4: 180°
X Coordinate = Cos(180) = -1
Y Coordinate = Sin(180) = 0

Point 5: 270°
X Coordinate = Cos(270) = 0
Y Coordinate = Sin(270) = -1

Dimensions

The Sine and Cosine values for an angle are based on a circle with a radius of one unit. The formula for working out the X coordinate on a circle is:

radius * cos (angle)
and for the Y coordinate is
radius * sin (angle).

If you're using Flash4, which doesn't have these functions built into its scripting language, the first step would be to find a way to do these trigonometry functions and that is what this script in this frame deals with specifically You could do these calculations in real time using hideously long expressions, but this would slow things down considerably. Even if these functions were built into Flash4 (as they are in Director) it would still be quite CPU-intensive to do these calculations in real time. The alternative to this would be to create a lookup list or often referred to as the *lookup method*.

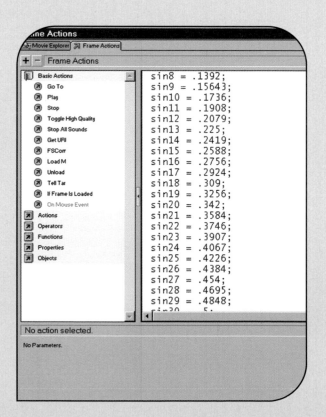

You can do this by setting the values for an array of variables to the values of the corresponding Sine or Cosine values. You could then extract this value whenever you needed it, without doing the calculations. You could also have used Math.Sin(x) to calculate this, remembering that the Flash 5 Math.Trig functions use radians, but we have left the original Flash 4 lookup intact. To create this lookup list, I used the following script to set an array of variables:

sin0 = .0;
sin1 = .01745;
sin2 = .0349;
sin3 = .05234;
...

sin89 = .9998;
sin90 = 1;

This sets the approximate Sine values for angles 0 to 90. From these values you can derive the values for angles 91 to 360. You can see in the graph below that the Sine and Cosine values for angles 0 to 360 range from 1 to -1 and that the Cosine value of an angle equals the Sine value of the same angle plus 90 degrees. The Sine and Cosine values are thus offset by 90 degrees.

Because Flash 5 now includes math functions, we will only briefly touch on how the full 360° lookup table was produced. You can set the Sine values for the next 90 degrees by counting backwards, setting the values of variables: sin90 through to sin180 to the values of variables sin90 to sin0.

To arrive at Sine values for the remaining 180 degrees, you simply need to set the values of variables sin180 through sin360 to the minus values of variables sin0 through sin180.

To set the Cosine values I use the following script that sets the Cosine value for an angle to the Sine value of the angle, plus 90 degrees. So the values of variables cos0 to cos270 are set to the values of variables sin90 to sin360.

And the values of variables cos270 to cos360 are set to the values of variables sin0 to sin90.

When you run the script, two sets of arrayed variables will be set in the movie: variables: sin0 to sin360 and variables cos0 to cos360. To extract the Sine value of a particular angle (X) simply use eval("sin" add X) and eval("cos" add X) for Cosine.

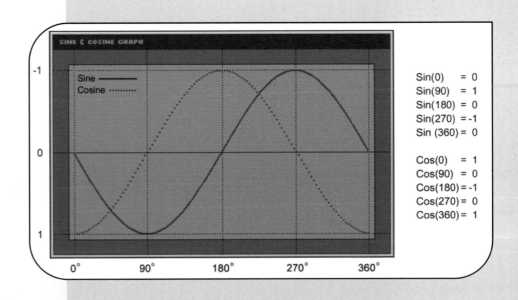

Dimensions

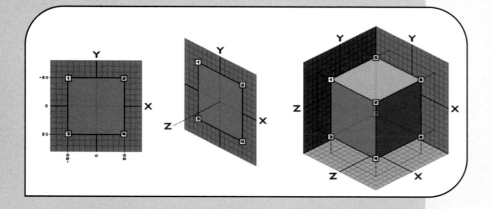

The script in frame 2 is responsible for setting the initial starting coordinates for the individual vertices.

3D objects are made up of vertices that are basically reference points in 3D space. In a 3D environment, vertices have a Z co-ordinate as well as X and Y. The figure shows the vertex - co-ordinates for a two-dimensional square of 100 units high and wide, with its center point at co-ordinate 0,0. Its co-ordinates consists of:

Point 1: x=-50, y=-50
Point 2: x=50, y=-50
Point 3: x=-50, y=50
Point 4: x=50, y=50

To extrude this square into a cube, each vertex would also need a Z co-ordinate.So, the co-ordinates for a cube with the dimensions of a 100 units high, wide and deep with its centerpoint at co-ordinate at 0,0,0 will look like this:

Point 1: x=-50, y=-50, z=-50
Point 2: x=50, y=-50, z=-50
Point 3: x=-50, y=50, z=-50
Point 4: x=50, y=50, z=-50
Point 5: x=-50, y=-50, z=50
Point 6: x=50, y=-50, z=50
Point 7: x=-50, y=50, z=50
Point 8: x=50, y=50, z=50

For our purpose, these co-ordinates can be stored by using an array of variables (Variables: "x", "y" and "z") that would later be used to do the 3D calculation.You can do this manually by setting the value for variables "x", "y" and "z" individually.

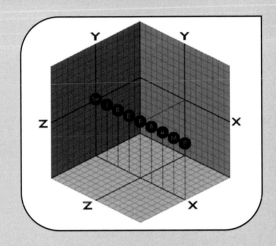

Alternatively, you can write a looping script to do this. In this specific example, when the movie begins, I wanted all the points to line up in a line along the X-axis to spell out the name W-I-R-E-F-R-A-M-E. I wanted the first point (W) to be set at coordinate −80,0,0 (XYZ) and the last one at coordinate 80,0,0.

I did this simply by running the following script, which uses −80 as a starting point and increments the next point's X-coordinate by 20, until point 9 is set at 80, while the Y and Z coordinates are set to 0.

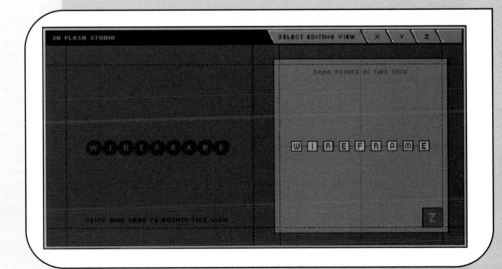

Dimensions

You can use script to create other geometric forms. For instance, for a spiral that twists around the X-axis, you can use the Sine and Cosine values that were set on the first frame.

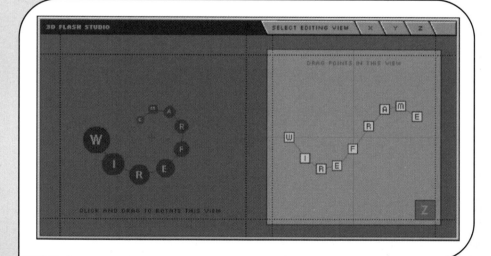

Frame 3: (label Set-up)Setting up the Scene

The script in frame 3 duplicates the lines and points into the appropriate levels and sets initial values for some of the variables that will be used in the movie. It also sets some stage objects to invisible until they're needed later in the animation.

Of special note is the variable "perspective" which has a value that will be used to calculate the 'camera lens angle' or the amount of perspective distortion. The lower the number, the more perspective distortion will occur. It is used in conjunction with "depth" in frame seven to distort the view to simulate a depth of field effect.

The next series of frames are responsible for the actual animation, user interactivity, 3D calculations etc. and consist of two frames that continually loop while calling scripts from the remainder of the frames. They are:

2. Main Looping Script

Frame 4 (label: Main Looping Script):
This frame contains the main looping script that calls the scripts to be executed in frames 6,7 and 8.

Frame 5 (label: Loop):
A frame that is responsible for telling the movie to jump back to frame 4, and in doing so, creating a continuous loop.

Frame 4 (label main looping script) and 5 (label loop)
Frame 4 contains the main looping script that calls the scripts to be executed in frames 6,7 and 8.

Frame 5 tells the movie to jump back to frame 4, creating a continuous loop.

The script in frame 4 looks like this:

```
if (drag)>0 {
    call ("Refresh 3D View");
}
call ("Mousetracking");
call ("Calc3d");
```

This script loops through a sequence of Call actions. The Call action is used to execute a script that resides in a frame other than the current frame. This is particularly handy when you need to execute the same script from a number of different frames or buttons. Instead of copying the script onto each frame, you can create one frame that contains the script and simply 'calls' the script whenever needed by pointing to the frame where the script is resident. It's important to note that the movie doesn't go to that frame. It simply executes the script and, once finished, returns to execute the remainder or scripts in the current frame.

In this case, I've used the Call action so that I could separate the different functions by placing them on separate frames (just to neaten things up a bit). So, in the script we've just seen, if variable drag>0 it will call the script in frame labelled "Refresh 3D View" (frame 8). It also calls the script responsible for doing the mousetracking and then the script that is responsible for doing the 3D calculations and drawing the 3D object.

Frame 5 contains a script that simply tells the movie to go to and play the previous frame:

```
prevFrame ();
play ();
```

This way the movie jumps between the two frames to create a continuous loop of calling the mousetracking and 3D calculation scripts. Notice the Play command; without this the movie will jump to the previous frame and stop instead of play.

Dimensions

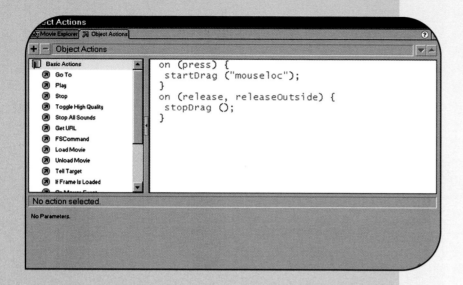

```
on (press) {
  startDrag ("mouseloc");
}
on (release, releaseOutside) {
  stopDrag ();
}
```

Frame 6: (label Mousetracking) Mousetracking

This frame contains one of the three scripts that are called from the main looping script. This script deals specifically with tracking the mouse pointer location and converting the mouse pointer's X and Y screen coordinates into degrees for the X and Y rotation of the 3D object.

When the invisible button receives a click and drag action, it tells "/Mouseloc" to be dragged from its original position. "/Mouseloc" is a blank movie clip that tracks the movement of the mouse, but is not directly used to set the rotation.

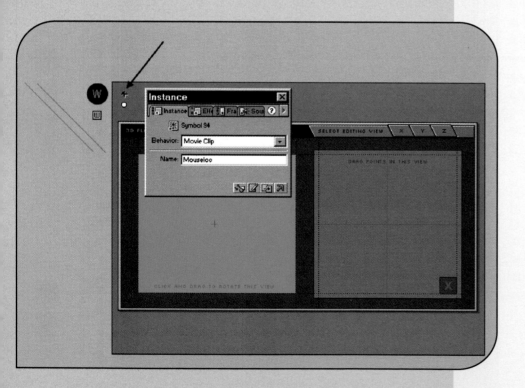

I wanted the rotation to have a delay effect so that the 3D object would slowly rotate to its new position. I did this by using a second object named "/TrailerObj", that follows "/Mouseloc" with a delayed action. It is this delay that is seen in the animation. The delay in the movement of "/TrailerObj" is achieved by first calculating the distance between "/Mouseloc" and "TrailerObj" for their X and Y positions.

By dividing Variable: "DifferenceX" by 5, a value can be derived which is added on to the X position of "/TrailerObj" so that "/TrailerObj" starts moving towards "/Mouseloc". The effect is that "/TrailerObj" will always move towards the position of "/Mouseloc". The larger the number one use to divide Variable: "DifferenceX", the longer "/TrailerObj" will take to reach the X-position of "/Mouseloc". The same also applies to Variable: "DifferenceY"

The rest of the script on this frame deals with converting the X and Y position of the mouse to X and Y angle values which can be used for rotation in the 3d view. I did this in two parts, first setting Variable:"Yangle", the value of which represents the rotation angle around the Y-axis and then Variable:"Xangle" for the X-axis.

Frame 7: (label Calc 3d) 3d Calc

This frame contains the script that is responsible for doing the 3D calculations, drawing the vertices and connecting them with lines.

The script on this frame is also called from the main looping script and is responsible for doing the actual 3Dcalculations and converting the 3D coordinates (X, Y, Z) to 2d X, Y) coordinates so that the points can be drawn on screen. It is important to understand that any 3D environment on a computer screen is an illusion of 3D space. A screen is essentially a 2D surface and the trick is to arrive at X and Y coordinates that can be used to draw the point's position on screen, and a Z coordinate that can be used to scale the points in order to create a sense of depth.

The script uses the "x", "y" and "z" coordinates for each point (set in frame 2) and the rotation angles (Variable: "Yangle" and "Xangle" to arrive at values for the X, Y and Z positions.

The calculations for rotation around all three axis will look something like the equation below and requires a value for the X rotation, Y rotation and Z rotation and values for "x", "y" and "z". The calculation is done nine times (once for each vertex with the value of Variable: "c" corresponding to the vertex number). This is where the Sine and Cosine values (set in frame 1) comes into play.

Note that the below equations contains the formula for calculating the X and Y coordinates on a circle on a single plane. I covered this earlier (remember: **radius * cos (angle)** for X 0and **radius * sin (angle)** for Y.The reason for this is that we are basicly calculating a points position on a circular path, not only for one plane, but for three (one for each axis) with "x","y" and "z" representing the radius or the distance away from the center of rotation on each axis (the coordinates set in frame 2):

Rotation around X-axis:
ypos = y * cos (Xangle) - z * sin(Xangle)
zpos = y * sin(Xangle) + z * cos(Xangle)

Rotation around Y-axis
xpos = x * cos(Yangle) + zpos * sin(Yangle)
zpos = -x *sin(Yangle) + zpos * cos(Yangle)

Rotation around Z-axis:
xpos = xpos * cos(Zangle) – ypos * sin(Zangle)
ypos = xpos * sin(Zangle) + ypos* cos(Zangle)

Dimensions

Because the X and Y position of "/TrailerObj" was used to generate the rotation angles, there is no value set for the rotation around the Z-axis. You can therefore take a bit of a shortcut and only calculate the rotation around the X and Y-axis. You'll see the difference between the two methods in the way the 3D object reacts when rotated.

Calculating the rotation for X, Y and Z as I've shown you would be a more thorough way to do it, but since I was quite happy to lose two lines of calculations, I missed out Z and did it this way:

Rotation around Y-axis

zpos = z * cos(Yangle) − x * sin(Yangle)
xpos = z * sin"(Yangle) + x * cos(Yangle)

Rotation around X-axis

ypos = y * cos(Xangle) - zpos * sin(Xangle)
zpos = y * sin(Xangle) + zpos * cos(Xangle)

Now that the individual vertices are drawn and scaled according to their depth, it's time to give these floating points some structure by connecting them with lines. Because it is not possible to plot individual vertex coordinates for a line in Flash we have to find another way round. This can be done by using a movie clip that contains a single diagonal hairline. The idea is to duplicate "/line" and to put the new instance at the same coordinate as the first point and then scaling it to stretch across to the next point. Because the line is 100 units high and wide its scale percentage and actual size has the same value, in other words, if we set its Y scale to 50% of its original height of 100 units, it would scale down to 50 units etc. Note that that the movie clip won't scale a negative value unless it is duplicated. (Scaling a movie clip that is not a duplicate with a negative value can yield some unexpected results.)

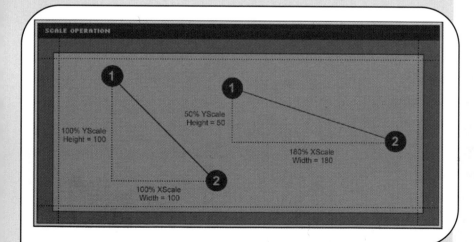

144

Frame 8: (label Refresh 3d View) Moving the Object Around in the World

The script contained in this frame refreshes the coordinates of the points in the 3D view when one of the draggable points in the editing view is being dragged.

Each of the draggable points contain a button which gives variable:"drag" a value of 1 when pressed. If drag has a value of 1, the script in this frame is called from the main looping script (frame4)It's important to note that all the scripts up to this point have dealt with setting static point co-ordinates for the vertices that makes up the 3D object (frame 2), and that the rotation values (Variable: "Yangle" and Variable: "Xangle") set in frame 6 ("Mousetracking") is used to rotate the "world" in frame 7("3d Calc") and not the actual "object". What we're actually doing is orbiting the 'camera' around the 'world's' center point rather than rotating the 'object'. The 'object' has a relationship to the 'world' that is set through its individual point coordinates. To move the object or its individual vertices around in the world we need additional calculations to set new values for its x, y and z co-ordinates (the ones initially set in frame 2).

Also note that the basic 3D engine has already been covered in frame 7 and that frames 8 and 9 deal with the added feature of changing co-ordinates of the individual points on the fly. In fact, if you delete frame 8 and 9 all together you'll still be left with a fully functional 3D engine, which allows you to set the initial co-ordinates in frame 2 and still be able to rotate the view.

I've included the last two frames to illustrate a method of moving the points around within their 'world', which opens up possibilities for numerous applications. I'll touch on these a little further down.In my example, I wanted to play with the idea of a mini-3D application that would allow the user to drag points around in an editing view to create his/her own 3D forms (albeit very simple). This application is so specific that I doubt whether you would want to duplicate it. For this reason I'm going to move through this quite quickly, focusing on the general concept. I'll extract a few key points towards the end of this chapter.

The movie starts with the object being viewed along the Z-axis and the editing view also showing the same view. The view in the 3D window is set through the combined rotation angles on the X and Y axis (Variable:Xangle and Variable:Yangle). If we recap, these angles were set by the position of "/TrailerObj" (frame 6) which in turn, gets its position from "/Mouseloc". In frame 3 we set the X and Y coordinate of "/Mouseloc" to 0. In other words, when the movie starts, the rotation value of both variables: "Xangle" and "Yangle" will be 0 which is the view along the Z axis.

Dimensions

To change the view when one of the X,Y or Z buttons are pressed, I simply set the X and Y position of "/Mouseloc", which usually represent the mouse position, to a new coordinate and "/TrailerObj" follows setting new values for Variables: Xangle and Yangle. The coordinates of "/Mouseloc" for the 3 views are as follows:

Along **X- axis**: "/mouseloc" X position = **90** and "/mouseloc" Y position = **0**
Along **Y- axis**: "/mouseloc" X position = **0** and "/mouseloc" Y position = **90**
Along **Z- axis**: "/mouseloc" X position = **0** and "/mouseloc" Y position = **0**

The appropriate position for "/Mouseloc" is set as part of the action on each one of the X,Y anf Z buttons in the top right-hand corner.

So, now that we know how to rotate the view to the appropriate angle, the following rules apply:

When editing along the Z-axis: the Horizontal (X) and Vertical (Y) distance of "/dragpoint" away from the center point of the editing view, would correspond to the distance of the X and Y coordinates of "/Vertex" away from the centre point of the world.

When editing along the X-axis: the Horizontal (X) and Vertical (Y) distance of "/dragpoint" away from the center point of the editing view, would correspond to the distance of the Z and Y coordinates of "/Vertex" away from the centre point of the world.

When editing along the Y-axis: the Horizontal (X) and Vertical (Y) distance of "/dragpoint" away from the centrepoint of the editing view, would correspond to the distance of the Z and X coordinates of "/Vertex" away from the centre point of the world.

The X, Y and Z buttons each contains a script that looks like this:

```
on (press){
    axisx = "z";
    axisy = "y";
    Yaxisneg = 1;
    setProperty ("mouseloc", _x, = 90);
    setProperty ("mouseloc", _y = 0);
    tellTarget ("xyz") {
        gotoAndStop ("x");
        }
    call ("Refresh Editing View");
}
```

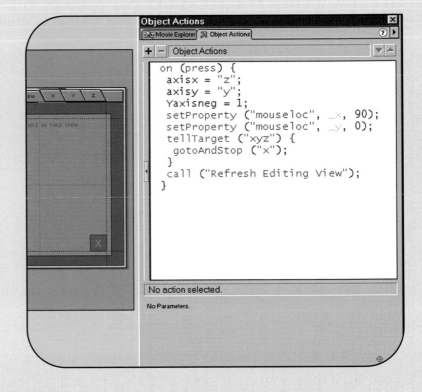

When the user presses one of these buttons, Variable: "AxisY" is set to a value either "x", "y" or "z". This tells the movie which axis of "/Vertex" should be affected when manipulating the Y position of "/dragpoint" for each view. It also sets Variable: "AxisX", which does the same except that it tells the movie which axis to affect on manipulating the X position of "/dragpoint". It also sets Variable: "Yposneg" to –1 if the Y-Axis is selected. This simply mirrors the view when editing on the Y-Axis (without this the editing view along the Y-Axis would appear upside down). It also gives "/Mouseloc" a new position, as already explained above. This rotates view to the new view.

Dimensions

The script in frame 8 looks like this:

```
dc = 0;
while (dc < 9) {
    dc = dc + 1;
     set (AxisY add dc (getProperty("DragVertex" add dc,_Y)-EditingCenterY)*Yaxisneg);
     set (AxisX add dc (getProperty("DragVertex" add dc,_X)-EditingCenterX);
```

The script is looped nine times (once for each point). If the "Z button" was the last one to be pressed, you will be editing along the Z-axis, according to our rule mentioned above, Variable: "axisY" will have the value of "y" and Variable: "AxisX" will have "x" as its value. Variable: "EditingCenterY" and "EditingCenterX" represents the coordinates of the centre of the editing view.

After the script has looped nine times:

Variable: **"y1"** will be set to the distance **"/dragpoint1"** is away from the centre of the editing view on the Y-axis.
Variable: **"x1"** will be set to the distance **"/dragpoint1"** is away from the centre of the editing view on the X-axis.

Variable: **"y2"** will be set to the distance **"/dragpoint2"** is away from the centre of the editing view on the Y-axis.
Variable: **"x2"** will be set to the distance **"/dragpoint2"** is away from the centre of the editing view on the X-axis.etc

The rest of the script on this frame is simply responsible for updating the lines that connect "/dragpoint1" to "/dragpoint9". This script is similar to the one used in frame 7 to scale the lines between the individual vertices in the 3D object.

Frame 9: (label: Refresh Editing View) Refreshing the Editing View

The script contained in this frame refreshes the editing view that the user sees when they press one of the XYZ buttons and is called from the script within these buttons.

Frame 9 is basically the reverse of frame 8. Where frame 8 reset the x, y and z co-ordinates of the individual points in the 3D view based on the positions of the points in the editing view, frame 9 sets the positions of the points in the editing view relative to the points in the 3D view. The script in this frame is executed when the viewer presses one of the X, Y, and Z buttons in the top right-hand corner.

The scripts used in frames eight and nine can be a bit hair-raising but let's look at how this could work for you. I'll recap and summarise what we've been doing throughout the movie.

First we set the individual vertex coordinates (Variables:"x1","y1","z1", "x2", etc.) which gave the individual points a position in the 'world' (frame 2).

Dimensions

Then we set rotation angles (Variable:"Xangle" and "Yangle") based on the position of "/Mouseloc" (frame 6).The above rotation angles, and the vertex coordinates and the "perspective" variable were then used by the script in frame 7 (3D Calc) to derive at a X and Y screen coordinate for each point, as well as a scale value. The point that I want to emphasize here is that the script in frame 7 (3D Calc) is continually executed, each time taking the vertex coordinates, rotation angles and perspective value and calculating new screen coordinates for each point.

So, essentially, you could change any of these variables at any time and the 3D view will be updated. This is what we did in frame 8, where we changed the original x, y and z coordinates for the individual points. These changed variables are then being used by frame 7 to calculate new screen coordinates.

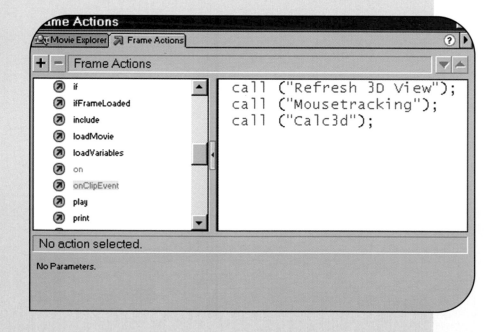

Let's do a little experiment:

Change the script in frame 4 (Label: "Main Looping Script") to read:

call ("Refresh 3D View");
call ("Mousetracking");
call ("Calc3d);

Delete the script in frame 8 (Label "Refresh 3D View) and replace it with the following script:

```
z5 = z5+madd;
if (z5 >100 or z5 < -100) {
  madd = -madd
}
```

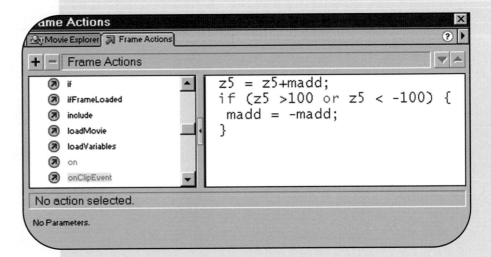

Add this line in frame 3 (label: "Setup"):

```
madd = -10;
```

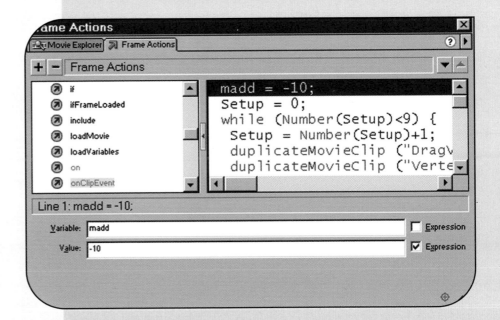

Dimensions

When you run the movie, you'll see that "/Vertex5" automatically moves forward and backwards on the Z-Axis. This is because we're continually adding the value of Variable: "add" (which starts out as −10) to Variable: "z5" which represents its z −coordinate. If the value of Variable: "z5" is smaller than −100, or greater than 100, Variable: "add" is set to −add. This constrains the movement to a limit of 100 units away from the center point.

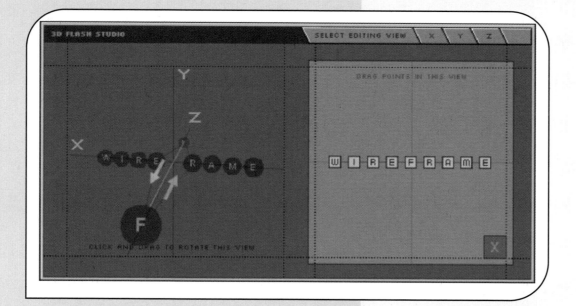

This is just a simple example of how the position of individual points could be controlled but you can create more complex movements. Experiment 5 on www.wireframe.co.za is based on this principal. If you're a game developer, you could base a number of interesting games on this method.

Whether you simply want to create a rotating 3Dmenu (remember, the individual points can contain any graphic or buttons, even text) or whether you want to pursue something more complex, such as the creation of a 3D game, this technique should come in very handy. When it comes to 3D there's quite a bit to wrap your head around, but once you've grasped the underlying concept, things get a little easier. From here, you could move on to experimenting with the setting of the initial co-ordinates for the vertices in frame2. This will give you a good grounding of how the 3D environment works. For instance, try to set up the coordinates needed for a cube, then see if you can create other simple forms. Then start experimenting with moving the points around in space, using simple scripts like the one above and see how you can manipulate the x,y and z coordinates of individual points.

" An effective piece of animation becomes a powerful form of communication, primarily because it has been given a *soul* by the designer. "

ERIC JORDAN
www.2advanced.com

System

As a child, I was awestruck by the well-crafted opening sequences of movies and greatly inspired by rare 3D animation videos that were just breaking into the mainstream. I grew up on science fiction, electronic music and at the dawn of efficient computer technology. This shaped the focus of my design techniques and the way in which I create them. As I was growing up I never anticipated creating animated art across a world-wide network. Sure, my destiny was always going to be art in some form, but the problem was deciding on a platform for my efforts. I was used to expressing my imagination through illustration, painting, writing and music video as an artistic toolset, but where was I going to find a space to exhibit my art created across so many varied media?

For me, that ideal exhibition space came from within my computer: a seemingly limitless tool that has broken the boundaries of conventional methods of composing art and music. That canvas has been widened by the Web, bringing the added dimension of a truly global audience - but with limitations. Rigid HTML constraints and non-standardized browser formatting make it difficult for businesses to communicate and for artists to express themselves. The way around this frustration is Flash web design. This is where the walls come down.

Flash has given me the canvas that I have been unconsciously seeking all along; the answer to combining a range of media to create a rich sensory experience. The word *sensory* is important for me here because I feel that our perception of the world depends upon our basic tools: the senses. Every memory we have is shaped by messages of sight, sound, taste, smell and touch. Textual content and images alone are a practical method for getting across a message, but they offer a limited 'experience'.

MEDIOR IS A HYBRID. IT COMES FROM THE WORDS 'MEDIA' AND 'METEOR'.

MEDI⊕R

EXPERIENCE

EMOTION

System

When they view motion graphics, our audience becomes involved in the essence of our message. To enhance that, we should always try to connect with the viewer on an emotional level, to stimulate them through the use of carefully planned sights, sounds and motions. An effective piece of animation will take into consideration how people respond to movements, tones and atmospheres. Quick-moving text and fleeting bursts of random light might simulate energy or power, while slow-fading text and the relaxed unveiling of objects may indicate serenity or patience.

An effective piece of animation becomes a powerful form of communication, primarily because it has been given a *soul* by the designer.

I like to think of motion graphics in terms of *web-scapes* rather than *web sites*. As a motion graphics designer I attempt to convey a sense of atmosphere in the sites I create. The concept is simple: if the site can sustain itself as a world in and of itself, I've succeeded in creating a tangible atmosphere.

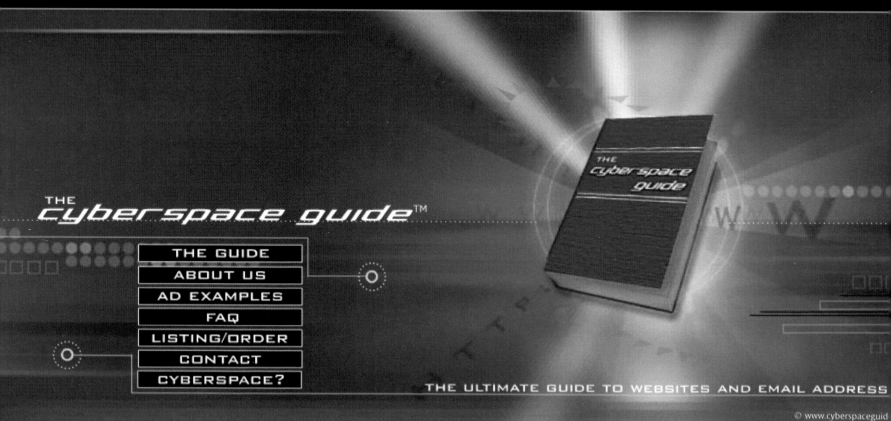

THE
cyberspace guide™

THE GUIDE
ABOUT US
AD EXAMPLES
FAQ
LISTING/ORDER
CONTACT
CYBERSPACE?

THE ULTIMATE GUIDE TO WEBSITES AND EMAIL ADDRESS

© www.cyberspaceguid

Eric Jordan

I remember once talking to a talented Flash designer and thinking of successful Flash sites in terms of a *sphere*. A sphere is a perfectly shaped orb which offers a central space where matter may exist and not be tainted by outside elements. A successfully realized site will follow the same general consistency. If it maintains its form and doesn't deviate from the intended purpose, the site exists as a self-sustaining form of media. The content it carries is justified independently of anything else. This is a powerful way to deliver a focused, streamlined message. You might be asking yourself, "What constitutes a 'sphere' in terms of a web site?" My answer is to think of the center as the content. This is the focal point of the site; the message that is being delivered. The outer shell of the sphere is the design and the way it wraps itself around the content aesthetically. The center is always protected by the shell. The main function of the design is to support the content. You'll see this implemented to the full extent in 2advanced (www.2advanced.com).

ERIC JORDAN PRESENTS

天

風

水

MOTION GRAPHICS DESIGNER
ERIC JORDAN
木火風龍

2 ADVANCED
WWW.2ADVANCED.COM
SOLACE IN TECHNOLOGY, BELIEF IN THE FUTURE.

2ADVANCED REQUIRES:

THE MACROMEDIA FLASH 4 PLUGIN & AN 800X600 RESOLUTION OR HIGHER
A FAST COMPUTER IS ALSO RECOMMENDED

DOWNLOAD FLASH HERE

ENTER

System

As I built 2advanced, I set out to convey a sense of complexity, not only in thinking but also in function. I think that it's been a success because of its surreal atmosphere and the way in which I've made it deliver its message. I'm often asked where the vision came from and what it represents. I think that growing up in an era of new technologies and scientific breakthroughs has certainly had an influence on me. Today, our achievements as a civilization still astound me. I feel that we have come a long way in a relatively short period of time and it's this sense of monumental progress that I wanted to convey with 2advanced. To create a complete and honest vision, I needed to dig deep into my collective influences and bring them to bear on an interface that sang 'progress'. Much of my vision was inspired by the literary descriptions of cyberspace interfacing in William Gibson's novel *Neuromancer*, in which he describes complex GUIs and intelligent navigation routines, beautifully realized ways of interacting with the digital environment of the future. I did my best to emulate these technologies, which meant pushing the limits of Flash navigation. I wanted 2advanced to deliver a focused message of complexity and technological progress within a design shell that was complex but simple at the same time. My plan was for clear organization, flow and streamlined navigation to support a showcase of animated experimentation, concepts and theories about the nature of technology-aided design.

© Cover Illustration Rick Berry

VISION | FLASH WEBDESIGN | STATIC WEBDESIGN | GRAPHIC DESIGN | EXPERIMENTAL | AUDIO | MULTIMEDIA | ✻ | CON

SOLACE IN TECHNOLOGY, BELIEF IN THE FUTURE.

IN PROGRESS

SOLACE IN TECHNOLOGY, BELIEF IN THE FUT

2ADVANCE
WWW.2ADVANCED.C

ICS DESIGNER: ERIC JORDAN

DVANCED? | AWARDS | ENVISION | METHODS & INSPIRATION | THE 2ADVANCED MACHINE V2.0 : REBIRTH OF

Eric Jordan

At a time when draggable windows and second level movies were a rarity, 2advanced made these techniques shine. Some Flash designers denounce draggable windows as a useless and gratuitous element, which, in most cases, is true, but I wanted to use them within 2advanced to show utility, function and intricacy.

I designed the content windows as floating boxes which the viewer could move around the interface. They fall under the sphere concept, but in a more interesting way. Each content box can be seen as a sub-sphere which falls under the main shell of the entire interface. This allows the viewer to focus solely on the message being presented in the window and not be distracted by navigational elements in the parent interface. The viewer still retains a sense of being within the 2advanced sphere, but is focussed on the information within the draggable windows. This is a very simple, yet effective technique to communicate information clearly from within a complicated interface.

The success of a Flash site depends on how well we as designers use our innovative animation techniques to express the client's message. Although clear communication is the goal of all motion graphics, the style in which we present them is unique to each of us, based on our own stylistic impressions. This style will ultimately set the tone for the delivery. Balancing delivery issues with design aims was, for me, an important consideration as I built 2advanced.

Although I had no client brief to satisfy with the project, I had a message of my own to communicate.

Too many of today's Flash intros use extraneous text just for the sake of having something to animate. To avoid this, I wanted to portray my message through graphics and carefully calculated movements. I focused on the speed and easing of my elements to give an overall sensation of awe and relaxed discovery.

You can see the best example of this focus in the 2advanced introduction, before the actual interface is revealed. It begins with a quick, fleeting burst of soft gradient circles and then eases into a tranquil progression of text and images. The text, though, is very minimalist. It never strays from the concentrated message of the site. Each animated segment is meticulously planned and flows into the next. **Everything has a reason to be there.**

Simplicity is a way of conveying calculation and awareness; a whisper can convey more emotion than a scream. I feel that it's the minimalist elements of 2advanced that strengthen its message and make the delivery more genuine. This is where my voice comes through in the design. One of the most difficult aspects of becoming fluent in the language of motion is finding a unique voice. I feel that I've found mine because I was lucky to solidify my style in the early stages of my design career. That has helped me to build a successful portfolio of well-branded projects.

System

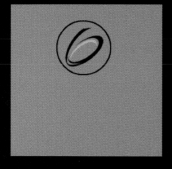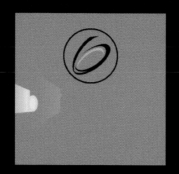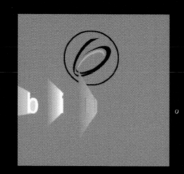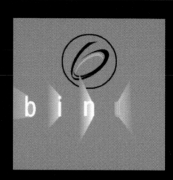

My design voice is a reflection of the world I perceive around me. Anything and everything has an effect on the way I create and express myself. I don't list my influences simply from art or other forms of design, but also from what surrounds me every day. Impressions may come from freeway lights receding in the darkness, industrial machinery contrasting with nature, even the shape of ocean waves as they roll in on the shore. There are so many ways to draw from the world around you, to take elements from life and incorporate them into your design. It's a way of helping people relate to your message, whether or not they are conscious of it.

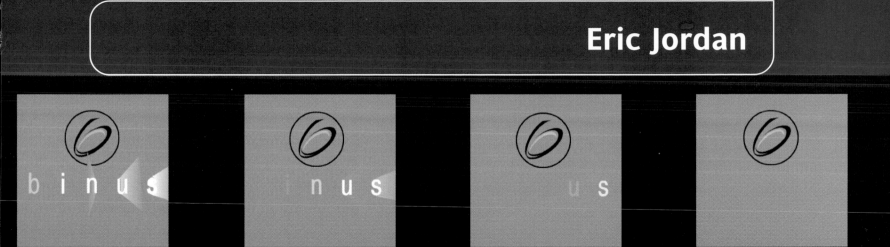

b i n u s

i n u s

u s

System

To begin giving life to the 2advanced introduction, I laid down an array of custom effects with a Roland JP-8000 synthesizer. This powerful keyboard has the ability to tweak waveforms and almost every aspect of a sound, from its envelope to its reverb level. Once I had found an instrument or sample that best exemplified the 2advanced vision, I played a few different notes on the keyboard and captured the sound in Sonic Foundry's Sound Forge. From there I modified the timing and attack of each effect to match the movement of the animation segments. Finally, the sounds were optimized at 22,050Hz with an anti-alias filter. This kept the file size down to a minimum while still maintaining an acceptable level of quality. In the main movie, the sound elements added up to about 27k - not bad at all. The soundtrack, however, was to be loaded as a separate movie on top of the main interface so that it could be controlled with an audio on/off trigger button. Its file size turned out to be around 45k which would be streamed at a rate of 56k a second.

Eric Jordan

Apart from my custom-built soundtrack, I had a series of sounds ready to be mapped out to the intro animation. Planning the visual and auditory aspects for the site was like directing a movie (not that I've ever done that...yet). To help myself keep the focus of the interface as streamlined as possible, as I built the site I needed to go through a bit of storyboarding. Using the simplest of tools - a pencil and a pad of paper - I mapped out the navigation. I also roughly sketched the design layout but left myself room to create most of the final aesthetics in Flash. I decided on an 800x400 interface because, for me, that matches the wide-screen movie format and gives the site a sleek, larger-than-life feel.

For the most part, 2advanced is a combination of imported images and native Flash graphics. Flash is great for minimal design elements, but to achieve extremely complex effects with shading, gradients and lighting, you really need to use something like Adobe Photoshop. You can construct amazing sites when you combine the power of vector animation and the beauty of raster graphics. This is the typical route I take as I create a site because it allows me to create a complex and eye-catching foundation but still utilize the animation and interactivity of Flash. I created the background element of the 2advanced layout using Photoshop 5.5 and mported it as a jpeg file at quality level 7. It's an 801x281 pixel image, consisting of complex gradients and interlaced lines, so a bitmap file wouldn't cut it. I created and imported several other smaller jpeg backgrounds into each of the content Flash files that make up the draggable windows. Using Photoshop, I gave each one its own hue to create a sense of individuality for the content sections. Because Photoshop can handle complex layers, I was able to modify my main background and move elements around to create the series of unique backgrounds you see on 2advanced. I then created a new

layer over each individual file and modified its color and transparency. This established the theme that holds the site together. Apart from the portfolio screenshots of web work and other graphics, I created all other elements of the interface within Flash.

I focused on targeting medium-bandwidth users with a relaxed animation speed (though I used a high frame rate), in order to ensure that my vision would reach a wide audience. I did my best to reuse symbols as much as I could to avoid inflating the file size. My aim was to keep the primary file below 200k, which is a target I have for most of my web-based projects. This size limit is in no way an industry standard. It simply seems to be the best balance between load time and the quality of animation you can achieve. I have to admit that I've found this artistically restricting sometimes, but I've learned to use Flash in such a way that if I plan ahead, I can normally realize my full vision and keep it within the boundaries of an acceptable file size. On a broadband connection, the time it takes to load a 200k file seems to be virtually nothing. A 56k connection doesn't have too many problems either. In the end, I landed at a very acceptable 168k for 2advanced. Though a very small file size by today's standards, it still had to be preloaded in order to avoid any problems during the streaming of the file. Now, I typically only preload about half of an entire Flash movie because it greatly reduces download time and doesn't have a noticeable impact on streaming. The first half of the movie's frames are loaded before the file plays and, as it begins, the second half of the frames are being downloaded in the background. This proved to be very effective with 2advanced. I tested it on a range of machines, varying in CPU speeds and memory amounts, and it ran pretty smoothly on all systems. Recent versions of Netscape and Internet Explorer all appeared to run 2advanced without a hitch.

System

If there is one thing I want people to pick up on when they visit 2advanced, it's the fact that the site is a 'system'. 2advanced design is based on a conceptual GUI that I developed while considering the stylistic elements of operating systems in the far future. Hence the name, 2advanced.

I believe that as technology progresses, we will see simple interactive systems, such as ATMs and other task-specific kiosks, which focus on the use of sub-panels and draggable palettes for their navigation. It allows the user more control over his workspace. If someone is at ease with their environment and its toolsets, they are likely to be more productive. With this in mind I designed 2advanced using straightforward navigational tools and floating palettes that hold specific content matter. It functions much like an operating system, pushing the user to interact with the environment and to be productive with whatever she gets out of the content.

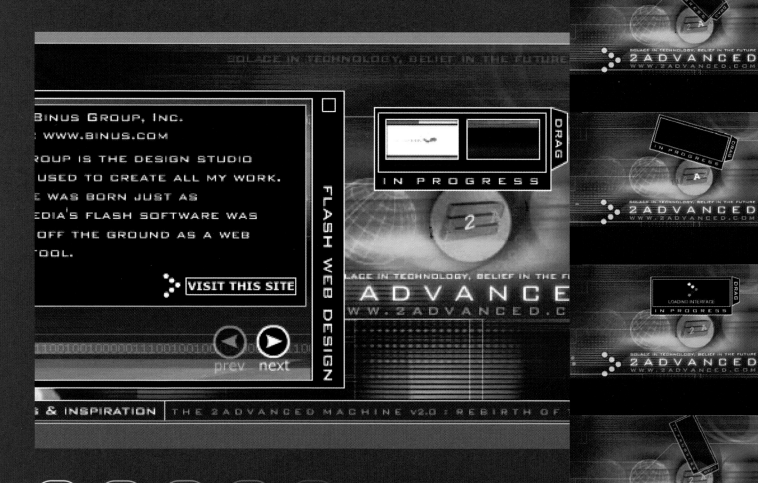

the feedback that I've received on 2advanced, seen that it's these characteristics that give the ng of an operating system that people seem to most fascinating. Most of the questions have about the draggable windows: how I make them (open, close, etc.) and how external Flash files oaded into the interface. As a response to these tions I'm going to take you to the core of the anced system and show you how I've simulated I think could be the operating systems of the e. Although rather common now, draggable e clips are a useful element in interactive media.

They provide a way for the user to have a bit of control over what he is viewing and how he views it. This gives the sense of truly interacting with the environment. Let us look at the draggable content windows which make up the heart of the 2advanced system, and the way in which they function. Over the next few pages I will deconstruct the interactivity and action scripting that I used to create these external movie clips. I've said that I originally created 2advanced within Flash 4, but I have updated my instructions to reflect the changes that you've seen in Flash 5.

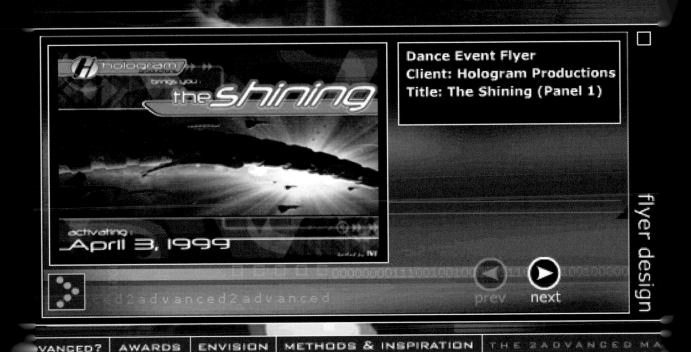

Dance Event Flyer
Client: Hologram Productions
Title: The Shining (Panel 1)

flyer design

prev   next

System

If you're not familiar with the site, let me give you a brief synopsis of what happens in the interface. A row of main menu items (symbols assigned as buttons) appear above and below a theoretical 'load space' where the content is to open. Hitting a button launches a floating box (I'll call them *panels*), which preloads its contents and then opens to the available information. The panels contain a framed background, navigational elements, content and a drag tab. The viewer can use the drag tab to move the panel anywhere within the interface, much like you move dialog boxes around within Windows. In the upper right corner of each draggable panel is a close button which the viewer presses to close the window. Pretty straightforward navigation, but how does it work?

At first glance, the 2advanced interface may appear to be a single Flash file but, if you take a closer look, you'll notice that the panels each preload their contents before actually showing them. This is because each panel is actually an external movie. When I say *external* I mean that the content windows being launched by the menu options are separately published .swf files that are being loaded into different levels of the main movie. This is called the **load movie technique**.

It allows you to insert one or more external .swf movies on top of one another, which can help your design in several ways. One advantage is that you can build in the capability to have two windows open in the interface at the same time. Another is that it doesn't bump up the file size of the main movie too much. Loading movies into the upper levels also gives you control over each movie's timeline independently, which you don't get if you use GOTO commands - that is unless you use some pretty complex ActionScripting. Using GOTO commands in a scene with several independent content windows is basically just going to make things more complicated than they need be. So, to summarize, loading separate .swf files gives you the freedom to control separate timelines while cutting down on primary movie load behind this function is assigned to the buttons in the main interface so that the menu items launch the external movies.

Let's take a look at how the Flash Web Design panel of 2advanced is initiated by the menu. In the Instance Properties dialog box, under the Frame Actions tab, I used the following command to load the external .swf into level 1 of the main movie:

loadMovie ("flash-wd.swf", 4);

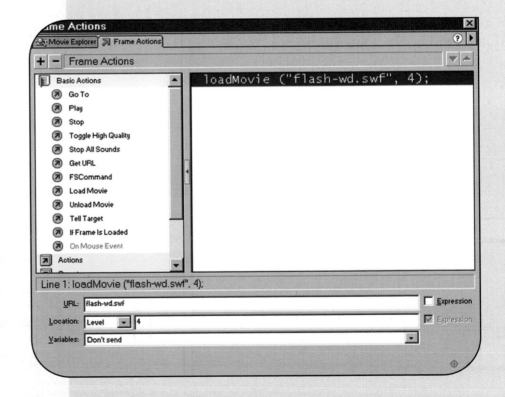

System

Drag-and-drop interactivity can get more complicated than this. For instance, you could want the Drag action to stop only once the user has dragged the movie clip over a certain spot in the main movie.

The ActionScripting for this type of advanced drag-and-drop function might look something like this:

```
on (press) {
 startDrag ("/object");
}
on (release) {
 stopDrag ();
 x  = getProperty (" /object", _droptarget );
 trace (x);
 if (getProperty(" /object",_droptarget) eq "/dropspace")
   tellTarget (" /status") {
     gotoAndPlay ("CorrectDropSpace");
   }
 } else {
   setProperty (" /object", _x, "80");
   setProperty (" /object", _ y, "120");
 }
}
```

where "/object" is the instance name of a movie clip containing the button., dropspace is a one-frame movie clip containing a shape that represents your drop area. If object is dropped in dropspace, then status is targeted to signify a 'correct drop'.

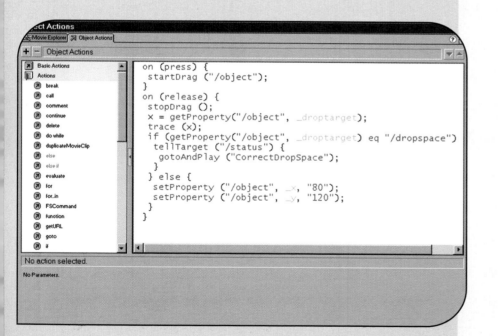

This is practical for games and complex interactivity because it allows for multiple cause and effect situations. But for the purposes of navigation and how I wanted 2advanced to show intricacy and progression, the simple draggable movie clip was enough for me.

OK, on to adding content.

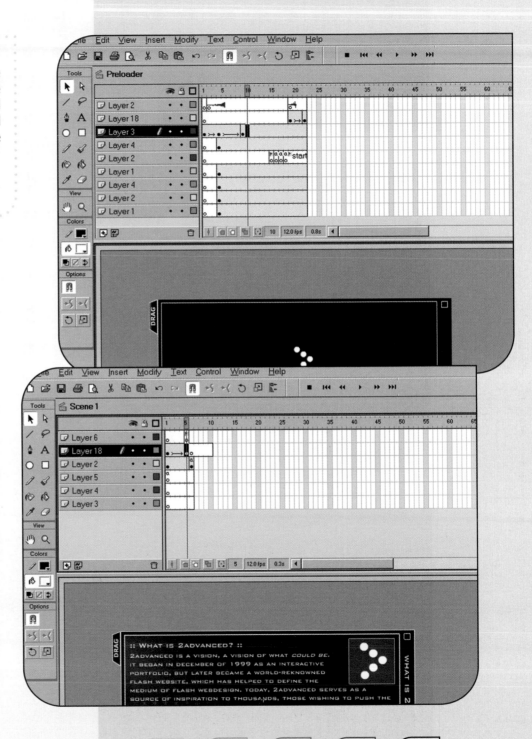

Before I could let the movie clip play I had to preload my content just as I would in my primary movie. The .swf file containing the movie clip consists of two scenes. One is the preloader scene which contains the panel and a preloading sequence. The other is the main scene which is used to display the content that has been loaded. Once the preloading sequence has completed, the movie clip continues on to the timeline of the main scene. From there, the content of the panel movie clip is displayed. The information within each panel is displayed and navigated using standard Flash interactivity, which, I guess, I don't need to go into here. Instead, I'll go on to the final stage of adding functionality to the 2advanced panels.

System

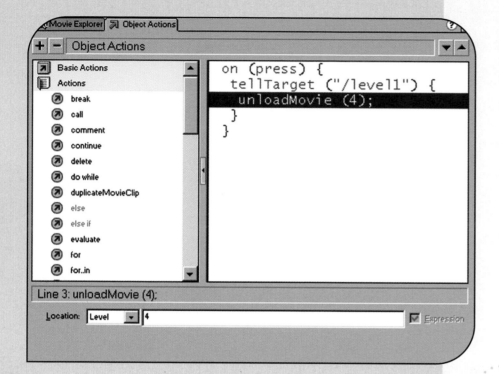

Line 3: unloadMovie (4);

Location: Level ▾ 4   ☑ Expression

Because I made it possible for the user to launch a window from the main interface, logic said that I had to let them close it. I had to embed into the movie clip a button which triggers a shutdown of the panel. For the 2advanced windows I designed a single square in the right-hand corner to serve as the close trigger. Still in the .swf file of the externally loading movie, I had to insert the button within the timeline of the movie clip. I added an action to this button under its Instance Properties:

```
on (press) {
  tellTarget ("/level1"){
    unloadMovie (4);
  }
}
```

The unload movie technique that I've used here communicates with the timeline of the parent .swf file (the file which has loaded the draggable panel on top of itself) and unloads the movie from the specified level. When the user presses the close button in the panel, level 1 (the main movie) is told to unload the .swf that has been loaded into level 4, and the window disappears from the main interface. The communication which goes on between separate movies and their timelines is dependent upon the tellTarget function, a significant addition to Flash 4 which added a great deal of interactivity. Using events to control targets gives you the freedom to control the timeline of the current movie, the timelines of other movies and external applications. The design implications for this new functionality are immense. It gives you valuable control over separate elements and the way in which they speak to one another.

I'll summarize the entire process and how things are arranged.

The main movie (the interface), loads an external .swf file containing to scenes into a new level. This loaded file contains a movie clip which plays according to what its timeline has been specified to do. The .swf now loaded in the current level may be unloaded from the main movie through the use of the close button.

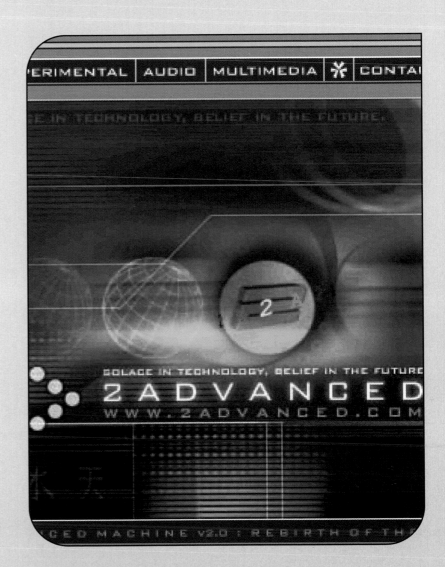

I have often been told that 2advanced certainly lives up to its name and I hope that my deconstruction of the site will shed some light upon the mysteries of its interface. The project has been a greater success than I could have ever imagined. 2advanced began in December of 1999 as an interactive portfolio, but has become a world-renowned webscape which has helped to define the medium of Flash web design. Today, 2advanced serves as a source of inspiration to those wishing to push the limits of this technology. Communicating concepts and visions to that global audience has become my passion. Since the debut of 2advanced.com, I have received a great amount of positive feedback from around the world, which pushes me to continue reaching out through motion and sound. Each project is a challenge and I strive to break new ground with each one I undertake. Flash is a powerful medium, which, once mastered, is capable of capturing the imagination of a worldwide audience. It combines the strengths of motion, sound and interactivity to create the ultimate user experience. In Flash I have found my ideal canvas and I intend to take it to its limits.

" ...the Lego feeling should be something that happens every day, not something to feel nostalgic about as you grow up. "

MANUEL CLEMENT
www.mano1.com

Looping

Sheep Standing next to Large Lego
© Bob Krist/CORBIS

There are two things from my childhood that have had enormous significance on what I do today. The first is the seven years of classical music training I had. Although I didn't realize it then, my music study has had a big impact on the way I feel now about energy, images, vibrations, motion, time and space. The rules that govern music - the transitions between major and minor chords, and the way vibrations work, for example, can be applied to everything around us.

The second is Lego. I always feel fantastically alive when I'm creating things, realizing thoughts and visions in a physical, real-world medium. Creating things now makes me feel like I did when I was a child, making Lego spaceships, or sandcastles on the beach.

Manuel Clement

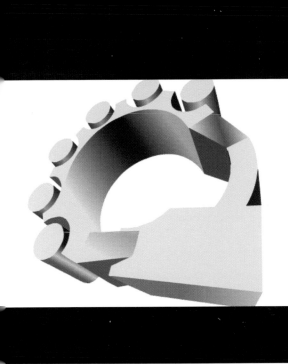

Three years ago I discovered Macromedia and, more particularly, Flash. For the first time in years, I recognized that 'Lego feeling' - I could mold and create my visions and dreams on the screen. Flash was much more to me than another piece of new software. As I played with it, I realized that I had been right to feel frustrated sitting behind my desk at school, that the Lego feeling should be something that happens everyday, not something to feel nostaligic about as you grow up.

When you are creating, you're making a representation, a digital print, of who you are and what you feel. I guess you've already noticed this yourself - this *crystallisation*. When you look back at your work, you can recall the state of mind, the whys and wherefores behind it. I find this crystalization of my past can be a very valuable learning experience.

The work for which I get most recognition is my three dimensional Flash animations and graphics. My artwork has always been about perspective, deconstructed architecture, mechanical devices and structures, so one of the first things I did when I got Flash was to work with those ideas as best I could.

Looping

Because of the technical limitations of Flash at that time, I had to draw a lot of images by hand, working around the two dimensional nature of Flash to create illusions of depth. The process was very time consuming, results were hard to control, and I created everything in a one-shot process that left little room for enhancement or change. Today, the separate tools that automate many of these processes (like Swift3D, Vecta3D and Illustrate) make things much more interesting - and quicker. I can improve my methods of designing environments and structures on the job, because the technology enables me to organize time more efficiently. I guess the scope of a designer's work will always be restricted to some degree by the tools avaiable, but those limitations are becoming more

and more transparent, allowing us to materialize our visions with much more simplicity, and with less consideration for the technical process.

Flash 5's fully integrated programming environment really pushes those limitations. While these new features might at first appear a bit unfriendly if you're not comfortable with code, you'll find getting to know them is well worth the effort; you'll be able to put form to your visions faster and more efficiently, and your creative output can't help but rise dramatically. These features will become intrinsic and essential to your relationship with the medium - unless someone comes up with a better way to transfer human vision to machine.

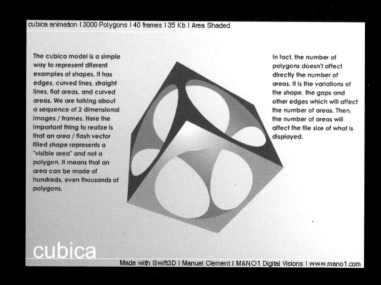

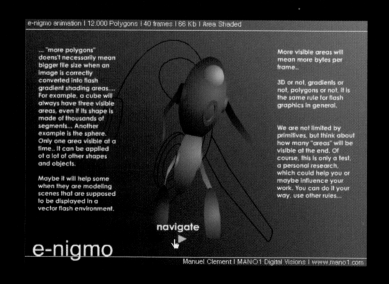

Manuel Clement

For the last few months I've been working with exploding objects and environments. I started by simulating explosions in 3D Studio MAX, and observing how the objects and scenes I had sculpted broke up according to various factors and parameters. While the word *explosion* is often used to signify destruction, it can also be about freedom, new beginings, life and origins, and it was within these parameters of meaning that I was working.

I called the concept behind the new visual identity of mano1.com *oriship*. It's a ship built from a pit that has exploded. I paused the explosion to represent crystallisation. The explosion itself can be taken to represent a lot of things; the process of creation, getting something out of your head (the pit), or the explosion that began everything - the big bang (origins). I think we all have the power to explode and output a world of visions, a micro universe.

Music plays an important part in my current work - in fact soundtracks play a major part in all my web design projects, so I'll discuss sound loops over the next few pages. I'll also talk about the Load Movie action, and using loading locations to help deal with slow loading movies.

Looping

I'm going show you how to create sound loops and switch sound playback, without any gaps or glitchs on the switch, between four different tracks. (You can of course include more sound tracks if you want to.) My .fla files are included on the CD, if you'd rather look at that than build it from scratch.

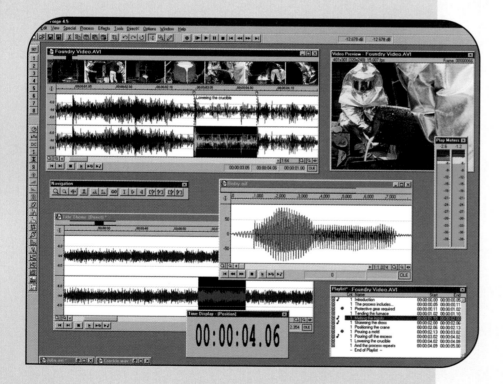

First prepare your sounds in an external WAV editor, like Sound Forge. In order to loop well a sound needs to be timed correctly. The best way to do this is to compose the tracks yourself and then cut the loops out. I wouldn't recommend that you record loops from commercial music, because you might find yourself on the wrong side of copyright law, but if you don't want to set about composing yourself, you can buy sound loops from the Internet, or look for some public domain ones, (www.loopz.com or www.sonicfoundry.com are good sources).

Open Flash and import these sounds (File>Import). Make sure that the sounds are in your Library and that you don't have any sound events set on your main timeline (double-click on a keyframe, and check that the Sound tab displays None). For this example, I'll call the sounds **track1.wav**, **track2.wav**, **track3.wav** and **track4.wav**.

Create a standard button and make four copies. Align them as you like and add some labels (X, 1, 2, 3, 4).

Now we need to add some actions to the buttons. Click on the first one (X) and in the Object Actions window add:

```
on (press) {
   /:current = "none" ;
}
```

Add this action to the other buttons, replacing none with track1, track2, track3, and track4 as you work through buttons 1,2,3 and 4 respectively.

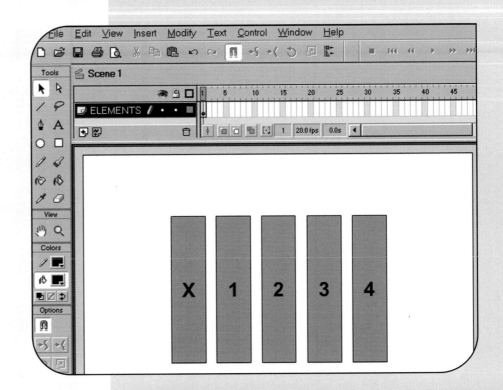

It's important to understand what the /:current variable does.

/:current controls the choice that the user has selected. The colon plays a vital part in defining current as a variable. Without that colon, current would just represent a movie clip, or something similar.

The five buttons are setting this variable value to:
none : no sound is played, all tracks are stopped
track1: track1 plays, all other tracks are stopped
track2: track2 plays, all other tracks are stopped
track3: track3 plays, all other tracks are stopped
track4: track4 plays, all other tracks are stopped

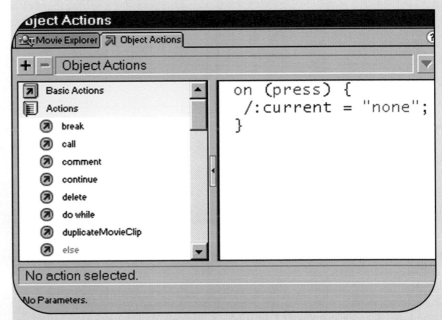

Looping

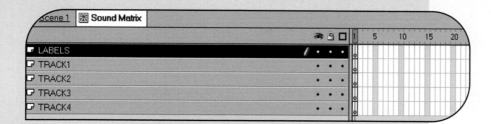

The next thing to do is add in a sound matrix, a system that will start to play the selected track and stop the previous one.

Create a movie clip symbol and call it **Sound Matrix**. Create five layers and name them as I've done here.

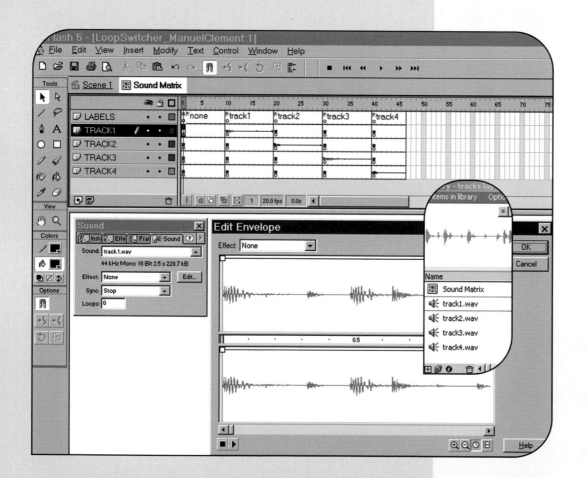

Put a blank keyframe on each of the layers. On the top layer, **LABELS**, click keyframe 1 and in the Frame Panel add the label **none**.

Now add the sound events that stop the four tracks in order. Each track has its own layer, so beginning with **TRACK1**, click keyframe 1, select the Sound Panel and choose the sound track1.wav from the sound pop-up menu. Set the Sync to Stop and hit OK.

Repeat the exact same process for **TRACK2**, **TRACK3** and **TRACK4**, selecting track2.wav, track3.wav and track4.wav respectively.

Now select the column of keyframes on frame 1 from the top layer, LABELS, down to TRACK4, and copy these keyframes so that you can reuse them.

Select the column of frames at frame 10 and paste in the keyframes. The columns of keyframes at frame 1 and frame 10 should be identical. Paste in the keyframes again at frames 20,30 and 40. You should have five identical columns.

We need to rename the labels on four of the five columns. Click on frame 10 of the LABELS layer, and change the label's name to track1 via the Frame Panel. Change the other labels as appropriate, at frame 20 to track2, at frame 30 to track3 and at frame 40 to track4.

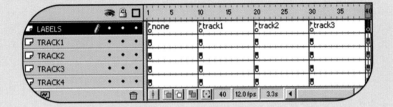

We'll change the sound events so that the right sounds begin at each label.

Go to frame 10 and click on the keyframe of the TRACK1 layer. On the Sound Panel change the Sync from Stop to Start. Repeat that process at frame 20 on the TRACK2 layer, at frame 30 on TRACK3 and at frame 40 on TRACK4.

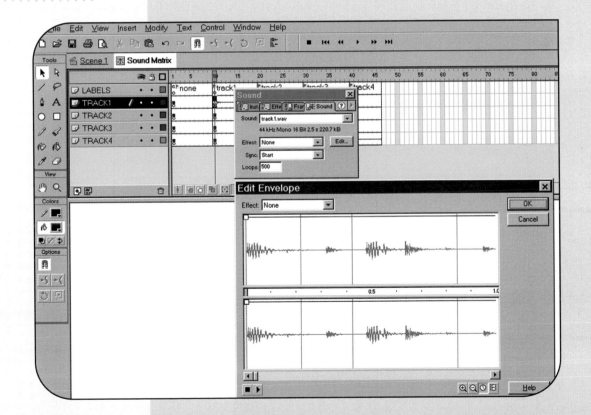

Looping

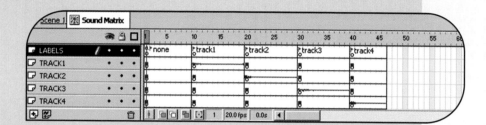

The Sound Matrix timeline should look like this. Don't worry about the extra keyframes, they won't increase the size of the final movie.

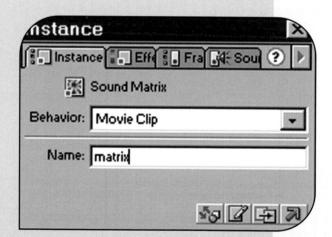

Drag the Sound Matrix from your Library onto the main timeline. Before we can assign Tell Target actions to the Sound Matrix we need to give it an instance name. Select it, and on the Instance panel type the name **matrix**. Now you can assign Tell Target actions to the matrix by specifying the path /matrix.

So far, we've created the user interface with five buttons on the main timeline, set the /:current variable value, and created a Sound Matrix that starts and stops the tracks. We still need to create a device that continuously checks the value of /:current and tells the Sound Matrix (/matrix) to go to a label. Basically, that's the device that links the user interface with the Sound Matrix.

Create a new movie clip symbol and call it **controller**. The first job of the controller is to set a default choice. For this example, we'll set the default user choice to none, which means that no sound will play in the Flash movie until the user presses one of the buttons.

Select frame 1 and add this action:

/:current= none

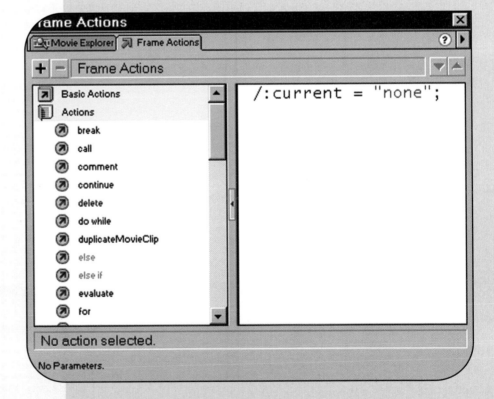

Looping

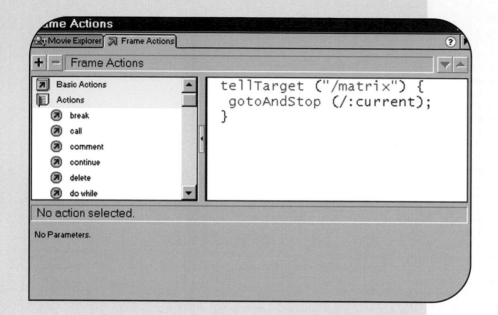

Now we need to add the continuous action that will change the state of the Sound Matrix (/matrix) when the user changes the value of the variable /:current. So add a keyframe to frame 5, select it and add this action:

```
tellTarget ("/matrix") {
  go toAndStop (/:current);
}
```

The action tells the movie clip /matrix to go to the label named with the variable value of /:current. The labels in the /matrix movie clip match the values the user buttons are set to (none, track1, track2, etc.).

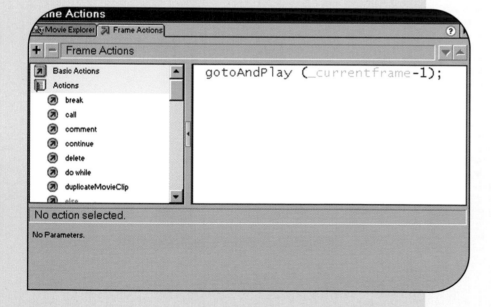

To make this action run over and over when the .swf plays, add a keyframe on frame 6 and add in this action:

```
gotoAndPlay (_currentframe - 1);
```

This action tells the the movie clip to go to the previous frame and play it. I chose to use an expression rather than a frame number because it makes the system easier to customize. If you wanted to move your keyframes to another place, for example, the _currentframe - 1 expression would ensure that the loop still works.

We need to put the controller movie clip on the main timeline.

Select the controller symbol from the Library and drag it onto the main stage. Double-click on it and enter a new instance name, **controller**. Specifying an instance name on the controller isn't particularly important for this example, but might be useful if you are tweaking the system at a later date.

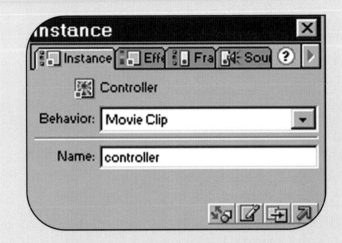

We're almost done... How about making a small screen to show the track selected by the user?

Select the Text tool. Activate the Text Field button to make a text field that will display the variable. Create a text area on the main timeline under the user interface (the five buttons that you created earlier). To edit the properties of this text box bring up the Text Options panel.

In the Variable field, type current. Untick Selectable and tick Border\Bg.

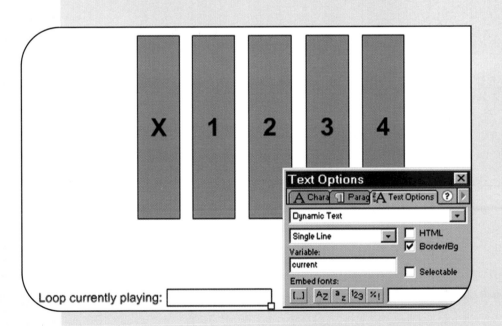

Looping

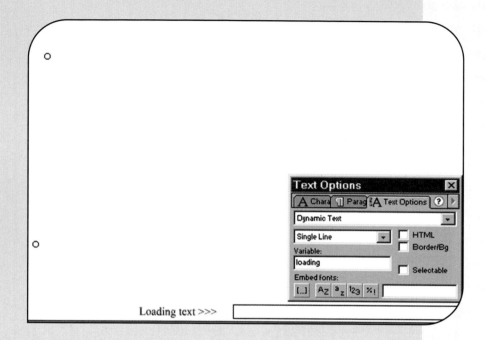

Text Options ×

A Chara | ¶ Parag | ₌A Text Options | ? | ▶

Dynamic Text ▼

Single Line ▼ | ☐ HTML
| ☐ Border/Bg

Variable:
loading | ☐ Selectable

Embed fonts:
[...] | A_Z | a_z | 123 | %! |

Loading text >>>

But I'm not here to focus on problems, so let's build the solution. We'll send a string value to a variable text field visible on the main .swf stage of the first frame of the .swf we'll load. Once the .swf is loaded, we'll send an empty string value to the same visible variable located on the main movie that will stop to display the loading messege. This will give you a small file size (just a few lines of ActionScript). It's efficient (the loading messege is displayed instantly, even if no graphic or text has been loaded) and, if you use it across your site, brings consistency to your design. This method also makes changing the location of any loading messege on your project very simple.

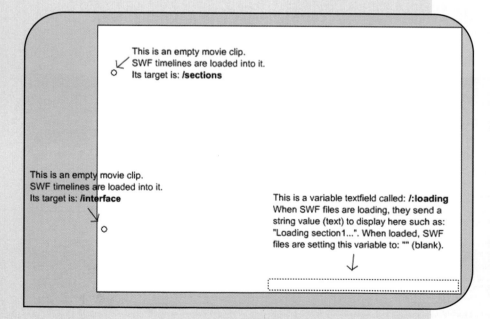

This is an empty movie clip.
SWF timelines are loaded into it.
Its target is: **/sections**

This is an empty movie clip.
SWF timelines are loaded into it.
Its target is: **/interface**

This is a variable textfield called: **/:loading**
When SWF files are loading, they send a string value (text) to display here such as: "Loading section1...". When loaded, SWF files are setting this variable to: "" (blank).

Before we start, let's go through all the elements that we'll be using in the project.

The main movie (main.fla>main.swf) will be the .swf that's embedded onto the HTML page, the root of your project. This movie has to be very small so that it will load quickly. This is the movie that will hold all the other .swf files the user will display or load. There's no need to create a loading sequence for it because it should be no bigger than 1-5k, which should stream on even the slowest connection.

The interface (interface.fla>interface.swf) is the movie that loads right after your main movie. It contains the navigation of the site. In this particular example, it will be made up of three rectangular buttons labelled **load section1**, **load section2** and **clear.**

Section 1 (section1.fla>section1.swf) is a template for the content you would like to put there, and **Section 2** (section2.fla> section2.swf), likewise.

You can extend the system to include as many sections as you need. For this example, we'll use two.

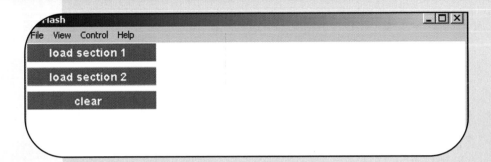

Blank (blank.fla>blank.swf) is an empty .swf that enables us to avoid the Unload Movie action and its disadvantages. Loading the blank.swf into a location makes things look exactly the same as if you were using the Unload Movie action, but no file is removed from the user's cache.

So that's the plan. Now we'll go through the process.

First, create a new Flash movie, edit the movie properties and change the frame rate to 20. That's the fps rate that I use in most of my Flash projects.

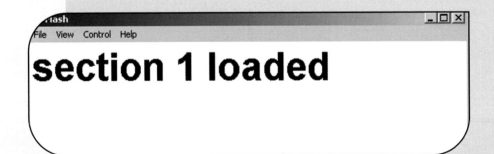

Looping

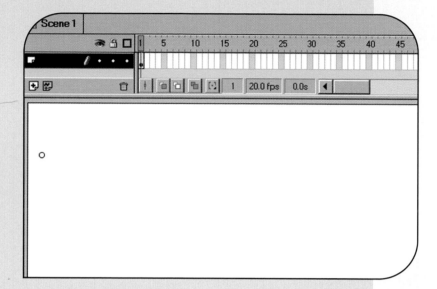

Now create the only symbol that you'll need. Insert a new movie clip symbol and call it **blank movie clip**. Don't create anything in this symbol, but go back to editing the main stage timeline.

Next, create the locations for the section loading. Drag the blank movie clip symbol that you've just created from the Library onto the main stage.

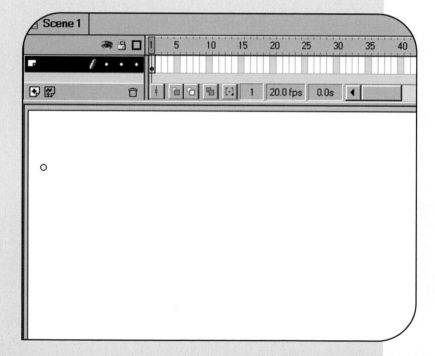

Select the empty movie clip and on the Instance Panel type the name **sections**. The path to this empty movie clip is now /sections.

Now you need a second empty location to load the user interface. You don't need to create a new symbol. Just reuse the same blank movie clip and give it a different instance name. Drag another blank movie clip symbol from the Library and place it on the main stage where we'll load the interface, like I've done here. Call it **interface** in the Instance panel Name field.

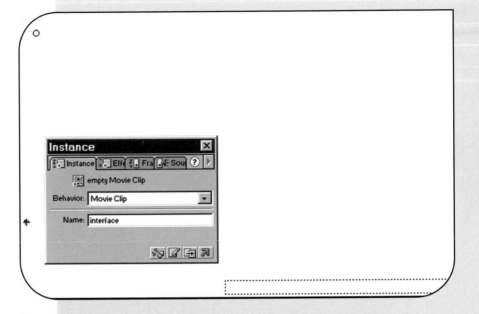

We're going to create a variable text field to display the loading messages instantly. Select the Text tool, and then choose Right Alignment and Dynamic Text from the Text Options panel. I usually use the _sans font in text fields that are going to display variable values because it is aliased and very readable. If you decide to use a different font make sure that it will display correctly by activating the outlines.

Create the variable text field on the main stage area.

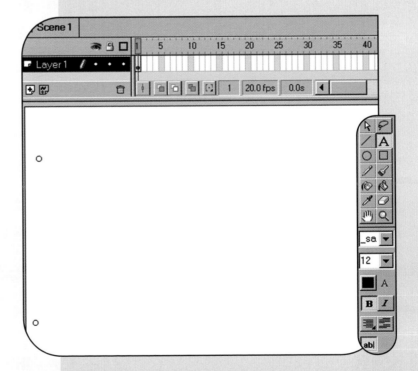

Looping

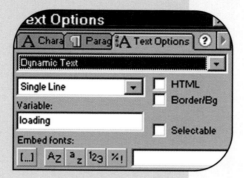

Edit the properties of the text field using the Text Options panel as I've done here.

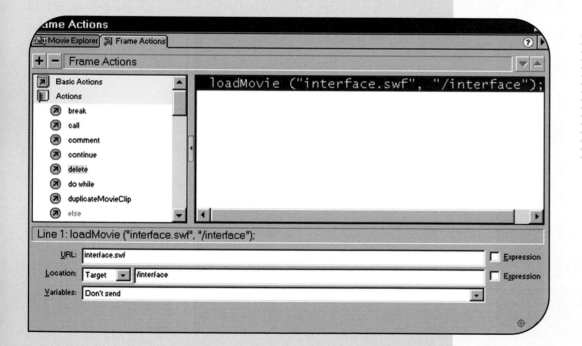

You need to add an action to the main movie that will load the interface movie (interface.swf) into its empty target (/interface). Add this action to frame 1:

loadmovie ("interface.swf","/interface");

Save your document as **main.fla** and export your movie as **main.swf**.

Your main stage area should look like mine here on the right.

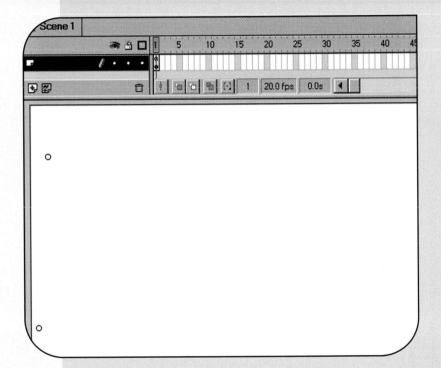

The next stage is to build the interface.

Create a new Flash document.

Create a blank keyframe on frame 1, frame 2 and frame 3. Frames 1 and 2 will be the loading sequence, while frame 3 will be the keyframe where everything is displayed.

Looping

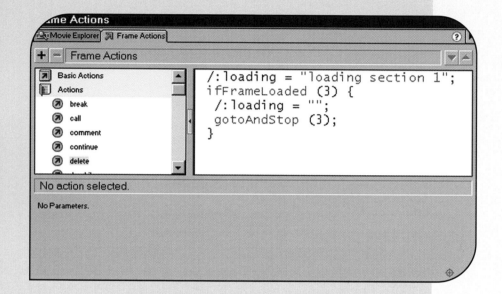

```
/:loading = "loading section 1";
ifFrameLoaded (3) {
    /:loading = "";
    gotoAndStop (3);
}
```

No action selected.

No Parameters.

On frame 1, add this action:

/:loading = "Loading section 1" ;
if FrameLoaded (3){
        /:loading = "";
        gotoAndStop (3);
}

The first action is sending a string value Loading interface to the variable /:loading which is visible on the main stage.

The second action will occur once the frame 3 (which contains our content) has loaded. The movie will send a blank string value "" to the variable /:loading, (i.e. clear it), then go to frame 3 and stop. The contents (interface) will be displayed and the loading message will disappear.

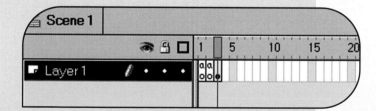

We want the action on frame 1 to repeat itself until the contents (frame 3) has loaded. On frame 2, add this action:

go toAndPlay (1);

Select frame 3. This is where the interface will be located.

Now you can create a basic button on your user interface. Draw a rectangle, (these are 9X1 on the default 18px grid) make it a button and call it **generic button**. Copy and paste to create two more buttons and arrange all three like this.

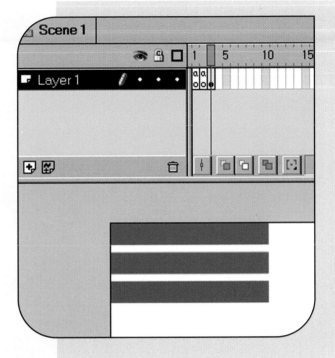

Now give these buttons some names. Create centred text labels, using the names **load section 1**, **load section 2** and **clear**.

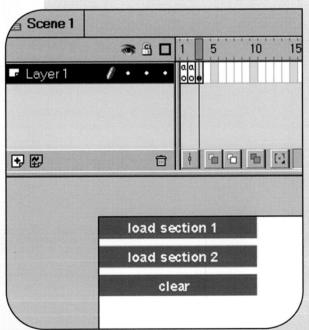

Looping

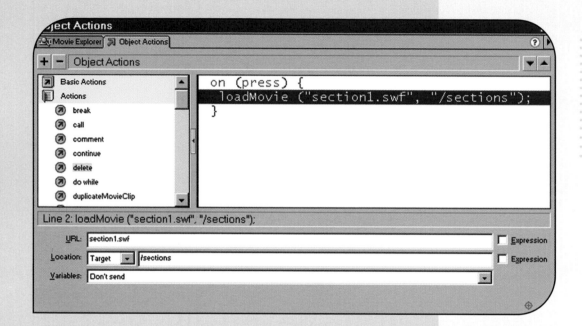

To load section 1, add this action to the first button:

```
on (press) {
loadMovie ("section1.swf","/sections";
}
```

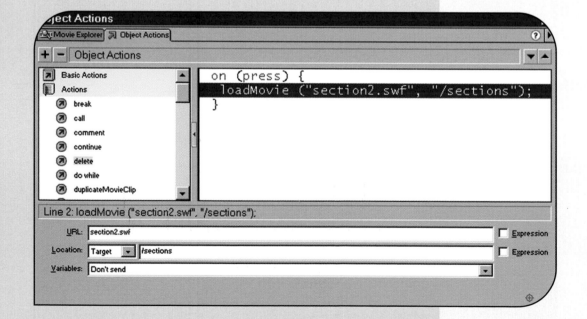

When the user presses the button, the specified URL (section1.swf, in this case) is loaded into a target, which is an empty movie clip located on the main stage area, /sections. Add the same action to the second button (load section 2) but replace section1.swf with section2.swf. In the third button, insert blank.swf.

Export your movie as **interface.swf** and save your document as **interface.fla**.

The next stage is to build section 1. This is a template that will include your content. The only content I'm using here is some text - **section (number) loaded** - but, of course, you can customize this.

So, create a new Flash document. Use the same preloader that you built for the interface on frame1. You'll see in the screenshot that everything stays the same, except the loading message, where **loading interface** becomes **loading section**.

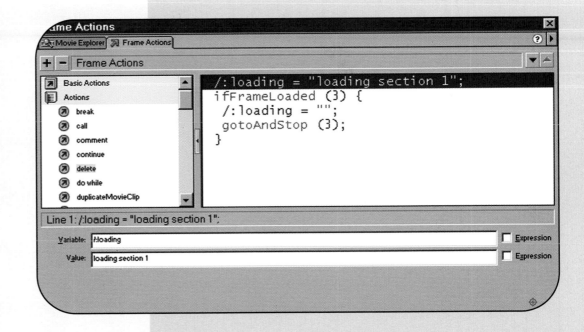

Select frame 3, where your content will be. For this example, simply create a text object. Select the Text tool, and make sure the Text Field option is disabled. Click on the stage and type **section 1 loaded**. Your timeline should look like this.

Export your movie as **section1.swf**. Save your document as **section1.fla** and close.

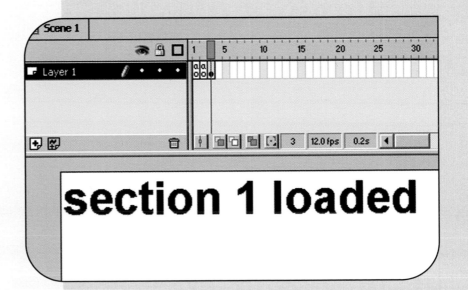

Looping

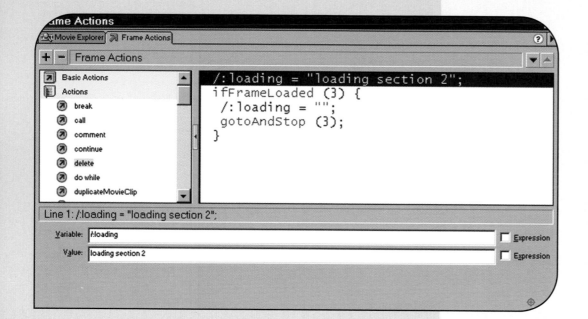

Now build section 2.

Open section1.fla. On frame 1, change the action to:

```
loading = "loading section 2";
if FrameLoaded (3){
  /:loading ="";
  gotoAndStop (3);
}
```

On frame 3, change the text that's displayed to **section 2 loaded**

Export the movie as **section2.swf**. Save the document under a different name, **section2.fla**. Close the document.

To build the blank movie, create a new Flash document and export it as **blank.swf**. Save it as **blank.fla** and close it.

All the elements of our system are now ready. Go to the folder you've exported all of the .swf files to. Open the file main.swf, which should give you this screen:

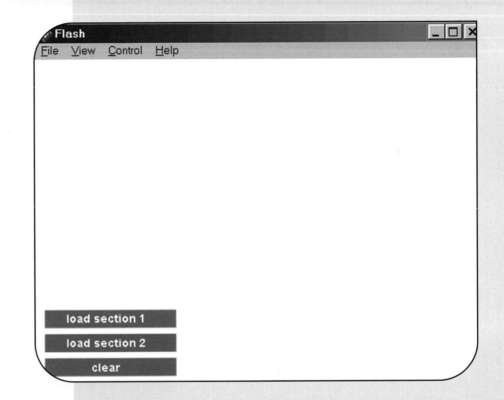

Click on the button called load section 1. You'll see the section1 loaded in the empty location we've created on the top left corner of the stage area. Note that you won't see the loading message. This is because you're playing the file locally. When the system is loaded from the Internet, and if your sections are containing a lot of content, the loading message will appear on the screen and remain until loaded.

The system that we've built is very easy to expand. Each element is loaded separately and, even if you clear the sections from the screen, they are still in the user's cache (via the blank.swf replacement). By using target locations instead of levels, you can change the location of every element by editing one file (main.fla) and moving the empty movie clips around.

" Cinema allowed a new breed of designers to express their creativity in a novel way, using motion. Now Flash and the Web allow us to explore new coupling that same motion graphic design with interactivity. "

BRENDAN DAWES
www.saulbass.com

React

I can remember the first time I saw truly great motion graphics on screen as if it were yesterday. Feeding my passion for sixties spy movies, I was taping everything that even vaguely sounded like it might give me my much-needed fix. If it had plot twists aplenty, shady characters and mad gadgets, I had it labeled and boxed. *Charade* sounded like it would fit the bill perfectly. Starring Cary Grant and Audrey Hepburn, the film was a roller coaster ride full of white-knuckle twists and turns.

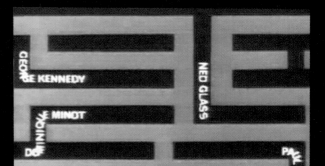

Brendan Dawes

I sat down to watch the 1963 movie without any idea that the first two minutes would make such an impact on me. Spiraling arrows pulled me into the movie as Henry Mancini's perfect 'spy jazz' score held me hypnotized. The arrows accelerated, and a maze of scurrying cast names slid onto the screen, getting lost as the lines spun faster and faster. This was no ordinary title sequence, this set the theme for the entire movie: simple graphical shapes and lines, with hectic momentum setting the chaotic theme for the movie, being chased and being lost.

The man responsible for this title design masterpiece was Maurice Binder, best known for his work on the James Bond titles. His work has showed me how graphics together with motion can convey messages and themes much more emotively than simple print. I had to know more about what we now call Motion Graphics, and it wasn't long before I came across the father of motion graphic design, Saul Bass.

React

Were Saul alive today, I feel sure he would be using Flash as his creative medium. You only have to look at his stunning titles for movies like *Psycho* (lines slashing across the screen) and *Vertigo* (hypnotic spirals) to recognize his work as the forerunner of many of today's Flash web site sequences, even if the creator doesn't know it.

I created a web site in homage to this design legend. I developed Saulbass.com entirely in Flash, as an exercise in using Bass' work as inspiration for the interface and general look and feel of the site. I've kept text to a minimum, relying on simple graphical shapes for navigation. The color scheme is predominantly red and black, based on the poster design for *Anatomy Of A Murder*.

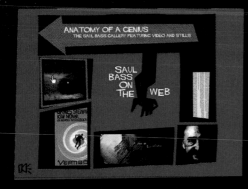

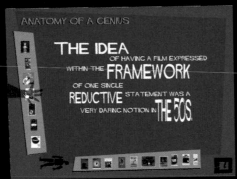

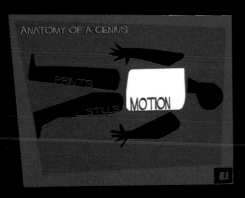

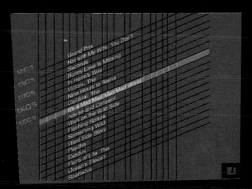

Each section of the site uses different areas of Saul Bass' work as inspiration. The Filmography section is based on the title sequence of *North By Northwest*, the films from each decade sliding in top to bottom, bottom to top, like a typographic elevator, above lines that suggest compass points. I used the dead man cut out graphic, also from *Anatomy of A Murder*, as a navigational device in the gallery section. Motion is used to cut between the different sections, though it's not overplayed. I really don't like those long-winded interface designs that do a better job of showing off graphical tricks than getting you where you want to be! How many times have you used a navigation system that, after selecting an option, takes another ten seconds or more to open up, spin round, or carrying out some other fancy maneuver, before letting you at the content. It might be great the first time, but it soon gets frustrating, and eventually deadly dull! Saul Bass knew that "less is more" and that still holds true even today.

React

Using Flash as a medium for creating carbon copies of the work of designers like Bass, Binder and Pablo Ferro is perhaps doing this great piece of software a big injustice, and possibly missing the point. Cinema allowed a new breed of designers to express their creativity in a novel way using motion. Now Flash and the web allow us to explore new heights, coupling that same motion graphic design with interactivity. Cinema is a fairly passive medium, although there were some crazy initiatives in the fifties to electrify seats and the like! By contrast, Flash is an interactive medium and should implemented as such. This is not to undermine pure motion graphics work constructed in Flash, these are great too, but they are not the whole story. For

example, I was checking out one of the many Flash forums on the web not so long ago, and came across a post that said: "The future of the web is here!" Expectantly I clicked on the link, anticipating a great innovative work, but it turned out to be a 2 megabyte 3D-esque Flash movie. The whole experience was completely passive, I just sat back and watched. The truly depressing thing about this was that many people on the forum agreed that this was indeed the future, that as soon as broadband arrived we would be seeing more stuff like this. They had to be kidding! This work completely missed the point of the medium they were enthusing about, it may of well been on a TV screen for the lack of interaction.

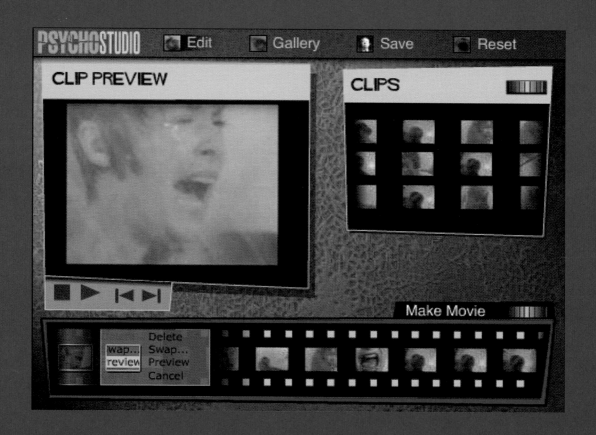

Brendan Dawes

When you're creating motion graphics in Flash you've got to think in Flash too. Think about the medium you're working in. Think about how you can involve user participation in your design, where the differences lie between this medium and a more passive medium like print or cinema. In the gallery section of the Saul Bass site for example, I didn't even try to choose between running a simple soundtrack in the background oblivious to the user and some rollover sounds, but put the two ideas together. I cut the jazz score from *Anatomy Of A Murder* into separate audio chunks that are triggered when a visitor rolls over a gallery thumbnail, the user is play-ing the score, and the sound and graphics work together in the interaction.

It is my personal belief that this interplay between motion graphics and interaction in Flash will give rise to truly interactive applications, or as I like to call them Flapplications. Think back to the days when Java was made out to be the application savior of the web, and we were told that we would all be using Java applets for our day-to-day web business. How many times do you use Java applets? When did you last see one of those terrible early Mac implementations that crashed or hung your browser? As the majority of front-end web development is done on Macs, it stands to reason that a bad implementation of the Java Virtual Machine together with the marked absence of a really good Java editor wasn't really going to help Java set the world on fire as far as graphical user interfaces and creative applications go. But now we have Flash 5. It's cross platform and it has its own virtual machine, only this time we call it a 'plug-in', which we know guarantees that as long as the user has it, your effect will run as you expect it to. But it also has many advantages graphical and interactive design advantages over Java: fonts are encoded with the file, you can throw graphics around easily, interaction is easily built in, sound can be added without any hassle, mp3 support, scalable etc, etc. What we're talking about here is media rich applications for the web and other delivery devices.

React

But what about object oriented programming techniques? Surely that's where Flash comes unstuck? Absolutely not! Using movie clips you can build reusable objects, or you can build your Flash movies in a modular fashion so they are made up of many separate movies working together, passing variables and commands to each other. Forget OOP (object orientated programming), the future is FLOOP!

And this is the key to the success of applications created in Flash. Flapp design does not constrain your design to the windows and buttons built into the core operating system; in fact you could even create your OWN operating system (FLOS anyone?) Maybe we'll at last come to the end of the Windows metaphor, and find something new and exciting created by a designer taking the forefront. Kai Krause, former chief science officer for Metacreations was trying to achieve something like this with his applications Soap and Kai's Power Tools, but he had a team of people working with him. Using Flash for your application design, you don't need more than a couple of people working together to turn everything on its head.

Brendan Dawes

So who will be designing these Flapplications? Personally I think we will start to see the rise of a new breed of interactive application designer, someone who has a handle on motion graphics techniques, but someone who is just at home with programming architecture. An uber designer for the 21st century.

Yes there will still be designers and programmers as separate entities, but the people who wish to embrace both disciplines and then mutate that into their work will be the ones to watch as technology becomes more and more advanced.

React

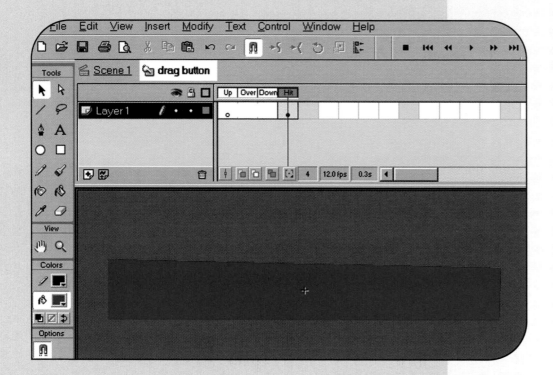

We need to make the button you've just created invisible, so double-click on the newly created button in the Library to edit it.

An invisible button is one that has a defined hit area, but nothing else in its other three button states. You'll see, when you first begin to edit the button, that it has a keyframe in the Up state. Drag the cursor over to the Hit state and press F6 to insert a keyframe. Now select the graphic in the Up state keyframe and delete it. Your invisible button is ready to be used.

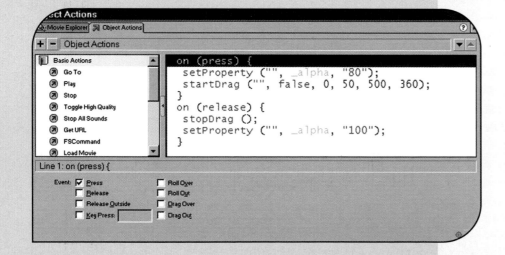

```
on (press) {
  setProperty ("", _alpha, "80");
  startDrag ("", false, 0, 50, 500, 360);
}
on (release) {
  stopDrag ();
  setProperty ("", _alpha, "100");
}
```

Back in the movie clip, main window, double-click on the newly created button, and select the Actions tab.

This is where we add the drag 'n drop actions for the window. Select On MouseEvent, and choose Press from the events

216

Click on the + sign at top left and choose startDrag. Leave the target box blank, because the button is contained within the clip we want to drag, so we don't need to specify a target.

We also want to stop the dragging as soon as the mouse is released. Click on the + sign, and choose On MouseEvent from the pop up box. From the event list on the right, choose Release.

Finally, select the on (release) { line in the box on the left. Click on the + sign and choose stopDrag. Your window is now draggable. To test it, go to the main stage, make sure the movie clip Main Window is on the main stage and choose Control>Test Movie from the menu bar. You should now be able to drag your created window around the stage.

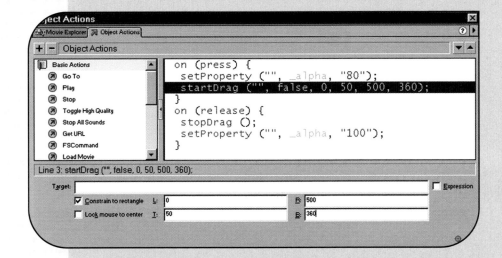

React

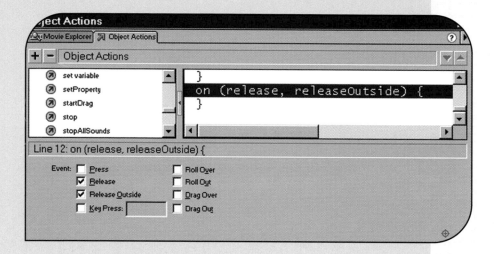

Next we should create a series of events that will execute when the user stops dragging and releases the mouse.

Create an on mouse event as before. This time choose two events from the checkboxes on the right, Release and Release Outside.

First we need to make our dummy clip invisible, so choose Set Property from the actions list. In the Set: dropdown, choose visibility and set the value to 0. Make sure the target is set to ../../icon. Finally we need to stop the dragging action. Choose Drag Movie Clip from the actions list and click the Stop drag operation radio button on the right.

This button now needs to be copied onto all the other thumbnails. But before we do that, we need to add one more piece of functionality.

Detecting Where the Clip has been Dropped.

So far we've created a draggable window, with masked content that we can drag outside of the window using a dummy clip. All this is great, but it's no good to anybody if we don't know where the clip has been dropped. In Psycho Studio, I needed to know if it had been dropped on the preview window or on the timeline. Let's take the timeline as example.

The timeline is made up of two movie clips. The first one is the parent movie clip, which is the basic timeline window. Inside this movie clip is another movie clip, which I've called **frames**. This movie clips actually contains thiry-one identical movie clips, and in fact it's the same dummy clip we used in the previous steps, containing all thirty-one thumbnails.

When a clip is dropped onto the timeline, some scripting inside the above button script detects whether this clip has been dropped onto another movie clip.

Note: you can only detect where things have been dropped on movie clips!

So how do we detect what has been dropped where? Well fortunately there is a built in property inside flash that will tell us all we need to know: _droptarget

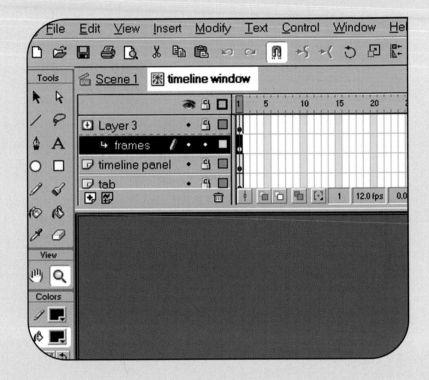

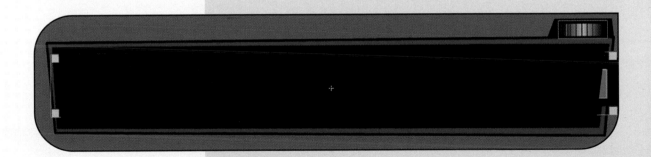

React

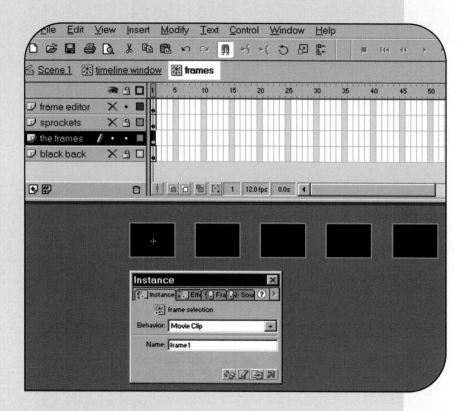

Before we detect the drop, we need to give all the frames the correct instance names. I named them **frame1**, **frame2** etc for all thirty-one frames.

The core scripting for the drop detection occurs in the same button from the previous step.

In the on (release, releaseOutside) { mouse event choose Set Variable from the actions list.

In the Variable: box on the right type:

../../:debug

To set the value of this variable, click on the Value: field of the set variable. Then under the Functions set of actions, select the getProperty action.

```
on (press) {
  selection = "clip1";
  // this is the main control action
  tellTarget ("../../icon") {
    gotoAndStop ("clip1");
  }
  startDrag ("../../icon", true);
}
on (dragOut) {
  setProperty ("../../icon", _visible, "100");
  setProperty ("../../icon", _alpha, "50");
}
on (release, releaseOutside) {
  ../../:debug = <not set yet>;
```

Line 14: ../../:debug = <not set yet>: [Value: An expression is required.]

Variable: ../../:debug

Value:

You will now see:

getProperty (target, property);

We need to replace the text that says target and property with the correct values. The target is the dummy icon clip so we replace the word target with:

../../icon

Next we need to get the _droptarget property of this clip, so we replace the word property with:

_droptarget

The final line should look like this:

getProperty ("../../icon", _droptarget)

Click OK.

```
on (press) {
  selection = "clip1";
  // this is the main control action
  tellTarget ("../../icon") {
   gotoAndStop ("clip1");
  }
  startDrag ("../../icon", true);
}
on (dragOut) {
  setProperty ("../../icon", _visible, "100");
  setProperty ("../../icon", _alpha, "50");
}
on (release, releaseOutside) {
  ../../:debug = getProperty ( target, property );
```

Line 14: ../../:debug = getProperty (target, property); [Value: Property name expected in GetProperty.]

Variable: ../../:debug

Value: getProperty (target, property)

React

To help to see what's happening when we drop the clip on something, we can put an editable text box off stage on the main movie timeline. When you've created your text box, make sure you name it 'debug' using the variable field in the Text Field properties box, Modify>Text Field. It's not essential that we do this, but I find it helps with debugging.

Test the movie. You should see when the clip is dropped that the text field is given the value of the clip's _droptarget property. If not, check your 'debug' box is on the main movie timeline and not contained in a movie clip. You may need to temporarily increase the movie size (Modify>Movie>Increase Height) to see the textfield.

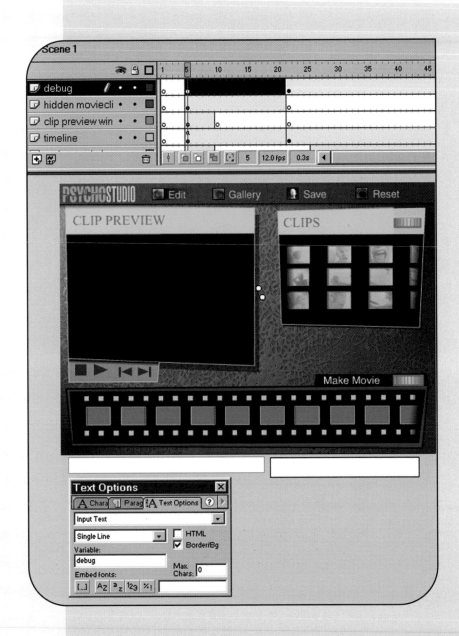

React

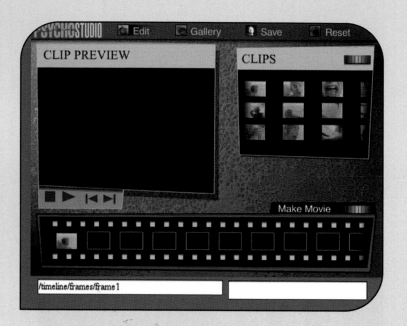

Now that we know where the clip has been dropped, we can then take that information and process it using if…then conditional statements to see if it's been dropped on anywhere specific, and act accordingly. For instance, this is the line of code in Psycho Studio which detects that the clip has been dropped on the preview window (it's attached to the buttons in the thumbnails movie that we looked at earlier):

```
if (getProperty( "../../icon", _droptarget) eq "/preview/screen") {
    setProperty ("../../icon", _visible) "0");
    loadMovie (eval("selection") add ".swf", "../../preview/screen");
}
```

/preview/screen is the _droptarget returned when the clip is dropped on the preview window. This is because the preview window is made up of two movie clips, one with the instance name **preview** and another inside that with the instance name **screen**. So we know if this value is returned from _droptarget, we need to load the relevant clip into the preview window.

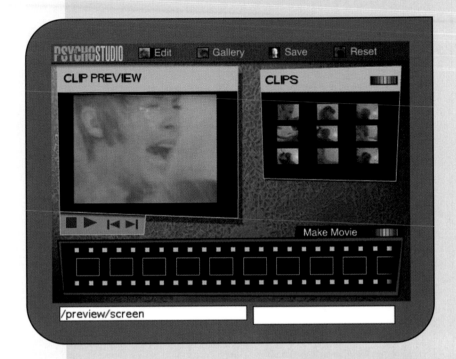

And that's it. I hope this technique will be useful for you when you're designing your own material, and I've included my fla files on the accompanying CD for you to download and experiment with, if you'll find that helpful.

TONY KE

"Imagination and creativity are very important...
There is always a way to work around a limitation,
but there's no solution to stunted creativity."

TONY KE
www.keicon.com

Illusion

Although accidents in real life can be disastrous, an accident in digital design may well turn out to be an asset. Some of the best ideas throughout history have originated as accidents, and this is certainly how my best ideas for Kedesign came about. In this chapter I am going to deconstruct one of my very first Flash projects that I completed in school, Project Kedesign. You can see Kedesign within my new site www.keicon.com.

As a new media designer, I was in frequent need of inspiration, particularly when I was creating for the Web. The limited capabilities of HTML, together with the limitations imposed by browser differences, didn't offer much room for maneuver. The advent of Flash has opened up a myriad of exciting ways for me to express myself freely on the Web. It comes at a price, however. Working with Flash requires careful coordination of motion graphics, sound and user interaction. You'll need good all-round media knowledge. But it's worth it. The more I design with Flash and the deeper my understanding of design using motion and sound becomes, the firmer my belief that the Web is fast becoming the designer's new playground.

Tony Ke

I came across Flash for the first time while visiting www.balthaser.com, completely innocent of the technology and its capabilities. I was mesmerized. That site woke me up. I realized that the Web no longer revolved around scrolls and clicks, or pages filled with ad banners and complex script liable to freeze your computer. I dropped everything, began learning Flash and soon realized that this new technology could really make my ideas come alive. With Flash, I could finally control sound, layout, typography, motion and interactivity.

I learned Flash the hard way; after two months of all-nighters and Kraft dinners, hacking the Flash 4 demo on a PC better suited to a museum showcase than my desk, Kedesign was born. I intended to use my first Flash web site to showcase my portfolio, hoping to land a job in the design field. Things turned out a little differently, though. The site won various design awards and people started asking about my design and style influences. It was all a bit of a shock!

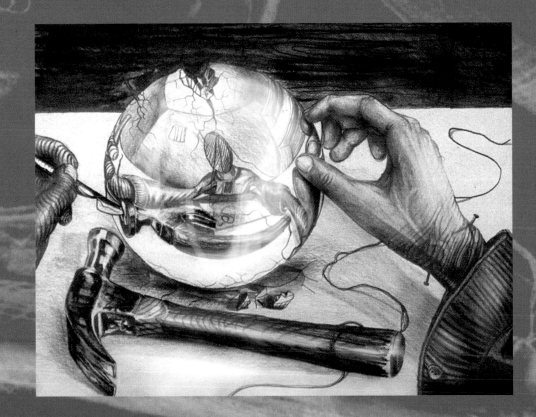

Illusion

Before I became a digital designer I worked as a traditional painter and illustrator using watercolor, oil and pencil. I focused on surrealism and realism; exploring the interaction between light and shadow, color and texture. Some of the fine art skills and understanding I acquired really helped me with my digital design. The digital toys that came about in the eighties gave me a wealth of inspiration. Videogames have definitely played an important role in the way I design - as a kid I was more interested in the character animation, depth and perspective they used than winning or losing.

Having studied motion and interactive game design since 1987, I'm currently using some of the techniques from the videogames of this era in my Flash designs. I've always felt that videogames are an art form in their own right, not simply another form of entertainment – a higher form of new media design. Some of the newer games on the market these days have incredible interface and motion design.

Many top videogame designers have also inspired me in my design. These include Hideo Kojima (Metal Gear), who redefined and revolutionized what interactive movies should be, and Shigeru Miyamoto, who designed the Super Mario game. I particularly love the way Miyamoto uses colors and visual interactivity. I intend to design a videogame in Flash before too long, particularly now that I've seen the more powerful ActionScript in Flash 5, and perhaps get involved with the game industry.

I love movies, so they naturally have a great influence on my design. Kyle Cooper, best known for his work in the main title intro design for the movie, *Seven*, and not so widely acknowledged for his redesign of the Netscape animated logo, is a master of motion design and typography. He was also one of Paul Rand's students – the famous graphic designer who created the ABC and Westinghouse logos. You can find some of Cooper's work at imaginaryforces.com. Although some people find it too dark, I think it is just beautiful, particularly in combination with his motion typography.

© Kyle Cooper and Jenny Shainin, Imaginary Forces

Illusion

When I design a web site I try to explore the possibilities first and then work around the limitations. This gives me a lot more creative freedom during the initial design stages. Imagination and creativity is very important. Don't let the limitations of the Internet inhibit your creativity. There is always a way to work around a limitation, but there's no solution to stunted creativity. I wanted to give my site an air of mystery and darkness, so I worked predominantly with dark gray colors, reserving the bright colors for the buttons and the interface. This color contrast guides the user from section to section. I also wanted the user to have a sense of exploration, to feel as if they were moving through a video rather that flipping through the pages of a book or traditional HTML, so I made the transitions between sections as smooth as possible.

realized that I ought to have a picture of myself on the site, to give it a more personal touch, but the idea really didn't appeal: in the first place my friends were bound to practice their Photoshop techniques on my face! Moreover, I wanted to keep the size of the project file size down. I tried converting the original picture to a vector, and using it for a background. The face came out incredibly flat and looked more like a pancake, so I decided to try and add some depth. I tried making a 3D model of my face but as a coupon-collecting student I hadn't any programs and little budget to

produce a 3D animation in Flash. In my student days, Swift3D and Vecta3D for Flash were not even in the alpha stage of development. Even if I had managed to stump up the money for new tools, it would have taken time to learn how to use them effectively, particularly for a 3D model as complex as a face. I had to find an all-Flash solution, and fast. The technique I came up with became one of the most unique effects on the site, about which I received most questions. In this chapter I will show you a more advanced technique than the one I used back then.

Illusion

You could use this 3D effect for surreal or plain 3D designs, either can be convincing. Which you use simply depends on your preferred visual style. I chose the flat shade 3D effect because it lies in interesting contrast with the design of the rest of the site. It also requires less space and CPU speed. You can generate this effect using Flash alone, as long as you can find an appropriate picture to begin with (there are 3D effects that this technique cannot produce without external resources).

The current technology available means although effects on the site might appear to be 3D, they are in fact 2D. It's not the dimension that makes successful site, but the design itself. You can find some great examples of vector-based 3D animation at www.kmpinternet.com and www.mtv2.co.uk. I like 3D interfaces because they can convey a very convincing sense of space and motion, but they increase file size significantly and appear choppy on slower computers. I used a 2D interface on Kedesign so that I could reach as wide an audience as possible, including those with slower computers.

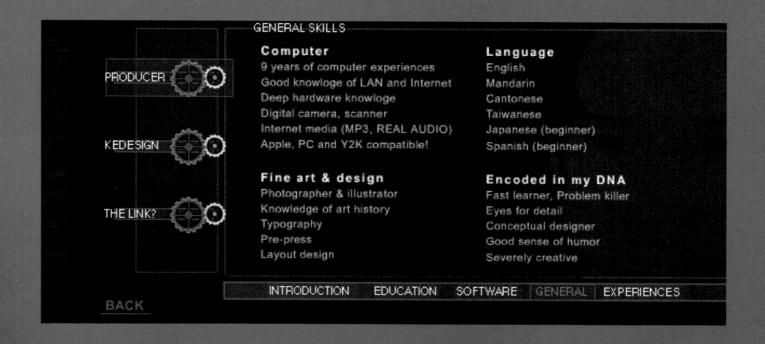

Tony Ke

Sound is, for me, one of the most important elements in Flash, but is also one of the most misused. Flash developers have a tendency to add sound to everything, which can be unnecessary, particularly when it's simply being used to punctuate mouseover states on every button on a stage. For example, suppose you're on a web site that uses six buttons. Each button fires a laser gun shooting sound when the mouse hovers over it, a different explosion sound when the button is pressed, and so on. If you yank the mouse from the first button to the last button in less then second, six audio clips of laser shooting explode. It's a sonic disaster.

Sound should be planned and implemented carefully, so that it guides the audience through the design, and should never be included simply for the sake of it. This can be confusing and unpleasant. Background site sound should fit with your design and content in the same way as your background graphics.

I intended the completed web site to be under 300k on a single .swf file; smaller than many other Flash sites that run between 400k and 600k with multiple .swf files. I aimed for this smaller size so that the whole site would fit on a floppy and would be a reasonable size for an e-mail attachment, so potential employers could retain a copy. A 300k web site should preload in less than six seconds on a 56k modem, and be able to stream the rest of the content without pauses or skipping. I highly recommend that if your web site is going to be larger than 300k, you break it down into multiple .swf files using the Load Movie action in Flash and load the movie as needed. That way users don't have to wait for information. Many people won't wait for more than ten seconds for a site to load unless they're sure that the information they're looking for will be there, so it's very important to have an effective preloader and then stream the content. The Kedesign site loads behind the introductory sequence, so while users are watching what might at first appear to be the loaded site beginning its work, in fact the introduction behaves as the preloader.

Illusion

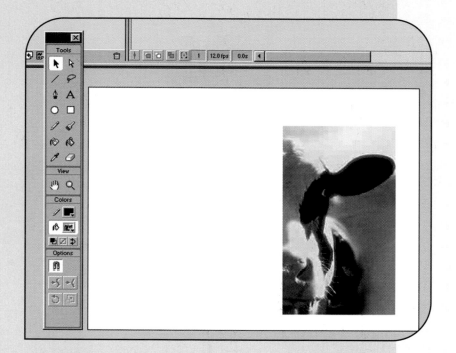

Once your image is ready, find the center point, highlight it and delete half. While you're cutting, keep in mind that the other side will be reconstructed later using the mirror image of the remaining half.

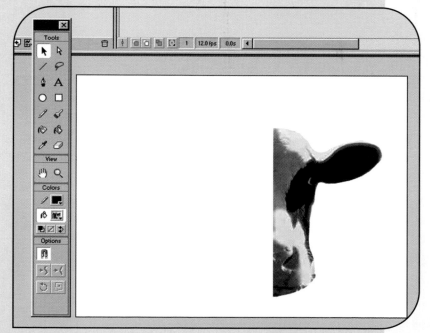

Now clean up the image, using the Eraser tool to take out the unwanted background. Our cow symbol is now ready to plug into a movie.

Create a new movie clip symbol and name it.

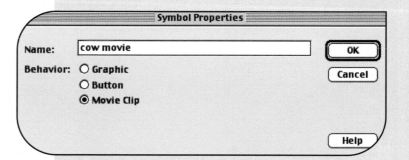

Now create three layers in the new movie clip that you've made and name them **Left**, **Right** and **Guide**, converting the last into a guide layer by right-clicking with the mouse and selecting Guide on the drop-down menu.

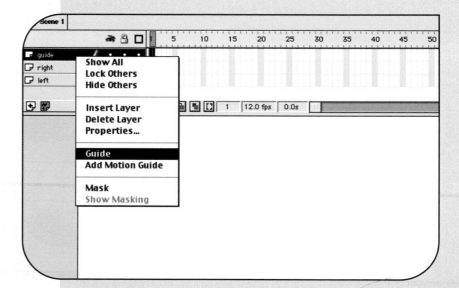

Illusion

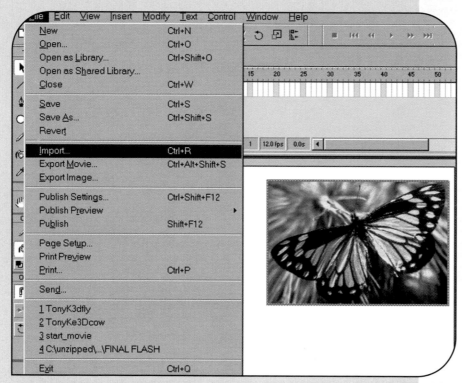

3D butterfly

You can also use this technique to make objects that are symmetrical from above, such as bees or butterflies.

Import an appropriate image.

Convert the image to vector by choosing Modify>Trace Bitmap in the Flash menu. In this step, I chose to convert to vector because this is scaleable, although you might choose to use the raster option, depending on the nature of your object.

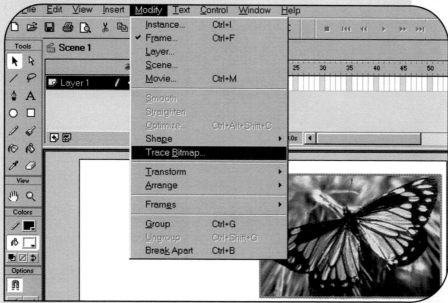

The smaller the number you set for the color threshold, the closer the colors will be to the original image. The smaller the minimum area you set, the more detail you'll see. I used 50 for the color threshold and a minimum area of 8 pixels; I also set the curve fit to Smooth and the corner threshold to Normal. The settings you choose will depend on the quality and style of the image you want to achieve. Remember also that the simpler the vector graphic, the better the animation will play.

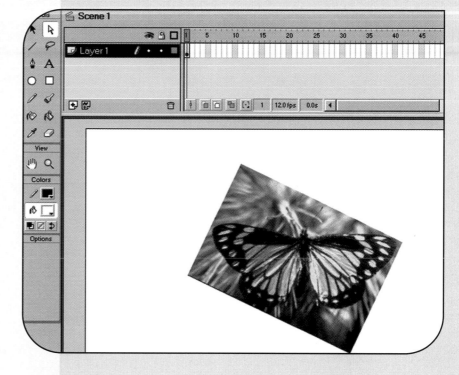

Now rotate the image so that the butterfly can be cut through the middle using a vertical line.

Find the middle of the object, highlight the unwanted side and hit delete.

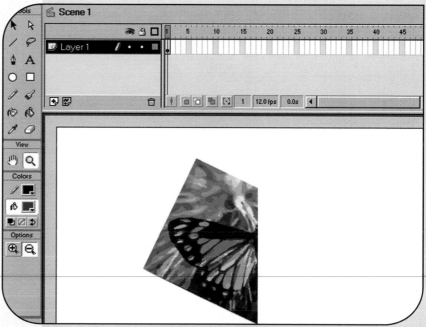

Illusion

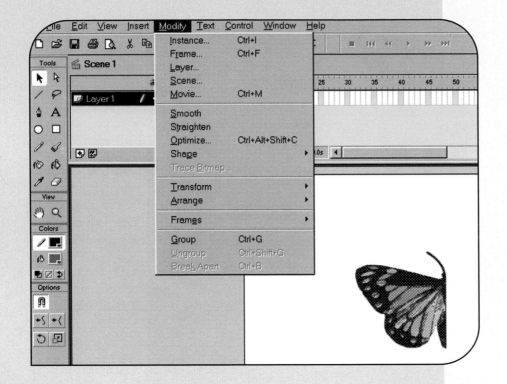

Clean the background away using the Eraser tool, highlight the object, then go to Modify>Optimize in the Flash menu.

If you use a raster image, you can skip this step. The best way to optimize a raster file is to use an image-editing program, like ImageReady or Fireworks, before importing into Flash.

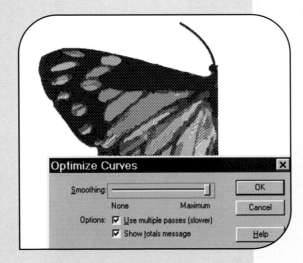

Go maximum on Curves>Optimize! This will help to reduce size and improves animation speed.

Following optimization, highlight the object, hit F8 to convert it to a graphic symbol and give it an appropriate name.

Create a new movie clip symbol and name it, then drag the graphic symbol from the Library to this movie clip. Enter a keyframe at 70 and create a motion tween. Then enter several keyframes between 1 and 70. In each keyframe, either scale down the wing, or scale it up horizontally to make the wing appear to move. When you're scaling down, turn the brightness of the symbol down, so that it lightens. Make sure the first and last frames are the same so that the loop is perfect.

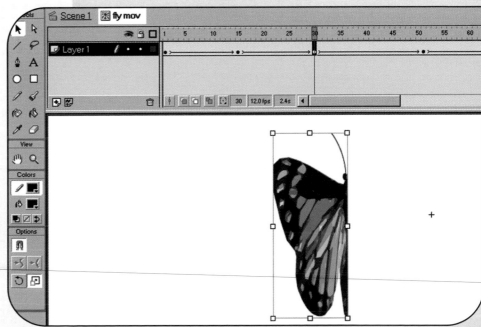

Finally, make sure to place the body of the butterfly in its original position when you're scaling the wing up or down. You can draw a guideline to help by drawing a vertical line along the body of the half butterfly.

Illusion

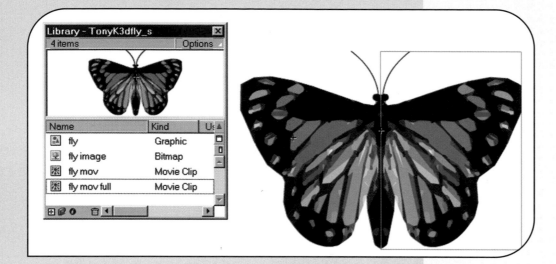

Now create another movie clip symbol, name it **fly-mov-full** and drag in the movie clip, fly-mov, from the Library. Then copy and paste from right side to left side and flip horizontally to make a full butterfly.

You can drag the fly-mov-full movie clip into your main movie to use the 3D butterfly. Below is a screen shot from an intro I put together for an up-coming design community site called Exit925.

You can use these techniques to convert all sorts of things to 3D using Flash. All you have to do is find objects you want to convert. The process may take a few tries to be convincing, but the final result is often rewarding.

I hope that you find a use for the techniques that I've shown here.

My final tips are in the first place, to always plan before you design: paper first, then computer. Also, know what you're aiming for before you start, or you'll get lost in the middle of development.

As I developed Kedesign, I also learnt to remember that the speed the Flash movie will play on someone else's computer is just as important, if not more important, than the file size of the final project. Your audience might be prepared to wait for your site to load, but they're not going to buy a new, faster computer to view it.

Reuse your Flash symbols by all means, but don't over-use! You'll pay the price for a larger file size. If you need convincing, try this simple experiment:

In a new Flash window make a simple box in your main movie; convert it to a graphic symbol. Then copy the box symbol ten times in your movie to form a line of boxes and group them. Now animate them, left to right from frame 1 to 10, and publish.

Now open another new Flash window, create the ten boxes in a line and then convert to a graphic symbol (so you end up with one graphic symbol containing ten boxes), then animate as you did for the first movie. Publish the file and compare file sizes. Most designers today are still designing for low-end computers and slow Internet connections. With the emergence of broadband connections such as cable and ADSL, designers can finally tap into the true potential of Flash technology and their creativity. Until then keep optimizing your Flash movies!

IRENE CHAN

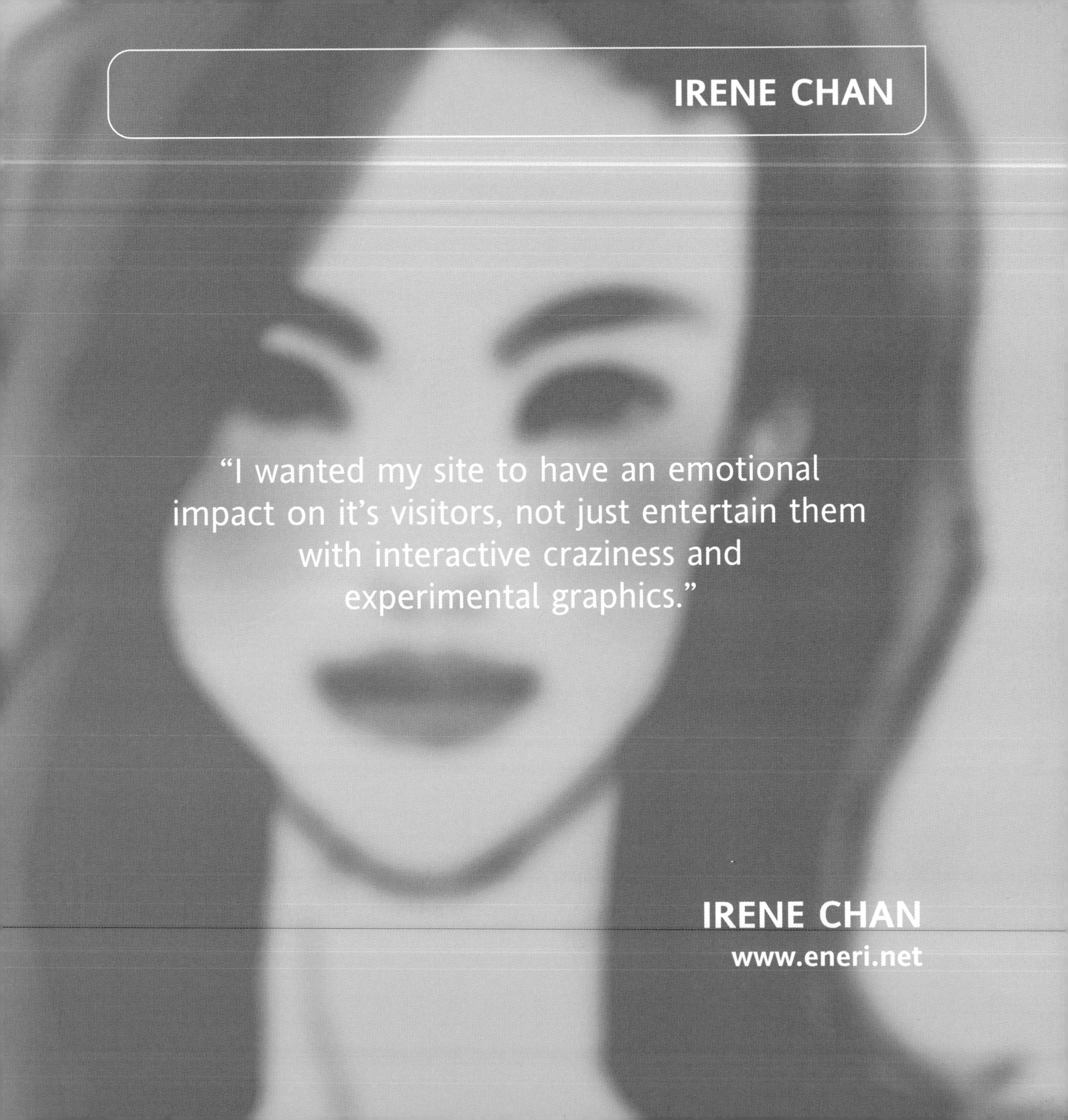

"I wanted my site to have an emotional impact on it's visitors, not just entertain them with interactive craziness and experimental graphics."

IRENE CHAN
www.eneri.net

Rainfall

Different people see different things in eneri.net. Some people appreciate the rich colors and design; others enjoy the motion graphics. The aspect of the site that has generated the most controversy, however, is the content. While it works for some, others have challenged whether such emotive, personal material based on feminist philosophies should be portrayed on the Internet at all – multiple visual narratives examining, not without a flavor of irony, those private hopes, dreams, fears in life and love. Some people have said that the level of intense personal privacy unsettles them; they were surprised to see something so intimate exhibited in such a public forum. But we're familiar enough with artists using twisted, gory figures on their oil canvases to express themselves, so why would the Web, as an exhibition space, be treated any differently? Should it simply be an information exchange, an e-commerce marketplace, or a showcase for cutting-edge, experimental design, devoid of any sentiment or emotional content?

Irene Chan

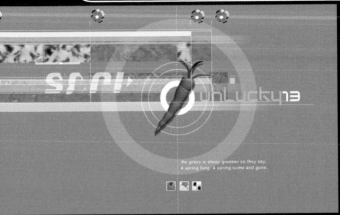

© www.volumeone.com

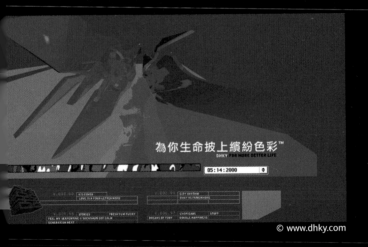

為你生命披上繽紛色彩™
DHKY FOR MORE BETTER LIFE

© www.dhky.com

© www.typogRaphic.com

Eneri.net began as a New Year resolution back in 1999. I had always wanted to publish art about myself – about things that I have observed and learnt at certain points in my life. My admiration for the first generation of well-executed, experimental web sites, such as volumeone.com, dhky.com and typographic.com, motivated me to use the Web as my exhibition space.

Unlike some other web sites that concentrate on playing with what Flash and other web technologies can do as tools, my main purpose for eneri.net was to express intense personal sentiment in rich design. I wanted my site to have an emotional impact on its visitors, not just entertain them with interactive craziness and experimental graphics.

Rainfall

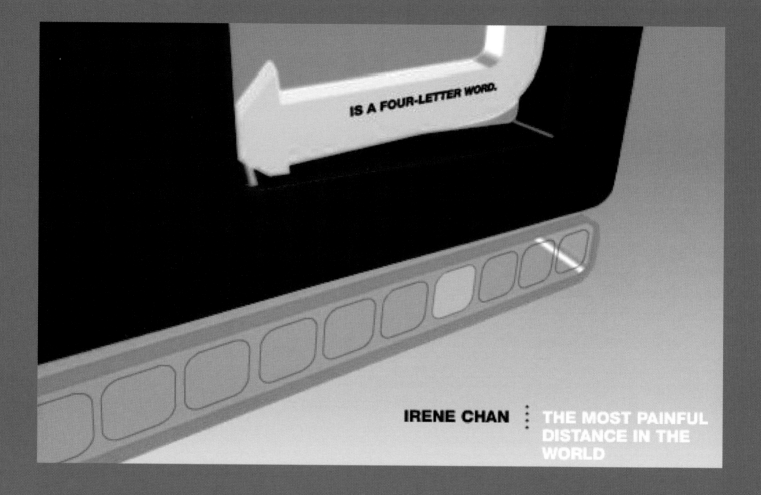

IS A FOUR-LETTER WORD.

IRENE CHAN : THE MOST PAINFUL DISTANCE IN THE WORLD

I didn't deliberately pursue a predominantly feminist theme. In the end it was inevitable, though, both because I am a woman, so I can't really help seeing things from a female perspective, and because I've been highly influenced by two of my favorite feminist artists, Frida Kahlo and Barbara Kruger.

Frida Kahlo portrayed her life experiences using surreal self-portraits and writings, and Barbara Kruger protested her feminist ethics through a powerful juxtaposition of symbolic photographic imagery and words. In the same vein, at eneri.net I wanted to share with the audience the way I see the world.

Irene Chan

As I began to build eneriwomaninterface (EWI) I set out to explore the dynamics between male and female from a feminine point of view. I used the Yin-Yang symbol as a primary design element throughout the site, to tie design elements together both visually and conceptually. In Chinese philosophy Yin-Yang represents the relationship between the harmonious yet distinct polarities of the Moon (feminine) and the Sun (masculine) and how there is never one without the other.

Rainfall

With that as my starting point, I planned the framework of EWI as a very simple, linear navigation system around a series of short animated Flash narratives. This was an important design decision for me because I wanted to leave the audience free to visually engage with the Flash movies and not be distracted by a complex navigation system. Despite this simplicity, I had to take the framework through two major revisions to make it work visually with all seven different Flash movies.

I had to maintain the vision of the entire site as I built each Flash movie. I mocked up the initial designs, briefly, in Photoshop, giving each its own narrative ingredient and metaphor, while ensuring they cohered with my main theme. The concept behind each movie remained constant as I took them through a number of design revisions to make sure they looked good inside the navigation framework. That completed, I was ready to bring in Flash to pull each piece together using motion and interactivity.

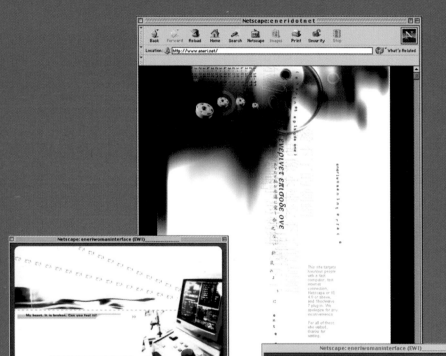

Because I've never been too concerned with getting massive exposure for my site, I didn't let bandwidth issues affect my thinking too much during the planning and building process. On the first version of the eneri.net splash page, I stated that the site was targeted at "people who have a fast computer, fast Internet access, Netscape or Internet Explorer 4.0 or above, with Shockwave Flash plug-in" - and those with enough time and the right frame of mind. I did, however, try to limit each individual Flash movie to somewhere around 200k or less, so that it would still be a reasonable download size for people on a 28.8k

modem. It's fair to say that this size is still quite heavy, compared to the normal 60k limit that a 28.8k handles smoothly, but testing on 28.8k modems showed that most movies on eneri.net download within 1-2 minutes – which I hope is worth the wait.

You can see in the graphics here that I made EWI lie in a separate window launched from within a larger piece. I called that piece The Most Painful Distance and put it together in around five weeks, a few months after the launch of eneriwomaninterface.

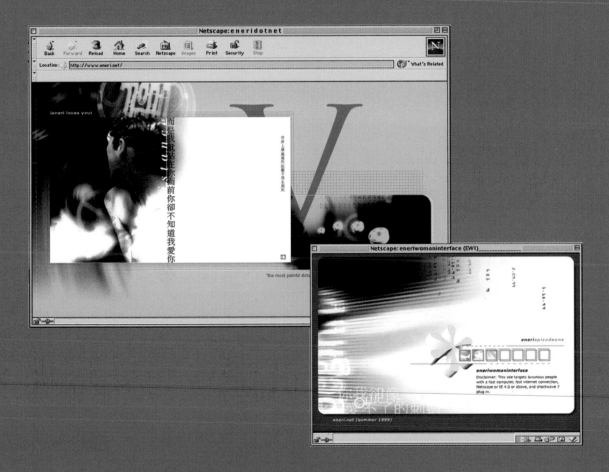

Rainfall

Flash played an important part in giving life to this piece, integrating strong rhythm and movement with different Photoshop layouts and the background music that I had chosen. Just as I had done with my previous designs, I developed three scenes with complementary elements and color schemes, intending to introduce animation in between. I chose the 'restriction' symbol (the circle with a slash that goes across in the middle) to unify the whole design concept. The animation hits onto the main stage like rain (imagine looking down on the ground from above when it's raining), or like a big rubber stamp, suppressing and breaking the freely animated typography and graphical elements as they explode below. The animation effect complements the concept of the poem itself with all the irony and oxymoron between 'the living and the dead', 'when you can't see that I love you', and 'when two hearts love, and cannot be as one'.

the most painful

the most painful

The music that I chose to tie in with the design has a touch of irony to it. Instead of underpinning the general feel with mournful music, I used a soft and dreamy piece. The music contradicts the atmosphere generated by the twisted figures and harsh words of the movie. I think that the unease that this contradiction engenders in fact contributes to the atmosphere of anguish. This technique of contradiction and irony is a continuation from EWI. Examples include the light-hearted lounge music for "You Don't Give Me Flowers" (about a woman's disappointment in love), and the use of the choir music for "Eneri Prayer", praising God (symbolizing the male power) on the surface while protesting subtly behind.

Now that I've laid out the general background to the site, over the next few pages I'll talk about importing graphics and how to use Flash as an animation tool with typography, using a couple of animation designs from within eneri.net.

Rainfall

For both eneriwomaninterface and The Most Painful Distance, I've talked about importing graphics from within Photoshop. For me, a successful motion graphics animation piece in Flash needs to have a good balance between vector and bitmap animation design.

You should start by planning out your storyboard, and then design a couple of static scenes that go together both visually and conceptually, and lay them out in Photoshop. When you're designing, try to visualize how these static scenes are going to animate and morph into one another. Start with a blank screen and imagine how the different elements of your design will fade in and come together as a whole. This is an example of how static scene designs for a Flash motion-graphics animation might look.

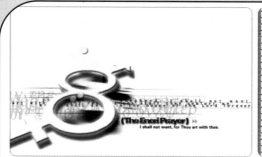

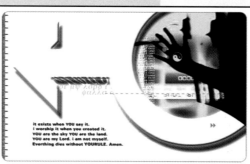

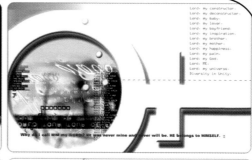

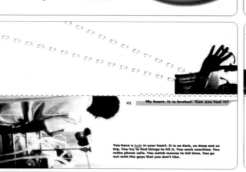

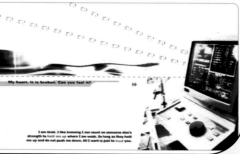

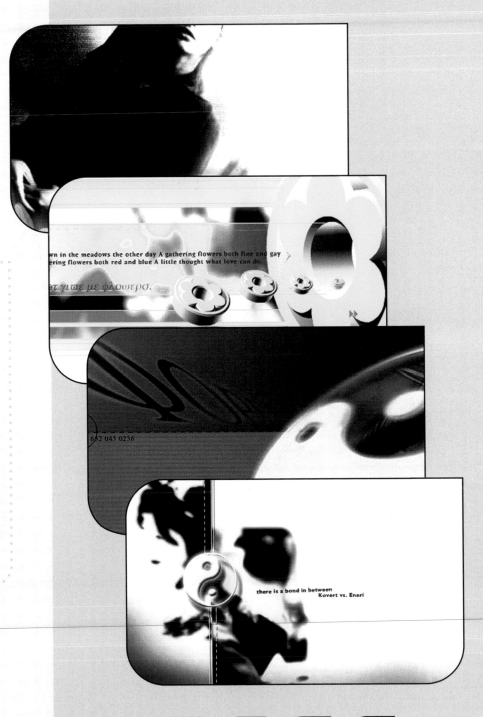

Once you've laid out the static scenes and the storyboard, dissect them into the individual elements that correspond with the animations and reproduction effects you'll use Flash to produce. Reproduce all possible elements of your design in vector format. Elements that wouldn't show up well if they were imported as bitmap graphics, such as screen lines, typographic elements and icons, should all be traced and recreated in vector format, either using Flash or another vector program, such as Adobe Illustrator or Macromedi Freehand. When you import vector elements into Flash from an external vector program, always make sure that you break them apart by going to Modify>Break Apart. This knocks down the memory of the vector element that you've imported.

Rainfall

If your static storyboard designs are laid out in Photoshop and are made up of multiple layers, the guide layer image will provide a flattened version. This guide image won't affect the size of the whole movie because it will be placed on its own guide layer and won't be exported. It merely serves as a visual guideline in Flash when you're working on the animation on top of it.

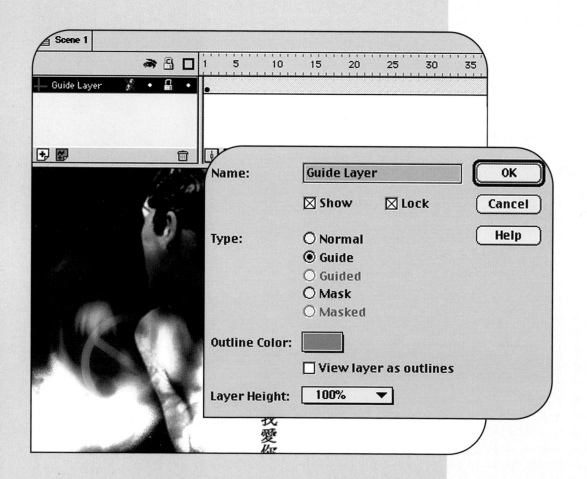

Remember to change the layer type to Guide instead of Normal in the Layer Properties dialog box (it comes up when you double-click on the Page icon on the timeline layer you're on). You can lock this layer by checking the dot under the Lock icon when you're working above the guideline layer. By doing this you'll never accidentally move the guide layer image around when you're moving and animating the elements on top of it.

Import other Photoshop graphics into Flash, according to your animation intentions. In Photoshop, turn off the layers that contain the elements you're going to recreate in vector format. Save the rest of the image out in PICT format (or any lossless image file format), and import them into Flash.

Most people use Photoshop bitmap images in Flash for the static design of their movies to enhance the visual quality. Although Flash isn't made for bitmap animation, we can always push the borderline of bitmap graphics in Flash to create certain photographic motion design effects that vector-based animation can't achieve alone.

Bright Glow/Explosion Effect

Now we'll look at how you might build the 'over-exposed' bright-out effect in Flash that you see here. This is a 13-frame sequence of the Flash movie that glows rapidly to white and falls back to its original color in only 0.5 seconds.

Rainfall

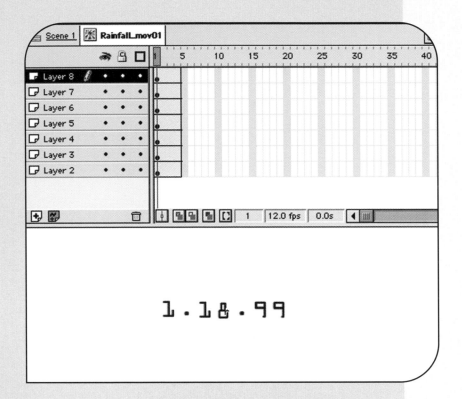

1.18.99

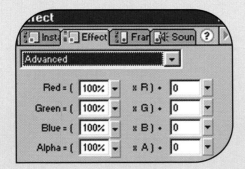

Begin with a white background on your Flash file. Create a blank graphic symbol by going to Insert>New Symbol. Name your symbol **Image01**. Import your image on the stage inside the symbol. Then create a new layer and put Image01 onto it.

On your timeline, leave between five and eight frames blank and insert the duplicate keyframe. Double-click on the duplicated Image01 symbol on the stage area. An Instance Properties dialog box will show up.

Under the Effect Panel, go to Advanced. Here you need to adjust the saturation of the symbol to make it look as if it's being exposed to extremely bright light.

Tip: extreme brightness may also cause the object to change color as it gets lighter. It might become more orange, red or blue, depending on the light source.

With this in mind, adjust the three upper bars that control the threshold of RGB on your object to the right. I usually give a more reddish-orange tone to the image when it's turning bright white. The shades you put on your object will depend on the original tone of your image. Click OK when you're done adjusting.

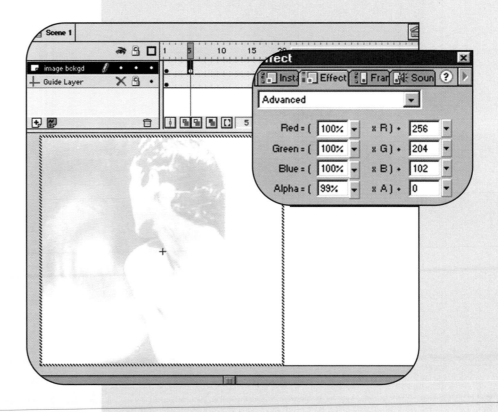

Rainfall

Rainfall Effect

One particular typographic character-by-character animation that I loved putting together for eneri.net is the rainfall effect. Here, words are treated individually, like raindrops falling from the upper part of the screen. Unlike the explosion effect, the rainfall animation works better on typographic elements with simple structures, say, numbers, the English alphabet or even Japanese Hiragana and Katakana characters.

Create a blank movie clip symbol. This will loop itself later when it's used on the main stage. In the symbol, type in the text that you want to animate.

Symbol Properties

Name: Rainfall_mov01

Behavior: ○ Graphic
           ○ Button
           ◉ Movie Clip

OK

Cancel

Help

Once you have the text, break it down by going to Modify>Break Apart. Make every single character into a symbol and put each symbol onto its own layer, as we did before with the dissolve effect.

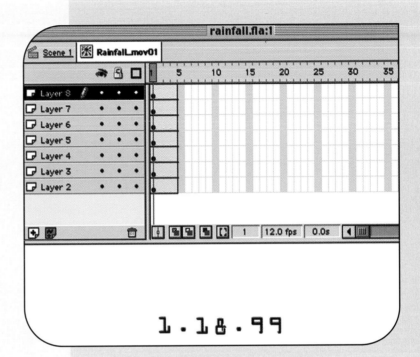

You should have a number of keyframes lined up vertically in separate layers. Duplicate your keyframes twice on your timeline. The distance between the original keyframe and the first duplicated keyframe is the length of time you wish the characters to stay still. The animation will take place between the first and the second duplicate keyframes.

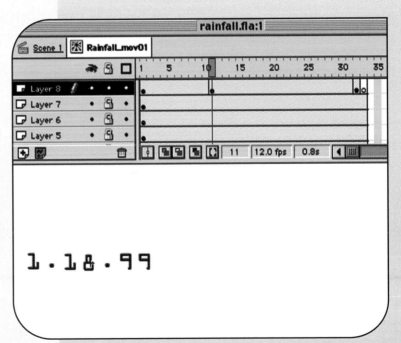

On your stage area, press and hold down the Shift key and drag each character horizontally from the first to the second duplicate keyframe. As you do this, add a gentle slant to the angle, to make the final effect more interesting, but make sure that the angle is different for each character.

Rainfall

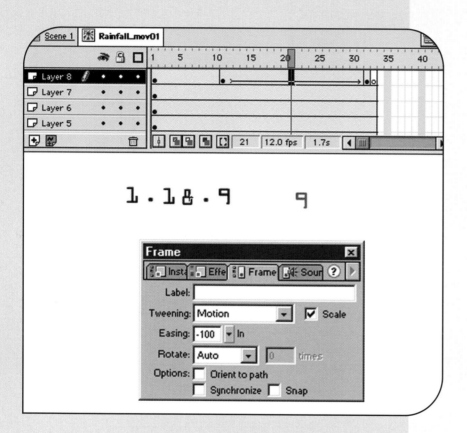

Change the opacity of the alphabet on the second duplicated keyframe to 5% by double-clicking the symbol on your stage and adjust its opacity level in the Frame Properties dialog box. Put in a blank keyframe right after this keyframe on your timeline.

Motion tween between the two duplicated keyframes. Adjust the ease-in/ease-out level accordingly.

Repeat the process on every layer you have. It doesn't have to line up on the timeline or follow a sequence as you animate it, but keep playing back and forth to check and see what looks best. When you play the timeline, you should see the sentence flowing away like smoke as the characters fade out and disappear one by one.

On your timeline, add a Stop command on the last keyframe for this whole sequence. This ensures that it stops when it reaches the final frame and has totally faded away.

Create a couple of movie clips using the steps that I've described to create visual variations.

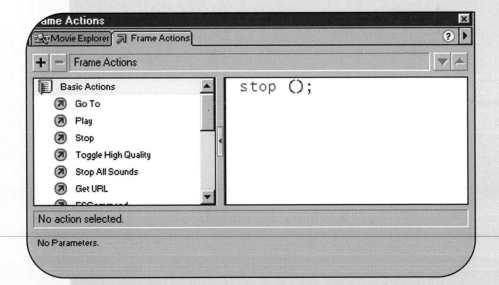

Rainfall

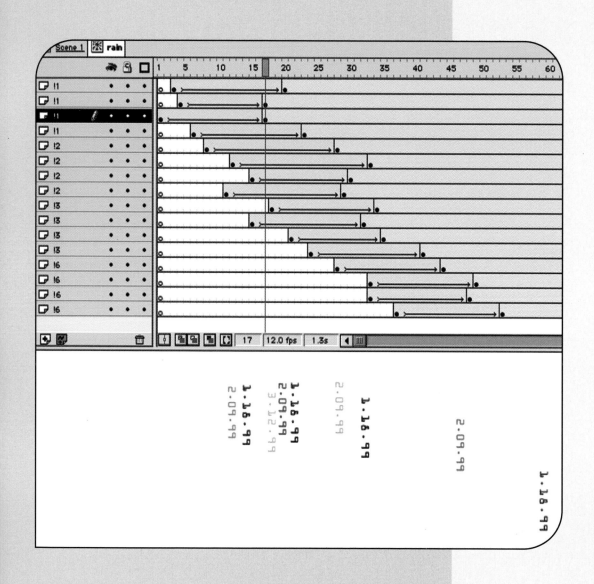

Create a new movie clip symbol and call it **Rain**. Drag all the individual alphabet movie clips that you've just created from the library and onto the stage area of Rain. Put each one on its own separate layer. Rotate them vertically so they will be pointing vertically down. Fade them in individually by duplicating the keyframe on your timeline; change the opacity of the original keyframe to 5% and motion tween between the two keyframes.

Instead of lining them all up, spread these keyframes randomly across your time line so that the individual raindrop clips don't appear on the stage simultaneously. Put twenty or thirty blank frames before the end to allow each raindrop to fully animate itself and disappear from the stage.

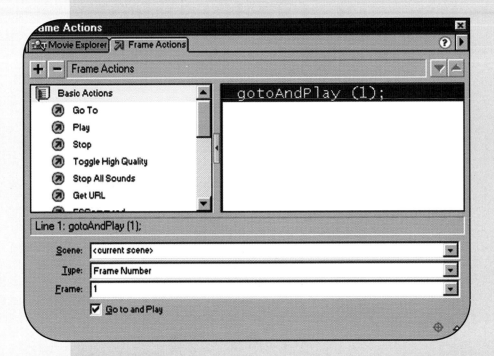

Add an action frame to the last keyframe of the rain sequence by double-clicking on it. To loop the movie, go to the Properties dialog box and tell it to play from frame one.

Go back to your main stage area. On top of your background layer, drag the whole Rain movie clip symbol onto the stage. Export the movie. Now you'll see the rainfall effect. It should look as if the sentences fade in, one after the other, fall like autumn leaves and dissolve from sight. This will loop very gently as the movie goes on.

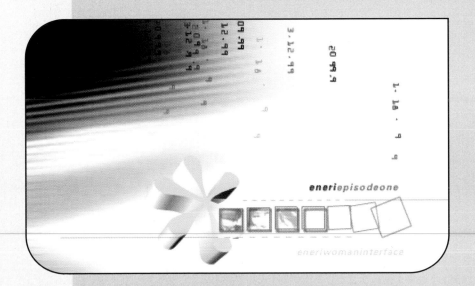

Rainfall

I'll conclude with some miscellaneous animation tips. These are several things you may need to keep in mind when you're creating a motion graphics piece in Flash.

There should always be more than one animation sequence going on in your movie at any one time so that the whole motion scene is visually attractive.

Although there are different sequences going on, it's important to keep one dominant animation as the focal point of the whole movie, while others are only supplementary motions. In other words, the supplementary motions should be kept subtle compared to the major one.

When you're animating vector elements on a photographic background, try to match the color and tone of this object to the background graphic (in other words, be wary of using bright white lines or shapes against a dark shaded background unless you're trying to create a certain kind of visual effect!).

Like many of the other experimental design web sites out there, I look forward to seeing eneri.net having a totally new appearance every once in a while, introducing new personal philosophies with stunning visual effects. As web technology changes almost daily and bandwidth grows, the Internet may soon be a totally different thing, enabling a totally new audience experience. Who knows what eneri.net will become five or ten years from now?

But before all that happens, I wanted to show you some of the techniques that I've tried out at eneri.net. I wanted to show that bringing a few Flash elements together, with no advanced scripting or motion capture, is a simple way to produce effects that look a lot more complicated than they really are and make your audience wonder how you've achieved them.

The rest is up to you. Enjoy your exploration of Flash capabilities within your own designs.

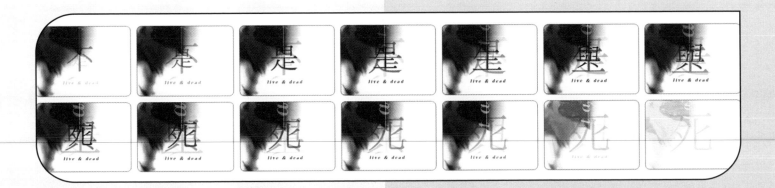

"What I was trying to capture was the reflection, the impression of the real human being conveyed through the way time flowed between the keystrokes."

YUGO NAKAMURA
www.yugop.com

Nervous

Before I begin, there's something I want to deny. I want to deny that I am in any way the sort of person you would call a master of Flash.

I'm conceited enough to think that, by now, I've acquired a good deal of familiarity with some of the technical aspects. As far as my thoughts and comments about the Web go, however, I would have to admit to

not having any intractable, deep-rooted design ideas, or indeed a systematic approach. Ultimately, what I think and what I say is only consistent in that it's liable to constant change. The ideas and working approaches that I hold so firmly one day, suddenly seem uninteresting the next, and I let them go without a thought of regret. I simply go along by trial and error.

semi-automatic
description
about:MONO*crafts TOKYO, JAPAN

```
»GetProperty ("/drag", _x )
»GetProperty ("/drag", _y )
tom)and(_level0:press=1))
et" =int((mY-top)/pitch)+1
&target)+(mX-center)/a)/b
                        End If
        Set Variable:"i" =1
        Loop While (i<n)
"c-(eval("x"&i)*(2+c)))/ax
"v"&i +(eval("v"&i)+rv)/bx
&i =eval("x"&i)+eval("v"&i)
&i, X Position) =eval("x"&i)
eval("x"&i)-center)/5+100
I00-(eval("x"&i)-center)/3
        Set Variable:"i" =i+1
        End Lo
```

KIRIYA
ON | JL

KIRIYA.COM :: BEYOND PHOTOGRAPHY

beta

I guess you could say that isn't really such a bad working method, given that the Web is a different place from one day to the next, even from moment to moment. With things changing as quickly as they are, there doesn't seem to be a lot of point in devoting time and effort to crystallizing my own thoughts at any given moment. I half expect the things that I have to say about the Web to be out of date as soon as I've said them. The incessant upheaval and change is, though, the one thing I really love about the Web and I hope that it stays as vibrant, dynamic and energetic as it is now for a good while to come.

Nervous

When I was at school, my focus of interest was the environment around me. I wandered around gardens and buildings, mountain villages and towns, trailing my camera. I was still reading all sorts of books about landscape and environment when I wrote my university dissertation, and it was at about that time that I finally grasped an extremely simple truth.

I realized that my impressions of the environment I was seeing depended entirely on what I *perceived* of my surroundings: how I viewed it. The things I see are determined by the relationship, the *interaction*, between me and the environment that I'm a part of. I realized that what I had thought of as an environment, existing outside of me was in fact entirely bound to what was going on *inside* me.

We all encounter things that are extraordinary, things that amaze, surprise or even shock us. At such a moment, the things around us that we previously regarded as mundane suddenly acquire a significance they didn't have before. They *look* different. The simple truth I recognized back then was that, when these things happened and I tried to understand the way my environment had changed to my eye, I was actually looking at what has changed inside myself. I have unfettered respect and gratitude for the things that have triggered changes in my environment and for the people who have created them. I hope that one day I will be able create such things and I work each day to accumulate experience to allow me to do so.

Yugo Nakamura

This concept of the perception of environment is found in an even more extreme form on the Web. I believe that the perception that any given person has of the Web environment is dictated by what they have already encountered there. I suspect that some designers see it as an endless exhibition of pages with fabulous design features, and that some users think of it as something that grows in response to the countless messages scattered on countless bulletin boards. I wouldn't be surprised if there are novice users out there that think Yahoo! and AOL are all there is to the Web. I think that one of the key features of the web environment is that it in a constant state of flux; it evolves from moment to moment, according to the user's intentional browsing activities, and the accidental discoveries she makes on the way.

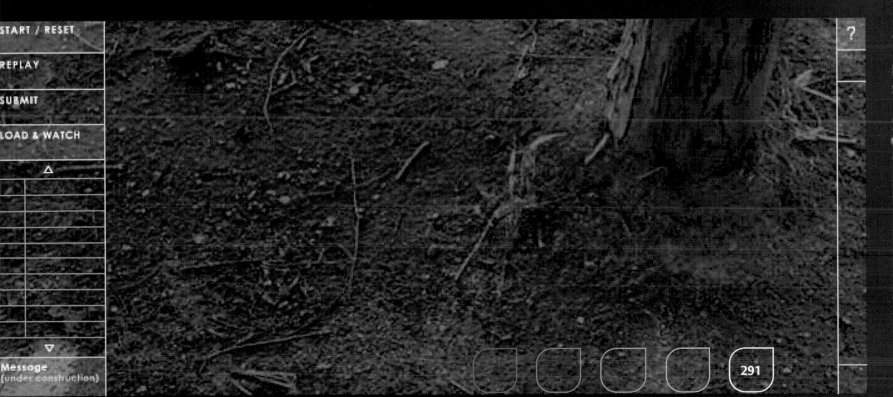

START / RESET

REPLAY

SUBMIT

LOAD & WATCH

△

▽

Message
(under construction)

Nervous

Of course, I'm no exception to this rule, and my own perceptions of the web environment also change from moment to moment through a myriad of chance discoveries. For example, it was through a collection of works of great artists and designers such as John Maeda, Tomato and dextro that I chanced upon the pure environment *within* the machine in front of me, the computer. Sensorium.org, was another site that brought to me a net environment completely unique to any I had imagined before. As I discover more and more sites similar to these, my perception of the web environment changes continually, which I find so richly, terribly exciting. I hope, one day, to myself create sites that affect people in the same way.

Yugo Nakamura

At the moment, I am experimenting with an alternative form of web communication that breaks through the restrictions of current browsers. Browsers are the bars of the cage that restrict web communication, restricting the user's freedom and the designer's expression. I have to say, though, that some of these restrictions might well be something expert web designers thrive on. I am working towards finding a way outside of these constraints using Flash, because it is, quite simply, the most powerful tool I've come across.

I am not particularly interested in using Flash to create cool motion graphics. What I do want to create is a unique communication experience, or interface environment, a **reactive field**. This interface will allow give the user complete communicative freedom. It will respond instantaneously to any user action, in a manner entirely appropriate to that particular user's pattern of action and behaviors within the environment. The sort of interface I am hoping to build is one where the **essence** of the individual user, existent in the background of the field, behind the business of the web page that we're accustomed to, becomes apparent and real through his or her interaction.

My design rationale is to uncover and emphasize this essence. Of course, graphical design, like typography, layout and motion graphics, are important, but the aspect of the user's encounter with a website that I currently regard as absolutely intrinsic to their experience, is in the **field** itself; the basic environment in which these elements are placed. To take a painting analogy, rather than consider what subject to paint and what sort of picture to create, I am focusing in on the more basic level of the decision making process: the sort of canvas the picture will be painted on.

I consider computers and the Internet together create a medium that allows for the creation of a multitude of different fields. In the face of the many different concepts embraced by the Internet - spatial concepts, time flow, even our existence and interconnectivity - my own belief is that we should also be experimenting with different approaches to the field itself.

Nervous

But all of this rather abstract. I'd like to show you a concrete example of an experiment I carried out on primarily a time-flow editing - a guest book called **BOOK OF TYPOBEAT**.

When a visitor types on the keyboard, the corresponding letters float up in a line on the screen. The visitor's keystroke intervals are recorded by the millisecond, so the exact keystrokes can be reproduced if the visitor presses the REPLAY button. Should the visitor choose to SUBMIT the data, the keystrokes will be recorded on the server.

I was playing with the way that, in a typical guest book, time is condensed into an instant: the instant the user presses the SUBMIT button. In my guest book I was trying to capture real-time time-flow, a continuum of keystrokes typed by the visitor. Because the logged data encapsulates the flow of real-time moments, it begins to feel like an entity in its own right, in a way that write-in data fails to do. The rhythm of the timing conveys all sorts of impressions. Like breathing, it conveys the state of mind of the operator at the other end of the network. What I was trying to capture was the reflection, the impression of the real human being, conveyed through the way the time flowed between the keystrokes.

Yugo Nakamura

This guest book is a field, carefully designed to bring out the essence of the impression of a real entity lying hidden in the Net. To repeat the point, the technical aim of my designs is not to produce some hugely attractive motion graphic or eye-pleasing layout, but rather to work out how to really bring out this essence.

I am still in the first stages of exploring this area and I'll admit that I haven't achieved even half of what I want to. There is still a wealth of unexplored avenues and possibilities. As long as the Web continues to develop, there will be endless new sources of inspiration.

As I began by writing, I have no more idea than anyone else of the way things will go in the future, but I do know that, as far as I'm concerned, the way events are shaping up at the moment is extremely enjoyable and exciting. And that's something I hope we'll never lose sight of.

ONE AUDIO THE ONLY ONE MUSIC PORTAL FOR YOU.

ONEAUDIO IS COMING IN NOVEMBER

AN OSINTERNET CREATION

WATCH MODE

Nervous

The way in which I create my Flash content is a little idiosyncratic. But I believe that this method in itself helps give individuality to my work, and with that in mind I would like to focus this tutorial on my creative method.

I have more or less turned my back on conventional frame-based animation methods. Instead, I use ActionScript extensively, and control almost all of actions and events using scripted formulae. And, of course, I am always refining my ActionScript technique.

I worked out a number of basic Flash ActionScript techniques that are now becoming more widespread during a seemingly never-ending development period. Incidentally, the site at MONO*crafts, www.yugop.com, was my attempt to fuse diverse elements organically into a single interface world.)

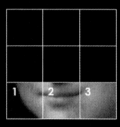

NOW LOADING KEY-COMPONENTS...

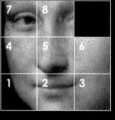

NOW LOADING KEY-COMPONENTS...

Yugo Nakamura

READY... CLICK TO START.

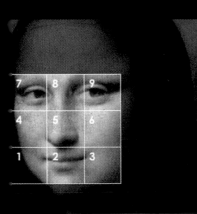

It's not just Flash; the Web itself is an extremely technically restrictive medium. However, I would guess that none of the Web designers who I respect ever regard this as a restriction on their freedom, but derive huge enjoyment from working out and and around the rules of the game. I'm trying very hard to foster this attitude myself - I want to draw positive enjoyment from the forest of restrictions that confront me.

I would like to give some idea of the spirit of the way in which I actually create my work. The example I will give is the movie Nervous Matrix which is the initial screen of MONO*crafts.

Nervous

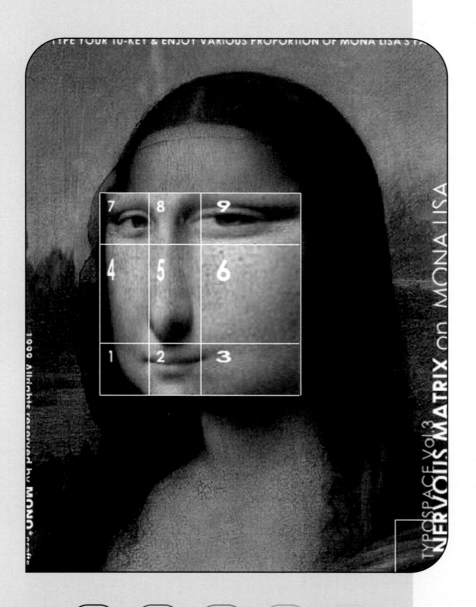

This movie is a very simple and easy to understand interactive toy. A 3x3 matrix is mapped over Leonardo da Vinci's Mona Lisa. The elements of the matrix correspond to the elements of the numeric keypad on the keyboard, and by pressing one of the keys the corresponding cell in the matrix expands and Mona Lisa's face is distorted in real time. The cells do not move independently but interfere with each other, repeatedly fluctuating between expansion and contraction, so that the proportions of the matrix vary in an infinite pattern depending on the timing with which the numeric keys are pressed.

This means that it is not a sequential movie, with a predetermined plot line, but rather it has been designed to be a *reactor*, infinitely responsive to user input.

The .swf movie one on my site is actually script controlled to a rather high level of detail, and it would be superfluous or even positively counter-productive to describe it all. So I will limit myself to describing the underlying thinking, and the main aspects of the script. I'm assuming a certain level of Flash and ActionScript knowledge in the commentary that follows. Regrettably there is not enough space to write this tutorial giving consideration to everybody, so all I can do is ask the beginners amongst you to forgive me if you find yourselves struggling to understand.

Yugo Nakamura

The main processes within .swf file are divided into two phases. First, a field is created that specifies the interrelationship between the cells in the matrix. Then the correspondence between the numerical key input and the screen is established.

I will describe, in sequence, the specifics of the actual operations in these stages. A source file for the tutorial has been included on the CD-Rom, filename, monalisa-tutorial.fla, and you should first refer to that for details of the basic movie configuration.

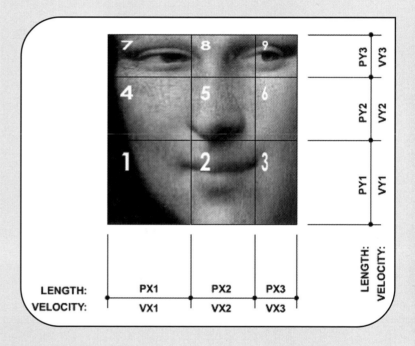

Establishing a Field

We will first establish the field that specifies the relationships between the cells.

As you can see from the diagram, the lengths of a total of six edges, i.e. three vertical and three horizontal, specify the shape of the 3x3 matrix. These are respectively defined as:

Horixontal edge lengths: PX1, PX2, PX3
Vertical edge lengths: PY1, PY2, PY3

In addition, these are assumed to be continuously moving, and the speeds of change of the edge lengths are:

Speeds of change of the horizontal edge lengths: VX1, VX2, VX3
Speeds of change of the vertical edge lengths: VY1, VY2, VY3

These are the basic variables. The dynamic relationship between the edge lengths and their speeds is determined within Flash ActionScript, and you need do nothing more than create an arrangement in which this is reflected by the sizes of the cells.

Nervous

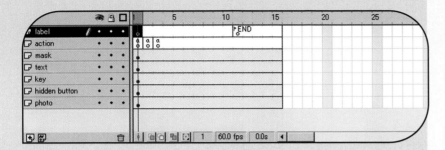

The frame configuration in the movie is extremely simple, as you can see from the diagram. I'm going to focus on the **action** layer. In frame 1, the initial variables are set. Frame 2 holds the main process that we've talked about and frame 3 simply jumps back to frame 2

So let's look at the main processing in frame 2. There are three phases. The first controls the speed of change in the lengths of the edges of the cells (VX1 to 3, VY1 to 3), the second controls the lengths of the edges of the cells (PX1 to 3, PY1 to 3), and phase three alters and displays the sizes of the cells.

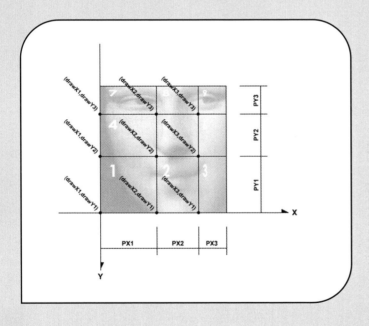

Controlling the Speed at which the Cells Change

The expansion and contraction of the cells is extremely smooth, as you will see if you look at the sample. The speed of expansion and contraction of the cells, which is accelerated by pressing the numeric keypad, is not constant but gently fluctuates, accelerating and decelerating while the system gradually settles into the original cell size. This movement is controlled using this formula:

set variable VX = [VX + (L-PX)/accel]/slow

VX	Speed of change of the cell
PX	Current size of the cell
L	Default value for the size of the cell (60 in this example)
accel	Acceleration parameter (100 in this example)
slow	Deceleration parameter (1.075 in this example)

Yugo Nakamura

So, when there is a difference between the current cell size, PX, and the default value L, the speed of cell change, VX, changes in acceleration proportional to this difference, in the direction in which the difference is made up. Smooth fluctuating movement is created by repeating this at length in a 20fps frame loop.

The acceleration of the fluctuation is specified by the value of the constant, accel, so, the lower the value of accel, the more rapid the acceleration. Conversely, the higher its value, the slower the acceleration. In addition, slow is the parameter which specifies overall attenuation. Again, the higher its value the more rapid the attenuation, the lower, the more gentle. You will get good results if you set target values similar to these:

accel = 10 to 100
slow = 1.01 to 1.50.

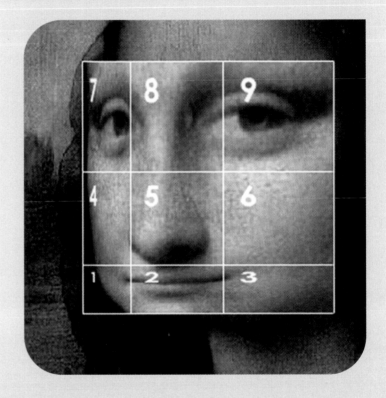

Nervous

I have applied this formula to other areas of MONO*crafts, because it is a useful way to create a common feel for movement across the site.

For the Mona Lisa effect, I applied this formula to VX1 to 3 and VY1 to 3, which gave me this script to build the expansion and contraction of the cells:

```
i =1;
while (i<=3) {
set ("VX" add i = (eval("VX" add i)+(L-eval("PX" add i))/accel)/slow);
set ("VY" add i = (eval("VY" add i)+(L-eval("PY" add i))/accel)/slow);
i = i+1;
}
```

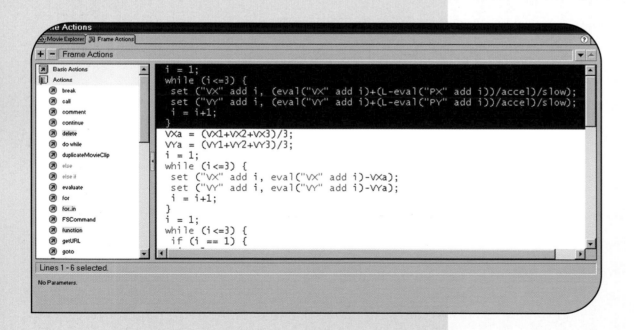

However, this script alone is not enough for the cells to interact with each other. Left like this, they would simply expand and contract in isolation. However, you can see from the way the matrix moves that the cells are not independent. They fluctuate as if they were jostling each other. If one of the cells expands, other cells contract to accommodate it, and if one cell contracts others expand. I built in this interactivity by adding this script to what I have just shown you:

```
VXa  = (VX1+VX2+VX3)/3;
VYa = (VY1+VY2+VY3)/3;
i =1;
while (i<=3){
set ("VX" add i = eval ("VX" add i)-vxa);
set ("VY" add i = eval ("VY" add i)-vya);
i  =i+1;
}
```

VXa and VYa are averages of the speeds of change of the cells, VX1 to 3 and VY1 to 3. If these are subtracted from the respective VX and VY, the sum of the speeds of the cells will always be 0 and the relationship which results means that, if the speed of one cell accelerates, the speeds of other cells reduce. This is the relationship that produces the jostling fluctuation that we're aiming for.

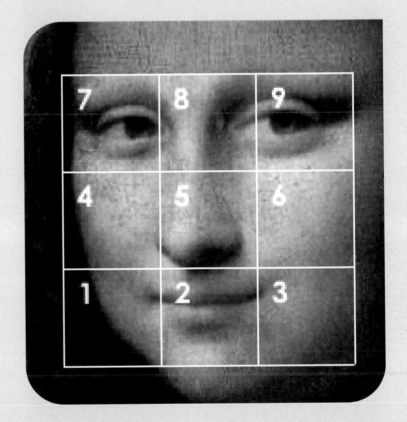

Nervous

I have added another element to aid the fluctuation as a whole on the site, but I have rather reluctantly decided not to talk about this to avoid complexity. With the script discussed up to here, the matrix as a whole stays a constant size and does not expand and contract.

Controlling the Lengths of the Edges of the Cells

Once you've established the speed at which the lengths of the edges change, it's a simple step to add speed to the edge lengths and constantly update them:

$$PX=PX+VX$$

This is employed in PX1 to 3 and PY1 to 3, just as before.

```
i =1
while (i<=3);
set (PX add i = eval("PX" add i)+eval("VX" add i));
set (PY add i = eval("PY" add i)+eval("VY" add i));
i = i+1;
}
```

```
do while
duplicateMovieClip
else
else if
evaluate
for
for.in
FSCommand
function
getURL
goto

set ("PX" add i, eval("PX" add i)+eval("VX" add i));
set ("PY" add i, eval("PY" add i)+eval("VY" add i));
i = i+1;
}
i = 1;
while (i<=3) {
setProperty ("/tenkey/key" add i, _xscale, eval("PX" add
setProperty ("/tenkey/key" add i, _yscale, PY1*100/L);
setProperty ("/tenkey/key" add (i+3), _xscale, eval("PX"
setProperty ("/tenkey/key" add (i+3), _yscale, PY2*100/L
```

ines 27 - 29 selected.

Parameters.

Altering and Displaying the Sizes of the Cells.

Finally, we need to think about setting and placing the nine movie symbols to predetermined sizes and positions, based on the lengths of the edges of the cells established in the previous step. The movie clip placement and the instance name are as shown in the earlier figure. For the sake of convenience, the whole of the matrix comprising the nine cells is set as a movie symbol with the instance name **tenkey** (the standard Japanese term for the numeric keypad), and the movie symbols **key 1** to **key 9** of the different cells are placed in the lower layer.

"TENKEY"

7 "KEY7"	8 "KEY8"	9 "KEY9"
4 "KEY4"	5 "KEY5"	6 "KEY6"
1 "KEY1"	2 "KEY2"	3 "KEY3"

Nervous

First, let's look at setting the cells' sizes, which involves nothing more complicated than setting PX1 to 3 for the vertical edges and PY1 to 3 for the horizontal edges. The next piece of script designates, in sequence, percentages for the sizes of cells grouped by row as follows: key 1 to key 3, key 4 to key 6, and key 7 to key 9. These are the default values for the cell sizes, with the initial setting at frame 1 being a constant designated as 60.

```
i =1
while (i<=3) {
setProperty ("/tenkey/key" add i, _xscale, eval("PX" add i)*100/L);
setProperty ("/tenkey/key" add i, _yscale PY1*100/L);
setProperty ("/tenkey/key" add (i+3), _xscale) eval("PX" add i)*100/L);
setProperty ("/tenkey/key" add (i+3), _yscale) PY2*100/L);
setProperty ("/tenkey/key"add (i+6), _xscale) eval("PX" add i)*100/L);
setProperty ("/tenkey/key" add (i+6), _yscale) PY3*100/L);
i =i+1;
}
```

If you have more matrices, you'll have to build a more elegant multiple loop, but, since we're looking at three rows and three columns, I have used this rather less elegant but easy to understand script.

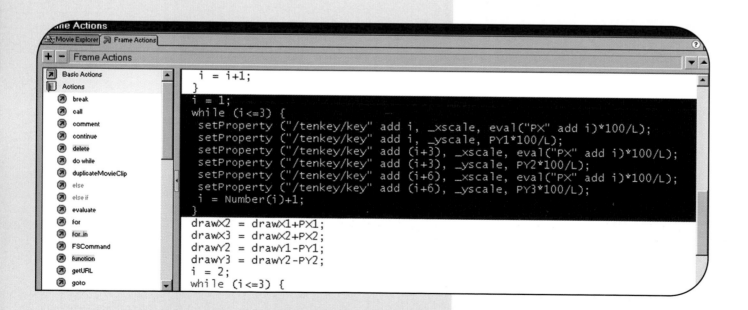

Next, we'll look at placing the cell in the desired position. For this, we need to achieve a seamless line up, in accordance with the sizes of the cells, from the bottom-left position of the matrix, in sequence vertically and horizontally.

First of all, the term for the initial setting of frame 1 is:

drawX1 =getProperty ("/tenkey/key1", _x);
drawY1 =getProperty ("/tenkey/key1", _y);

```
drawX1 = getProperty("/tenkey/key1", _x);
drawY1 = getProperty("/tenkey/key1", _y);
L = 60;
i = 1;
while (i <=3) {
  set ("PX" add i, L);
  set ("PY" add i, L);
  set ("VY" add i, 0);
  i = i+1;
}
accel = 100;
slow = 1.075;
plusV = 5;
```

Nervous

```
setProperty ("/tenkey/key" add i, _yscale, PY1*100/L);
setProperty ("/tenkey/key" add (i+3), _xscale, eval("PX" add i)*100/L);
setProperty ("/tenkey/key" add (i+3), _yscale, PY2*100/L);
setProperty ("/tenkey/key" add (i+6), _xscale, eval("PX" add i)*100/L);
setProperty ("/tenkey/key" add (i+6), _yscale, PY3*100/L);
i = Number(i)+1;
}
drawX2 = Number(drawX1)+Number(PX1);
drawX3 = Number(drawX2)+Number(PX2);
drawY2 = drawY1-PY1;
drawY3 = drawY2-PY2;
i = 2;
while (Number(i)<=3) {
setProperty ("/tenkey/key" add i, _x, eval("drawX" add i));
setProperty ("/tenkey/key" add (i+3), _x, eval("drawX" add i));
setProperty ("/tenkey/key" add (i+6), _x, eval("drawX" add i));
setProperty ("/tenkey/key" add (i*3-2), _y, eval("drawY" add i));
setProperty ("/tenkey/key" add (i*3-1), _y, eval("drawY" add i));
setProperty ("/tenkey/key" add (i*3), _y, eval("drawY" add i));
i = Number(i)+1;
}
```

The bottom left co-ordinates, drawX1, drawY1, are designated as constants. Next, the placement is done in accordance with the sizes of the cells. This is how it looks when converted into script:

drawX2 =drawX1+PX1;
drawX3 =drawX2+PX2;
drawY2 =drawY1-PY1;
drawY3 =drawY2-PY2;
i = 2;
while (i<=3) {
setProperty ("/tenkey/key" add i,_x, eval("drawX" add i));
setProperty ("/tenkey/key" add (i+3), _x eval("drawX" add i));
setProperty ("/tenkey/key" add (i+6), _x eval("drawX" add i));
setproperty ("/tenkey/key" add (i*3-2), _y =eval("drawY" add i));
setProperty ("/tenkey/key" add (i*3-1), _y =eval("drawY" add i));
setProperty ("/tenkey/key"add (i*3), _y =eval("drawY" add i));
i =i+1;
}

With that, the main script is fully complete. This is the entire script:

Frame 1: Initial settings of the variables

drawX1 = getProperty("/tenkey/key1", _x);
drawY1 = getProperty("/tenkey/key1", _y);
L = 60;
i = 1;
while (Number(i)<=3) {
   set ("PX" add i, L);
   set ("PY" add i, L);
   set ("VY" add i, 0);
   i = Number(i)+1;
}
accel = 100;
slow = 1.075;
plusV = 5;F

Frame 2: Main Processing

```
i = 1;
while (Number(i)<=3) {
   set ("VX" add i, (eval("VX" add i)+(L-eval("PX" add
i))/accel)/slow);
   set ("VY" add i, (eval("VY" add i)+(L-eval("PY" add
i))/accel)/slow);
   i = Number(i)+1;
}
VXa                                        =
(Number(Number(VX1)+Number(VX2))+Number(VX
3))/3;
VYa                                        =
(Number(Number(VY1)+Number(VY2))+Number(VY
3))/3;
i = 1;
while (Number(i)<=3) {
   set ("VX" add i, eval("VX" add i)-VXa);
   set ("VY" add i, eval("VY" add i)-VYa);
   i = Number(i)+1;
}
i = 1;
while (Number(i)<=3) {
   if (Number(i) == 1) {
      j = 2;
      k = 3;
   } else if (Number(i) == 2) {
      j = 3;
      k = 1;
   } else if (Number(i) == 3) {
      j = 1;
      k = 2;
   }
   set ("PX" add i, eval("PX" add i)+eval("VX" add i));
   set ("PY" add i, eval("PY" add i)+eval("VY" add i));
   i = Number(i)+1;
}
```

```
 i = 1;
while (Number(i)<=3) {
   setProperty ("/tenkey/key" add i, _xscale, eval("PX"
add i)*100/L);
      setProperty ("/tenkey/key" add i, _yscale,
PY1*100/L);
      setProperty ("/tenkey/key" add (i+3), _xscale,
eval("PX" add i)*100/L);
      setProperty ("/tenkey/key" add (i+3), _yscale,
PY2*100/L);
      setProperty ("/tenkey/key" add (i+6), _xscale,
eval("PX" add i)*100/L);
      setProperty ("/tenkey/key" add (i+6), _yscale,
PY3*100/L);
   i = Number(i)+1;
}
drawX2 = Number(drawX1)+Number(PX1);
drawX3 = Number(drawX2)+Number(PX2);
drawY2 = drawY1-PY1;
drawY3 = drawY2-PY2;
i = 2;
while (Number(i)<=3) {
   setProperty ("/tenkey/key" add i, _x, eval("drawX"
add i));
      setProperty ("/tenkey/key" add (i+3), _x,
eval("drawX" add i));
      setProperty ("/tenkey/key" add (i+6), _x,
eval("drawX" add i));
      setProperty ("/tenkey/key" add (i*3-2), _y,
eval("drawY" add i));
      setProperty ("/tenkey/key" add (i*3-1), _y,
eval("drawY" add i));
      setProperty ("/tenkey/key" add (i*3), _y,
eval("drawY" add i));
   i = Number(i)+1;
}Frame 3: Jump to Frame 2

gotoAndPlay (2);
```

Nervous

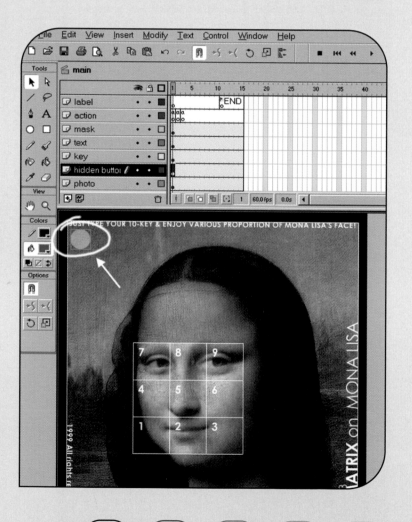

Setting the Correspondences with Numeric Keypad Input

The script up to this point sets the fields with organically corresponding cells. The rest is simple. We need to set up the correspondences you want when the keys are pressed. In order to get the cells to expand when a key is pressed, all you need to do is to add some form of increment to the speeds of the edge lengths of the cells (VX1 to 3 and VY1 to 3), which were so laboriously set in the preceding sections.

More specifically, all you need do is insert scripts such as the following into a dummy button (located on the hidden button layout in this sample).

```
 On (Key: 1)
VX1 =VX1+plusV;
VY1 =VY1+plusV;
}
```

Here, plusV is the increment added to the edge lengths of the cells when the keys are pressed.

This script means that when the key 1 is pressed, VX1 and VY1, which is to say the speeds of the lengths of the edges of the cell corresponding to key 1 accelerate by an amount equivalent to the magnitude of plusV.

In addition, from frame 2 onwards, animation involving a slight change of color is added to the movie symbol of the cell corresponding to key 1, (a stop is put on Frame 1. See Figure 3-5), and a small degree of coloring can be added by Tell Targeting using the following script:

```
Begin Tell Target ("/tenkey/key1")
Go to and Play (2)
End Tell Target
```

The cell color changes when a key is pressed.

To summarize, the script when the key 1 is pressed is as follows:

```
on (keyPress: "1") {
  VX1 =VX1+plusV;
  VY1 =VY1+plusV;
  tellTarget ("/tenkey/key1") {
   gotoAndPlay (2);
  }
}
```

Then the operation simply needs to be repeated for the other keys (2 to 9). And that's it. The following script is incorporated into the dummy button.

Nervous

```
 on (keyPress "1") {
VX1 = Number(VX1)+Number(plusV);
VY1 = Number(VY1)+Number(plusV);
tellTarget ("/tenkey/key1") {
gotoAndPlay (2);
}
}
on (keyPress "2") {
VX2 = Number(VX2)+Number(plusV);
VY1 = Number(VY1)+Number(plusV);
tellTarget ("/tenkey/key2") {
gotoAndPlay (2);
}
}
on (keyPress "3") {
VX3 = Number(VX3)+Number(plusV);
VY1 = Number(VY1)+Number(plusV);
tellTarget ("/tenkey/key3") {
gotoAndPlay (2);
}
}
on (keyPress "4") {
VX1 = Number(VX1)+Number(plusV);
VY2 = Number(VY2)+Number(plusV);
tellTarget ("/tenkey/key4") {
gotoAndPlay (2);
}
}
on (keyPress "5") {
VX2 = Number(VX2)+Number(plusV);
VY2 = Number(VY2)+Number(plusV);
tellTarget ("/tenkey/key5") {
gotoAndPlay (2);
}
}
on (keyPress "6") {
```

```
 VX3 = Number(VX3)+Number(plusV);
VY2 = Number(VY2)+Number(plusV);
tellTarget ("/tenkey/key6") {
gotoAndPlay (2);
}
}
on (keyPress "7") {
VX1 = Number(VX1)+Number(plusV);
VY3 = Number(VY3)+Number(plusV);
tellTarget ("/tenkey/key7") {
gotoAndPlay (2);
}
}
on (keyPress "8") {
VX2 = Number(VX2)+Number(plusV);
VY3 = Number(VY3)+Number(plusV);
tellTarget ("/tenkey/key8") {
gotoAndPlay (2);
}
}
on (keyPress "9") {
VX3 = Number(VX3)+Number(plusV);
VY3 = Number(VY3)+Number(plusV);
tellTarget ("/tenkey/key9") {
gotoAndPlay (2);
}

gotoAndPlay ("loop1");
}
```

This is almost all the scripting I used to build the Nervous Matrix. As I mentioned earlier, I have simplified things and reluctantly had to leave out a few of the elements from the sample actually running on my site. There, I have smoothed the fluctuation of the matrix as a whole, although the example that I've used here is static. I also used processing to avoid errors when the viewer presses the same key repeatedly to make a single cell particularly large. My aim here has been to give you all the basic script that you need to create a similar effect of your own. The attached CD-Rom includes a source file for this tutorial, so please take a look at this if you feel so inclined.

"...take in what's out there, learn how it's done, adapt it, add to it, but remember that the best ideas are in your own head. "

JAYSON SINGE
www.neonsky.com

Pointillism

I want a huge LCD monitor. I daydream about it when I'm staring into my 19-inch CRT at 2 a.m., bathing in radiation, my eyes tired and dry. I'm not thinking of one of those 22-inch jobs. I'm thinking meters. Too big to touch from end to end with my outstretched arms. Wall-sized. And when I see this thing in my mind, I never really see anything displayed on it: It's blank. Even turned off, it's beautiful. Monolithic and quiet. But as much as I would love to walk into my office someday and see this black hole covering an entire wall, I know it wouldn't help me a bit. It might inspire me for a few short moments, but it would no more make me a better multimedia designer than would having a new set of brushes make me a better painter. As if buying an expensive guitar would somehow improve my ability to play it. Sure, we need tools. And, yes, better tools make our work a lot easier. But tools are for solving problems, problems that arise when we try to translate what we create in our minds into something we can share.

Flash is a wonderful tool. But Flash can't create for us. Flash is but a means to an end. Our challenge is to create great problems. Solve them. And to create new problems again.

Jayson Singe

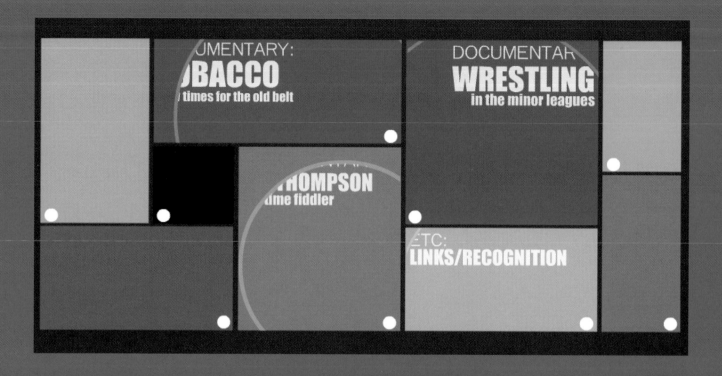

Ask yourself, "What do I want to see?" But don't forget to ask yourself "Why?" I see a lot of sites that don't interest me because they don't **do anything**. And I see a lot of sites that are an electrical storm of motion and interactivity, but I find myself asking "So what?" because they lack substance. Finding the balance is the real art. You will find that balance in design, not in 'cool' effects.

So many amazing new ideas are surfacing all the time that it's easy to get overwhelmed, caught-up in the latest effects. Be careful. I found myself deep into a project recently, designing a site around an interesting effect that I had been tinkering with. What I was really doing was designing backward. I should have

been building toward an aesthetic, but instead I was building around an effect that really had none on its own. It was frustrating to have worked on something for over a week and then to realize that I was approaching the project from the wrong direction, but it was an important mistake to make. It would be nice to know exactly where I'm going with every project before I turn on the computer. And it would be nice to know exactly how I would get there, step by step, without making all my mistakes, but I'd never learn anything. So, take in what's out there, learn how it's done, adapt it, add to it, but remember that the best ideas are in your own head. They are the ideas that are yet to come, and they are yours to find.

Pointillism

I really didn't get into Flash until version 4. My experience in web presentation was limited to Quicktime, which I had been using to mix photojournalism with audio to create multimedia documentaries. I had played with Flash 3, but its audio capabilities were weak, so I only learned enough to get frustrated. When Flash 4 was released with MP3 compression codecs I gave it a closer look. The new version had everything I was looking for, and, with the implementation of ActionScript, much, much more.

I created the NeonSky site as a home for my multimedia documentaries. The subjects of the stories contained on the site were going to be varied, each with its own individual look and feel, so I wanted the main interface to be a little more subdued. I wanted it to appear simple. That's about the extent of what I had in mind from the start.

I began with a horizontal rectangle, classically cinematic in proportion. I began to split it up into different parts, into smaller component rectangles and squares. And that's as far as I went. I liked the simplicity. I played around with the composition quite a bit, but I left the main rectangle intact. And I left the color palette simple too subtle variations of the three primary colors.

Jayson Singe

Within Neonsky, I decided to go with an intro for two reasons. One, I wanted to introduce the logo, the name of the site and at least something about its nature – new media. Second, I wanted to set the boundary for where everything would sit once the interface appeared. My message here is that if you don't have a reason to use an intro, don't make one, especially not a long one.

Because I was trying to stick with a simple geometric look, the logo presented a minor problem. I really wanted to give the illusion that the entire site is composed of geometric shapes, rectangles in particular. I needed to somehow build the logo out of shapes that I could use in the interface.

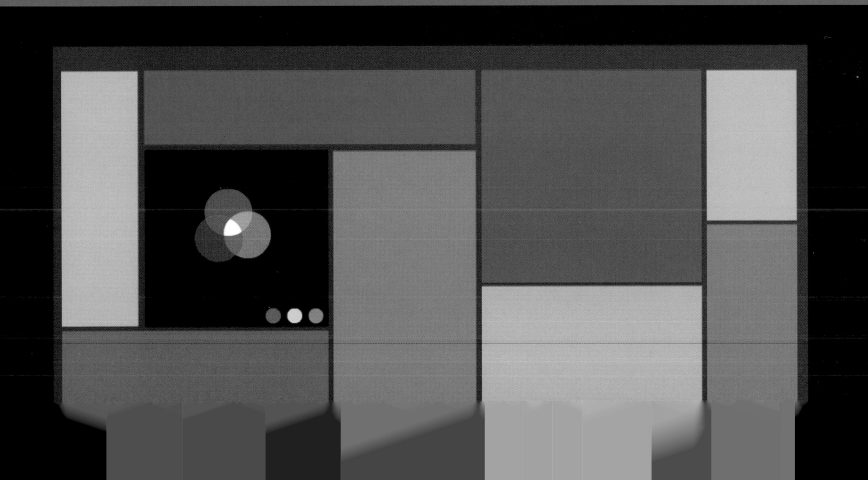

Pointillism

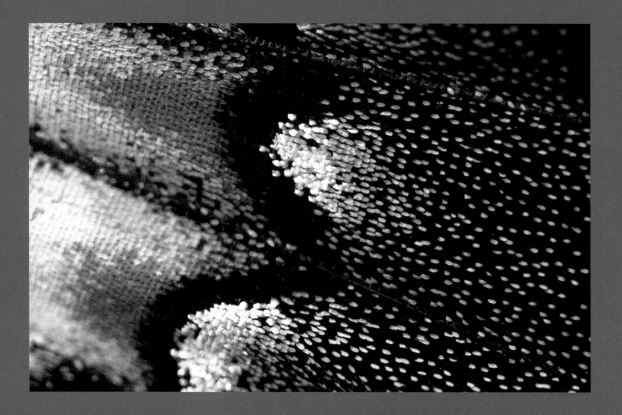

As a newspaper photographer, the solution was right before my eyes - and rubbing off on my fingers every day. It's also what I see when I'm staring into my monitor every night. Dots. Pixels. Bunches of very small things that create the illusion of something bigger, something solid. To reproduce photographs in the newspaper, pictures are converted into what's called a halftone, a pattern consisting of thousands of tiny dots or rings. And, of course, the images on our computer monitors are composed of thousands of tiny points of light - pixels. These patterns are everywhere in nature. In art too. Salvador Dali experimented with the halftone in several of his works. His oil, *Portrait of My Dead Brother*, was a major inspiration for NeonSky. I found that this theme of a complex pattern of smaller cells, or scales, was something that had emerged within my own work too, shown in my butterfly.

Jayson Singe

I put these dots to work in NeonSky, using them in animation and in the structure of the interface. The logo emerges as a grid of dots. The interface materializes as rectangles filled with dots. The navigation is controlled with dots. And so on.

Pointillism

Once you find something you like, stick with it. Play with it until you've squeezed everything out of it that you can. Everything you create has been influenced by something that you've seen or experienced. As you work through your designs, you become your own dominant influence and it's then that your creativity is really flowing. That flow is powerful. It will take on a life of its own, finding its way into your future projects. As an example, I can trace back the look and feel of one of my recent sites to the ideas I was exploring in NeonSky. The colors and shapes on ViviSys.com - even the dots pattern on the chair - are reminiscent of the style of NeonSky.

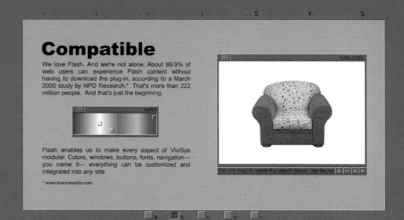

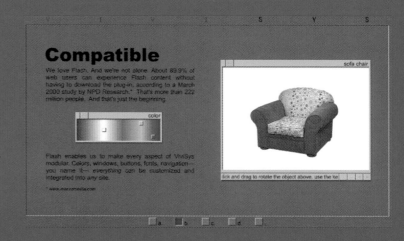

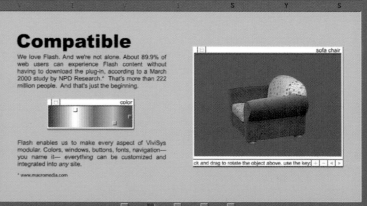

Jayson Singe

Trends in design are spreading so quickly that it's difficult to see where they're coming from. Flash design seems to be sprouting from the same collective unconscious. But it's not. We are influencing each other, but it's happening so quickly that it looks like we all have the same ideas from the start. Trends in art that used to take years – even decades – to move across continents are crossing the globe in the time it takes to download a page or send an e-mail. I get a lot of e-mail asking how I created the masking effect with the Neonsky logo. In the next few demonstrations, we'll work through this effect, more like pointillism in its construction than a true halftone. We'll start by using multiple copies of a single movie clip to create a wave effect. We'll build on that idea by using multiple instances of the same movie clip along a timeline and end up by combining the cascading movie clip effect with a little ActionScript to create an interactive, drag-and-drop interface. Here, we'll get into variables, drag-and-drop, setting properties and loading movies.

Pointillism

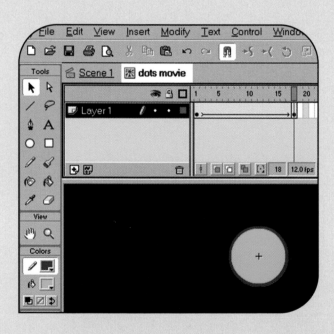

Draw a green circle with a diameter of twenty pixels. Make it a symbol and call it **dot**.

Create a movie clip, **dots movie**. Insert an instance of the dot symbol into frame 1 and in frame 18. Modify the instance of the dot in frame 1 to Alpha 0 and scale it to 20% of its original size.
Modify the instance of the dot in frame 18 to Alpha 100.

Tween the two frames (with a motion tween). Testing the scene shows the dot changing from small and transparent to large and opaque.

Insert a keyframe in frame 19, the first frame after the tween. Modify the instance of the dot in this new frame, changing the tint to an orange color (r250,g100,b25).

Create a new layer and call it **Layer 2**

Cut and paste the frames (frames 1-18) of the first tween of the green dot into frame 18 of Layer 2. Then reverse these frames.

Now paste the frames again into frame 37 of Layer 1. Reverse these frames, as well. Modify the instance of the first keyframe in this tween (frame 37), changing the tint of the dot to orange (r250,g100,b25).

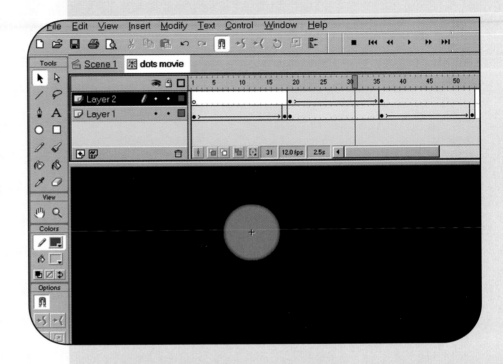

When you're modifying the color properties of the dot in the last keyframe (53) of this sequence, use the Color Effects Advanced option to set its tint and its Alpha. Set the Alpha to 0 and the color selections to red 250, green 100, blue 25. It's important to use the Special option when you want to modify more than one color property, as we do here when we tween an already tinted symbol to a specific Alpha.

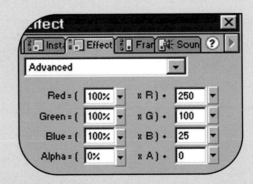

Pointillism

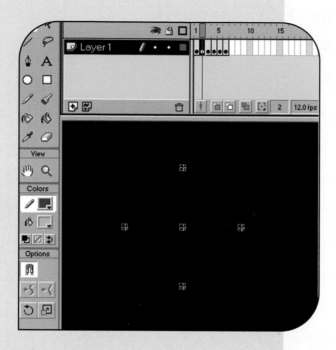

Insert a Stop action in frame 53 of the movie clip, dots movie.

Create a new movie symbol and call it **dots graph**. Place the movie clip, dots movie, in frame 1, centered on the stage.

Insert a keyframe in frame 2. In this frame, place four dots movie movie clips around the center movie clip. It's helpful to turn on the grid and show layers as outlines so you can see where you're positioning these movie clips.

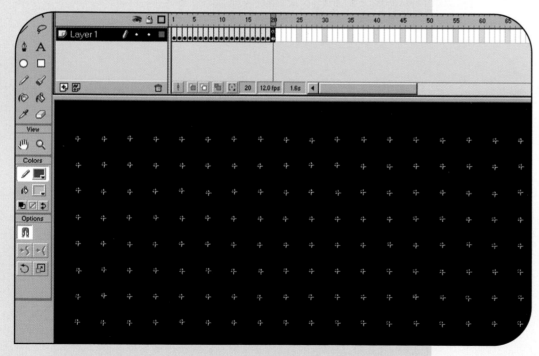

Continue to add dots movie movie clips in each subsequent keyframe, growing out from the center until you have completed a rectangle nine movie clips tall and twenty-one movie clips wide. Be careful not to cut and paste the movie clips, but to insert them from the Library. If you copy clips from previous frames you could copy more than one by mistake, ruining the cascading effect. When you've completed the rectangular grid, use the Align command to straighten the rows.

You'll know that the more animation you have on the screen, the slower the computer can process the presentation. If you put too many moving dots on the screen at once, the animation gets clunky and everything slows down. You can correct this to a certain degree by using audio through the animation sequence and setting the audio properties to stream. So, as well as enhancing the user experience, any audio loop that you add will help to keep your animation up to speed for viewers with slower computers. Streaming keeps the animation in sync with the audio by skipping animation frames along the way. A few missed frames in an animation like the dots graph is no big deal.

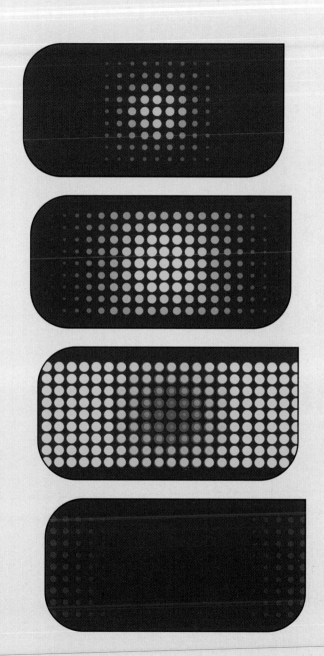

Setting the sound to stream won't correct everything. If there are just too many movie clips animating at once, instead of chugging along slowly, the stream setting will cause slower machines to skip over a lot of frames, and that looks even worse than being a little slow. Play around with the movie's fps setting as well. Speeding up the movie won't help a slower machine, but if you're used to setting your fps at higher speeds (more than the default twelve fps), you might try lowering it if you play with the stream sync technique.

Pointillism

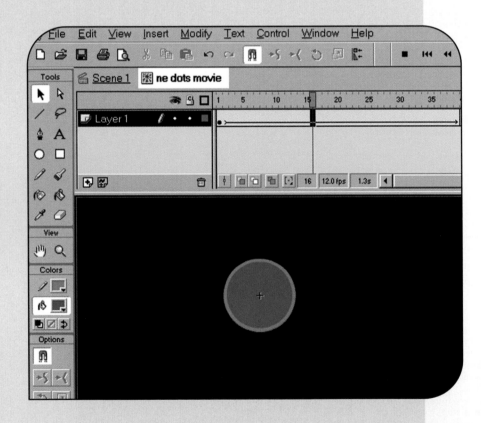

Adding a Mask

In the first demo, we created a movie clip, called dots movie, in which a dot tweens from a very small and transparent state to a larger size and solid color before it fades out at the end of the clip. We put this movie clip in the main timeline and added more and more instances of it in each subsequent keyframe. When we test the .fla, the colored dots appear to bloom out from the center and then fade out at the edge of the stage in the order they appear along the timeline. I'll extend that now by adding a mask to this effect to give the illusion that the dots are filling up whatever shape we chose to mask with. But by also enlarging the dots we'll create an entirely different illusion.

Just as we did in the first effect, draw an orange circle, make it a symbol and call it **ne dot**.

Create a movie clip, but this time call it **ne dots movie**. Within this movie clip set ne dot to tween from a small size at Alpha 0 to a large size at Alpha 100, over 40 frames. For this effect, at the end of the tween, make the symbol 250% larger than the original.

Next, insert a keyframe at frame 50, then another at frame 68. Tween the two frames.

Modify the tint of the dot at frame 68 to be the green color we've been using (r147, g215, b100.). We've used this color several times, and we'll use it again, so make a new color in the colors palette. Insert a keyframe at frames 95 and 140. Reduce the size of the dot in frame 140 and use the Color Effects Advanced dialog box to change its color to blue. Set its Alpha value to 0.

Insert a Stop command in the last keyframe.

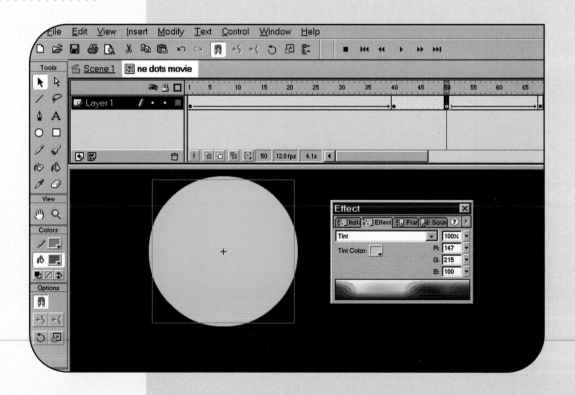

Pointillism

Now let's create a graph once again. Create a new movie clip, **ne dots graph**.

We could use the graph from the first demo, but the colors would bloom and change from the center outward. For this effect, we want the color to cascade diagonally, from the upper left to the lower right. It's easy to change the symbols that make up the graph, and, as we'll see, any number of effects can be achieved by playing around with that one simple clip. But unless you're just flipping the horizontal or vertical orientation, or changing the scale, changing the graph is very time consuming.

First, we'll make a mask layer. A mask behaves like a window. In the final movie, it will only show graphics contained within its shape, masking from view anything that lies outside. Make a new symbol from any shape or logo that you want to act as the mask. That shape will fill with the halftone pattern. I use the NeonSky logo from the site.

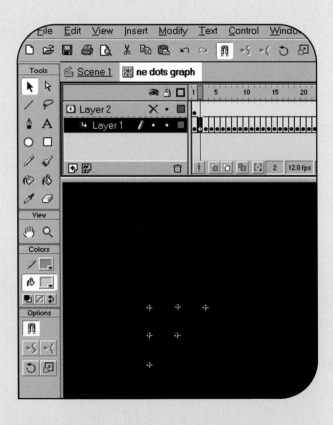

Place it in the first frame on Layer 1. Call the layer **logo**. To convert the logo layer into a mask layer, right-click or ctrl-click on the layer name bar and choose Mask from the pop-up menu.

Make a new layer called **ne dots movies**. Start the graph by placing one ne dots movie movie clip at the upper left.

Jayson Singe

Add two more in the next frame, moving diagonally from top left to lower right until the movie clips cover the area of your mask symbol. We'll go back later and remove unnecessary movie clips (as I've already done in the demo) that are not filling the areas of whatever mask we end up using. Add a Stop command in the last frame.

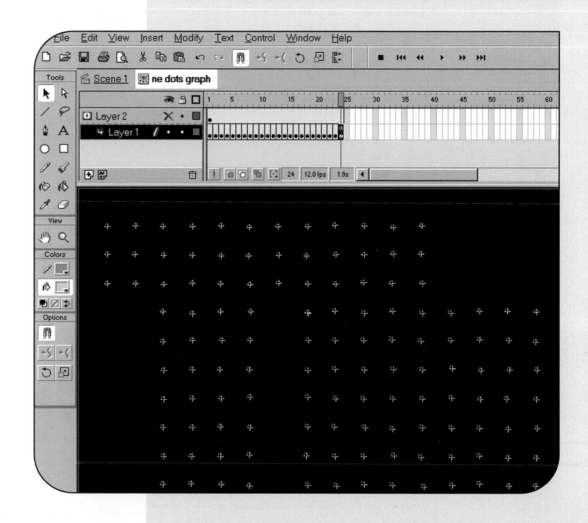

Pointillism

Test the movie. It should fill up with growing dots, diagonally from top left to bottom right.

Once the masked object has filled with the overlapping movie clips, it changes color gradually.

Drag-and-drop Interface

One of the effects on the NeonSky site that gets a fair amount of attention is the water droplet effect in the drag-and-drop Multimedia Tools section. That particular effect is really done in Photoshop, so to keep your mind concentrated on Flash, I've come up with an interface that uses the drag-and-drop script but creates something like the ripple effect by expanding on the dots movie ideas that we've been exploring in this chapter. So far, we've been using a graph to map out the paths of dozens of small movie clips. We're going to simplify that graph into one column, and then turn that column on its side so the movie clips stack vertically on top of one another.

We'll be working with two Flash files, one of which will load into _level1. The default level is 0 so level 1 will appear above it.

Create a new Flash file named **demo3**. This will serve as the _level0 .swf. Create a dot symbol (sound familiar?) but make this one gray. Insert that dot into a new movie clip called **dots movie**. Create a simple tween from a small size (modify/scale 20%) to a very large size (modify/scale 300%) over 20 frames, as we've done before. Insert a new keyframe at frame 35 and modify the color effect, Alpha=0, and up the scale by another 200%.

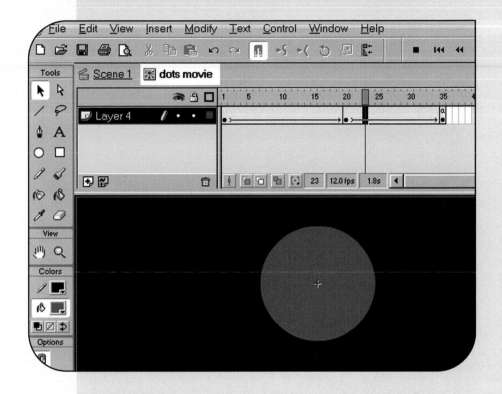

Next, instead of using a dots graph to space the movie clips out over a two-dimensional area as we've done before, we'll make a **drop sequence** movie clip, where they will all drop in on the exact same point.

Add the standard Stop action to the first empty frame of this new movie clip because it will sit on the stage, invisible until we tell it to go to and play frame 2 (the animation). Make a keyframe at frame 3 and insert the **dots movie** movie clip.

Insert a keyframe on every third frame until there are six movie clips on the timeline, as I've done here.

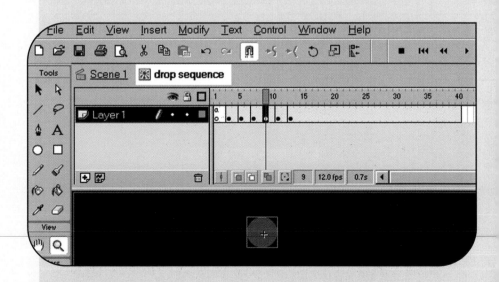

Pointillism

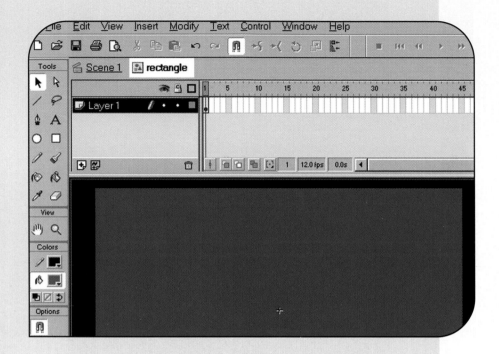

Create a new symbol of a rectangle and name it **rectangle**.

Create a new movie clip, called **background**, and, in frame 15, insert the rectangle symbol, centered on the stage. Tween the rectangle from Alpha 0 to Alpha 100 over fifteen frames. Insert a Stop action on the first keyframe. Add a new keyframe at frame 31 and delete the rectangle from this frame (the keyfrme will not show a hollow circle, signifying a blank keyframe). add a Stop action in this new frame.

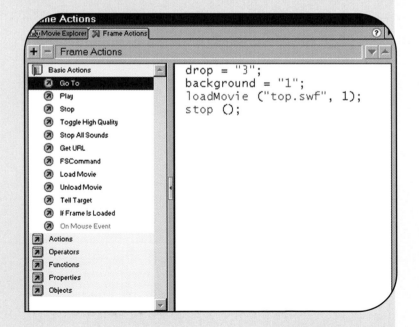

Go to the main timeline and create two layers: **background** and **dots sequences**.

Assign the following actions to the first frame of the top layer:

```
drop = "3";
background = "1";
loadMovie ("top.swf", 1);
stop ();
```

(We'll cover the top.swf that you see in the code on the next page.)

334

Insert the background movie clip in the background layer and center it on the stage. Modify its color effect to the same orange color that we've been using (r250, g100, b25). Name its instance **boxorange**. Copy the boxorange movie clip and paste in place. Name the instance of this new movie **boxblue**. Modify its color effect to a blue tint (r30, g142, b196). Paste in place again and name the instance of this new movie clip **boxgreen**. Modify its color effect to a green tint (r155, g211, b97). In the **drop sequence** layer, insert three copies of the **drop sequence** movie clip. Name one instance, **orange**, and modify its tint to r219, g60, b0. Name another **green** and make it green (r155, g211, b97). name the third, **blue**, and tint it (r30, g142, b196). Save the file, but leave it open for now.

Now we're ready to start the **top** file.

Create a new movie, called **top**. Create a new layer, called **dropzone**. Add the following actions to frame 1:

```
orangex = getProperty ( "/orangedrop", _x );
orangey = getProperty ( "/orangedrop", _y );
greenx = getProperty ( "/greendrop", _x );
greeny = getProperty ( "/greendrop", _y );
bluex = getProperty ( "/bluedrop", _x );
bluey = getProperty ( "/bluedrop", _y);
stop ();
```

Pointillism

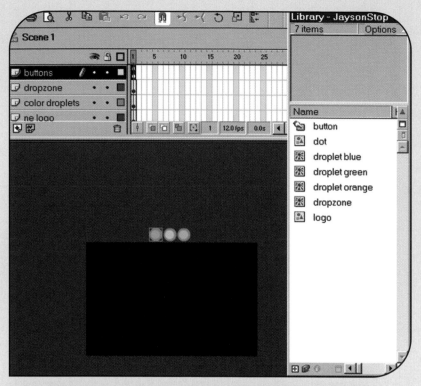

Go back to the **demo3** movie we just created and get the rectangle symbol. Paste it and center it on the stage, then convert it to the movie clip, **dropzone**. Name its instance **dropzone**.

Insert a new layer and call it **faux mask**.

Masks in Flash don't work across loaded levels, so, as the name suggests, we'll use this movie as a false mask by loading it into **_Layer1** to mask the animation in **_Layer0**. Draw a gray box around the entire stage, extending out slightly beyond the boundaries of the movie on all sides. Paste the rectangle into this layer and break it apart. Deselect it, select it again, and then delete it, knocking a rectangular hole in the gray faux mask. Now lock this layer so that it's out of the way. Go back to the Library for **demo3** again and insert three **dot** symbols in a new layer called **color droplets**.

Convert each to a movie clip and name their instances **orangedrop**, **greendrop** and **bluedrop**. Modify the color effect to make one our orange color, one our green and one our blue color, respectively. Go into the **orangedrop** movie clip and add a Stop action to the first frame. Tween the dot from 100% scale, down to 10% scale over frames 2 through 8. In frame 8 of the movie clip, assign the action:

duplicateMovieClip ("_level0/boxorange",_level0/:background,_level0/:background)

We're duplicating the colored background movie clip and setting its new name to a variable on the base level called **background**.

In the next frame, assign the actions to reset the drop position to its original coordinates:

setProperty ("/greendrop", _x, /:greenx);
setProperty ("/greendrop", _y, /:greeny);

Concatenate the string that specifies the level we are targeting, _level0/ and the new duplicate movie clip _level0/:background:

tell Target ("_level0/" & _level0/:background);
  gotoAnd Play (2);
}

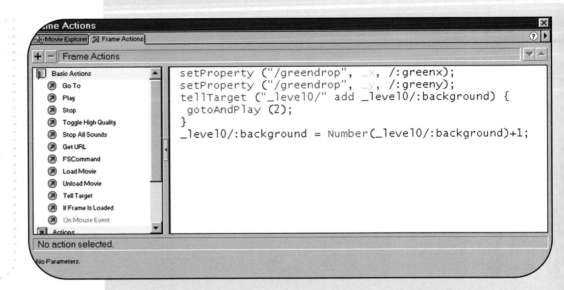

Finally, add 1 to the variable so that the next background box will play on the level above the previous one:

_level0/:background" = _level0/:background + 1;

Tween the dot back up to 100% scale over frames 15 through 28 Copy all the frames (1-28) in the movie clip, and paste them into frame 1 of both the **droplet green** and **droplet blue** movie clips. For the **droplet blue** you'll need to go into each of the assigned frame actions and change all the references of orange to blue. For droplet green, change all the references of orange to green. Create a new layer above the others called **buttons**. Make a new button, called button, with only a hit state containing a **dot** symbol scaled to 150%. Position a button over each of the three colored drops.

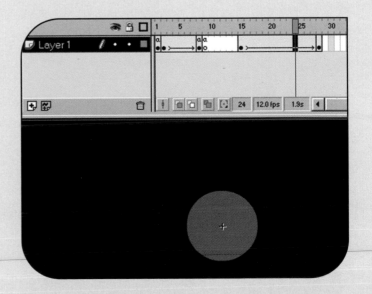

Pointillism

Apply the following actions to the button corresponding to the droplet orange.

```
on (rollOver) {
    setProperty ("/orangedrop", _xscale "125");
    setProperty ("/orangedrop", _yscale "125");
}
on (rollOut) {
    setProperty ("/orangedrop", _xscale "100");
    setProperty ("/orangedrop", _yscale "100")'
}
```

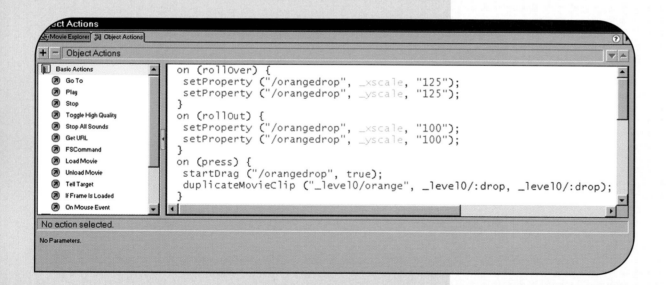

As we did with the background movie clips, we duplicate the color movies from _level0 into the next higher level so they will appear on top of any previous colored clip:

```
on (press){
 startDrag ("/orangedrop", true);
   duplicateMovieClip ("_level0/orange",_level0/:drop, _level0/:drop);
}
```

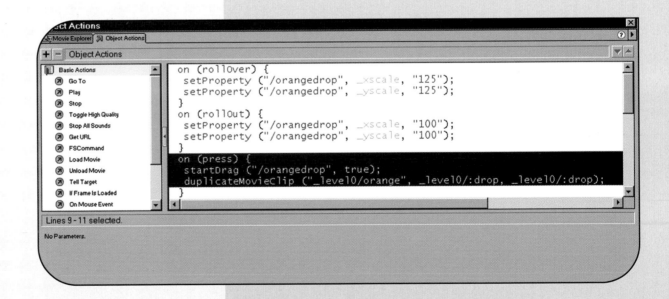

Pointillism

On Stop Drag, we check to see whether the drop is over its target. If it is, it will play the color movie in _level0. If it's outside the dropzone, it will reset to its original position:

```
on (release, releaseOutside) {
  stopDrag ();
    if (getProperty ( "_level1/orangedrop", _droptarget ) eq "_level1/dropzone") {
    setProperty ("/orangedrop", _xscale "100");
    setProperty ("/orangedrop", _yscale "100");
    setProperty ("_level0/" add _level0:/drop, _x, getProperty ( "/orangedrop", _x ));
     set Property ("_level0/" add _level0:/drop, _, getProperty ( "/orangedrop", _y ));
        tell Target ("_level0/" add  _level0:/drop) {
            gotoAndPlay (2)
            }
```

We add 1 to the drop variable so the next colored movie clip will play on top of the previous ones:

```
_level0/:drop = _level0/:drop + 1;
tellTarget ("/orangedrop") {
    gotoAndPlay (2);
  }
} else {
setProperty ("/orangedrop", _xscale "100");
setProperty ("/orangedrop", _yscale "100");
setProperty ("/orangedrop", _x, /:orangex);
setProperty ("/orangedrop", _y, /:orangey);
      }
```

When we play demo3.swf we can drag and drop the colored dots into the black area and watch that color fill up the window. Each color loads in above the last, giving the illusion of something like dropping dye in a pool of water.

" As a web designer, you have the power to make things appear to be something they're not, just like a mime artist who makes his audience think that he is sitting on a chair made out of thin air."

Matrix

Cut-and-paste.com was originally intended to simultaneously push the boundaries of a multimedia presence both in print and online. This was always going to be a challenge because, as you might expect, the design ideas we had for one medium did not easily translate onto the other. We didn't want to restrict our print edition to standard black ink on a white background. We wanted to play around with tactile details, like scratch foil, embossing, fluorescent and silver inks, things that wouldn't work on screen. On the cut-and-paste.com web site, we abandoned a magazine formula of text and pictures, but chose instead motion graphics, aiming to have everything move at its own pace, accompanied by ambient sounds. None of this could be translated into print.

The content is lifestyle based, reflecting elements of our personalities and interests, and is fueled by our collective desire to move away from press release media. Ultimately, quite an eclectic mix. We didn't design our material for a mass audience. Instead, from it's genesis, cut-and-paste.com was intended to appeal to the individual on a one-on-one basis, anywhere and at any time. Featured items were to have no boundaries and were to be as diverse as today's alternative lifestyles, ranging from plays committed to film, a digital film festival, through music, street art and on to commerce. The only theme that permeates the entire site is the digital world and technology. We decided that cut-and-paste.com shouldn't pin its colors to the mast as other alternative lifestyle publications were doing then. We wanted visitors to the site to drop in, not because they needed to find something in particular, but because they were curious to see what had changed.

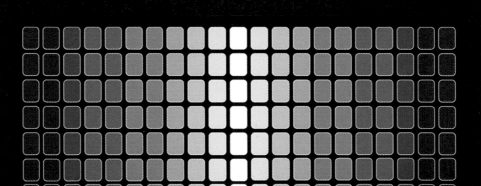

cut-and-paste.com

With this set of ideas as our starting point, we intended to design the cut-and-paste.com interface to reflect that changing nature of its content. Our artistic imperative was that things should be un-flagged, allowing the more curious viewers to search out things for themselves. We decided to avoid using a structural navigation grid. We managed to translate this particular 'look for yourself' idea onto the page in one particular cut-and-paste print edition when we hid a selection of Brian Eno's truisms behind silver blocks, without letting readers know that they could be scratched off. On one level, we could have put them there to be just a random selection of silver bars that looked nice, but readers inquisitive enough to scratch them were rewarded by Eno's Oblique Strategies. Aiden Grenelle Keith O'Toole and Tony Cudlip, the design team behind cut-and-paste.com created the interface as an illusion that would appeal to and reward the curious visitor in the same way as our silver blocks. When you visit the site, the first thing you see is a board of dominoes. If you do nothing, it does nothing. The screen remains still. If you're curious enough to begin rolling your mouse over the screen, you're paid for your efforts with a crash of chimes as the little dominoes start to turn over. We hope to stimulate your curiosity even more when you see that, as they rotate, some offer nothing, while others offer hotspots that link to sections deeper within the site. If you can't find anything of interest within those links, we hope that the interface itself, with colorful palettes, ambient sounds made up of chimes and gongs instead of irritating snaps, bells and buzzes, will be a hypnotizing, relaxing experience in itself.

Matrix

Aiden brought in the feel of illusion from his inspiration drawn from theatre, the art of illusion and magic. When you're creating something three-dimensional on screen, say a Philipe Stark chair, you can rotate it and see every leg on it right there in front of you. In animation, the backs and undersides of things aren't important – what matters is the illusion that they are there. It's also pure illusion that objects rotate and move on screen. As a web designer, you have the power to make things appear to be something that they're not, just like a mime artist who makes his audience believe that he is sitting on a chair made out of thin air. Aiden and the team learned to pay attention to even the smallest detail of their design in order to create the illusion that they were after, especially because there were so few details on the site to mask any inconsistencies.

For instance, little rectangles with squared edges don't look like they're moving when they are being turned over, so, to create the sense of movement and give the correct gradation of reflected light, they modified the corners with a curve.

cut-and-paste.com

Zen is fundamental to the design ethic behind cut-and-paste.com, hence the rural, raw, warm feeling that surrounds the site. The colors that we've used are earthy: a contrast to the lurid fluorescent shades of green, orange and yellow usually associated with computers and web art. To fit with our Zen, almost solemn feel for the site, we chose quite somber colors to give the individual objects a semi-precious quality, rather than a flippant, tiddly wink feel.

There are two sets of colors: a gradation of blue to purple on the front and blue to green on the flipside. We chose these from the 256 indexed as safe for the web. Rather than choosing colors that looked amazing on a 22inch screen and lost their punch on a 15inch, we went with ones proven to be effective regardless of the color option selected by the user on their screen set up. Although, at a glance, it might look as if the interface as quite pop-ish, like Bridget Reilly's work or Andy Warhol's 1960s repeats, there's actually a lot more going on. The initial bank of dominoes has a very symmetrical central line, giving the impression of a horizon waiting for something to happen. Then the little stones look and feel real in that they turn in this delayed motion, sweeping along the line, creating a hypnotic wave effect.

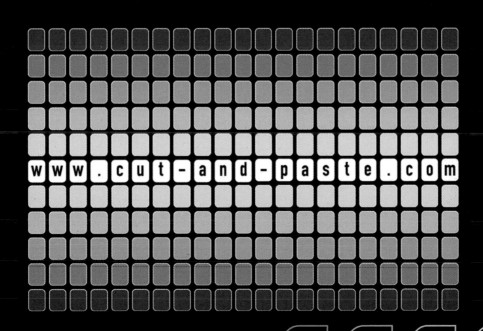

Matrix

The artistic hopes for cut-and-paste.com remain buoyant, although our redesigned site has a more structured approach. The content falls more easily into categorized zones. We feature web music and radio, web TV, giveaways, magazine articles and links to other sites – either sites that we think have a similar feel to our own, or sites that are just amazing in their own right. They range all the way from commercial sites to a student's online portfolio. When we first began, we weren't sure how long cut-and-paste.com would last; it was an embryonic - experience site. Now, ten months later, we're up and running with a content-heavy informative gallery. We now want to make it easier for people to access specific content, be that a special feature, experimental work, text articles or a particular DJ mix.

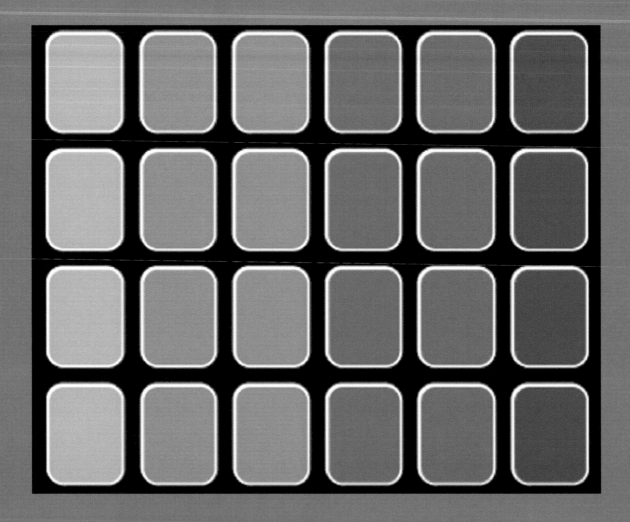

We're happy now to expand on the curiosity for curiosity's sake element and give users the opportunity to be able to access exactly what they're looking for without having to turning over every stone on the front page to find it. We also intend to play around with the illusion of dimension, maybe building something like a doll's house in which you move objects around.

It's the design process of this domino animation on our present site that designer, Keith O'Toole is going to walk through next. Tony Cudlip will conclude with a few notes on the audio authoring and production that we added to tie up the feel of the interface.

Matrix

Our design for the board began with a pretty obvious constraint – we had to limit the dimensions to the number of dominoes required to spell out www.cut-and-paste.com across the center.

Before I received the files to begin my work within Flash, the first domino had been through a design stage in Adobe Illustrator and then Metacreations Inifini-d, where it was extruded and rotated and rendered as a Quicktime movie. Before I could trace each frame of the sequence in Flash, I needed to convert the .pict files that I'd received into a readable format. I chose jpegs.

I created the sequence of one domino turning over twenty-two frames. The recommended frame rate for web animation in Flash is 12 fps, so the domino takes almost a second to turn over once (180 degrees), and almost two seconds for a full rotation.

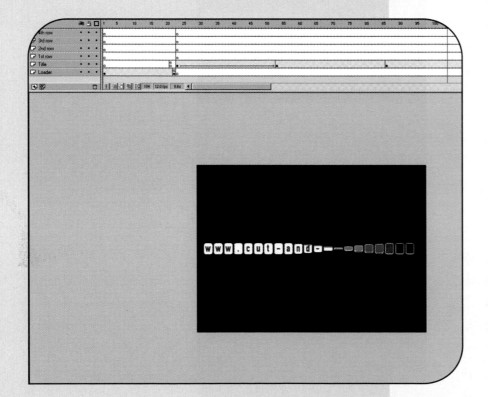

If you're still working with Flash 4 you'll know that it has no rounded corner tool, so you'll have to do as I did and create each corner using the Line tool. To do this you need to pick the start point of the curve on the vertical and the matching point on the horizontal, draw the line and then drag it to meet the curve of the underlying image. You need to repeat this for each of the four corners over the twenty-two frames. When you're tracing like this, it's useful to convert the image to a symbol and reduce the Alpha of the symbol to 60 or 80 per cent. To help you see clearly where you're placing your lines, lock the layer that the image is on and insert a layer above it to trace on. Now that we have the built-in Bezier curves in Flash 5, you can be a lot more accurate.

When I finished tracing the twenty-two images, I copied and pasted them all into a new movie clip on a fresh timeline. I colored each frame of the animation to show that there was a front and back to the domino. I then duplicated the movie clip for each of the twenty-two colors that appear across the board and colored them according to the gradient that Aiden had chosen, using a web-safe palette in Illustrator.

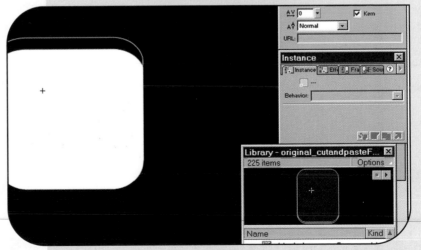

Matrix

The next stage was to create the row of twenty-one dominoes in the center of the board, each with a white backface, which, when turned, reveal the title www.cut-and-paste.com to introduce the site. I created a graphic symbol, called Dominoes, incorporating twenty-one movie clips that played over sixty-four frames.

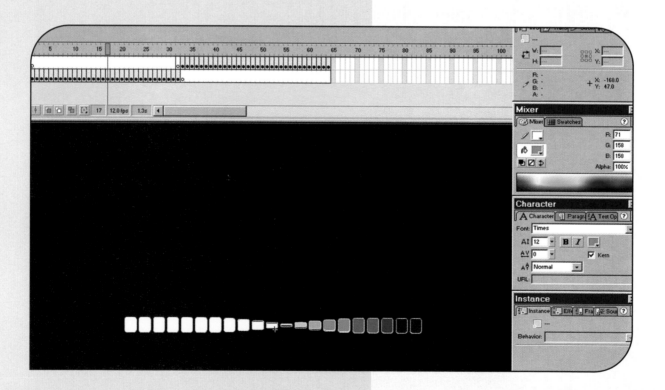

should be:

I added a keyframe to the same layer on the main movie timeline and inserted a copy of the Dominoes symbol, this time with an extra layer. On this layer, from keyframe 7 through keyframe 28, each letter of www.cut-and-paste.com appears one at a time in sequence. They then disappear in reverse order from keyframe 37 to keyframe 57. The effect is that the letters appear on the other side of the dominos as they turn, disappearing as they return to their original state.

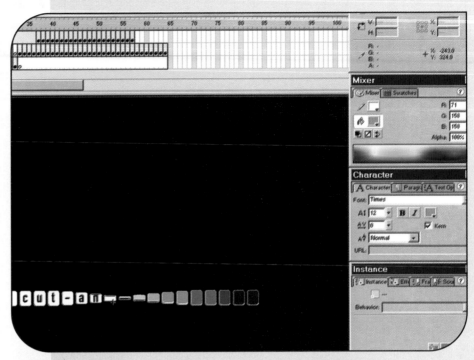

When the line of colored dominoes reappear, I converted one row to a static graphic symbol. At this point, I created eleven layers to show the board being created out of one row. Each row moves out of the previous row over a sequence of five frames.

When this sequence is completed, the set of eleven rows are replaced with the individual movie clips of each domino, and from then on each domino can be activated by the viewer moving the mouse over it.

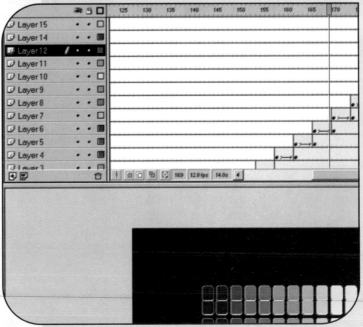

Matrix

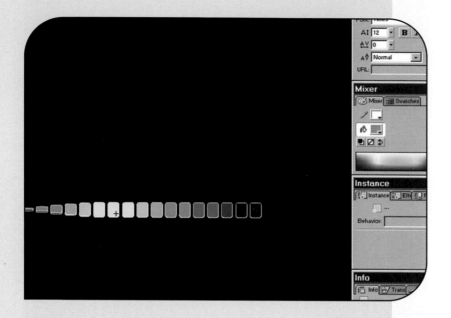

The dominoes at this point are rotating 360 degrees in continuous motion. To make each domino stop once it has turned 180 degrees, I added a Stop action to frame 1 and 12 of each movie clip.

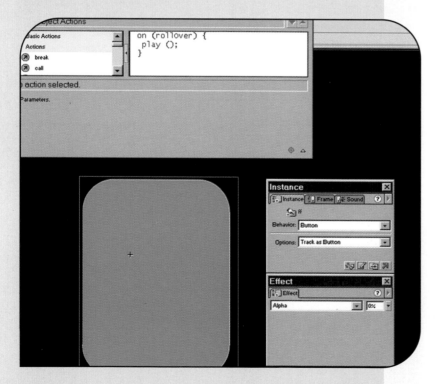

To activate the motion, I added a button inserting a layer inside each domino movie clip, above the layer containing the graphic. I create a solid black rectangle slightly bigger than the domino and converted this into a button symbol.

I reduced the Alpha of this symbol to 0 so that the underlying graphic is visible, and assigned to it this action:

```
on (rollover) {
  play ();
}
```

The domino turns because the movie clip time-line is instructed to play.

I added another layer to deal with the targets in the relevant movie clips, above the layer with the On (Roll Over) button on it. I made the target in Illustrator, and imported it directly into Flash as an .eps, breaking it apart using Modify>Break Apart. Then I converted the image into a button symbol and put it in the new layer at keyframes 7, 12 and 17. At keyframe 7, I set the Alpha of the symbol to 32. At keyframe 12, it's 100, and at keyframe 17, it's back to 0. (There's a blank keyframe at 18 so that the target is no longer visible). I used motion tweening across this sequence so that the target fades up and then out as the domino turns.

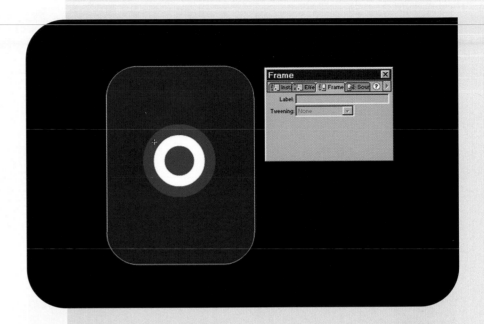

On keyframe 12, the target appears centered on the flip-side of the domino. To link that target to the relevant document, I added this action:

```
on (release) {
  getURL ("example.htm");
}
```

We deliberately chose to have the targets appear randomly across the board, rather than in any logical order, so that viewers have to make an effort to look for them.

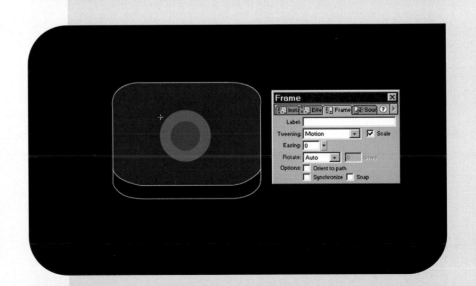

Matrix

I used a simple preloader that ran for twenty-two frames at the beginning of the scene (enough for one full rotation of the domino). To do this I inserted a keyframe at frame 22 with the action:

```
gotoAndPlay (1);
ifFrameLoaded (190) {
  gotoAndPlay (23);
}
```

This action sends the movie back to frame 1, causing the domino to loop, until frame 195 (the frame with the completed board) is loaded. When frame 195 is loaded, the movie continues to frame 23, and the introduction sequence begins.

I added a keyframe to frame 21, on a separate layer, with the action:

```
ifFrameLoaded (316) {
  gotoAndStop (316);
}
```

This sends anybody who had previously been to the site (if their file was cached) to the full board of dominoes so that they don't have to wait through the introduction if they've seen it before.

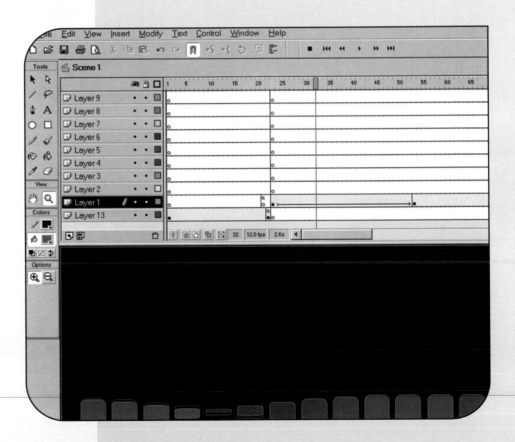

Matrix

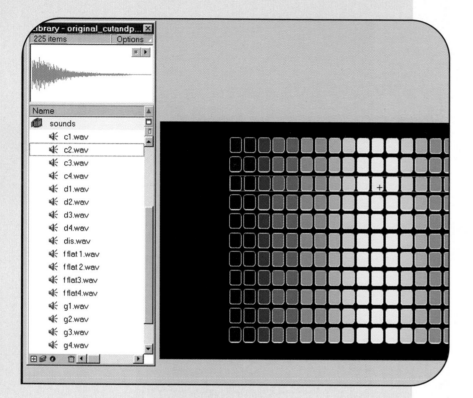

Adding the Chimes

In keeping with the Zen theme, we decided to base the audio around bells, and settled on a five-note wind chime that we created using MIDI and Sonic Foundry's Sound Forge 4.5.

To make the sound of wind blowing through a set of chimes, we transposed the chimes over three octaves and arranged them on the dominos in sequence. We felt that this, together with the domino's reaction to the cursor, created the right balance between control and chance.

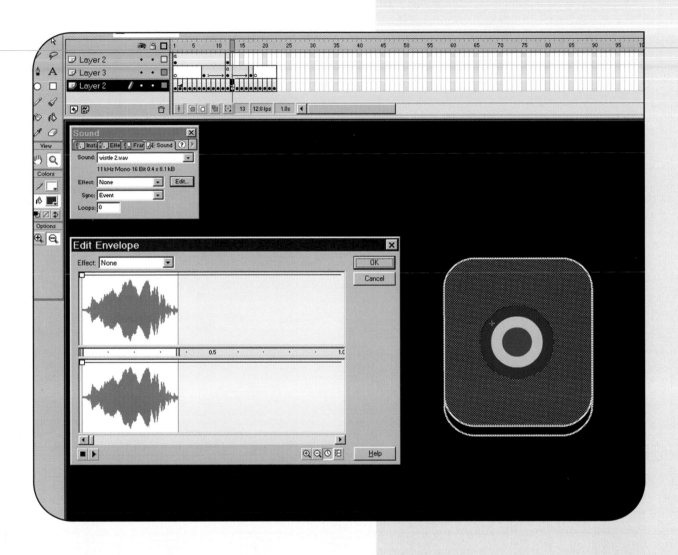

To achieve the effect, we put two .wav files in each movie clip, one on frame 2 and one on frame 13. We assigned a Stop action to frames 1 and 12 so that viewers only hear the sound effects as each domino turns.

Matrix

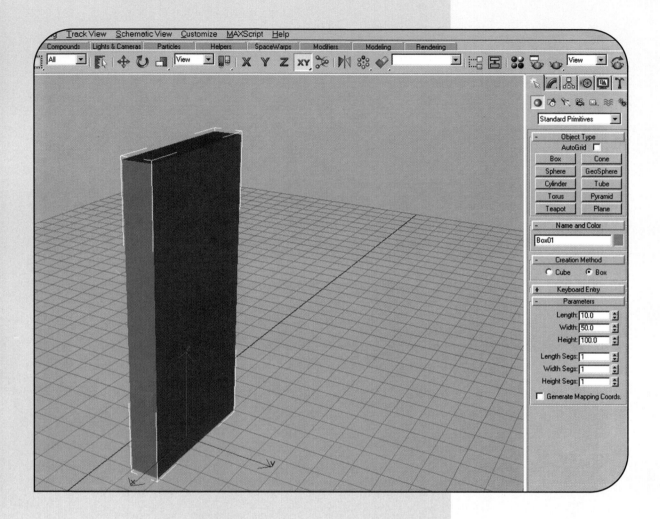

It's true that we'd do things a little differently now. If you try to do something similar, you may find that using one of the 3D Studio Max plug-ins, Vecta 3D or Illustrate, could help you create the domino rotation a little quicker. Vecta 3D and Illustrate both create 3D simulated gradient fills, which you may find effective.

When we put the effect together, we were concerned with bandwidth restrictions, but as things improve, you may find that you'll have room to use fully rendered images with correct light sources and surface materials. Bandwith problems also meant that we had to produce the sound at 11khz mono, but maybe one day, we could the same thing at luxurious 44khz stereo.

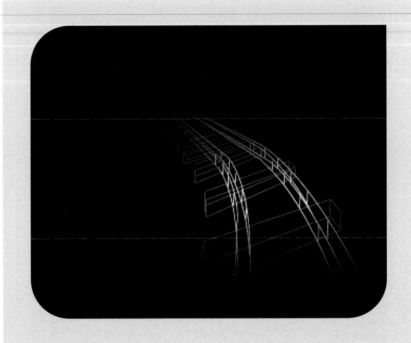

Cut-and-paste.com has become our ever-expanding gallery. In the real world, were we to build a gallery space to rival the Guggenheim in Bilbao, we would have to lay out millions upon millions of pounds, but the Web is all about illusion. On the Web, bricks and mortar don't matter, but time, concept and passion do. So, although a concept like turning over lots of little stones with their chimes to create anl intriguing and warming feel might, in the real world, cost thousands of pounds, on the Web it took us three days.

We hope that what we've shown you here will help you do things just as quickly.

Rules

When I came across Flash in 1998, I found that it allowed me to bring together three of my passions: interactivity, graphic design and animation.

I used to draw a lot when I was young, (all those years ago!) and I loved animated films and puppet shows like Jim Henson's Muppet Show. I was always struck by the evocative power that these simple objects and creatures exuded when they were animated with such talent. Some of my favorite artists are the genuine craftsmen of their medium: Jan Swankmayer (Alice, Jabberwocky) and Piotr Kamler's (Chronopolis) stop-motion animations, Yoichiro Kawaguchi's and John Lasseter's computer graphics.

Olivier Besson

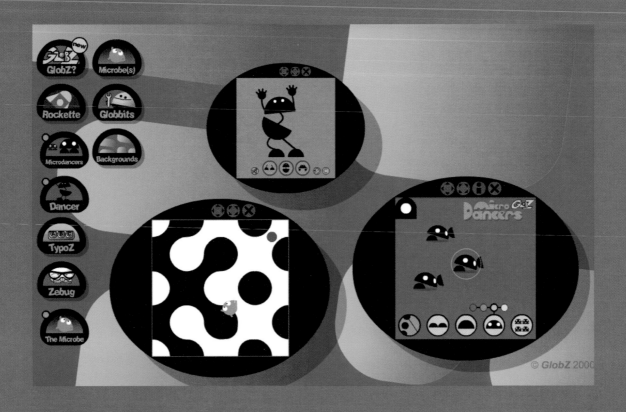

In my design work, I have always been fascinated by exploring shapes and contours, shadows and light, and textures. I particularly enjoyed drawing imaginary structures in the style of Moebius and M.C. Escher. Later, I became interested in stylization and cartoon-style line drawing, all of which stood me in good stead when vector animation arrived on the Web.

For years, I've also been interested in role-playing games (like Dungeons & Dragons) and board games. I spent time inventing a constant stream of board games of my own, testing them out with friends. Curiously, the most alarming, as well as the most effective, was a game in which the aim was to simply change the rules of the game itself. The real rules of the game, the underlying rules, merely stipulated how to propose and incorporate new rules. There was no aim to this game other than whatever occurred to the players each time they played it. I was, quite possibly, a little mad, but this early interest did enable me to create computer games later on; now good currency for new start-ups and the net economy today.

Rules

Despite my interest in games, the rules that govern them, and animation, I didn't work with computers until relatively recently. My influences come mainly from cinema, literature and intellectual or sporting pursuits. If you have passions outside of the PC and the Internet, I strongly advise you not to forget them while you work at your machine. The designs that we create are a product of our whole selves, influenced by everything that we do and see in our lives.

In 1995, during my engineering training at university, I found myself using 3D graphics to create a dynamic simulation program that would allow me to study particle interaction. I was surprised by the aesthetic quality of real-time interactions within a highly reactive system. You can see these animations at: www.multimania.com/goprof/simul/simul.htm

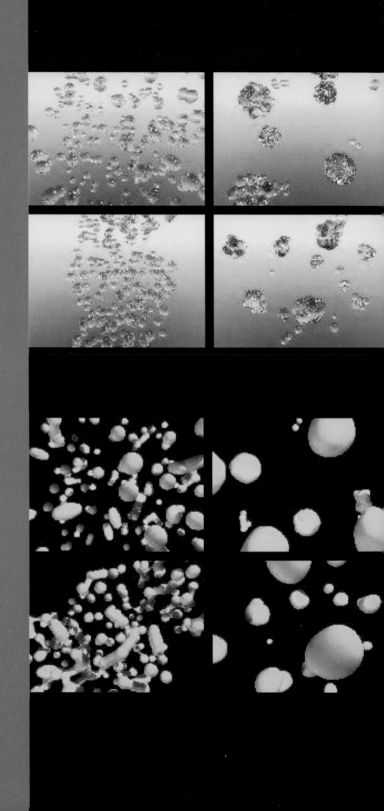

Olivier Besson

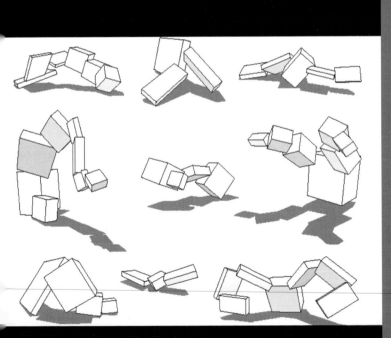

A large part of my work at university was research into the algorithms used for synthesizing images and behavioral animation (my primary source of information was the magazine Siggraph Computer Graphics). I found that those algorithms were usually simplified versions of methods used by mathematicians and physicists for decades. They can be used for all sorts of animation possibilities:

•to animate natural phenomena with the help of particles

•to animate movement with the help of reactive agents - flocks of birds in flight, for example. See Craig Reynolds' Boids www.red3d.com/cwr/boids/

•to simulate physical interactions (objects interacting)

•to generate natural forms such as fractals and arborescence

•to generate primitive creatures through genetic mutation. A good example is Karl Sims' Evolved Virtual Creatures at www.genarts.com/karl

These algorithms are simplified so that they can be executed more quickly in real-time software and video games. Scientific accuracy gives way to the equally plausible and realistic results that less exact algorithms can produce. Having said this, though, some of these algorithms can still only be executed on the most powerful of computers.

Rules

Interactive designers now have a rich heritage of patterns or models at their disposal, just waiting to be used in interactive programs.

Not being an outstanding storyteller myself, I draw on games and rules to think up systems with intrinsic functions. A user's interactivity is directed towards discovering the system's function, interacting with it, playing with it and exploring its possibilities, sometimes achieving an objective or final point. I think of these systems as a kind of linear fiction.

I've found that the best way to create autonomous systems is to take an object oriented approach. It allows me to create systems by modeling the objects that I'm going to use in the system in advance and makes subsequent programming much simpler. It's a very practical approach, free of complex theory, but it does require quite a bit of experience.

That my creations are minimalist is very much part of their conception. My creative process begins with

ideas, thoughts and notes doodled on scraps of paper: drawings, situations, assumptions, mechanics, and anything else that occurs to me. I carry on collecting and thinking until I find a couple of ideas that look like they might work together efficiently to make an interactive game or experience. Then comes the difficult part: working out the rules of the game. The rules have to be simple enough to make sense to a player, and it must be possible to program them with the tools available to me.

Simple rules don't necessarily imply simple interactions. In fact, it can be quite the opposite, because simplicity usually enables a greater variety of potential strategies and expressions. A good example is the game of Go, an Asian game of strategy with rules that you can pick up in ten minutes, but which remains unfathomable even after a lifetime of study. You can you can find some advanced Flash interactive courses on Go at www.multimania.com/goprof/go/go.htm

To find the *right rule* is an exercise that mixes logical rigor with unrestrained creativity.

Olivier Besson

At the moment, all my time is taken up with creating interactive content for my site, www.GlobZ.com. The Internet is already a tremendous medium for the distribution of animation and music by independent artists. The massive distribution of my first creation, the Flashy Dancer, encouraged me to design more content that was just as interactive, surprising and simple to use, and to make it widely available in the same way.

Computers and the Web are our tools to create and view interactive works. From a scriptwriting point of view, the interactive possibilities are countless. We can design interactivity into fiction-based narrative sites, adventure games and web experiences, but even these are still in their early stages of development. More excitingly, new genres keep appearing. I look forward to adding a new multi-user dimension to my interactive art and to developing new games and worlds that can truly evolve over the network.

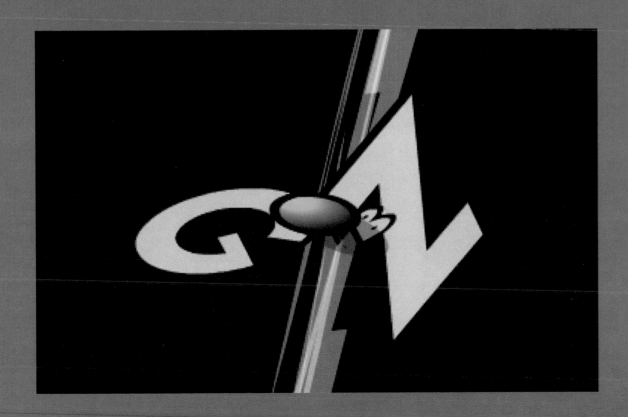

Rules

In this section I'm going to show you how I put together the moving-letters effect in the introductory animation on www.globz.com. I'll begin by looking at the idea behind the animation and how the math equations transition into Flash programming. Then I'll show you how to implement it using concrete step-by-step examples. You can find the corresponding .flas on the accompanying CD.

This animation's primary role is as the entry gate to the GlobZ site, but it also checks that the user has the correct Flash plug in. This chapter deals with the animation's role as an entry gate.

I set out to to create a dynamic logo that the user has to click in order to enter the site. The letters of the GlobZ logo move both randomly and dynamically, changing height, width and position. When a mouse rolls over the green O, the logo reverts to its normal appearance.

I did this by programming a script that changed the position, orientation and size of a movie clip frame by frame and then applied the script to each letter of the logo.

So why achieve this effect programmatically, and not simply use tweening? Excellent question!

I chose the programing option because it allowed me to make the object's motion truly unpredictable (using the random() function) and change the physical parameters in real time; so when the user moves over the O button, the stiffness parameter is increased and the logo returns to its normal appearance naturally. Finally, it made for a very light file because, generally speaking, scripts (constructive information) take up less space than graphical objects (descriptive information).

OK,now we're into a litle bit of kinetics.

Suppose we have an object that moves over a period of time. The rate at which the position of the object changes with time is called its *velocity*.

This diagram represents the change in position of an object at a position, x, in time, for a period of time, dt.

x_t is the position of the object when time is t, and x_{t+dt} is the new position of the object after the unit of time, dt, has elapsed. Time, or, t, is the time at which we begin to observe the motion. The object's velocity is responsible for the object's shift in position to x_{t+dt}, from its original position of x_t.

So, dt is the period of time between each successive recording of the movement of the object. This time interval has to be small enough and measurements made frequently enough to enable a realistic picture to be built of the motion that is being modeled. For example, a movie shown at the cinema might show at a rate of 24 images per second, making the interval between two images 41.7 milliseconds (ms) - small enough to create a lifelike moving image. I tend to use 20 images per second in my Flash animations.

$$xt+dt = xt + vtdt$$

Where vt is the velocity at time t

Formula 1: Velocity

You can think of the formula relating the velocity vt to the positions xt and xt+dt and the period of time dt like this: imagine a car moving away from you along a road. The car is 10 meters from you (xt=10) and is moving away from you at 20 meters per second (vt=20). So, after 2 seconds (t=2), the car will have traveled an additional 40 meters, and it will be 50 meters (xt+dt) away. Using the formula, xt+dt = 10 + (20 x 2) = 10+40 = 50.

So, using this formula, we can find the new position of an object, based on its old position and its velocity.

But, of course, velocity isn't necessarily constant. We can describe velocity relative to time in terms of acceleration. Here are a few rules for dealing with acceleration:

• when the acceleration is zero, the velocity does not change.

• when the acceleration is positive, the velocity increases.

• when the acceleration is negative, in other words, when we're dealing with deceleration, the velocity decreases.

Acceleration is governed by a similar formula:

• When the acceleration is zero, the velocity does not change:

• When the acceleration is positive, the velocity increases:

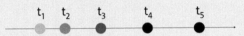

• When the acceleration is negative, in other words, when we are dealing deceleration, the velocity decreases:

$$vt+dt = vt + atdt$$

Where at is the acceleration at time t

Formula 2 : Acceleration

Rules

$$F = m*at$$

where : F denotes the total applied force and m denotes the mass of the object

Formula 3: Newton's Second Law

If an object being pushed, pulled or subjected to any kind of overall force in the real world, Newton's Second Law shows that the acceleration of the object is proportional to the forces applied to the object.

Although these formulae will be useful to you, don't worry if it isn't immediately obvious to you how it all works. In order to write succinct ActionScript code, we'll have to simplify them anyway.

Here are some examples of the sorts of formulae that might be used to model forces in computer games:

Constant forces (wind, gravity etc), F=c
A spring of stiffness k : F = -k ¥ (x-xdef)

xdef represents the pull of a spring on an attached object to its final rest position. We can use this force to model the attraction between two objects.

Viscosity (d) of a medium, like air or water: F =-d¥vt.

Viscosity acts in the opposite direction to velocity. This force is very important because, without viscosity, systems will oscillate indefinitely and never reach equilibrium. Think of it as a drag-like force.
Brownian Motion of strength b: F = b¥(random(200)-100)/100.

This force allows us to simulate unpredictable movement, (smoke particles in air, for example), and gives a value between –b and +b. This is the force used behind the movement of the letters of the GlobZ logo.

When you're building computer games, you should first calculate the total force that will be applied to an object (attraction, viscosity and so on) and, using Newton's Second law, (formula 3), calculate the acceleration that will be applied. Then use the acceleration (formula 2) to deduce the new velocity, and use the velocity formula (formula 1) to find the new position of the object.

OK, this is where I begin to show you how to implement all these equations in Flash.

Ultimately, we're going to simulate an object being attracted to its rest position by a spring-like force of stiffness 'stiff' (k in the spring definition on page twelve), coupled with a damping of viscosity 'damp' (d in the viscosity definition on that same page).

Rules

$$F = -\text{stiff} ¥ (xt - xdef) - \text{damp} * vt$$

The object is going to move back and forth until the damping force finally brings it to its rest position (Xdef), (we'll add the Brownian motion in later). Here is the sum of these forces:

To make it simple, suppose the mass we're using in Newton's Second Law is m = 1. The position in the current keyframe is represented by xt, and the position in the next frame by xt+dt, which can be, and is in the following equations, denoted by x'.

So according to Newton's Second Law:
a= -stiff ¥(x-x0) –damp ¥ v

Now let's suppose that dt=1 (to make it even more simple). According to the acceleration formula, 2, the new velocity (v') is:

v' = v -stiff¥(x-x0) –damp ¥ v
so:
v' = (1-damp)¥v - stiff¥(x-x0)

We apply this to the velocity formula (formula 1) to get the new position:

x' = x + v'

Bear in mind that I've written x'=x+v' instead of x'=x+v but has little effect upon the final result because the change in velocity from v to v' is trivial.

So the variable x would be computed in Flash like this:

x_speed= (1-damp)*x_speed – stiff*(x – x_def);
x = x + x_speed;

I've named the variable that corresponds to the speed of x as x_speed and the variable that is the default value of x as x_def.

We don't need to keep the acceleration value in a Flash variable and we'll suppose, for the sake of this example, that the physical parameters (damp, stiff, x_de) have already been initialized.

Now let's add in the Brownian motion of strength brown (replacing 'b' in the definition above) which we talked about before:

```
x_speed=(1-damp)*x_speed –(x–x_def)*stiff + brown*(random(20)-10)/10;
x = x + x_speed;
```

So how are we going to use this to shake a **Foo** movie clip? The following script does the job:

```
x = foo:_x;
x_speed =(1 damp)*x_speed–(x–x_def)*stiff + brown*(random(20)-10)/10;
x = x + x_speed;
setProperty("foo",_x)=x;
```

But this procedure will have to be executed in every frame, so we'll need a temporal loop.

We need to proceed in three steps.

Rules

First create a new movie clip. In frame 1, put this initializing code:

```
damp = 0.05;
x_def = GetProperty("foo", _x);
stiff = 0.2;
brown = 0.2;
gotoAndStop("Move_x");
```

This code sets the values of physical parameters damp, x_def, stiff and brown and goes directly to the temporal loop (see below).

Next, create a new keyframe in the timeline of your movie and label it **Move_x**. Add this script to the keyframe:

```
x = foo:_x;
x_speed = (1-damp)*x_speed–(x–x_def)*stiff + brown*(random(20)-10)/10;
x = x + x_speed;
setProperty("foo",_x)=x;
prevFrame ();
```

Then put an empty keyframe just before the Move_x keyframe, and put a Play action into it.

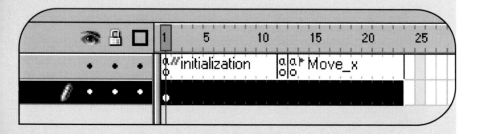

Creating Continuity

When the playhead reaches the Move_x keyframe, it jumps to the previous frame and the content is displayed in Flash. As soon as the new content is displayed, Move_x works its magic again, everything is reconfigured and the updated content displayed, and so on through the loop.

You can use this procedure every time you need a piece of code to display the screen. If you want to use several scripts independently, you can put the keyframes in separate movie clips. We'll see a little later how to apply this same script to the properties_y, _rotation, _width and _height.

Applying the Shaking Effect to Several Movies

If you need to apply this effect to several movie clips, a practical approach would be to create a 'shaker' clip to shake any clip into which it is inserted. This is easy because, in Flash, one clip containing another is called a **parent**, and can be referred to by its child using the ".." path syntax. I've put together a shaker clip for you to use: you can find it on the enclosed CD.

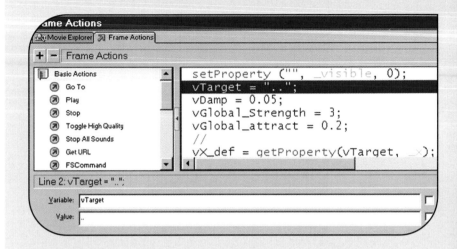

To make your clip shake, you should first open up the clip you want to use and then drag the Shaking Behavior clip from the Library into it. Each letter in the Globz logo is a movie clip that uses the Shaking Behavior movie clip. The hierarchy is as you see here,

Each Shaking Behavior movie clip independently animates its parent (i.e. a character of the logo). I'll take you through how I put them together.

First I put this initialization script into the first keyframe:

```
setProperty ("", _visible, 0);
target = "..";
damp = 0.05;
x_def = GetProperty(target,_x);
stiff = 0.2;
brown = 0.2;
gotoLabel «Move_all»;
```

The initialization makes the Shaking Behavior clip invisible and specifies the clip being shaken as the parent ("..").

Rules

Then I modified the code in the Move_all keyframe so that it changes the properties of the parent clip denoted by the variable target.

```
x = getProperty(target,_x);
x_speed=(1-damp)*x_speed–(x–x_def)*stiff + brown*(random(20)-10)/10;
x = x + x_speed;
setProperty(target,_x)=x;
```

Note that only the first and last lines have changed.

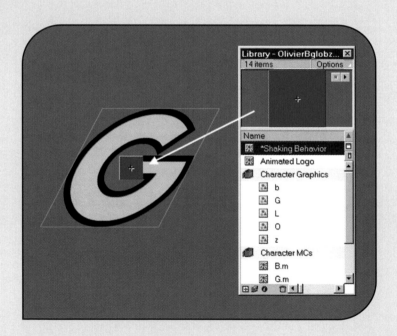

Now insert the Shaking Behavior clip into each of the letters.

Don't worry that they look red – they aren't visible in the final movie. And Voila! If you now test the animation you can see that each letter's _x position has been randomly modified.

See the X_GLOBZ.swf on the CD-Rom.

You can adapt this to create other effects. For example, you could create behaviors that make things appear/disappear, follow another clip, incorporate a transparency effect, resize things, and a lot more.

Putting the behavior clip inside another one allows you to change and update symbols quickly, which will be useful when you're working on big projects. Rather than changing each instance separately, you only need to change the clip inside the movie clip symbol.

Now let's look at how we can modify the **Shaking Behavior** clip to change the _y, _rotation, _xscale, and _yscale properties. This time, we'll put these actions in keyframe 1.

```
setProperty ("", _visible, 0);
vTarget = "..";
vDamp = 0.05;
vGlobal_Strength = 3;
vGlobal_attract = 0.2;
//
vX_def = getProperty(vTarget, _x);
vX_strength = 1;
vX_attract = 1;
vX = vX_def;
//
vY_def = getProperty(vTarget, _y);
vY_strength = 1;
vY_attract = 1;
vY = vY_def;
//
vXscale_def = getProperty(vTarget, _xscale);
vXscale_strength = 5;
vXscale_attract = 2;
vXscale = vXscale_def;
//
vYscale_def = getProperty(vTarget, _yscale);
vYscale_strength = 5;
vYscale_attract = 2;
vYscale = vYscale_def;
//
vRot_def = 0;
vRot_strength = 2;
vRot_attract = 1;
vRot = vRot_def;
//
gotoAndStop ("Move_all");
```

Rules

You will also see that Move_x keyframe has been relabelled to Move_all with the following code in that keyframe:

```
// vX
vX_speed = Number(Number((1-vDamp)*vX_speed)+Number(vX_strength*((random(200)-
100)/100)*vGlobal_Strength))+Number((vX_def-vX)*vX_attract*vGlobal_Attract);
vX = Number(vX)+Number(vX_speed);
// vY
vY_speed = Number(Number((1-vDamp)*vY_speed)+Number(vY_strength*((random(200)-
100)/100)*vGlobal_Strength))+Number((vY_def-vY)*vY_attract*vGlobal_Attract);
vY = Number(vY)+Number(vY_speed);
// vXScale
vXScale_speed = Number(Number((1-vDamp)*vXScale_speed)+Number(vXScale_strength*((random(200)-
100)/100)*vGlobal_Strength))+Number((vXScale_def-vXScale)*vXScale_attract*vGlobal_Attract);
vXScale = Number(vXScale)+Number(vXScale_speed);
// vYScale
vYScale_speed = Number(Number((1-vDamp)*vYScale_speed)+Number(vYScale_strength*((random(200)-
100)/100)*vGlobal_Strength))+Number((vYScale_def-vYScale)*vYScale_attract*vGlobal_Attract);
vYScale = Number(vYScale)+Number(vYScale_speed);
if (Number(vXscale)<0) {
        vXscale = -vXscale;
}
if (Number(vYscale)<0) {
        vYscale = -vYscale;
}
if (Number(vXscale)>500) {
        vXscale = 500;
}
if (Number(vYscale)>500) {
        vYscale = 500;
}
// vRot
vRot_speed = Number(Number((1-vDamp)*vRot_speed)+Number(vRot_strength*((random(200)-
100)/100)*vGlobal_Strength))+Number((vRot_def-vRot)*vRot_attract*vGlobal_Attract);
vRot = Number(vRot)+Number(vRot_speed);
//
setProperty (vTarget, _x, vX);
setProperty (vTarget, _y, vY);
setProperty (vTarget, _xscale, vXscale);
setProperty (vTarget, _yscale, vYscale);
setProperty (vTarget, _rotation, vRot);
```

Rules

```
  prevFrame ();
```
Note that the formulae have been adapted to allow for global parameters.

```
yscale_brown=10
yscale_stiff=0
```

The other brownian and stiffness parameters for all other properties (_x, _y, _xscale, _rotation) set to 0.

```
rot_brown=10
rot_stiff=0
```

The other brownian and stiffness parameters for all other properties (_x, _y, _xscale, _yscale) set to 0.

```
y_brown=10
y_stiff=0
```

The other brownian and stiffness parameters for all other properties (_x, _xscale, _yscale, _rotation) set to 0.

Working out suitable parameters really is fun for behavioral animation programmers. I can spend hours playing around with the values of these parameters: you can discover all sorts of exciting and original effects while you're debugging the code.

Bringing the Logo to a Halt during Rollover

When you move the mouse over the green button of the logo, the following script is executed:

```
vNewStrength = 0;
        vNewAttract = 1;
        vNewDamp = 0.7;
        //
Comment: modify strength parameter in each movie clip.
        ../G/bro:vGlobal_Strength = vNewStrength;
        ../L/bro:vGlobal_Strength = vNewStrength;
        ../O/bro:vGlobal_Strength = vNewStrength;
        ../B/bro:vGlobal_Strength = vNewStrength;
        ../Z/bro:vGlobal_Strength = vNewStrength;
        //
Comment: modify attract parameter in each movie clip.
        ../G/bro:vGlobal_attract = vNewAttract;
        ../L/bro:vGlobal_attract = vNewAttract;
        ../O/bro:vGlobal_attract = vNewAttract;
        ../B/bro:vGlobal_attract = vNewAttract;
        ../Z/bro:vGlobal_attract = vNewAttract;
        //
Comment: modify damp parameter in each movie clip.
        ../G/bro:vDamp = vNewDamp;
        ../L/bro:vDamp = vNewDamp;
        ../o/bro:vDamp = vNewDamp;
        ../B/bro:vDamp = vNewDamp;
        ../Z/bro:vDamp = vNewDamp;
```

This modifies the variables strength, attract, and damp in the shaking behavior of each letter movie clip in the Logo. (This clip is called shaker in each letter). Setting brown to 0 completely cancels out the shaking effect. The letters return to normal with little or no wobbling. (damp viscosity is set to a high value).

A similar piece of code resets the original values for the three variables in the On (Roll Out) action. It uses the default values for the attraction and the Brownian Motion equations, and a much weaker viscosity value, so the letters become less responsive and appear to be slowing down.

```
on (rollOver) {
  vNewStrength = 0;
  vNewAttract = 1;
  vNewDamp = 0.7;
  //
  ../G/bro:vGlobal_Strength = vNewStrength;
  ../L/bro:vGlobal_Strength = vNewStrength;
  ../O/bro:vGlobal_Strength = vNewStrength;
  ../B/bro:vGlobal_Strength = vNewStrength;
  ../Z/bro:vGlobal_Strength = vNewStrength;
  //
  ../G/bro:vGlobal_attract = vNewAttract;
  ../L/bro:vGlobal_attract = vNewAttract;
  ../O/bro:vGlobal_attract = vNewAttract;
  ../B/bro:vGlobal_attract = vNewAttract;
  ../Z/bro:vGlobal_attract = vNewAttract;
  //
  ../G/bro:vDamp = vNewDamp;
  ../L/bro:vDamp = vNewDamp;
  ../O/bro:vDamp = vNewDamp;
  ../B/bro:vDamp = vNewDamp;
  ../Z/bro:vDamp = vNewDamp;
}
on (rollOut) {
  vNewStrength = 1;
  vNewAttract = 0.05;
  vNewDamp = 0.05;
  //
  ../G/bro:vGlobal_Strength = vNewStrength;
  ../L/bro:vGlobal_Strength = vNewStrength;
  ../O/bro:vGlobal_Strength = vNewStrength;
  ../B/bro:vGlobal_Strength = vNewStrength;
  ../Z/bro:vGlobal_Strength = vNewStrength;
  //
  ../G/bro:vGlobal_attract = vNewAttract;
  ../L/bro:vGlobal_attract = vNewAttract;
  ../O/bro:vGlobal_attract = vNewAttract;
  ../B/bro:vGlobal_attract = vNewAttract;
  ../Z/bro:vGlobal_attract = vNewAttract;
  //
```

Lines 2 - 22 selected.

No Parameters.

Rules

```
../Z/bro:vGlobal_Strength = vNewStrength;
//
../G/bro:vGlobal_attract = vNewAttract;
../L/bro:vGlobal_attract = vNewAttract;
../O/bro:vGlobal_attract = vNewAttract;
../B/bro:vGlobal_attract = vNewAttract;
../Z/bro:vGlobal_attract = vNewAttract;
//
../G/bro:vDamp = vNewDamp;
../L/bro:vDamp = vNewDamp;
../o/bro:vDamp = vNewDamp;
../B/bro:vDamp = vNewDamp;
../Z/bro:vDamp = vNewDamp;
}
on (rollOut) {
vNewStrength = 1;
vNewAttract = 0.05;
vNewDamp = 0.05;
//
../G/bro:vGlobal_Strength = vNewStrength;
../L/bro:vGlobal_Strength = vNewStrength;
../O/bro:vGlobal_Strength = vNewStrength;
../B/bro:vGlobal_Strength = vNewStrength;
../Z/bro:vGlobal_Strength = vNewStrength;
//
../G/bro:vGlobal_attract = vNewAttract;
../L/bro:vGlobal_attract = vNewAttract;
../O/bro:vGlobal_attract = vNewAttract;
../B/bro:vGlobal_attract = vNewAttract;
../Z/bro:vGlobal_attract = vNewAttract;
//
../G/bro:vDamp = vNewDamp;
../L/bro:vDamp = vNewDamp;
../o/bro:vDamp = vNewDamp;
../B/bro:vDamp = vNewDamp;
../Z/bro:vDamp = vNewDamp;
}
on (release) {
getURL ("http://www.globz.com", "_self");
}
```

Once I'd finished the coding for this effect, I played around with different values for the parameters until I found ones that I felt worked. This final tuning allows you to be really creative because, depending on the values of the parameters, you can get very different effects: heaviness, liveliness, rigidity...

I also found that if the letters get too big they can slow down the movie, or make the letters swap positions: so I imposed a limit on the _xscale and the _yscale that keeps these two properties between 0 and 500.

The time spent testing also revealed some other, unexpected effects; if you move the mouse quickly over the green button, for example, it thrashes about and distorts violently. This animated logo seems to have been quite eye-catching, because I've had a lot of positive feedback from visitors to my site. Flashers have even asked about it on newsgroups - I hope this chapter has helped satisfy their curiosity.

I've tried to show that to create the effect you want, you need to plan and model before going ahead and implementing it. In this case I had to consider not only the properties, but also their relative rates of change. You also need to be pretty familiar with Flash before creating an effect. If you aren't sure about some effects, test them out first.

Finally, I've found that it pays to make an effect re-usable by putting it into a clip of its own. Some quite complex effects work well because they have been made up out of several smaller effects that are used as the building blocks of a more complicated structure.

"Solutions and whole pieces come to me just as I'm about to wake up in the morning, or as soon as I slip off to sleep at night. I think that, when I'm dreaming, my brain enters a sort of super Flash mode."

JAMES PATERSON
www.presstube.com

Sketch

Sculpture at Legoland
© Richard Cummins/CORBIS

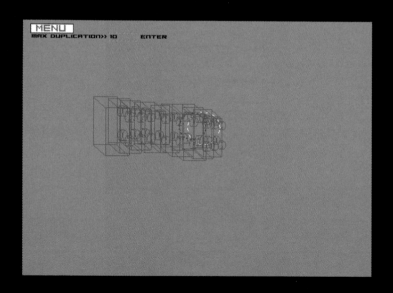

My love for Flash comes from the same place as my love for Lego: sitting down with nothing, then building and experimenting until I end up with something that interests me. I've been completely absorbed in drawing for about eight years now. I draw in a sketchbook for a couple of hours every day, letting one train of thought lead to the next, without much thought for where I'll finally arrive. I treat Flash exactly the same way. I play and experiment, building little toys and sketches, until they come together to form something more significant.

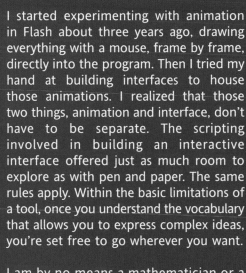

James Paterson

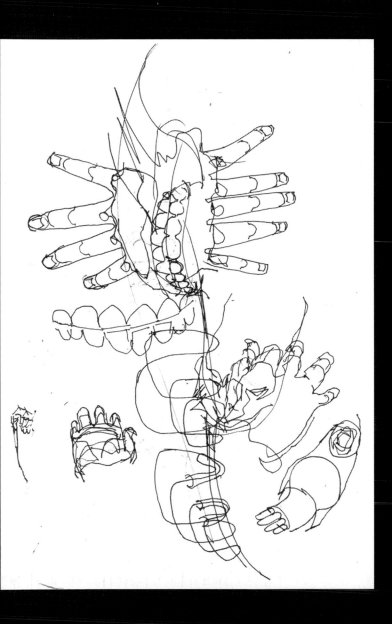

I started experimenting with animation in Flash about three years ago, drawing everything with a mouse, frame by frame, directly into the program. Then I tried my hand at building interfaces to house those animations. I realized that those two things, animation and interface, don't have to be separate. The scripting involved in building an interactive interface offered just as much room to explore as with pen and paper. The same rules apply. Within the basic limitations of a tool, once you understand the vocabulary that allows you to express complex ideas, you're set free to go wherever you want.

I am by no means a mathematician or a programmer. I draw. I learned ActionScript by experimenting and playing with each little action as I needed it. All of my Flash is based on common sense. I figure out what I want a script to do for me in plain English and then set about translating that into Flash syntax. I find myself slipping into basic physics from a completely homebrewed foundation. Attraction, trajectory, friction and chain reactions all just sort of start to make sense once I can see how they work visually, and how they fit into a project that I am doing. In this next section I am just going to talk about my process, and how I am using Flash to get the results I'm after.

Sketch

What inspires me to do what I do? Music has a huge influence on my visual style. I am a big fan of electronic music and Hip Hop. I get a lot of ideas from listening to music and making connections between sound and visuals. Some of the artists that float my boat are Aphex Twin, K-Rad, and Buck 65.

Norman McLaren has a direct visual influence on my current animation. He scratched animation directly onto film reels to get a super direct and organic look. His free and loose style of animation, and his constant self-reinvention has given me a lot of inspiration. After seeing a video of his work I realized that Flash was the ideal piece of software for exploring that area.

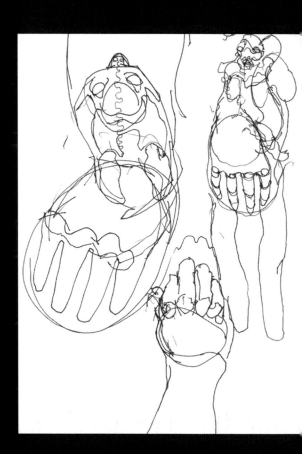

James Paterson

The online community is another big influence. Of course, there's a natural distance between my animations and the mainstream Internet design world, because my work comes from a completely personal place, but my knowledge of ActionScript, and my motivation to gain that knowledge, is definitely derived from things that I've only ever seen online. There are a couple of sites out there that are really setting standards and pushing the medium to new places. www.praystation.com was the site that drove me to tackle ActionScript in the first place. I went there and saw some stuff that made me drool, so I figured I'd have to learn this side of the beast. Of course, there are some other fabulous sites around.Check out these if you haven't already:

www.turux.org (art)
www.destroyrockcity.com (art, design)
www.yugop.com (art of interfacing)
www.hoogerbrugge.com (art, hilarious)
www.iamstatic.com (art)
www.wireframe.co.za (interfacing)
www.moock.org (R&D superman)
www.thesquarerootof-1.com (art, interfacing)
www.hi-res.net (art, design, interfacing)
www.kiiroi.nu (community)

Sketch

I also get a lot of ideas when I'm asleep. Solutions and whole pieces come to me just as I'm about to wake up in the morning, or as soon as I slip off to sleep at night. I think that when I'm dreaming, my brain enters a sort of super Flash mode. I think that once you have the basic Flash vocabulary, your brain uses that knowledge to make connections while you're asleep, so that no matter how complex the dream idea is, your subconscious easily breaks it down into chunks and methods that you already know and understand. I don't know how many of you out there experience this, or will, but it's a blast. It's like that dream where you find a bag full of money, more money than you've ever had in your life. Then you wake up and realize that you were just dreaming. In this Flash dream, though, when you wake up, you can keep what you've found - and who knows, maybe you'll still end up with the big bag of money.

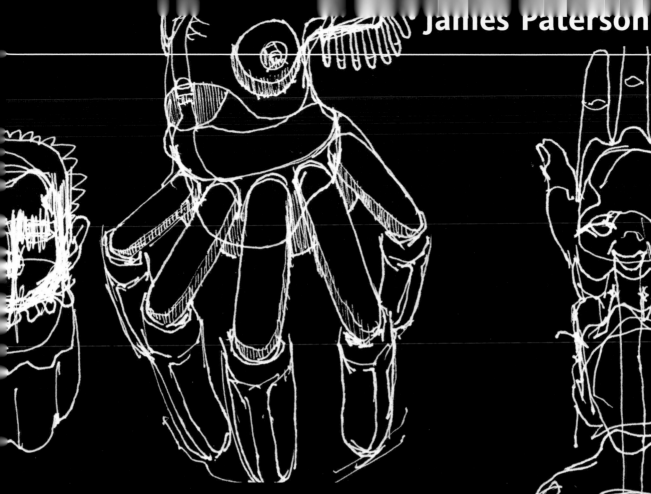

James Paterson

When I'm not just visually jamming and animating, I use a simple vocabulary of basic ActionScript functions to bring my drawings and ideas onto an interactive level. There's no point where the drawing starts and the interfacing begins, they steal and lend back and forth so much that the two have almost become inseparable. I'm constantly getting ideas for menu systems and interactive animations from the things I draw, and my sketchbook is starting to take on diagrammatic and systematic look and feel that wasn't there before. There's a constant push and pull between the organic and technology: figure drawings in loose relaxed positions, but broken down into modular volumes to be better understood and manipulated, and interfaces that incorporate that same modular breakdown and universal systemization to keep them economic and functional. I'm really interested in this idea of cross training and cross-pollination. If I'm spending way too many hours in front of my machine and my eyes are going square, I try to get out into the sun or to a loungy bar to draw in my book. I get most of my best ideas when I'm away from my machine.

Sketch

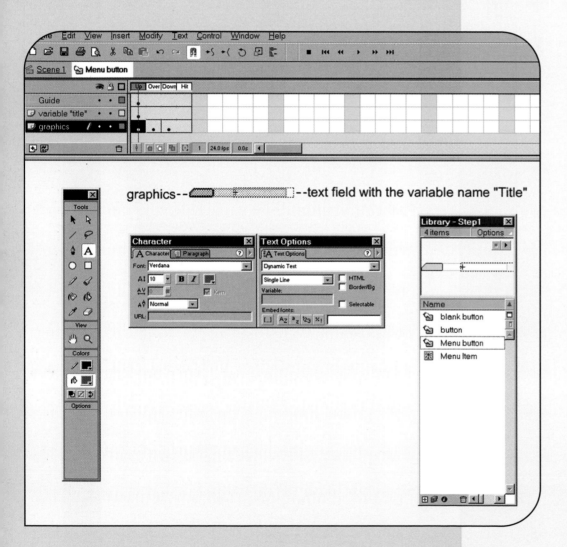

Which leads me into the next section of this chapter. We're going to build an interactive menu that will display ten pages from my sketchbook. One downside of complicated, rich Flash interfaces is that they are often very tedious to update. So, the primary aim of this menu (after making it work well and look dead sexy) is to use as few movie clips as possible and make full use of ActionScript so our lives become easier in the long run. A beneficial by-product of economic interfacing and dynamic ActionScript, as opposed to hard coding, is small file size. I'll walk you through building this menu step by step, breaking down each step into three parts. I'll and describe my intentions for this menu, show you all the code, and then translate it into plain English.

You can find the completed files on the accompanying CD. These are ten menu items we're going to work with:

Efudex
Plendil
Felbatol
Gonal-F
Polypred
Floxic-Otin
Propulsid
Mintezol
Nebupent
Liquabid

First create a button that contains a text field with the variable name **title**.

Then create a movie clip symbol, called **Menu Item**, which will have ten frames, one each for the ten pieces of content that we want in the final menu. Menu Item will also have a layer for the button you've just made, a layer to contain the variables , a layer for a drag button, and a layer for any extra graphics you want to add.

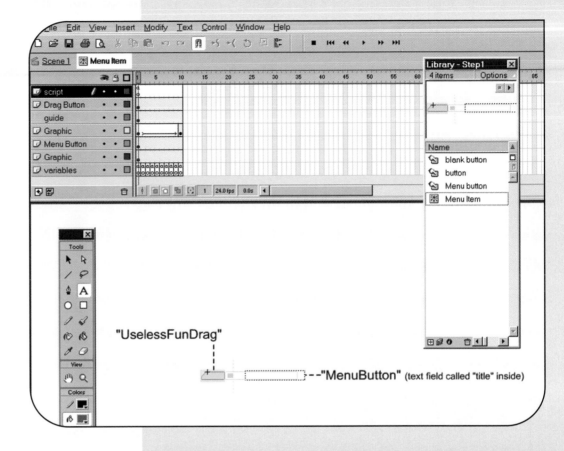

Add this action to the movie clip (I put it on the **script** layer, in frame 1):

gotoAndStop (getProperty ("",_name));

This tells the movie clip to go to, and stop on, the frame of its own instance name. So if the menu item instance name is 5, it will go to frame 5 and stop. The reason for doing this will become clear very soon.

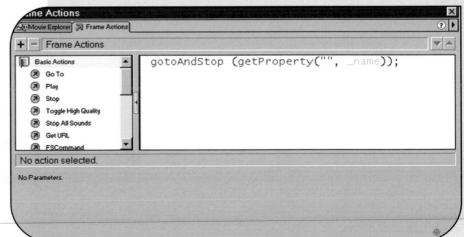

Sketch

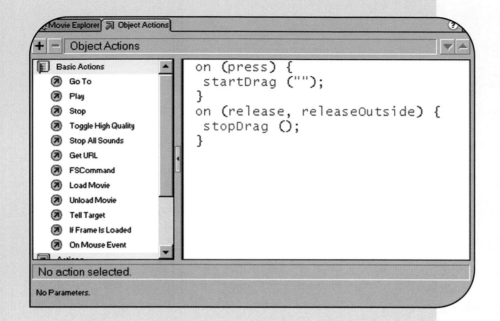

We're going to give our Menu Item movie clip a drag tab, called **Useless Fun Drag**, so that we can move it around in the Flash movie. For this, all we need is a transparent button that has this Drag action assigned inside it (I put it on its own Drag button layer):

```
on (press) {
  startDrag ("");
}
on (release, release Outside) {
  stopDrag ();
}
```

This does nothing more complicated than tell the movie clip to drag when the user presses the button and stop when he releases.

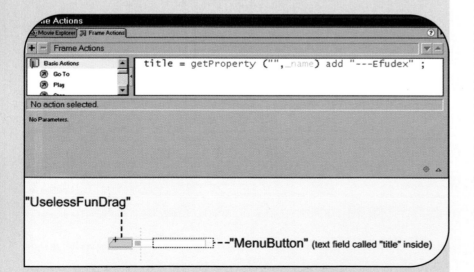

Now we need each frame of Menu Item to contain a title, in a Set Variable action, that will set the text field **title** (inside the first button that we made) to display whatever title we specify. Here's an example:

title = getProperty ("",_name) add "---Efudex" ;

Which means: "tell the text field, title, to display this timeline's current frame, and whatever title we specify. So when the movie is exported, the menu item with the instance name 1 would have a button that reads 1----Efudex. Similarly the menu item, 2, would read 2---Plendil. Frame 2 is identical, just with a different title:

title = getProperty ("",_name) add "---Plendil" ;

So, if we want ten menu items, we would have ten different Set Variable actions telling the button what to say. When the movie is exported, the menu item instance name 1 would have a button that reads 1---Efudex. Similarly menu item, 2, would read 2----Plendil.

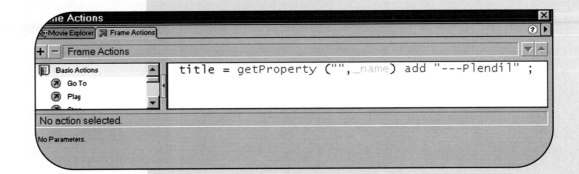

Drag a Menu Item movie clip symbol out of the Library and onto the canvas. Give it the instance name **1**. If you export the movie now, you'll have a lone button with the name 1---Efudex. If, for example, you had named that menu item **5** it would read 5---PolyPred. Setting the movie clip's properties to change like this, depending on its instance name, lets us have the ten menu items that we want, but with only one movie clip in the stage.

We want that single menu item, 1, to duplicate and create a full ten-tiered menu automatically, so the next step is to write a looping script to do that. I'll call it the **Auto Build** script. Take a look at it over the page and I'll explain what it means.

Sketch

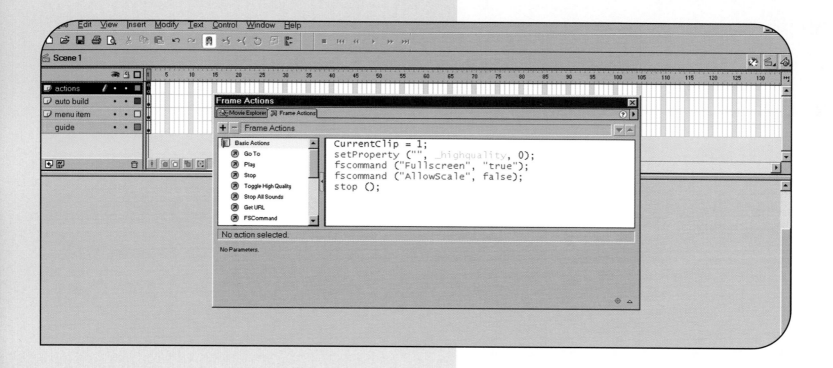

First, set a variable called CurrentClip in frame 1 of the main timeline to equal 1 (the current number of menu items)..

```
CurrentClip = 1;
setProperty ("", _highquality, 0);
fscommand ("Fullscreen" , "true");
fscommand ("AllowScale" , false);
stop ();
```

This variable will give us the current number of menu items on the stage. It will start out having a value of 1 and every time a new clip is duplicated (which happens in the next piece of script), it will increase by one. Once CurrentClip reaches 10, the script will shut off.

This is the script that increments CurrentClip

```
if (/:CurrentClip) < 10 {
  duplicateMovieClip  ("/" add /:CurrentClip, /:CurrentClip+1, /:CurrentClip+1);
  /:CurrentClip = /:CurrentClip+1;
} else{
  stop ();
}
```

The script will use this variable CurrentClip to get all of its information for the duplicating menu items. The new name of the duplications will be CurrentClip+1, so should there be only one menu item on the screen, the name of the new duplicate would be 2. If there were two menu items on the screen, the duplicate would be named 3. CurrentClip will also specify which depth the newly duplicated menu item should occupy. So, if there is one menu item on the screen, the new duplicate will occupy the depth 2. If there are two menu items, the new duplicate will occupy depth 3.

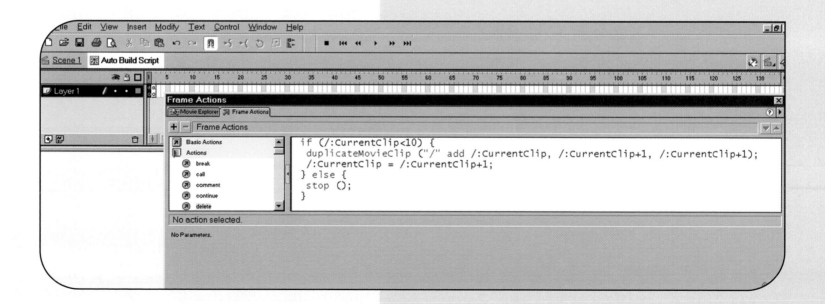

Sketch

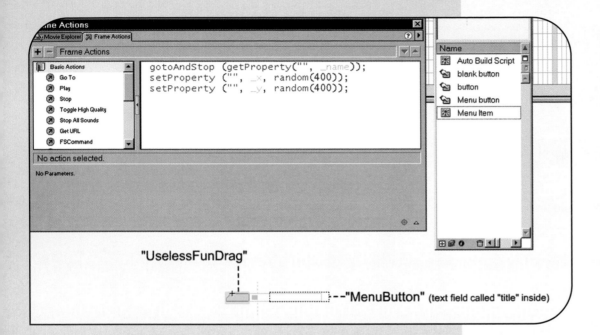

```
gotoAndStop (getProperty("", _name));
setProperty ("", _x, random(400));
setProperty ("", _y, random(400));
```

"UselessFunDrag"

"MenuButton" (text field called "title" inside)

Now we have an auto-building menu, spawning itself from one movie clip and one script. At this point, all of the menu items will be duplicating into the same physical position on the screen and sitting directly on top of each other. We'll make a small alteration to the action on the first frame of the movie clip, Menu Item, to correct this overlap problem so that the duplicated menu items will cascade.

This next piece of ActionScript will give Menu Item a random position on the screen once Auto Build has created it. The random location script looks like this:

```
setProperty ("", _x, random (400));
setProperty ("", _y, random (400));
```

Target "" means 'this movie clip', so it allows movie clips to apply actions to themselves without specifying an external address. So this script simply applies the movie clip's own x and y positions to a random number from 1 to 400.

When the menu items are spawned, they will be spread randomly across the screen.

The next piece of script is an attraction script that tells each menu item to gravitate towards its predecessor. So, 5 will move towards 4, 4 will move towards 3, 3 will move towards 2, and so on, creating a chain of attraction. We'll also create a draggable anchor point, I'll call it **0** (the bottom of the chain) to serve as our drag menu tab. When 0 is dragged, the menu will follow in a smooth, wave-like chain reaction.

To set up this chain reaction, we're going to have a new looping script that will live inside the Menu Item movie clip, a **Chain Script**:

```
Previousclip = "/" add (getProperty ("../",_name)-1);
 setProperty ("../", _x, getProperty("../",_x)+((getProperty(PreviousClip,_x)-getProperty ("../",_x))/2)+5);
 setProperty ("../", _y, getProperty("../",_y)+((getProperty(PreviousClip,_y)-getProperty ("../",_y))/2)+5);
```

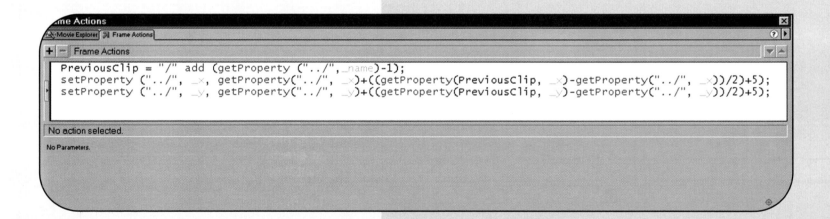

405

Sketch

The first line sets a variable, called PreviousClip, to the name of the parent movie clip, minus 1. So if I was to be sitting inside a movie clip with the instance name 5, the name of my parent movie clip minus 1 would equal 4. The forward slash at the beginning of (getProperty ("../",_name)-1) is the path for the main timeline, where PreviousClip will be. So, if I'm sitting inside the movie clip 5, my PreviousClip would equal /4.

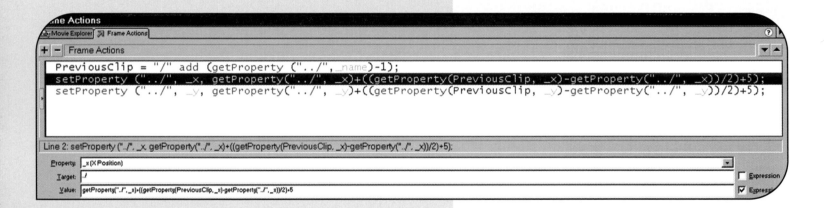

```
PreviousClip = "/" add (getProperty ("../",_name)-1);
setProperty ("../", _x, getProperty("../", _x)+((getProperty(PreviousClip, _x)-getProperty("../", _x))/2)+5);
setProperty ("../", _y, getProperty("../", _y)+((getProperty(PreviousClip, _y)-getProperty("../", _y))/2)+5);
```

Line 2: setProperty ("../", _x getProperty("../", _x)+((getProperty(PreviousClip, _x)-getProperty("../", _x))/2)+5);

Property: _x (X Position)

Target: ../

Value: getProperty("../",_x)+((getProperty(PreviousClip,_x)-getProperty("../",_x))/2)+5

The second line says, "Set the x position of my parent clip to move to half the distance from itself to its previous clip. Then add 10." If we didn't add 10 to the end, each menu item would move over the top of its previous clip, causing all of our menu items to sit directly on top of each other and, of course, we want them to cascade.

The third line contains the instruction to repeat the same script for the parent clip's y position, saying "Set the y position of my parent clip to move half the distance from itself to its previous clip. Then add 10."

Our 0 movie clip (the drag menu tab) is simply going to be a graphic with an overlaid button that has a drag action on it, just like Useless fun Drag.

So now, when the movie is started, it will build itself, spawning menu items to random locations. Each menu item will glide towards its previous clip, and the menu will settle into an evenly spaced cascade of items. When the user drags the drag tab 0, the menu will follow in a dynamic flowing chain reaction.

Now that we've finished the menu's action, it's time to start prepping the content and forging a connection between the two. First, we'll set the button actions inside the Menu Item movie clip to load a piece of content in the form of a .swf file into the interface. We want the button's Load Movie action to be dynamic, so that we can add as much content as we want in the future and never have to go back and change or update it.

```
On (release) {
    LoadMovie (getProperty ("",_name) add
".swf","/LoadTarget");
}
```

When the user releases the button, this loads the movie myname.swf into the movie clip called LoadTarget, which is in the main timeline. So, if the user presses the button with the instance name 5, it will load 5.swf. If the instance name of the button is 2 then it would load 2.swf. This is how we can add a Load Movie action to ten pieces of content with only one piece of code.

The menu would now load up content if we had some, but we want the menu to disappear while the content is up, so we'll add some script in this button to tell the menu to slide off the screen. We'll use a simple Set Property action to tell the menu drag tab, 0, to reposition itself off the right side of the screen. The menu will then follow it to make way for the content. Here's the script:

```
On (release)
    setProperty ("/0", _xPosition) = 820;
        loadMovie (getProperty ("",_name) add ".swf",
"/loadTarget");
}
```

This tells Flash to set the x position of the movie clip **0** (menu drag) to 850, so that it's off the right border of the piece and out of sight. Now, because of the Chain Script, the menu will follow **0** off the right side and we'll have the whole screen to view the drawing that we have loaded.

Sketch

Once the viewer has finished looking at the content, they'll probably want the menu back to make another selection. We need to make the menu slide back onto the screen into the same place it was when it left. If the menu always stayed in the same position, this wouldn't be an issue because we could simply hard code its return co-ordinates. But, given that the user can drag around and play with the menu, we'll need it to return to a dynamic location. To help the menu remember where it's supposed to return to, we must save its X and Y position in a variable. We'll set these variables in the button, so that they are triggered to check and store 0's position on release:

```
on (release) {
  /:Xreturn = getProperty ("/0",_x);
  /:Yreturn = getProperty ("/0",_y);
  setProperty ("/0", _x, 820);
  loadMovie (getProperty ("",_name) add ".swf",
"/LoadTarget")
}
```

This sets a variable called Xreturn in the main timeline to equal the movie clip **0**' s X position at the time that the button is released, and a Yreturn for the the Y position. Now, if we wanted the menu to return to its place on screen, we would just tell 0 to go back to its Xreturn and 1.

Technically the only thing left to do is prep the content and the interface will be complete. If you have kept your graphics reasonably economic up to this point, the menu won't be much larger than 2k.

Object Actions

Movie Explorer | Object Actions

+ − | Object Actions

```
on (release) {
  /:Xreturn = getProperty("/0", _x);
  /:Yreturn = getProperty("/0", _y);
  setProperty ("/0", _x, 820);
  loadMovie (getProperty ("",_name) add ".swf", "/LoadTarget");
}
```

Line 5: loadMovie (getProperty ("",_name) add ".swf", "/LoadTarget");

URL: getProperty ("",_name) add ".swf" ☑ Expression

Location: Target ▾ /LoadTarget ☐ Expression

Variables: Don't send ▾

"UselessFunDrag"

"ChainScript"- - - - - -"MenuButton" (text field called "title" inside)

The content we are going to display will be a zoomable, draggable, well-compressed drawing. We need to be able to replace this drawing easily, if we have to, so that adding new content is less of a headache. We'll use a template .fla that we can just drop drawings into and export as 1.swf and 2.swf etc. to be called up by the interface. This .fla will have four elements:

- a movie clip that contains the drawing

Drawing
- a movie clip with a zoom-in script

ZoomScript, and its trigger buttons
- a close button, to unload the drawing and bring back the menu

- a drag button to drag this .swf once it has loaded into the interface.

The movie clip Drawing will consist solely of an imported jpg, aligned at zero X and zero Y. Drawing will sit in the main timeline at 50 % of its full size. This way, when it has loaded, the whole image will be visible within the 800X600 viewing area.

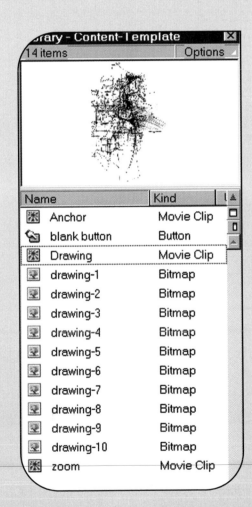

Sketch

We'll also have our drag button in the timeline. It is identical to the drag button in our interface, except much larger. This way, it will cover the whole drawing even when it has been zoomed to 100%.

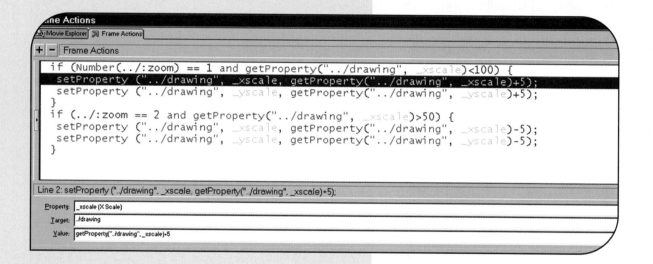

```
if (Number(../:zoom) == 1 and getProperty("../drawing", _xscale)<100) {
  setProperty ("../drawing", _xscale, getProperty("../drawing", _xscale)+5);
  setProperty ("../drawing", _yscale, getProperty("../drawing", _yscale)+5);
}
if (../:zoom == 2 and getProperty("../drawing", _xscale)>50) {
  setProperty ("../drawing", _xscale, getProperty("../drawing", _xscale)-5);
  setProperty ("../drawing", _yscale, getProperty("../drawing", _yscale)-5);
}
```

Line 2: setProperty ("../drawing", _xscale, getProperty("../drawing", _xscale)+5);

Property: _xscale (X Scale)

Target: ../drawing

Value: getProperty("../drawing", _xscale)+5

The zoom-in and zoom-out controls need to have a looping script to deliver their actions, which we'll call **Zoom Script**. Zoom Script will run in accordance to a variable that we'll call zoom. If the variable zoom equals 1, the script will zoom in on the drawing. If the zoom variable equals 2, the script will zoom out the drawing, and if the variable zoom equals 0, the script will not do anything. This script will also check the size of the Drawing movie clip to make sure that it hasn't zoomed in or out too much. If the drawing is at 50 %, its smallest size (the size it starts at), it won't zoom any smaller. If it is at 100%, (its full size), it won't zoom any larger.

```
if ((../:zoom ==1 and getProperty ("../drawing",_xscale) < 100) (
    setProperty ("../drawing", _xscale, getProperty ("../drawing",_xscale)+5);
    set Property ("../drawing", _yscale getProperty ("../drawing",_yscale)+5);
}
if (../:zoom=2 and getProperty ("../drawing",_xscale) > 50) {
    setProperty ("../drawing", _xscale getProperty ("../drawing",_xscale)-5);
    setProperty ("../drawing", _yscale getProperty ("../drawing",_yscale)-5);
}
```

So the first if loop checks whether the zoom variable in the previous timeline,equals 1, and the movie clip Drawing, also in the previous timeline, is less than 100%, 5% will be added to its _xscale and _yscale.

The second loop does the same sort of thing in reverse, so if zoom equals 2 and the movie clip is larger than 50%, 5% is subtracted from its _xscale and _yscale.

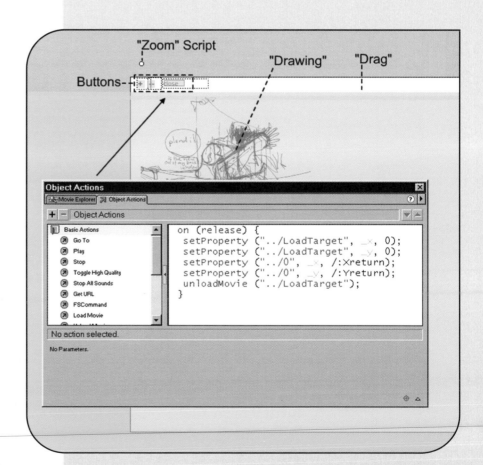

Sketch

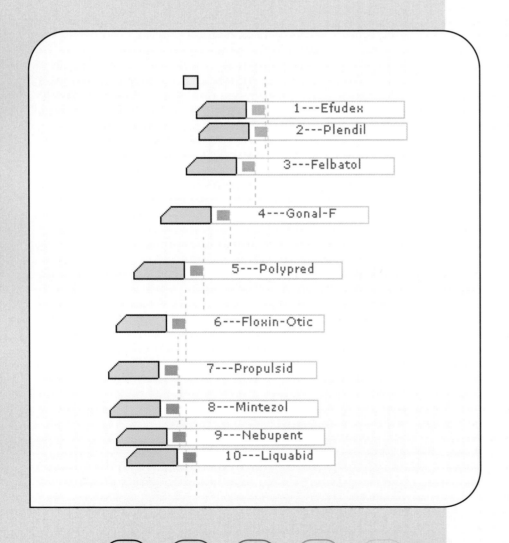

This next script will tell the Close button to unload the content from the movie clip LoadTarget, and tell the movie clip 0 (menu drag tab) to return to its Xreturn and Yreturn co-ordinates. It will also move the movie clip LoadTarget back to its original position, 0 0 (top left). The menu will follow 0 back onto the screen, and the interface will be ready for the user to make another selection.

```
on (release) {
  setProperty ("../LoadTarget", _x, 0);
  setProperty ("../LoadTarget", _y, 0);
  setProperty ("../0", _x, /:Xreturn);
  setProperty ("../0", _y, /:Yreturn);
  unloadMovie ("../LoadTarget");
}
```

Which means the x and y position of LoadTarget are set to equal 0, the x and y positions of **0** to their previous position, and the drawing unloaded from LoadTarget.

And that completes out interface. We have built an interactive menu system that is easily updated and changed. We've used script as efficiently as we could, together with as many dynamic elements as possible, so that this menu has a great deal of power and flexibility. This is a good example of how I go about working on a project technically from start to finish.

James Paterson

I don't know whether I will ever get bored of Flash, or the Internet for that matter. The power of this medium is its immediacy and ultimate flexibility. Artists don't have to wait to be approved and recognized before they can show. They don't need much more than $30 a month and a cheap computer to have a 24 hour international gallery. No one needs to qualify you, or to review you. The only factor that affects whether your work is going to have an impact on people is its quality.

You can just do what you do because it's what you want to see and, inevitably, people will discover your work because it is genuine and they can relate to that. As long as you like what you do, nothing else really matters. This equipment is bringing about a revolution in independent publishing, and I'm loving it.

"WackedUSA was my Internet playground,
a place I could design anything I wanted... "

VINCE SURIANI
www.wackedUSA.com

Puzzle

When I left college, I took a job as a web designer. I knew as much about web business as you might expect from a new graduate – pretty much nothing, but I soon realized that Internet real estate was up for grabs by anyone willing to drop $70 on a URL. And so WackedUSA.com was born.

WackedUSA.com was my Internet playground; a place I could design anything I wanted without having to worry about clients with their own ideas ("Wow. That looks great. But can you move the navigation from the top to the side and make everything red? Hey, thanks"), or my boss breathing down my neck ("Wow. That looks like crap. MOVE the navigation from the top to the side and make everything red."). Without having to follow unrealistic guidelines ("Hey, the site doesn't work on my DOS 6.1 desktop running Mosaic. What kind of web designer are you!?"). On WackedUSA.com, the only person I had to please was myself.

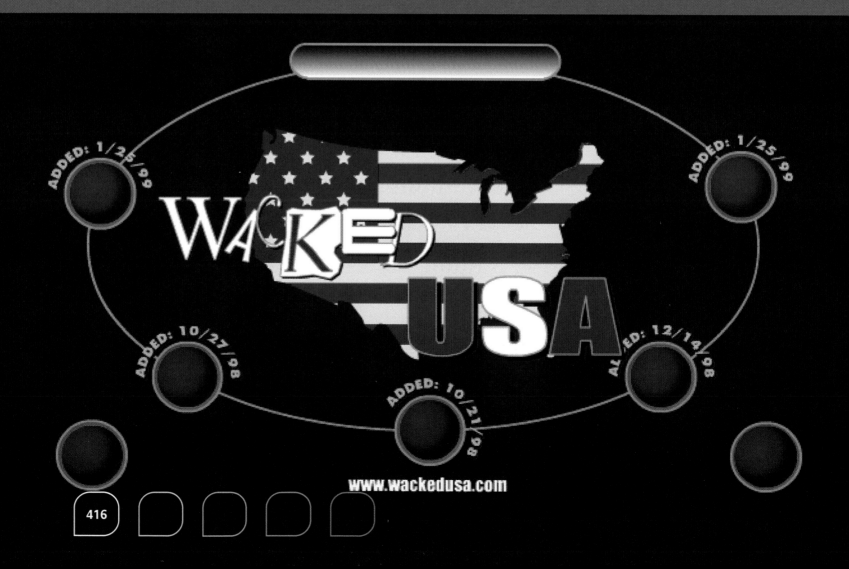

ADDED: 1/25/99

ADDED: 1/25/99

ADDED: 10/27/98

ADDED: 10/21/98

ALED: 12/14/98

www.wackedusa.com

416

Vince Suriani

I saw my first fully Flash web site at the Mac Expo in New York in '97. I was enthralled. I remember begging my boss to buy it for the agency and although he did, we never used it (he didn't think it mainstream enough). So I bought myself a copy of the software, quit work and started hanging around a Flash message board called the FlashPad. This sent me to the Matinee site, a fabulous piece of design, full of little gold and silver spinning 3D icons. It was beautiful, quite extraordinary, and I had no idea how they'd got those icons so perfect. (Although this was the original Matinee site, the new site could still be cited as an example of awesome 3D Flash and Design.)

Puzzle

We all started discussing how to go about making 3D flash on Flash Pad. There weren't many options, a situation made all the more frustrating because Nobody, from the**void**, was constantly updating his 3D Flash gallery using his Adobe Dimensions technique, which depended on an old version of Dimensions that I couldn't get my hands on. Mano1's hand traced pieces were stunning and tiny, but they took hours to create. The only thing I could come up with was to use Adobe Dimensions 3.0, which gave vector output. So I set to work on the first 3D Flash Demo Of Death.

Vince Suriani

Ok, first off, the reason it was called the Demo Of Death was because back then, before I knew what I was doing, I had said something to the effect of "Doing 3D in Flash is DEATH!" because it really was a pain. It was just a joke that stuck. But DOD1 did display some 3D in Flash. The design itself wasn't all that good, but then the only people who went to it were other Flash designers who I'd been chatting with on FlashPad. It still really wasn't about what people thought of it; I was just enjoying having my own site.

In the end it turned out pretty good and I'm still rather proud of it. Then a couple of months later, as I was hanging out with a friend of mine getting drunk, he asked me why all my 3D stuff was just spinning around. "Why don't you make it interactive, you know? It's the internet, not TV or a movie." He had a point. A good one.

So I started on the second 3D Flash Demo Of Death, trying to build more complex 3D Flash effects that did more than spin around.

WACKEDUSA'S 3D FLASH DEMO OF DEATH

Ok, ok... so it's not really all that deadly... it's just that everyone keeps saying that doing 3D in Flash is hard... which it is, but if you follow some simple rules everything always works out in the end...   More...

Then maybe a drop shadow on the ground to help with the illusion of depth, kinda like this:

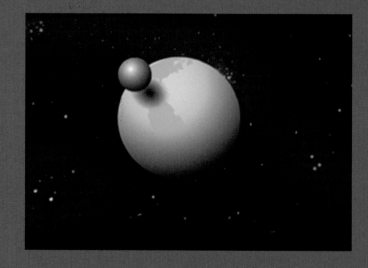

DOD2 was a moderate success. I had put together some more complex models that did more than spin, like the Gears of Death and the Title, and used interactivity with the Balloons of Death, which popped up when the mouse pointed at them. But I really had come to the end of what Dimensions could do for me. It is a great program, but it couldn't keep me up to speed with other 3D Flashers who were releasing awesome work at a relentless pace. I was totally against hand tracing, as it took forever and the only option I could see was to use Flash auto-trace bitmaps, and this was only effective if you turned the

contrast up to 100% in your image, making it black and white like the EgoMedia site.

Fortunately there was a sudden explosion of 3D Flash tools; first Illustrate came along, then Vecta3D, and most recently Swift3D. It was the capabilities of Swift3D that really inspired me to make the latest Demo Of Death. It freed me up from tons of laborious symbol tweaking and 3D headaches. And with Flash 4, I could use ActionScript to make truly interactive 3D Flash pieces. Probably my greatest success with this is the 8 Queens of Death.

The 8 Queens Of Death

This simple puzzle is really a training exercise for people who are starting to learn to play chess. The object is simple. Place eight queens on a regular chess board so that they are not attacking each other. Simple.

Although this Flash file may look complex, it's really not that bad. There are just a few key parts to it: the queens sinking down into their squares (also played in reverse to raise them up), some ActionScripting that moves any queens in check, the board itself, and the background. Let's just do it and you'll see.

OBJECTIVE: SIMPLY PLACE 8 QUEENS ON THE BOARD. CLICK ON THE SQUARE TO RAISE OR LOWER A QUEEN. IF A QUEEN IS IN THE LINE OF ATTACK OF A NEW QUEEN IT WILL BE REMOVED.

NUMBER OF QUEENS: 4

WACKEDUSA PRESENTS THE 8 QUEENS OF DEATH

3D FLASH DEMO OF DEATH III and ActionScript

Puzzle

I take care of the 3D work I need before I get into Flash. It's a good idea to make sure that you can actually create the 3D pieces before you start to code. I'm using Swift3D in these examples, but you can use whichever 3D program you're into. The method should be pretty similar, if not the same.

We're going to make one solid row of the board. First make a square using Adobe Illustrator (or Macromedia Freehand, or even Flash). Then duplicate it seven times so that you have eight in total, touching in a horizontal line, and save the file as an .eps for import into Swift3D.

You also need a queen object. You can model this yourself, or find a free object on the net. I made mine by lathing the profile of the queen in Ray Dream Studio and exporting it as a .3ds file (which Swift3D can import). I'm hoping that Swift3D 2 is going to include a lathe option.

Now that we've got the only things we need for Swift3D we'll import them. First open a new blank document in Swift3D. Then choose File>Import and load in your set of squares. (Leave the default settings for the width and bevel alone for a minute.) Color every other square a different color, so it looks like … a chessboard.

Open a new document in Swift3D, keeping the first one open. Choose File>Import and load in your queen object. Color the queen object however you like in this window, and once you're happy with her, select and copy. Return to the original Swift3D document and paste the queen into the image with the eight squares.

Move, scale and rotate the queen so that it is positioned on the first square. (Make sure you rotate the queen to point towards you, and don't rotate the squares. You'll see why later on.) If you're having trouble positioning the queen, open a second camera window in Swift3D to help.

Once you have the queen in position, copy it again, and paste it a square along in the same document. Now select both queens, group them, and copy/paste them into the next two squares. Carry out the same process once more, and you should have eight queens in eight squares, with the main camera looking down on them.

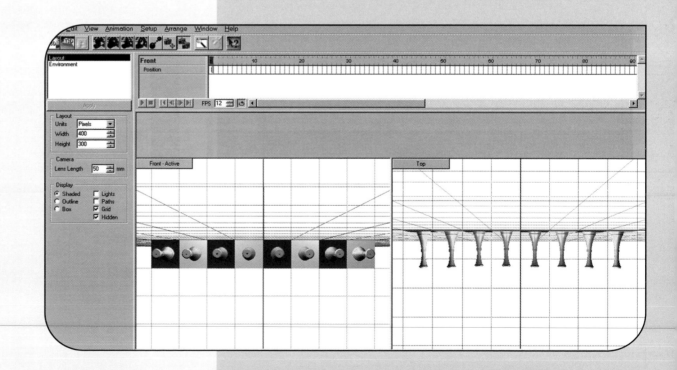

Puzzle

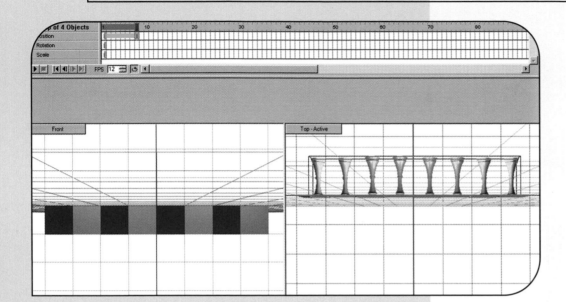

Now we need some animation.

If you haven't yet turned the second camera on, do so now and set it to top view so you're looking at the queens from the side. Click on frame 8 on the timeline and set a keyframe. (You could use more frames, but the more there are the bigger it gets. Eight is nice.) Now, move the queens down into the squares so that none of them show through, but not so far as to make the motion too quick when it is played.

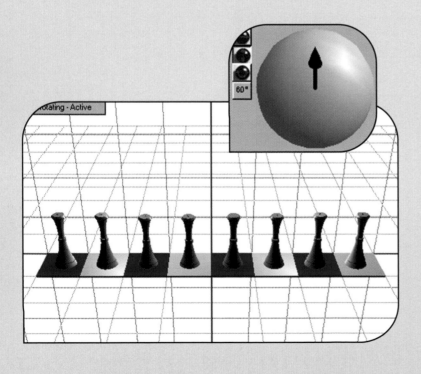

Click on frame 1 of the time line. Deselect the queens by clicking in an empty space. Set the main window (which should say Front) to rotating. This will let us rotate the camera without touching the objects in the scene. Constrain the rotation to only up and down by clicking on the vertical arrows by the crystal ball and set it to 60 degrees instead of 0.

Drag down in the crystal ball until it tilts once. Then click on the Fit to Camera button and be sure to save your Swift3D file. You will be using it as the starting point for the next few steps.

Export the animation of all the queens moving down, and make sure you're happy with the lighting and colors – it will take a lot of work to return to this point and change them later. Choose Edit>Select All, and while you're holding down the ctrl key DESELECT the first queen and the first square she is on. Hit delete. You should now have only one queen and one square. Choose File>Export and save the animation as a .swf (no outlines).

You might be wondering why we just did that. It's because we need Flash to do most of the 3D work, or rather, we want to import the least amount of 3D into Flash, so the file size is kept down. Then we'll just make movie clips of these animations and re-use them. So, if you've been following along, you can probably guess the next few steps.

Open the file that contains all the queens again, select all, deselect the second queen and her block, and hit delete. Export this animation, and repeat these steps for the next two queens.

We don't need to export the last four, because we can just flip the movie clips of the queens we've just exported to simulate the other side.

The last thing we need to do in Swift 3D is export the board. Delete all the queens (but not their blocks) by ctrl-clicking on them. Choose File >Export, set it to current frame only and turn the outlines on with the hairline setting.

That's all the 3D work we need to do. Now we'll start building our Flash File.

Open a new Flash file. Then import each of the queen swfs you've created into individual layers. You should end up with four layers, each one containing a different queen animation.

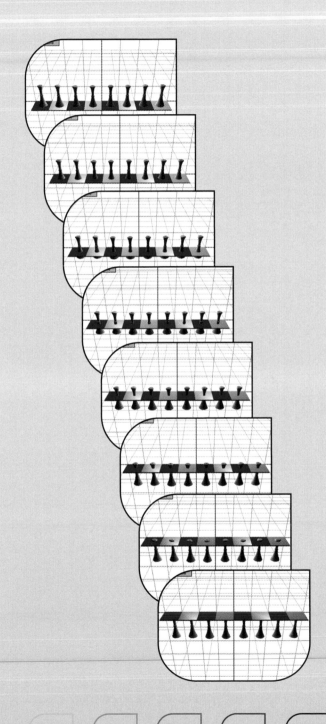

Puzzle

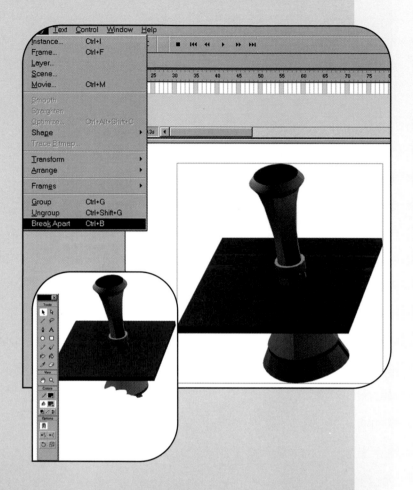

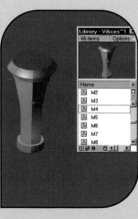
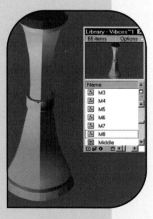

Each one of these animations needs to be in its own movie clip (so we can re-use them), so the next step is to right-click, or ctrl-click, on one of the queen layers and choose Hide Others. Then go though each frame, breaking apart the symbols until you have loose Flash shapes.

After you've finished that, you need to delete the part of the board in each of those frames, and any piece of the queen that is sticking out of the bottom of that board. Each frame should only contain one queen, which appears to sink into the board. Strange I know, but this is necessary so that Flash can do a lot of the 3D work for us.

So now we're ready to make the queen movies. Once you've cleaned each layer, you need to select all the frames on one layer (by clicking on the first frame of the layer and then moving to the last frame and Shift-clicking on it.), and copy them (Edit>Copy Frames).

Next create a new movie clip and paste those frames into it (Select the first frame and Edit>Paste Frames). You also need to select all (Edit>Select All) and to make a symbol for queen (give them any name you want. It doesn't matter). We're doing this so that we can duplicate the queens and fade them for the reflection we're going to fake.

Vince Suriani

Once you've created symbols out of each of the queens, create a new layer in that movie clip. Then copy and paste a queen into the new layer. Flip it vertically and then rotate it slightly to make it look like the reflection. Take a look at this image:

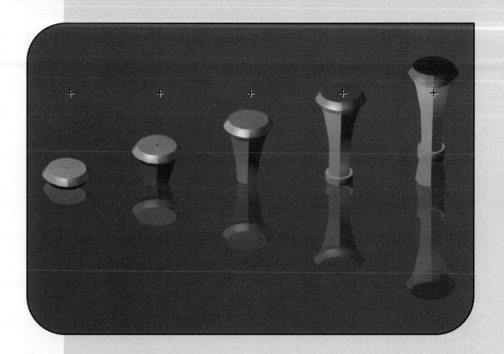

It's important that the layer with the reflection is under the layer with the actual queen. Otherwise the reflection would look... well, funny. Do this for every frame, so that each queen in each frame has its own instance flipped and transparent underneath it.

While you're still in the queen movie clip, select all the frames and copy them. Before you deselect those frames, reverse them by choosing Modify>Frames>Reverse. Next, click on the blank frame right after the last key frame in this animation and paste those frames in. So now your animation should be of the queen rising and then sinking. Pretty cool, huh? (If your queen is sinking and then rising, reverse the frames again.)

Just a few more steps and then this queen animation will be finished. Make a new layer, and on the first blank key frame give it the label **down**.

Now for a bit of ActionScript. Make another layer (you should have four in total now: one with labels, one with the main queen animation, one with the reflection of the queen, and this final one for the ActionScripts).

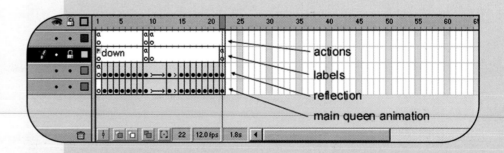

427

Puzzle

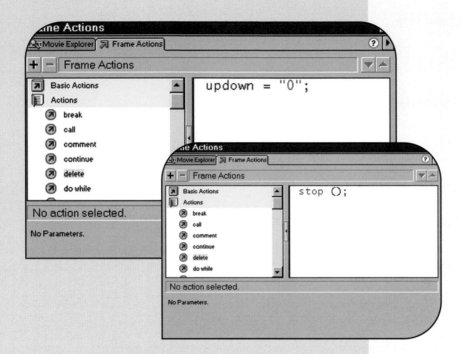

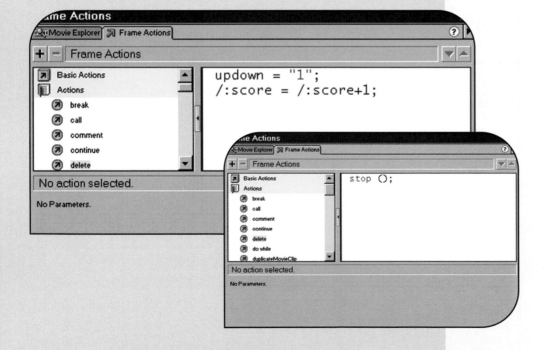

On the ActionScript layer double-click the first frame and add this ActionScript:

updown = "0";

This stops the queen animation before it starts and also sets the variable updown to 0, which will tell the ActionScript we're about to write that this movie's queen is down. It'll make more sense once we're done with the grunt work.

Now find the last frame of the animation of the queen rising up. Add a blank key frame to the ActionScript layer. In that frame, you need to add this ActionScript:

updown = "1";
/:score = /:score + 1;

This will stop the queen once it's raised and increase the score by 1 (a score of eight is going to be a win). It will also set the updown variable to 1, which will let us know that this movie's queen is up.

NOTE ON VARIABLES: placing a /: before a variable will set that variable in the main movie. Without that /:, the variable would be set in the movie clip only. This, again, will make more sense a little later on.

Create a new blank key frame next to the key frame you've just created. This one should be right above the first frame of the animation of the queen sinking down: Add this command:

/:score = /:score - 1;

This removes one point from the score since the queen is being lowered down (either by the user clicking on it or by another queen attacking it). Finally, add a key frame to the last frame in the ActionScript layer. It needs this command:

gotoAndPlay ("down");

This will reset the queen and prepare it to be raised again if need be. That's it for this movie. Now that you're finished with it, you can go back to the main timeline and delete the original layer that you imported this queen from (which is now a movie symbol in your Library.)

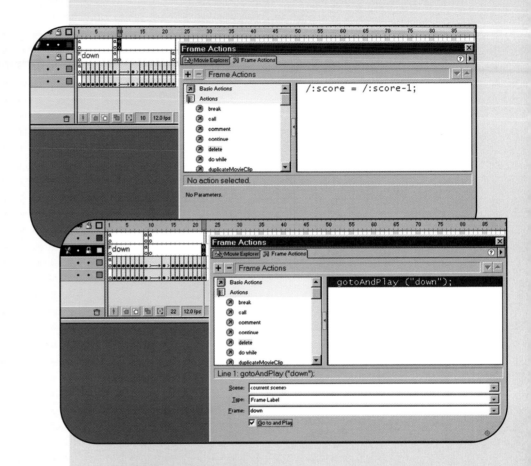

The best part of this is that you get to do it all again for the remaining three queens. Just repeat the instructions for making the Queens movie for each of them, and insert the same ActionScripts.

So, in the end, you should have a blank main movie, one movie symbol and eight individual queen static symbols per queen animation. Each of those symbols should be a different movie clip containing the four queens and their respective ActionScripts.

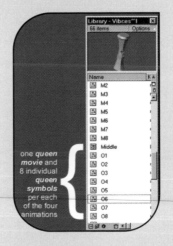

one *queen movie* and 8 individual *queen symbols* per each of the four animations

Puzzle

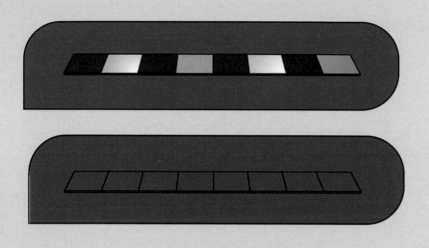

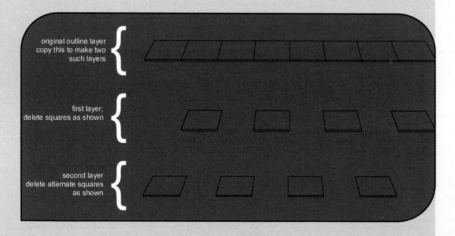

original outline layer
copy this to make two
such layers {

first layer;
delete squares as shown {

second layer
delete alternate squares
as shown {

Making the Board and the Buttons

Ok, so we're back on the main time line. Now you should import the one-frame swf you made with the eight squares of the board on it. Once you've got it imported, select all and move it to the middle of the stage.

Break the graphic apart and double-click the outline of the squares to select the entire outline, but not the fills. Cut the selected outlines out and paste them back into exactly the same spot you cut them from but on a new layer. Then make a third layer and paste the same outlines there too. You should now have one layer with just the fills, and two other layers both containing the same outlines.

Now we need to make each one of the outlines of the squares into its own button. The easiest way to do this is to hide all but one of the outline layers and delete every other square's outline. Then just drag select around one of them, hit the F8 button and save it as a button. Then drag select around the next one and hit F8 and save that one as a button.

After you've made those four buttons, hide that layer and show the other layer with the original outline pasted into it. Delete every other square's outline (but do the opposite blocks to those you did the last time so that when we're finished you'll have all eight buttons but four on one layer and four on the other.)

Once you've made all of them into buttons, show the two outline layers only (but not the filled layer) and select all. Cut them from those layers (you can delete them once they are gone) and then Shift-paste them back into the fill layer.

After all this you should have the eight square fills under the eight square outlines that are now buttons. We now need to do a little button work. Go to your Library, which should contain four queen movies and now eight wireframe buttons, and open one of the new buttons you've just created for editing. The first frame (the Up state) should have the outline in it. Click and drag that layer into the Over state, leaving the first frame blank, and then ctrl-drag to copy that frame into the Hit state as well.

The Hit state defines the area of the button that responds to a pointer's movement, so fill the outline in the Hit state with a color (any color - no-one will ever see it.) Go back to the Over state and apply whatever stroke treatment you want to that outline. I made mine two points wide with a nice bright blue to stand out. (Don't fill the outline.)

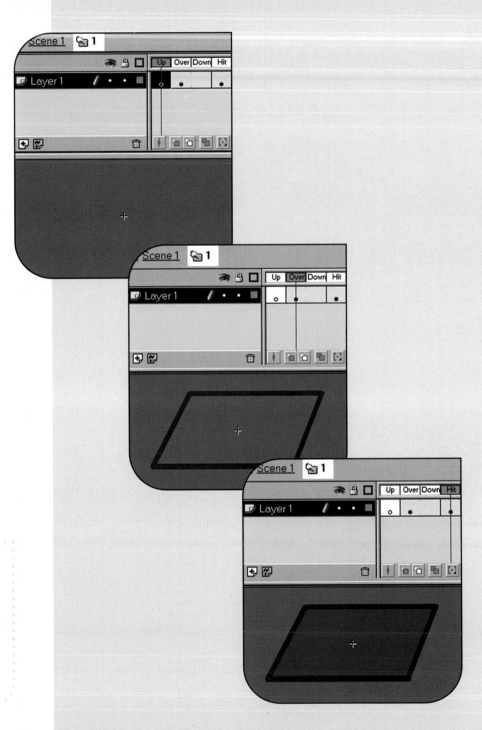

The button is invisible until the mouse rolls over it, when it will display a bright outline signifying the square the queen will land on. Carry out the same procedure for the remaining seven buttons, and when you've finished, return to the main timeline and stage. Note the transparent blue outlines representing the hidden buttons we've made.

Puzzle

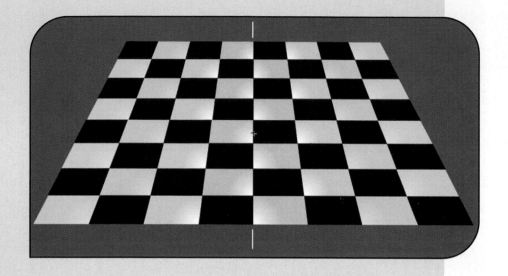

Because we made this the way we did, the middle line, in between the two middle squares, should be perfectly straight up and down. What you need to do is select all and copy the eight squares and their outlines. Create a new layer under the current one and paste the eight squares there. Move it until the bottom of the new set touches the top line of the old set. Center both middle lines on each other. Choose Modify>Transform>Flip Horizontal. (We need to do this since the pattern of the board is checkered.) Then all you need to do is scale the new eight squares down until the lines match up. There really is no precise way to go about this so just use your eye and zoom in to make sure everything is lined up right. It's not hard. Once you've finished you should have two rows of the board that are in perspective.

The rest is easy. Select All again, copy it, make a new layer and paste the two new rows in, move them to line up and scale them to match. Now do the four rows. Select ALL, copy, make a new layer, paste and scale and line up the board. You should now have all eight rows, each row smaller and further away than the last.

We're going to put everything on one layer for now, for organizational reasons.

Select All and. copy. Make a new layer. Right click, or ctrl-click on the layer and Hide Others. Paste the board back in and delete all the hidden layers.

Now we need to get all the wireframe buttons off this layer and into their own. A bit of clicking involved in this: click on the first wire frame and then move towards your right, Shift-clicking to add all of them into the selection. Cut them once you've selected them all, make a new layer and Shift-Paste them into it. Name the layer **WireFrame Buttons**.

After all this you should have one layer containing the checkered board pattern alone, and one layer with the outlines of the board that are in fact hidden buttons. (And, of course, the button layer should be ON TOP of the board layer...)

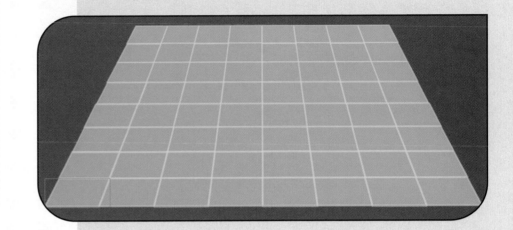

Now for the queens. We need to do something temporarily to the four queen movies. Currently the first frames of the queen movies are blank, and it's going to be hard to try and position them like this.

Open a queen movie. Find the frame with the queen in the up position. Copy that frame. Make a new layer. On the first frame of that new layer paste the queen frame. Do this to the other three queen movies. After we're done positioning them we'll just delete these layers to return the queens to their original state.

Puzzle

Before we go on we need to name the spaces of the board. It's going to get confusing in a while, so it will help with the explanation if we get this settled right now. We'll use a simple naming convention. The rows will be letters and the columns will be numbers. Simple. So if you're looking at the board top down, the top left corner space is A1, with A2 to the right of it and B1 below, and so on.With this simple grid method we'll be able to do quite a bit.

But back to the queens. First, add another layer to the main movie,and name it **H-Queens**, since this is going to be the front row of the board. Get the queen that goes on the left side of the board. (It should be the most tilted to the left). Drag the movie clip from the Library and place it so that it looks like it's resting on the board on H1. Just use your eye. It doesn't have to be mathematically exact; it just has to look right. Next, get the queen that's only slightly tilted and put it on H2. Do the same for H3 and H4.

When you've done this you should have four queens, one in each of H1, H2, H3, and H4, all on the same layer. Now we'll do the flip trick again.

Right-click on the H-Queens layer and choose Lock others, Select All, copy and Shift-Paste. While they're still selected, Modify>Transform>Flip Horizontal and drag them to the right so that they're sitting in the H5, H6, H7 and H8 spaces respectively. (It might be an idea to hold down Shift while you're dragging to make sure they're lined up.)

Boom. The first row of queens done... Now let's just name the instances of these movies before we go on. Double-click the H1 queen and give it an instance name of H1. H2's instance name is H2 and H3's is H3 and so on. Name them all. Simple.

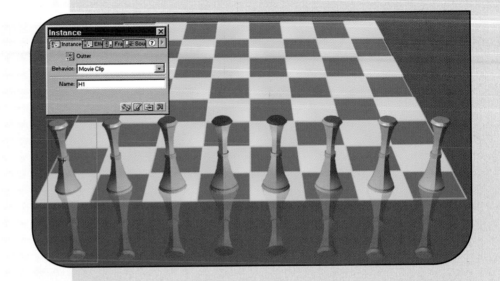

The rest of this is easy. After you've given every queen movie an instance name, Select All, Copy, make a new layer under the H Queens layer and name it G Queens

Right-click on that layer and lock others. Shift-Paste the H Queens into the G Queens layer, and while they're selected, move them onto the G row and Modify >Transform>Scale them to the right size. They should fit perfectly. Double-click all of them and give them instance names of G1, G2, G3, etc... Keep following this pattern till you finish the A Queens layer.

So now our Flash file is getting pretty nice. The bottom layer should be the checkered board pattern. The layer on top of that should be the WireFrame Buttons layer. Then on top of that should be the A Queens layer, with all the queens in that layer having instance names of A1, A2, A3, etc. Above that should be the B Queens, then the C Queens and so on till the H Queens layer. The stage should look like a chess board with every space filled with a queen. Pretty cool, huh?

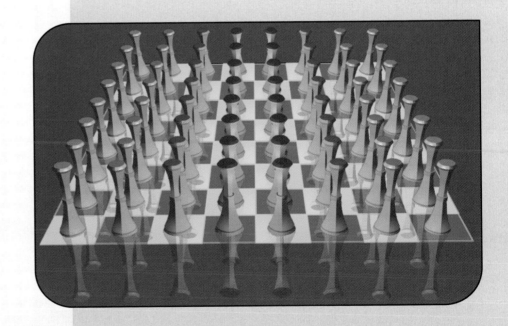

Puzzle

Now for the hard part: the ActionScript. Just kidding, it's not hard. Although, I'd like to say that I had help from my programmer friend Ollie von Gerbig. We were hanging out one night talking shop and I showed him what I had so far with the Queens Of Death. We started talking about the math of chess and similar things, and he really devised the logic of the ActionScript we're about to go over. It's really amazing what he could program considering how drunk we were. I recommend not being drunk while coding ActionScript. I would also like to say that some of my variable names might get a bit, well, odd. This is just a leftover from the trial-and-error process I went through when I was writing this thing - sorry about that.

Right-click on the WireFrame Buttons layer, and lock or hide others. Double-click the wireframe button at H1, and put in this Action Script:

```
on (release) {
  tellTarget ("/H1") {
   play ();
  }
  gotoandPlay ("wait");
  queenname1 = "H1";
}
```

This is what's going on here. First we tellTarget /H1, which is the queen movie for this square, to play. If you remember, the movie stops at both the down and the up state. This will reverse that. So if it's down, the queen will go up. If the queen is up, it will go down.

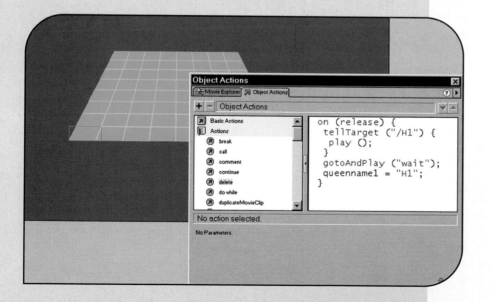

436

The next command, Go to and Play ("Wait"), we'll get to in a minute, but needless to say this is where the movie will check to see whether there are other queens in the way. And by setting the variable queenname1 to H1, our code will know which queen is the new one and not to remove it. (Because we want the queen that was just placed to stay and any queens that are being attacked to disappear.)

Unfortunately for you, you need to do this to the other 63 wire frame buttons. So, double-click the H2 button and put in this ActionScript:

```
on (release) {
  tell Target ("/H2"){
   play ();
  }
    gotoandPlay ("wait");
    queenname1 = "H2";
}
```

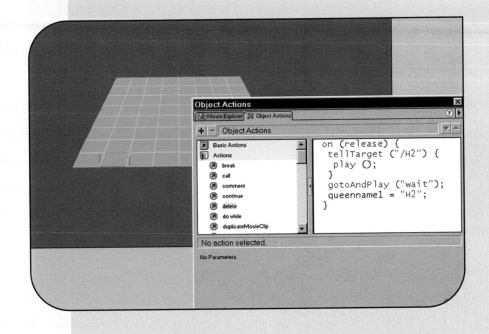

Note that you can now copy this code and paste it into all of the buttons, remembering to change the two H2's to what ever block you're on. Don't leave any out!

One last thing before this bad boy will work. The ActionScript layer.

Puzzle

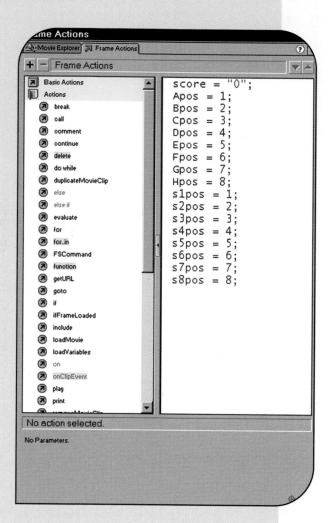

Create a new layer and name it ActionScript. Then in the first frame of that Layer add the following ActionScript:

```
score = "0";
Apos = 1;
Bpos = 2;
Cpos = 3;
Dpos = 4;
Epos = 5;
Fpos = 6;
Gpos = 7;
Hpos = 8;
s1pos = 1;
s2pos = 2;
s3pos = 3;
s4pos = 4;
s5pos = 5;
s6pos = 6;
s7pos = 7;
s8pos = 8;
```

What this code does is set the score to 0, (since the user hasn't started playing yet), and then sets the variables we'll need to make the check program work. We're going to use a Cartesian grid. What this means is that A1 will equal 1,1 and A4 will equal 1,4 and F3 will equal 6,3 and so on. It will make more sense in a minute. (Note that Flash won't let you start a variable name with a number so that's why those s's are there in front of the number positions.)

Add two blank frames at frame 3 and frame 4 on the ActionScript layer. Give frame 3 the label name **mainloop**. In frame 4 add this ActionScript:

gotoAndPlay ("mainloop");

So now once the movie starts it will get caught in a loop until the user clicks on one of the wireframe buttons.

Anyway, on frame 5 of the ActionScript layer add yet another blank keyframe, and give the new frame the label **wait**. This is where the movie jumps to when they click on one of the buttons.

After the code is done running we need the movie to jump back to the main loop, so in frame 24 of the ActionScript layer add a blank frame and this command:

gotoAndPlay ("mainloop");

If you're feeling adventurous, you could add this to mean that if they've scored less than eight, they go back to the main loop to continue playing, but if they have reached eight, they jump to a You Win screen:

```
if (/:score = 8) {
  gotoAndStop("youwin");
  } else }
  gotoAndPlay("mainloop");
```

Puzzle

Now for the logic of all this. In the ActionScript layer at frame 14, add a blank key frame.
Then add this ActionScript (I'll explain it below):

```
loopage = 1;
queennum = 1;
while (loopage<9) {
    if (eval ( "/A" add loopage add ":updown" ) == 1) {
        if ("A" add loopage ne queenname1) {
            queennum = queennum+1;
            set ("queenname" add queennum, "A" add loopage);
        }
    }
    loopage = (loopage)+1;
}
loopage = 1;
while (loopage<9) {
    if (eval ( "/B" add loopage add ":updown" ) == 1) {
        if ("B" add loopage ne queenname1) {
            queennum = queennum+1;
            set ("queenname" add queennum, "B" add loopage);
        }
    }
    loopage = loopage+1;
}
loopage = 1;
while (loopage<9) {
    if (eval ( "/C" add loopage add ":updown" ) == 1) {
        if ("C" add loopage ne queenname1) {
            queennum = queennum+1;
            set ("queenname" add queennum, "C" add loopage);
        }
    }
    loopage = loopage+1;
}
```

```
loopage = 1;
while (loopage<9) {
    if (eval ( "/D" add loopage add ":updown" ) == 1) {
        if ("D" add loopage ne queenname1) {
            queennum = queennum+1;
            set ("queenname" add queennum, "D" add loopage);
        }
    }
    loopage = loopage+1;
}
loopage = 1;
while (loopage<9) {
    if (eval ( "/E" add loopage add ":updown" ) == 1) {
        if ("E" add loopage ne queenname1) {
            queennum = queennum+1;
            set ("queenname" add queennum, "E" add loopage);
        }
    }
    loopage = loopage+1;
}
loopage = 1;
while (loopage<9) {
    if (eval ( "/F" add loopage add ":updown" ) == 1) {
        if ("F" add loopage ne queenname1) {
            queennum = queennum+1;
            set ("queenname" add queennum, "F" add loopage);
        }
    }
    loopage = loopage+1;
}
loopage = 1;
while (loopage<9) {
    if (eval ( "/G" add loopage add ":updown" ) == 1) {
        if ("G" add loopage ne queenname1) {
            queennum = queennum+1;
```

```
        set ("queenname" add queennum, "G" add loopage);
      }
    }
    }
    loopage = loopage+1;
}
loopage = 1;
while (loopage<9) {
    if (eval ( "/H" add loopage add ":updown" ) == 1) {
      if ("H" add loopage ne queenname1) {
          queennum = queennum+1;
          set ("queenname" add queennum, "H" add loopage);
        }
      }
    loopage = loopage+1;
}
```

What we did there was simply detect which queens are up. We're faking arrays in Flash by using variables with numbers at the ends of their names, so we can rotate through numbers and change variables. These are the first few lines of the code you just typed:

loopage = 1;

Prepares the loop.

queennum = 1;

Set queennum to 1 since the button the person just clicked sets queenname1 to the current queen and we don't want to overwrite it. This will make more sense in a minute:

while (loopage < 9) {

Loop until loopage (which is one now) is less than 9.

if (eval ("/A" add loopage add ":updown") == 1) {

Remember the variable in the queen's movie clips that sets the variable updown to 1 if the queen is up, and to 0 when it's down. This is checking that. "/A" add loopage add ":updown" when the loop first starts is equal to /A1:updown. This is the variable in the movie instance A1 called updown. Each of the movies has this variable set in it. As we move through this loop we check A2:updown, then A3:updown, and every time it's 1, which means the queen is up, the following commands happen:

if ("A" add loopage NE queenname1) {

Puzzle

```
    checkloop = checkloop-1;
}
```

Now let me explain what each piece of this code does:

```
if (queennum > 1) {
  holder1 = queenname1;
  holder2 = eval("queenname" add queennum);
  queenname1 = holder2;
  set ("queenname" add queennum, holder1);
}
```

This just reverses queenname1 and "queenname" add queennum, which is the last queen in the set. This illustrates nicely my point about not writing your code when you're drunk. It might seem a bit pointless, but the code below uses the last queen to start the checking and we want the queen that was just placed to stay, so we needed to reverse them. Oh well.

```
loopage = queennum;
```

We need to check all the queens except the one that was just placed down.

```
xname2 = substring (eval("queenname" add loopage), 2, 1 );
yname2 = substring (eval("queenname" add loopage), 1, 1 );
```

This sets xname2 to the NUMBER in the grid coordinate of the placed queen, and yname2 to the LETTER in the grid coordinate of the placed queen.

```
queenx = eval("s" add xname2 add "pos" );
queeny = eval( yname2 add "pos" );
```

This sets queenx and queeny to the number system we need to use for the Cartesian plane. Remember those variables that were set in the first frame of the movie? This gets the number values for the letters.

```
while (checkloop > 0) {
```

Loop through all the standing queens.

```
xname = substring (eval("queenname" add checkloop),
2, 1 );
yname = substring (eval("queenname" add checkloop),
1, 1 );
checkx = eval( "s" add xname add "pos");
checky = eval ( yname add "pos");
```

Get Cartesian coordinates of the queen currently being checked.

```
if (checkx == queenx) {
  // annnnnnnt
  tellTarget (eval("queenname" add checkloop)) {
    play ();
  }
```

If the queen being checked has the same x value of the placed queen then it is inline and being attacked. Tell Target that movie to play, which will lower that queen. (Note the comment, // annnnnnnt which is pronounced like the "incorrect" buzzer of a game show).

```
if (checky == queeny) {
// annnnnnnt
tellTarget (eval("queenname" add checkloop)) {
  play ();
 }
}
```

If the queen being checked has the same Y value of the placed queen then it is in line and being attacked. Annnnnnnt!

```
xdiff = queenx-checkx;
ydiff = queeny-checky;
xdiff = xdiff*xdiff;
ydiff = ydiff*ydiff;
if (xdiff == ydiff) {
// annnnnnnt
tellTarget (eval("queenname" add checkloop)) {
  play ();
 }
}
```

This is the code to check the diagonals. It's a bit of geometric math. Now, bear with me. Queens attacking along a diagonal are in a square. The code takes advantage of this. Look at the example. The x of the top queen is 3, the bottom one is 6. The code xdiff = queenx–checkx would set the xdiff to –3. (3 – 6 = -3). The y of the top queen is 3, the bottom 6. The code ydiff = queeny–checky would also produce a –3.

Then it squares them with the lines xdiff = xdiff*xdiff and ydiff = ydiff*ydiff so now, xdiff = 9 and ydiff = 9.

If xdiff = ydiff then ANNNNNNNT since we know it's on the diagonal.

Then the rest of the code just finished the loop until it checks every standing queen:

```
checkloop = checkloop-1;
}
```

That's really it. Some final touches: Make sure you have all frames of all layers going out to at least frame 24, so that the board and stuff doesn't disappear while you're checking the queens. Also, you should stick a blank key frame in the Wireframe layer at frame 5 (where the wait label is) so that people can't raise any queens until you've checked them and lowered the victim queens. Oh and don't forget to go back through the four queen movies and delete the placement layer, so that the queens are always standing.

Maybe you can model yourself a board, drop in the appropriate background and objectives. Maybe, make a pay-off animation for the people who solve the thing. You can do that on your own. That's the fun part.

Well, I hope you got something out of this. And as a final parting I'll leave you with one last puzzle: A2, B5, C7, D1, E3, F8, G6, H4 – there is another code like this one. Can you figure it out?

JOEL BAUMANN

"I only want a menu to be a menu when
I need a menu. I like to leave traces of my
existence in spaces that I leave. Words are only
words when you need to read them."

JOEL BAUMANN
www.tomato.co.uk

Wobble

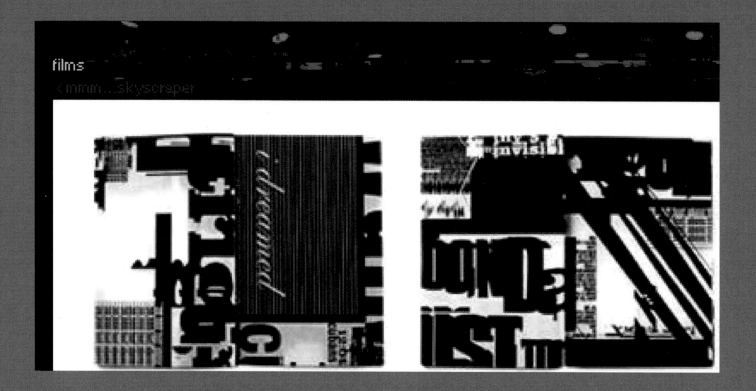

Tom, ant and I had been working together in the tomato building for one year, as part of Antirom, when we decided to set-up tomato interactive. It was a good idea and we haven't looked back since.

Our ideas and ways of working may differ, but we do have something in common: we're all interested in interactivity. We love the adventure of creating interaction between users and content, whether it be on the Web, on a CD-Rom, at standalone kiosks, or within interactive installations.

To cut to the chase: It is more important to understand the use and the functionality of the wobbler, the scroller, the wiggler and all the other effects or combinations of effects than to understand one single program. This might sound strange written in a book concentrating on Flash, but in my view it is a shorter step for a master of interactive design to become a master of Flash, than it would be for a master of Flash to understand interactive design in depth. This is why we see lots of Flash sites on the Internet that are well executed but few which are truly inspiring. So we do need to understand the tools of interactive design in depth, but to focus all our attention on learning only the details would be wrong. Good interactive design is independent of platform or protocol. Whether a wobbler is good or not is determined by where it exists and how it lives within an interactive project, not by whether it was made in Flash, Director, Java, C++, OpenGL, etc.

Joel Baumann

I use Macromedia Director for most of my work. This makes me feel that, since Director 7 I have been using Flash without knowing it, simply because all vector-based media in Director is handled by the Flash assets extra. Recently I have been integrating little animations made in Flash into Director movies and I've started to make Flash movies communicate with Director movies via scripts.

The wobbler came about through an odd sequence of events. It's even stranger to be writing about it in this particular book for the simple reason that my source of inspiration for it is writing in it too: Yugo Nakamura.

About a year ago, I received an e-mail from a dear friend of mine suggesting I have a look at www.yugop.com.

So I did. "Fascinating," I thought; "So you can make highly interactive and interesting sites in Flash after all!" I told my colleagues ant and Tom to have a look. Tom was particularly taken by the wobbling face of DaVinci's Mona Lisa. He suggested adapting this movement for a navigation system. We did. What we came up with was the navigation system that you find at www.tomato.co.uk.

Wobble

In this chapter I want to describe to you how we travelled from this inspirational beginning to that final effect.

It was of great importance for my journey that I took the right things with me along the way. You need to do that too. Make sure you bring with you a sound understanding of OOP, a bit of math and a good sense of logic along with you. They never seem to fail me. Oh, and make sure to leave all the "this is not for me, this is rocket science" thoughts at home. They just get in the way of that natural flow of thought.

Now, start by looking at the whole picture and its parts at the same time. In the first picture we see the static image and in the second we see the wobbled image. If we now think of the image as a set of smaller parts of an image, let's say nine pieces of an image laid out on a 3x3 grid, then we understand what is actually happening. You can see them here in equal proportion, but below you'll see the grid as it wobbles. So the grid shifts. AAAhhh, that's what's happening or, well, at least half of what is happening. This is what I call a *shifting matrix*. Now, when the matrix shifts, it doesn't go directly from equal distribution to the state of uneven distribution that you see in these two images; it wobbles a bit to get there.

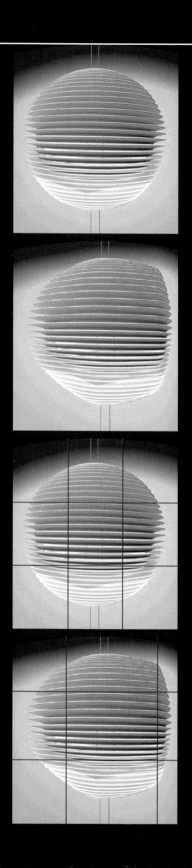

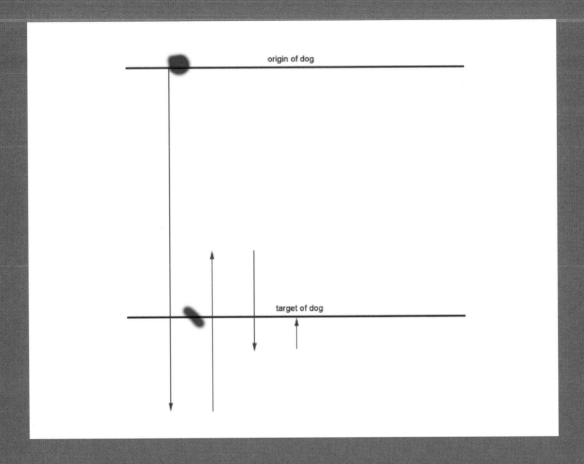

origin of dog

target of dog

To describe the wobble I will use a parable. Imagine a dog on a slippery floor and yourself with a stick in your hand. You throw the stick and it lands somewhere and stays there. The dog shoots off at top speed to get the stick. Being a dog he is guided by instinct, not by logic, so he doesn't slow down and slides past the stick by a good few feet. He spins around and shoots back towards the stick, again accelerating furiously. This time he travels a shorter distance and so has less time to pick up speed. This means that he overshoots by less, but he still overshoots. Around he goes again and this time he just about slips past the stick. All he needs to do is turn around and jump back one pace. He has reached his target. But, between his point of origin and his target, he has wobbled. I've tried to illustrate this dog to stick movement here. This is the second important hurdle of understanding on the way to the wobbler and I call it *inertia*.

As a matter of fact, once we understand this, we have a precise map of the way we need to go. Let's act on this map in our chosen environment. I chose Director, but I'm sure that you will be able to translate this to any other environment with a bit of work.

Wobble

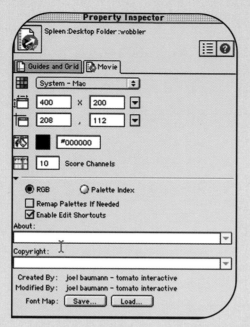

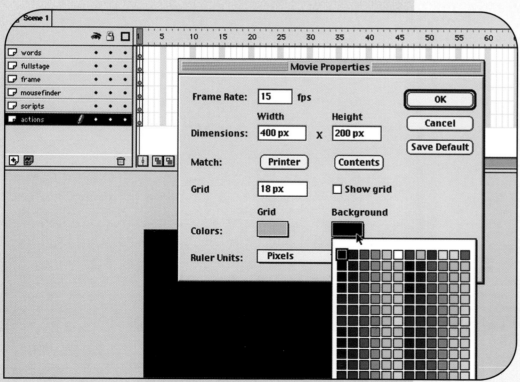

452

The Wobbler in Director

Director is a great animation package. You can lay images, video clips, sounds, etc. out in the timeline and trigger simple behaviours from all kinds of events. We're going to use it more like a coding environment and database than as an animation package, which shows how versatile Director actually is.

To set things up, open Director, open the Movie Properties window. Set the background colour to black, set the stage size to 400 x 200 and set the alignment to Centred. Save your movie.

Open the wobbler Score window and double-click frame 4 in the timeline of the script sprite. A script window should appear with the on exitframe/end exitframe handler set up for you to fill in. Between on exitframe and end exitframe type hinit. Now you're calling a handler hinit when your movie exits frame 4.

We still need to create the hinit handler. Close the Script window.

In the wobbler Score window double-click frame 5 in the timeline of the script sprite. Again a Script window will open with the on exitframe/end exitframe handler pre-set. This time, write two lines into it: hupdate and go the frame. Now you're calling a handler named hupdate. Again, we still need to create the hupdate handler.

You're also telling your playbackhead to go to this frame again. The movie now loops on this frame constantly, calling the hupdate handler in intervals of the speed you set the movie to playback at (providing your CPU is capable of executing the frame at that speed).

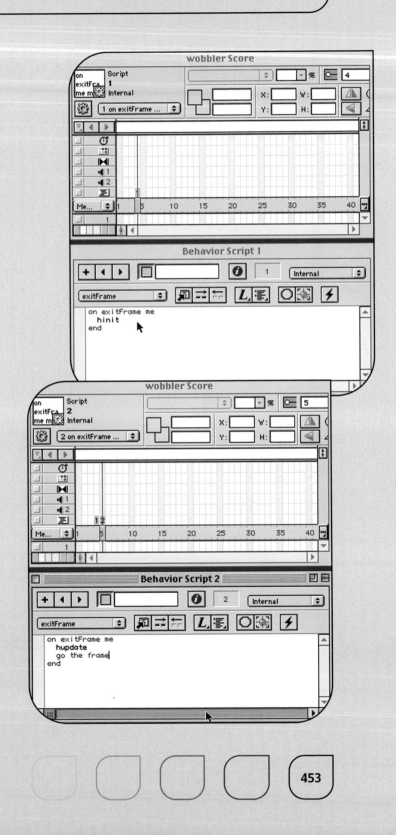

Wobble

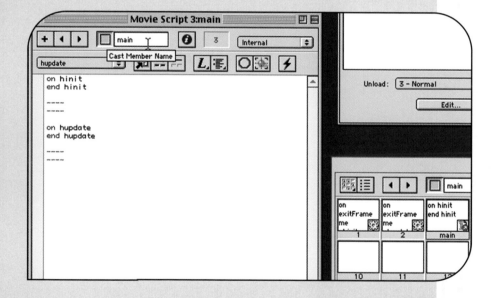

Open the Internal Cast window and have a look. You'll see the two script members that you created in the score earlier on. These members are behaviour scripts.

We now need to make a movie script cast member. (On the top left of the Cast window there is a button to switch the view style of the cast. Make sure that you're viewing the cast as icons, not as a list.) As it's empty at the moment, select member three and open the Script window. A new cast member appears in the Cast window and an empty script window opens. In the cast member name field, give it the name **main**.

Write this into the new script window:

on hinit
end hinit

This is the hinit handler that we were calling earlier. At the moment, it doesn't do much. Add a few minus signs as delimiters to keep your code tidy.

— —

Now add the hupdate handler:

on hupdate
end hupdate

Select empty member 4 in the Cast widow and open the Paint window. Call this member **placeholder**. Now select the pencil tool and make a one-pixel dot on the canvas. If you find that you can't be accurate enough with the pencil, draw a filled box and choose modify>transform bitmap>dimensions 1w 1h.

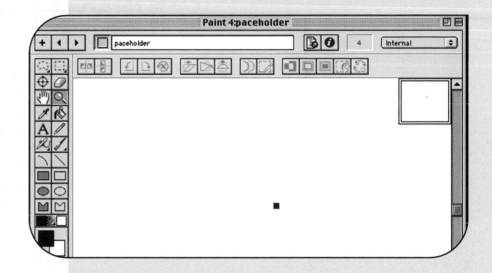

Drag the member placeholder from the Cast window to the Score window and into sprite 1, starting from frame 1. Change the vertical and horizontal position in the sprite Properties dialog box. Set the x position of sprite 1 by selecting it and writing −100 into the Reg Point Horizontal field at the top of the Score window. Do the same to the y position of sprite 1 by writing −100 into the Reg Point Vertical field.

Now copy the entire sprite 1 and paste it into sprite 2,3,4,etc., depending on the number of sprites you think you'll need for your movie. I think about ten will do for us.

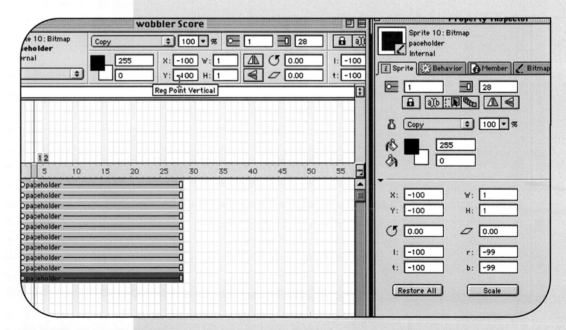

Wobble

Bring up the Cast window again. Select a cast member, leaving some space between it and placeholder. I've used member 21. Import the Flash movie that you're going to wobble. Here it's ToWobble.swf. If you're going to wobble more than one Flash movie, import them in sequence. member(21), member(22), member(23), etc.. For the moment, we're going to use the Flash movie as embedded media because it makes things a whole lot easier during authoring. We'll need to change it to linked media and give it an absolute path name later.

This is the basic set up that I go through for most of my Director movies.

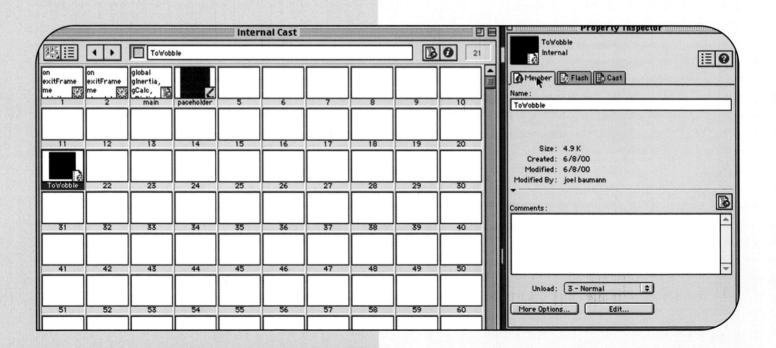

Now, let's get more specific.

The hinit handler is called first in the movie and it is called only once. Its purpose is to set up the variables and objects that we'll need in the movie. Here we go.

Local variables are containers that we need to hold values during an execution of a handler only and that can be disposed of after that execution. They don't need to be remembered for later use. A global variable is a container that holds values that need to be remembered for use in other handlers or other multiple executions of the same handler.

I find that a useful way to remember the difference is to think of phone numbers. You call 411 (directory enquiries) for the telephone number of a restaurant. They give you the number, which you only need to remember until you have successfully reserved your table. After this you won't need it again. That's your local variable. Your global variable is the directory enquiries, 411, number. You need to remember this permanently because you could want to use it again and again to find the number for a restaurant, a mechanic or a good Lingo coder.

We have to declare global variables. All objects are instances of a script. Since we need to address them, we'll birth them into variables. If we need the object to be remembered so that we can address it after the end of the handler it is birthed by, the object's container or variable will need to be global too. Proper naming of variables is important.

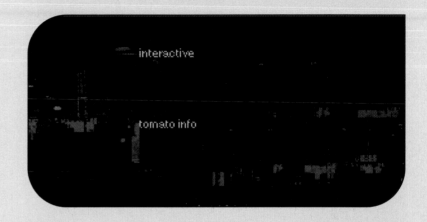

Wobble

We'll need four global variables: gInertia, gCalc, gPicList and gBeginSprite. Open the main movie script, called main member, and go to the beginning of the first line. At the moment, this line should be on hinit. Write:

global gInertia, gCalc, gPicList, gBeginSprite

Press Return a few times to get some space between this line and the hinit handler. You'll thank yourself for tidy code when scripts become very complex.

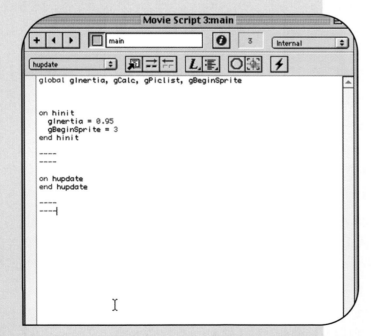

Let's initialise our movie. We'll need to give gInertia a value. I want that value to be a fraction of one, which means that when it is used as a multiplying factor, the original value diminishes. 0.95 sounds about right to me. Set the value in the hinit handler.

gInertia = 0.95

We'll now need to give gBeginSprite a value. This value represents the first sprite in the score that we'll fill with content and use in our movie. I usually leave a few sprites empty so that I can add content in the background at a later point if I need to. Let's initialise gBeginSprite at 3, leaving us two sprites that we can use in case of background emergency.

gBeginSprite = 3

We'll need to get some local variables going because we're about to calculate a bit of the set up routine on the fly. Setting up right is half the job, because you can get stuck later on in your program if your initial preparation doesn't allow for future necessities. Imagine what the variables are that determine the grid you will make. Asking questions helps. How high will the grid be? (lGridHeight). How wide will the grid be? (lGridWidth). How many rows will there be? (lRows). How many columns will there be? (lCols). How high will the rows be? (lRowHight). How wide will the columns be? (lColWidth). How much do I want the wobbled area to enlarge from its unwobbled stage to its target stage? (lHPressure, lVPressure). I also add some little calculation helpers, since it's often easier to do more complicated calculations in stages. After all, what are local variables for if not to aid my short-term memory? I usually need local variables to keep the stagewidth and the stageheight during initialisation. (lStageWidth, lStageHeight).

```
                                          Movie Script 3:main
+  ◄  ►   □ main

hinit          ▼   🗗 ⇄ ⇤   L ▤   O ✦   ⚡
global gInertia, gCalc, gPiclist, gBeginSprite


on hinit
    gPicList = []
    gInertia = 0.95
    gBeginSprite = 3

    lSpriteNum = gBeginSprite
    lMemberNum = 21


    lGridWidth = 400
    lGridHeight = 200
    lRows = 2
    lCols = 2

    lColWidth = lGridWidth/lCols
    lRowHeight = lGridHeight/lRows

    lHPressure =  100
    lVPressure = 50

    lStageWidth = the stageright - the stageleft
    lStageHeight = the stagebottom - the stagetop

    lHInit = lStageWidth/2 - lGridWidth/2
    lVInit = lStageHeight/2 - lGridHeight/2

end hinit

----
----

on hupdate
end hupdate

----
----
```

Wobble

I also need to calculate the topleft point of the grid to be made, as we are working with a Cartesian co-ordinate system and the topleft is therefore the starting point of my shifting matrix. (lHinit, lVInit). As we're going to repeat through a loop to create an object for each instance of a wobbly image, we'll need to use containers to keep track of which member to attribute to which sprite. This will become more obvious in a moment when we create the repeat loops. For the moment, we'll create the local variables to help count through a sequence of cast numbers and sprite numbers. (lSpriteNum and lMemberNum). Let's give all of these variables values before we get too confused.

We should start with lSpriteNum because we're going to start counting from gBeginSprite, remember?

lSpriteNum = gBeginSprite

It's good practice to keep the counters together, so next on the list is lMemberNum. The value that we give this variable corresponds to the number the first cast member that we'll attribute to a sprite. We imported ToWobble.swf into member 21, so:

lMemberNum = 21

Now we'll describe the grid we are going to use.

lGridWidth = 400
lGridHeight = 200
lRows = 2
lCols = 2

To get the width of each column, we have to divide the width of the grid by the number of columns we are going to have. We get the height of each row by dividing the total height of the grid by the number of rows.

lColWidth = lGridWidth/lCols
lRowHeight = lGridHeight/lRows

How much larger a wobbled cell of the grid gets is entirely up to us. I suggest a horizontal enlargement of 100 pixels and a vertical enlargement of 50. I keep the 2:1 ratio by choice, not by necessity.

lHPressure = 100
lVPressure = 50

To determine the stagewidth and the stageheight, we use a set of Lingo commands and a bit of easy logic:

lStageWidth = the stageright - the stageleft
lStageHeight = the stagebottom – the stagetop

I always want my shifting matrix to be centred on the stage. so I need to determine my topleft starting point from the centerpoints of both grid and stage. By subtracting half the grids width from the horizontal centerpoint of the stage, I should get the leftmost value of the grid. By further subtracting half of the grid from the vertical centerpoint of the stage, I can deduce the topmost point of the grid.

lHInit = lStageWidth/2 – lGridWidth/2
lVinit = lStageHeight/2 – lGridHeight/2

Before using gPicList as a list (the Director term for *array*), we need to declare it as such. For good practice, we should do this right at the top of our declaration of variables.

gPicList = []

Now we've described our grid well enough to make it, and it's time to get some help.

Joel Baumann

We're now at the point of declaring one of the major actors in this project that we will rely on for most of the calculations done here. For this reason, he has the name, gCalc. His container or address has been declared as a global variable already, so now we need to specify him. We'll need to address a script that acts like a manual, describing exactly how gCalc should be built, what he can do and how we get him to do it. We'll write this script later, but first, let's birth him.

```
Movie Script 3:main

main                                              i

hinit     ÷

global gInertia, gCalc, gPiclist, gBeginSprite


on hinit
  gPicList = []
  gInertia = 0.95
  gBeginSprite = 3

  lSpriteNum = gBeginSprite
  lMemberNum = 21


  lGridWidth = 400
  lGridHeight = 200
  lRows = 2
  lCols = 2

  lColWidth = lGridWidth/lCols
  lRowHeight = lGridHeight/lRows

  lHPressure =  100
  lVPressure = 50

  lStageWidth = the stageright - the stageleft
  lStageHeight = the stagebottom - the stagetop

  lHInit = lStageWidth/2 - lGridWidth/2
  lVInit = lStageHeight/2 - lGridHeight/2

  gCalc = new(script"Calc", lHInit, lVInit, lColWidth, lRowHeight, lRows, lCols, lHPressure, lVPressure)

  repeat with myCol = 1 to lCols
    repeat with myRow = 1 to lRows
      gCalc.mAddGridPos(myCol, myRow)
      add(gPicList, new (script"PicBox", lSpriteNum, lMemberNum, gInertia))
      lSpriteNum = lSpriteNum + 1
    end repeat
  end repeat

end hinit

----
----

on hupdate
end hupdate

----
----
```

GCalc's main task is to calculate the state of our grid at any moment during execution and to calculate changes to the grid when asked. As a starting point, we need to give gCalc an initial description of the grid, which is called **passing attributes**. In Director, we create an instance of a script by calling the new command on the parent script and passing all the needed attributes with it.

gCalc = new(script"Calc", lHInit, lVInit, lColWidth, lRowHeight, lRows, lCols, lHPressure, lVPressure)

Remember, we've not yet written the Calc parent script, so, right now, we're just preparing for it.

Wobble

Now it's time to explore one of the really powerful features of OOP. We need to make an instance of a script for each cell of the grid so that we can address each one individually and get it to perform changes to its content. All cells have the same kind of actions and properties. They just don't act in synchronicity; some get wider while others get thinner and so on. So, if we make one script that describes how a generic cell is made, what it can do and how to ask it to perform, we just need to birth multiple instances of it and ask them for different performance at different times (for instance one cell to be fat and all the others to be thin). So, we need to repeat through the columns and, inside this loop, repeat through the rows to birth an instance of a script for each cell. Again, we'll pass each instance its own bespoke set of attributes that we'll derive from the current positions in each loop and from our counters.

We'll also need to send gCalc a reference of each cell instance made, so that it knows in which order to birth the instances. Let's say I go through the rows, birthing each column for the current row. It would go something like this:

(row1, col1), (row1, col2), (row2, col1), (row2, col2).

We don't get the same result going through columns birthing the current row:

(row1, col1), (rwo2, col1), (row1, col2), (row2, col2).

gCalc needs to know the grid location for each sprite. As we sequentially increase the spritenum by one with our counter, we can mirror this sequence in a list in gCalc. So, we inform it of each instance and its row and column position.

The loops will look like this:

```
repeat with myCol = 1 to lCols
repeat with myRow = 1 to iRows
gCalc.mAddGridPos(myCol, myRow)
gPicList.add(new(script"PicBox"),lSpriteNum,
lMemberNum, gInertia)
lSpriteNum = lSpriteNum + 1
end repeat
end repeat
```

We'll need to include a method in gCalc that will take the two values we pass it and act on them accordingly. A method is similar to a handler, except that it's contained in an instance of a script. We are asking gCalc to mAddGridPos, for which we pass it two values. When we write the Calc parent script, we'll need to make a mAddGridPos method from which gCalc was birthed.

We add an instance of the parent script PicBox to the array gPicList and pass customised attributes along in the birthing process. As we did the Calc parent script, we still need to write the parent script PicBox. The local variable lSpriteNum is incremented each time we go around the second loop, while the second loop is called in each repetition of the first loop and the current position in both loops are passed through to the instance of the PicBox script. Therefore, each instance is birthed with its own bespoke set of attributes.

Note: If you want to pass each cell a different lMemberNum reference because you're using different castmembers for each cell, you'll need to increment the lMemberNum right there with the lSpriteNum.

We'll need to add a few things to the hinit handler further down the line, but this will become apparent when we're setting up the parent scripts. So far, our initialisation is finished; we have declared everything we need.

We're now going to build gCalc to be a helper who keeps track of the state of our grid and helps calculate. Select the empty cast member next to placeholder and open the Script window. Name the script Calc in the cast member name field and press the cast member properties button (the i button). In the Properties Inspector window, select **parent** in the drop-down menu labelled **type.**

When an instance of a parent script is birthed, the on new me handler is the first part of the script that is called. And all the attributes are passed to it. All the attributes that we want to remember must be stored in containers.

```
property pHPressure
property pVPressure
property pGridPos
property pHInit
property pVInit
property pColWidth
property pRowHeight
property pXWidthList
property pYHeightList
property pRows
property pCols
property pHPosList
property pVPosList

on new me, passHInit, passVInit, passColWidth, passRowHeight, passRows, passCols, passHPressure, passVPressure

  pHPressure = passHPressure
  pVPressure = passVPressure
  pGridPos = []
  pHInit = passHInit
  pVInit = passVInit
  pColWidth = passColWidth
  pRowHeight = passRowHeight
  pXWidthList = []
  pYHeightList = []
  pRows = passRows
  pCols = passCols
  pHPosList = []
  pVPosList = []


  repeat with x = 1 to pCols
    add(pXWidthList, pColWidth)
  end repeat

  repeat with y = 1 to pRows
    add(pYHeightList, pRowHeight)
  end repeat



  return me
end
```

Wobble

```
Parent Script 5:Calc
Calc
mAddit

on mAddGridPos me, passCol, passRow
  pGridPos.add(point(passCol, passRow))
end mAddGridPos

----
----

on mAddit me, passTarget
  localtarget = getat(pGridPos, passTarget)

  repeat with x = 1 to count(pXWidthList)
    temp = getat(pXWidthList, x)
    if x = getat(localtarget, 1) then
      temp = temp + pHPressure
    else
      temp = temp - (pHPressure/(count(pXWidthList)-1))
    end if
    setat (pXWidthList, x, temp)
  end repeat

  repeat with x = 1 to count(pYHeightList)
    temp = getat(pYHeightList, x)
    if x = getat(localtarget, 2) then
      temp = temp + pVPressure
    else
      temp = temp - (pVPressure/(count(pYHeightList)-1))
    end if
    setat (pYHeightList, x, temp)
  end repeat

  pHPosList = []
  localh = pHInit
  add(pHPosList, localh)
  repeat with x in pXWidthList
    localh = localh + x
    add(pHPosList, localh)
  end repeat

  pVPosList = []
  localv = pVInit
  add(pVPosList, localv)
  repeat with y in pYHeightList
    localv = localv + y
    add(pVPosList, localv)
  end repeat

end

----
----
```

```
on maddit me, passTarget
localtarget = getat(pGridPos, ptarget)

repeat with x = 1 to count(pXWidthList)
temp = getat(pXWidthList, x)
if x = getat(localtarget, 1) then
temp = temp + pHPressure
else
temp = temp - (pHPressure/(count(pXWidthList)-1))
end if
setat (pXWidthList, x, temp)
end repeat

repeat with x = 1 to count(pYHeightList)
temp = getat(pYHeightList, x)
if x = getat(localtarget, 2) then
temp = temp + pVPressure
else
temp = temp - (pVPressure/(count(pYHeightList)-1))
end if
setat (pYHeightList, x, temp)
end repeat

pHPosList = []
localh = pHInit
add(pHPosList,localh)
repeat with x in pXWidthList
localh = localh + x
add(pHPosList, localh)
end repeat

pVPosList = []
localv = pVInit
add(pVPosList,localv)
repeat with y in pYHeightList
localv = localv + y
add(pVPosList, localv)
end repeat
```

The obvious thing for us to have next is some kind of method to get this information out of these very useful lists and pass them to the right place. For this we we'll create the mQuad method. This method again passes an attribute pTarget that corresponds to a position in the pGridPos. Once we retrieve the value at that position in pGridPos, we know which cell is asking us for its corners. Remember how we filled pHPosList and pVPosList from the topleft? Use the value at pTarget position in list pGridPos as a lookup value. If, for example, the value in list pGridPos at position pTarget is point (1,2) we can deduce that the corner positions for that cell are in our lists pHPosList and pVPosList as follows:

Topleft = first value in list pHPosList because of the 1 and second value in list pVPosList because of the 2.

Topright = second value in list pHPosList because the next position along horizontally is at the second value in pHPosList. The vertical value is still the second value in list pVPosList.

Bottomright = the second value in pHPosList and the third value in pVPosList.

Bottomleft = the first value in pHPosList and the third value in pVPosList.

Wobble

Once they've been calculated, we'll return the values to the handler that triggered the method so that it can react accordingly.

By now, you should have all of this on code:

```
on mquad me, passTarget
localCell = getat(pGridPos, passTarget)
localh = getat(localCell,1)
localv = getat(localCell,2)
localone = point(getat(pHPosList, localh),getat(pVPosList, localv))
localtwo = point(getat(pHPosList, localh+1),getat(pVPosList, localv))
localthree = point(getat(pHPosList, localh+1),getat(pVPosList, localv+1))
localfour = point(getat(pHPosList, localh),getat(pVPosList, localv+1))
localquad = [localone, localtwo, localthree, localfour]
return localquad
end
```

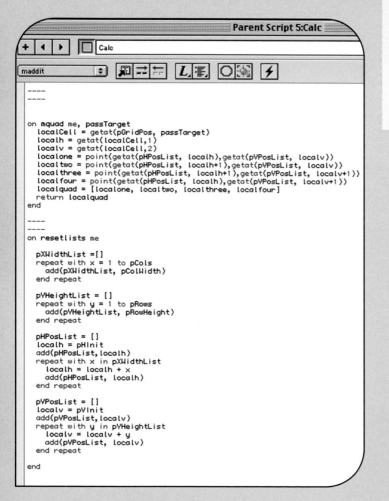

The last method that we need for Calc to work is an easy, but very useful one. It's called mResetLists because that is exactly what it does.

It's no more complicated than using bits of code from above to reset the two width and height lists and the two position lists:

```
on resetlists me

pXWidthList =[]
repeat with x = 1 to pCols
add(pXWidthList, pColWidth)
end repeat

pYHeightList = []
repeat with y = 1 to pRows
add(pYHeightList, pRowHeight)
end repeat

pHPosList = []
localh = pHInit
add(pHPosList,localh)
repeat with x in pXWidthList
localh = localh + x
add(pHPosList, localh)
end repeat

pVPosList = []
localv = pVInit
add(pVPosList,localv)
repeat with y in pYHeightList
localv = localv + y
add(pVPosList, localv)
end repeat

end
```

That's it for our helper.

Wobble

Now we'll now create the parent script PicBox that will lay down the workings of all the cells of our grid. Open the Cast window (and select the empty cast member next to Calc. Open the Script window and name the script PicBox in the cast member name field. Press the cast member properties button (button i) and select parent in the drop-down menu labelled type in the Properties Inspector window.

As we've done for Calc before, we now need to declare all properties that the instances of this script will need:

property pSprite, pCast, pQuad, pInertia, pTarget

The properties pSprite and pCast hold the sprite number and the cast number corresponding to the cell that an instance of parent script PicBox should describe. The property pQuad will be a list and we'll fill it with instances of the parent script Quad. We still have to write this parent script because I want to be able to ask each cell to update its own corners. It's easier to keep control of things in one script because the properties and functionality of each corner will be so similar. We know pInertia. It simply holds the same value as gInertia. I have set this property so that each cell could have a different value set for its wobble.

We need one more property to hold the four point values that make up the rectangle our cell inhabits on stage. Point values are Cartesian co-ordinates that Director uses to locate assets on the stage. Point(0,0) is the topleft of the stage.

In the birthing handler of parent script PicBox we set the values of the declared properties and the sprite of each cell. The sprites ink is set to background transparent (36) and it is informed of the member it is to hold.

```
on new me, passSprite, passMember, passInertia
pInertia = passInertia
pQuad = []
pSprite = passSprite
pCast = passMember

x = sprite(pSprite)
x.ink = 36
x.membernum = pCast
return me
end
```

The first method we need to write will fill pQuad. It will repeat through pTarget, filling a local variable x with the value of each position in pTarget. On each repeat, we'll birth a new instance of Quad and send the value of x to it as an attribute.

```
on mSetPquad me
repeat with x in pTarget
add(pQuad,new(script"Quad",x))
end repeat
end
```

You'll notice that pTarget has not yet been attributed a value. Remember that we still need to add some lines of code to the hinit handler. We'll come to that later.

The next method will repeat through the list attributed to the property pQuad. Each position of the pQuad list is filled with an instance of the parent script Quad. On every repeat, we'll call a function of the instance of Quad. A **function** is a method or handler that returns a value. We'll add that value to a local variable and use it to determine the rectangle that our cell will occupy on the stage.

```
on mset me
localquad =[]
localcount = 1
repeat with tempObj in pQuad
localquad.add(tempObj.mCalc(getat(ptarget,
  localcount),pInertia))
localcount = localcount + 1
end repeat
topleft = localquad[1]
bottomright = localquad[3]
sprite(psprite).rect                          =
rect(topleft[1],topleft[2],bottomright[1],
  bottomright[2])
end
```

Remember, we still need to create the Quad script and the mCalc function within it.

We still need a little method to set the pTarget property.

```
on mSeTtarget me, passTarget
pTarget = passTarget
end
```

Now the PicBox script is complete.

Let's finish with the parent scripts now. The last one we need is Quad. Open the Cast window and select the empty member next to member PicBox. Open the Script window and name the member Quad in the cast member name field. Press the Cast Properties button and select parent from the type drop-down menu in the Properties inspector window.

We are only passing one attribute to the birthing handler of the Quad script. This attribute is a list in itself, so we need two properties to hold its values pQH and pQV. We'll need two more properties to hold velocity values that will work on the horizontal and vertical movement of each corner of each cell. We'll call these properties pHVelocity and pVVelocity.

```
property pHVelocity , pVVelocity, pQH, pQV

on new me, passQuad
pQH = getat(passquad,1)
pQV = getat(passquad,2)
pHVelocity = 0
pVVelocity = 0
return me
end
```

Wobble

The only method within the Quad script is mCalc, which is actually a function because it returns a value. We've called the mCalc from the PicBox script, sending along an attribute and awaiting a returned value that we stored in a list. Now we're going to write the mCalc function appropriately, as a function that wobbles the corners rather than letting them go to their target point location immediately. The formula looks something like this:

Velocity = Velocity *Inertia
Velocity = Velocity - ((Position - Target)/variable)
Position = Position + Velocity

We'll need to add an if statement to make sure that our grid doesn't keep wobbling around one pixel while trying to divide ever smaller fractions.

```
on mCalc me, passTarget, passInertia
localpqh = getat(passTarget,1)
phvelocity = phvelocity * passInertia
phvelocity = phvelocity - ((pqh - getat(passTarget,1))/12.0)
pqh = pqh + phvelocity
if abs(localpqh - pqh) < 1 then
pqh = localpqh
end if

localpqv = getat(passTarget,2)
pvvelocity = pvvelocity * passInertia
pvvelocity = pvvelocity - ((pqv - getat(passTarget,2))/12.0)
pqv = pqv + pvvelocity
if abs(localpqv - pqv) < 1 then
pqv = localpqv
end if

return point(pqh,pqv)
end
```

As you can see, we're returning the point value awaited by the method calling the mCalc function.

The handlers that we'll create or update now will use all the functions, methods and handlers that we have created. The first thing we need is a handler to call the mSetTarget method in the instances of PicBox. This same handler should call resetlists in the instance of Calc so that we can use it every time we need to reset the targets.

```
on hSetReset
gCalc.resetlists()
repeat with lcount = 1 to gPicList.count
localquad = gCalc.mQuad(lcount)
localobject = gPicList[lcount]
localobject.mSetTarget(localquad)
end repeat
end
```

We need to call this handler straight away in the hinit handler. Add hSetReset() right under the last end repeat. We also need to call mSetPquads() in all instances of PicBox. Repeat through gPicList and call mSetPquad on each instance right after the hSetReset() call.

```
hSetReset()
repeat with x in gPicList
x.mSetPquad()
end repeat
```

The last new handler we need does the same thing as the setReset handler, with the exception of calling the mAddit rather than the resetlists method in the Calc script. This makes the grid wobble rather than reset to the unwobbled position.

```
on hsettargets  hitIm
passhit = (hitIm - gBeginSprite) +1
maddit gCalc, passhit
repeat with lcount = 1 to count(gPicList)
localquad = mquad(gCalc, lcount)
localobject = getat(gPicList, lcount)
msettarget localobject, localquad
end repeat
end
```

At last we can call the mset method in each instance of PicBox in the hupdate handler. This will keep setting and updating the positions of the corners of all cells. If one of the cells' target rectangle is enlarged, the whole grid will wobble.

```
on hupdate
repeat with runner in gPicList
mset(runner)
end repeat
end hupdate
```

If you run this movie now, the grid will be filled with the corresponding cast members. It won't wobble. That is because we still need one more ingredient.

We are missing a behaviour that will call the hsettargets when a mouseenter is detected, and the hSetreset handler when a mouseleave is detected. Open the Cast window and select the empty member next to member Quad. Open the Script window and name the member **roll action** in the cast member name field. Now press the cast member properties button and select **behaviour** in the drop-down menu labelled type in the Properties Inspector. Add the mouseenter and mouseleave handlers.

```
on mouseenter me
target = me.spritenum
hSetTarget(target)
end


——
——


on mouseleave me
hSetReset()
end
```

Now all we need to do is open the Score window and select all the sprites that are filled with placeholder. Make sure to select all frames in all of these sprites. From the Behaviour drop-down menu at the top left of the Score window select rollAction.

That's it. You might want to up the frame rate in the Control Panel window but the wobble should work.

Wobble

Once you're satisfied with the movie, open the Cast window, select member ToWobble and press the Cast Properties button in the Properties Inspector, select the Flash tab and press the More options button. Leave the Linked and Image options ticked. In the linf file field, enter the absolute path to the .swf file you want to load into the Wobbler. Save the movie and publish it. You can now upload it anywhere and it will search for the .swf file and load it and play, but none of the buttons in your .swf file will be able to load new HTML files into frames.

Flash will have to tell Director which files it would like to open and which is the target window. Director will then load the page with a Lingo command. You'll need to add a handler to your main movie script. This handler will be triggered by the .swf file.

```
on flashURL me, textfromflash
localURL = "http://www.myWebAddress.com/directory
/directory/"
localtarget = "_target"
localpage =  localURL & textfromflash & ".html"
gotoNetPage localpage,localtarget
end
```

Fill in the placeholder values in localURL and localtarget. Now all you need to do is to call the following in your Flash movie netURL field :

event: FlashURL "nameOfPage"

Leave the target field blank. That's it, now the Flash calls will load the pages that you want into the target windows.

Setting up Flash

Open up Flash and save your project as ToWobble.fla. Open the Movie Properties window and set the movie frame rate to 15, its width to 400, its height to 200 and its background to black.

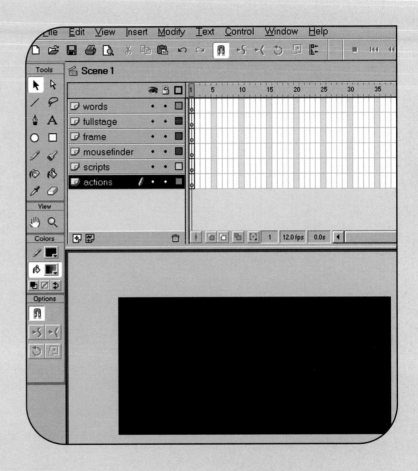

Because, in Flash, we can only control named instances via ActionScript, we'll be using movie clips at the heart of our OOP structure.

The first step is to make six layers in the main timeline. Name your layers from top to bottom as follows:

> **words**,
> **fullstage**,
> **frame**,
> **mousefinder**,
> **scripts**,
> **actions**.

Wobble

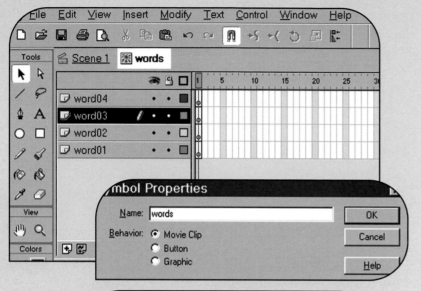

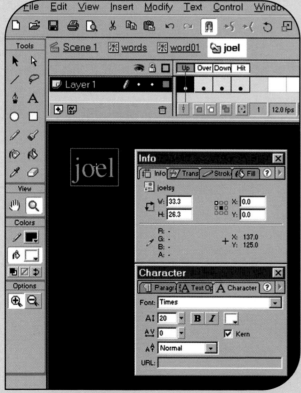

Then make five new movie clip symbols, calling them **words**, **frameMC**, **fullstage**, **mousefinder** and **scripts**.

Go into the Library and open the movie clip symbol, words. Make four layers on the timeline, calling them **word01**, **word02**, **word03** and **word04**.

Add a blank movie clip to each of the layers and give them instance names word01, word02, word03, word04, respectively. Using the Info Panel, place them all at x=0, y=0.

Double-click on the word symbol to edit it. choose the text tool and set the font to Times, 20 point, color white. Type JOEL in the center of the screen. Now select the text again and in the InfoPanel enter 0 for x and 0 for y and click Apply. Convert the text, JOEL, to a button symbol and give it the name **joelB**.

Repeat these steps to create button symbols within the other movie clip symbols, as listed here:

Movie Clip	Text
word02	TOM
word03	ANT
word04	LIZZIE

Double-click the frameMC symbol to edit it and draw a rectangle on the stage, with line color light gray, line thickness 1.0 and no fill color. Don't worry about the dimensions or placement of the rectangle; we'll set them with set values. Select the whole rectangle. In the Info Panel, set both x and y to 0, enter 399 into the w field and 199 into the h field (the dimensions of the stage -1). Keep the rectangle selected and convert it to a graphic symbol. Call it **framesy**.

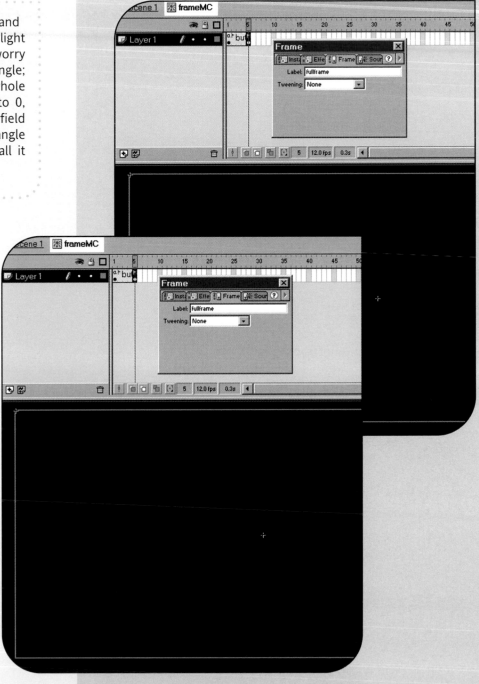

Add a new keyframe to frame 5. Select frame 1 again and, in the Effect Panel, set Alpha to 0% to make it invisible. With frame 1 still selected, use the Frame and Frame Actions Panels to label the frame **buttonframe** and add a Stop action. Now double-click frame 5 and, using the Frame Panel, label it **fullframe**. We'll be using the labels in our scripts to send the playhead of the movie clip symbol back and forth between the two frames.

Wobble

We need to make a transparent button, called **fullstageB**. A transparent button is one which only has a Hit state. The Hit state needs to be the same size as the stage. Set this via the Info Panel: x = 0, y =0, w = 400, h = 200.

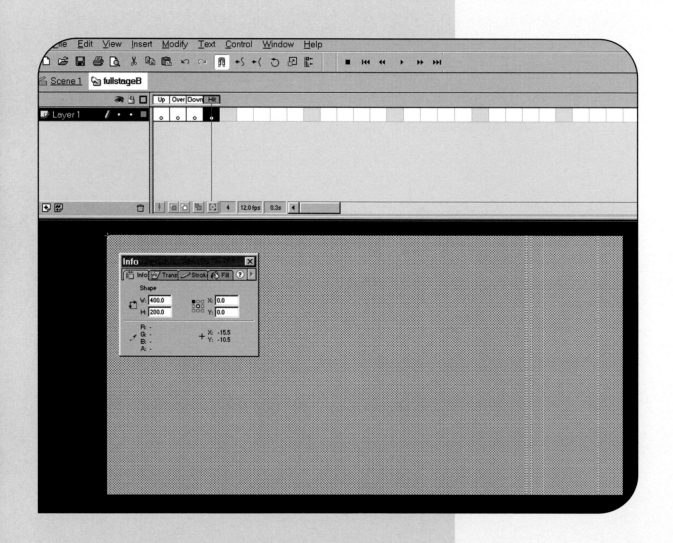

We're now ready to put these bits together.

Now that we have set up our environment and created the main actors in our piece, we'll write the code that brings the whole thing to life. All buttons need two states, signaling a roll on or a roll off state. The first stage is to make the text in the buttons into graphic symbols themselves. We are doing this so that we can dim or brighten the button text via instance effects to give visual feedback to the user.

Double-click the JOEL button symbol to open the button's timeline window. Select the text, JOEL, and convert it to a graphic symbol, named **joelsy.** Fill each frame with a keyframe so that the Up, Over, Down and Hit frames are all filled with an instance of the joelsy symbol.

Select the up frame and, in the Effect Panel, select Alpha and set it to 60%.

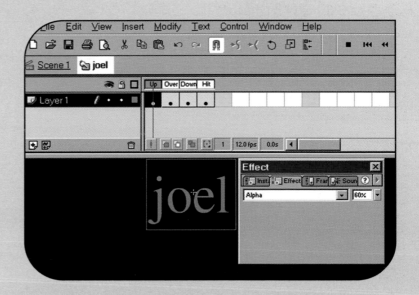

Wobble

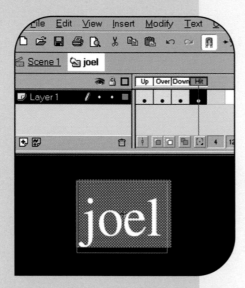

Add a filled rectangle around the word, as shown.

Without this rectangle, the button would only work when the cursor was actually in the text areas.

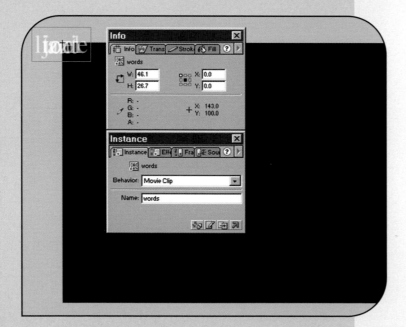

Go back to scene one of our movie and select frame 1 of the layer, words. Drag and drop the movie clip symbol, words, onto the stage and position it at 0,0 using the Info Panel. In the Instance Panel, name this instance **words**

Do the same for the fullstage layer and the fullstage movie clip symbol. Again, remember to name the instance something that you will remember. I use the layer name, in this case, **fullstage**. Repeat this for the layer, frame, and the movie clip symbol, frameMC, calling the instance, **frame**. For the layer, mousefinder, and the mousefinder movie clip symbol, call the instance **mousefinder**. Follow this right through until you've created a scripts instance of the scripts movie clip symbol on the layer... you know which one.

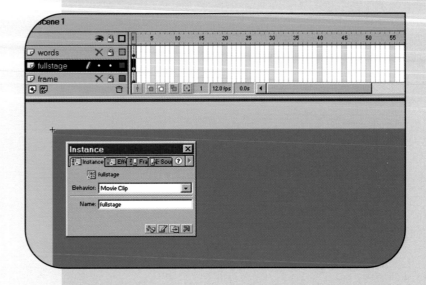

Now all we need to do is to go to frame 5 in scene one and to make a second keyframe in each layer.

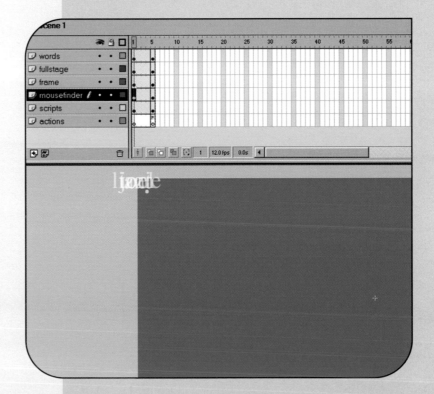

Wobble

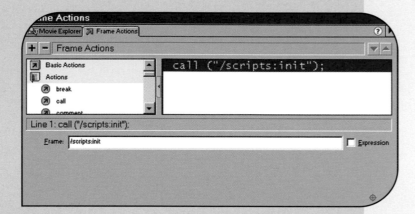

Adding that Bit of Code

Click frame 1 of layer, actions, and label it **init**. Now open the Frame Actions window and chose **call** from the + menu. Add "/scripts:init", to the Frame window. This means that we're calling a script in a movie frame labeled **init** in the timeline of an instance named **scripts**.

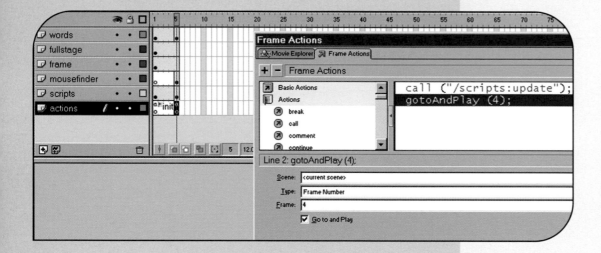

Now click frame 5 of the layer, actions, and using the Frame Panel, label it **update**. As we did with frame 1, we'll now add an action to this frame. In the Frame Actions window and choose call from the + menu (it's the second one down in Actions). On the right side, add "/scripts:update".

But that's not all. Chose Go to from the + menu and make sure that FrameNumber is selected from the Type pull-down menu. Enter 4 as the number. Don't forget to tick the Go to and play box at the bottom. We've now created a loop in which a script in an action of frame, update, in an instance called scripts is executed each time around. The loop makes the playback head jump back to frame 4 and, because we chose Go to and play, comes right back here to frame 5.

Now we need to make those scripts. Double-click the scripts movie clip symbol in the Library. There is one layer with one frame on the timeline. Click that frame and, in the Frame Actions window, add a Stop action.

Now go to frame 5 and add a keyframe. Give it a label, **init**. Go on to frame 15, add a keyframe and label it **update**. Go to frame 25, add a keyframe and label it **setVars**.

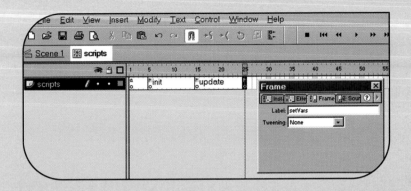

Select frame, init, and in the Frame Actions window add a Set Variable action. Call the variable **onstage** on the right-hand side. Make sure that Expression is checked and write 0 into the value field.

Next add a Call action and write /scripts:setVars into the frame field on the right

Finally chose startDrag action and write /mousefinder into the target field. Lock mouse to center should be checked.

What have we done here? We've set a variable to 0. This variable will determine whether the highlight we created in the frame layer will be on or off. We've called a script in the actions of frame setVars in the instance, script. This will set up a load of our variables, as the label of the frame indicates.

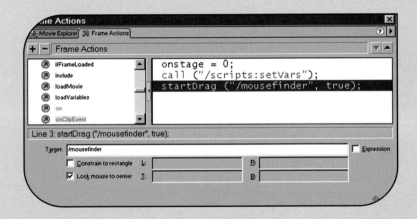

Wobble

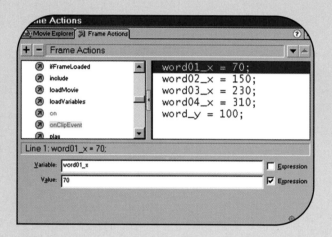

Click frame 25 (labeled setVars) on the timeline of movie clip symbol, scripts. Chose Set Variable from the Frame Actions window. On the right-hand side, call the variable word01_x, make sure that Expression is selected and set the value to 70. Repeat these steps for four more variables and values. Set variable word02_x equal to 150, variable word03_x equal to 230, variable word04_x equal to 310 and word_y = 100.

Now we have to check for cursor position and react to it. It is possible to create an array in Flash 5, but since we're animating only four words I think that it's best to repeat my code.

Click frame 15 on the timeline of movie clip symbol, scripts, and in the Frame Actions window chose Set variable. Name the variable mouseh in the Variable field..

Next, place the cursor in the Value field and click inside it as if to enter text. Select the action getProperty (it's in the Functions list).

The getProperty expression appears with two attributes that need to be filled in. Replace the word target with "/mousefinder", leaving in the quotation marks. Replace the word property with _x, without the quotations. (You could have also selected the property, _x, from Properties in the Actions window.

By capturing the x-position of the mousefinder instance, we capture the x-position of the cursor, because, as you might remember, we told the mousefinder instance to be dragged around by the cursor. We want to keep our variable, mouseh, in a range, so the words don't leave the stage.

We will now set our limits via an IF-else construct.

Enter the code:

```
if (mouseh < 20) {
   mouseh = 20;
} else if (mouseh > 380) {
mouseh = 380;
}
```

Frame Actions window:

```
mouseh = getProperty("/mousefinder", _x);
```

No action selected.

No Parameters.

Frame Actions window:

```
mouseh = getProperty("/mousefinder", _x);
word_y = 100;
if (mouseh<20) {
   mouseh = 20;
} else if (mouseh>380) {
   mouseh = 380;
}
```

Lines 3 - 7 selected.

No Parameters.

Wobble

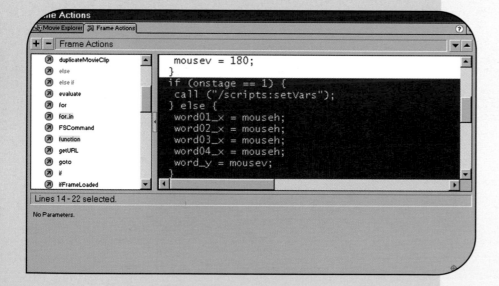

```
mouseh = getProperty("/mousefinder", _x);
word_y = 100;
if (mouseh<20) {
  mouseh = 20;
} else if (mouseh>380) {
  mouseh = 380;
}
mousev = getProperty("/mousefinder", _y);
if (mousev<20) {
  mousev = 20;
} else if (mousev>180) {
  mousev = 180;
```

Lines 8 - 13 selected.

No Parameters.

```
  mousev = 180;
}
if (onstage == 1) {
call ("/scripts:setVars");
} else {
word01_x = mouseh;
word02_x = mouseh;
word03_x = mouseh;
word04_x = mouseh;
word_y = mousev;
}
```

Lines 14 - 22 selected.

No Parameters.

We will need to do the same check for the mouse y position.

```
mousev - getProperty("/mousefinder" , _y);
  if (mousev<20) {
   mousev = 20;
} else if (mousev>180) {
   mousev = 180;
}
```

Now we'll check whether the cursor is on the stage. We could do this with a tedious calculation from the variables that we just set up, but it's much quicker to use another variable set by a button. We have already encountered this variable. It is called onstage

The code looks like this:

```
if (onstage == 1) {
call ("/scripts:setVars");
} else {
word01_x = mouseh;
word02_x = mouseh;
word03_x = mouseh;
word04_x = mouseh;
word_y = mousev'
}
```

We need to create a variable that represents the difference between the word's actual position and the variables holding its target position. Then we just need to animate the word moving from the first position to the second.

The difference (disH,disV) is calculated by the code below. (I also divided it by three to create a smooth movement.)

This code is repeated for each of the four words:

```
disH = (getProperty("/words/word01",__x)–word01_x)/3;
setProperty ("/words/word01", _x, getProperty("/words/word01", _x)-disH);
disV = (getProperty("/words/word01", _y)-word_y)/3;
setProperty ("/words/word01", _y, getProperty("/words/word01", _y)-disV);
```

You can figure out the rest.

```
 word04_x = mouseh;
 word_y = mousev;
}
disH  = (getProperty("/words/word01", _x)-word01_x)/3;
setProperty ("/words/word01", _x, getProperty("/words/word01", _x)-dish);
disV = (getProperty("/words/word01", _y)-word_y)/3;
setProperty ("/words/word01", _y, getProperty("/words/word01", _y)-disV);
disH  = (getProperty("/words/word02", _x)-word02_x)/3;
setProperty ("/words/word02", _x, getProperty("/words/word02", _x)-disH);
disV = (getProperty("/words/word02", _y)-word_y)/3;
setProperty ("/words/word02", _y, getProperty("/words/word02", _y)-disV);
disH  = (getProperty("/words/word03", _x)-word03_x)/3;
setProperty ("/words/word03", _x, getProperty("/words/word03", _x)-dish);
disV = (getProperty("/words/word03", _y)-word_y)/3;
setProperty ("/words/word03", _y, getProperty("/words/word03", _y)-disV);
disH  = (getProperty("/words/word04", _x)-word04_x)/3;
setProperty ("/words/word04", _x, getProperty("/words/word04", _x)-dish);
disV = (getProperty("/words/word04", _y)-word_y)/3;
setProperty ("/words/word04", _y, getProperty("/words/word04", _y)-disV);
```

"Boundaries don't hold us, don't let them hold you... The only boundary is your imagination."

YASUTO SUGA
www.rayoflight.com

Rays

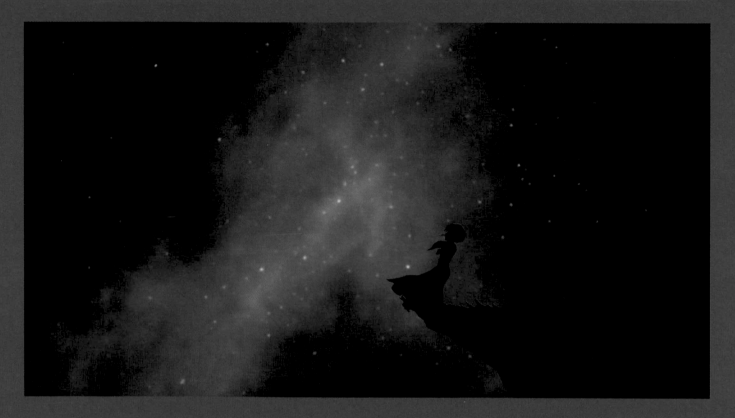

In the summer of 1998 I began Ray Of Light Productions (rayoflight.net), as a creative exercise using Flash on the Internet. My intention was then, as it is now, to create *experiences* on the web through animation, graphics and sound. At that time Flash and Flash web sites were still in their early stages of development, and much of the work being produced was considered revolutionary. There was no such thing as ActionScript, and most Flash effects were put together using clever tricks. Because I learnt Flash by battling through tutorials and online help, I worked completely oblivious to any best practices or particular authorial preferences; I just worked things out my own way. Many of the effects I put together on Ray of Light Productions were effects traditionally associated with the more widely accepted mediums like television and cinema.

My aim is to realize imagination and thought through the Flash medium, to tell viewers *the only boundary is your imagination*. Ray of Light Productions wasn't intended to be a web site and nothing but a web site, but to be an experience, an emotion, a feeling. I was trying to use motion and sound together to create something more substantial as a whole than as the individual visuals or moving components. I derived the aesthetic feel from the themes of Victorian England and H.G. Wells feel that I am very fond of. The sky, the stars, and the old clock, are all visuals that I enjoyed as much as a child as I do now. Starry night skies let your imagination run riot.

There are many influences on my work. I've always been fascinated by the things most people find simple and beautiful: nature, clouds, movement, cloth, the human figure. I try to work towards those moments in life when you feel both tranquil, peaceful, and at the same time, very much alive. The hand of God touches many things, and I think it can touch chords in us through our sensory experiences. The visual imagery that surrounds us is so vivid that it can become overwhelming, so it is sometimes through the other senses that we get these experiences, particu;larly sound and music If, when you're listening to a wonderful song, you close your eyes, you can sometimes feel yourself in a different place altogether. You forget that you're in the office, or in a traffic jam, and you find yourself somewhere in your subconscious, experiencing a different state of reality. That's the feeling I am trying to convey through Ray of Light: a sort of visual music.

I began work, not with a storyboard or even a visualization of what the page would look like, but by turning on my stereo and listening to music. The foundation and introduction of the site was built on Sarah McLachlan's *Fear* from the *Fumbling Towards Ecstacy* album; it is just one of the most beautiful songs I've heard. I just closed my eyes, and the imagery that popped into my head was what I began to try and create. Although the main part of the site is based on Madonna's *Power of Goodbye*, there is, in fact, no connection between this influence and the title of the album you can find it on, *Ray of Light*. It's just one of those weird coincidences. I thought of the name of the site before the album was released. That they both emerged at the same time certainly generated some confusion, but the site has officially nothing to do with Madonna. The *Power of Goodbye* is another extraordinary song, and the first fifteen seconds is stunning. I went through the same process and began constructing imagery around the song. Other music that I would love to create visuals around includes the British DJ Sasha's *Xpander*, German DJ Paul Van Dyk's *For an Angel*, Enya's work and Vivaldi's *Four Seasons*. Many of these have few words if any at all, which I feel is important too, because words can get in the way of your visualizations.

Rays

There a few artists who have already accomplished what I am trying to do, my favorite being Japanese animator Hayao Miyazaki, referred to as the Japanese Walt Disney. His works include *Nausicaa of the Valley of the Wind*, *Princess Mononoke*, *Laputa: The Castle in the Sky* and many more. Each of his movies has moments that bring you into new worlds of his own imagination, both visually and emotionally. One of the great features of his work is his portrayal of flight, beautiful and serene, and straight from a child's imagination. To fully understand his work you would have to watch some of his movies, but I hope that you will get a glimpse of what I am talking about on the Ray of Light web site. Miyazaki is truly inspirational, not only as an artist, but also as a human being.

Although the ethos behind my work is simple enough, there are, of course, implementation limitations in every medium. The first part of the site I built was the intro, which was an exercise not only in creativity but also in Flash. Building itshowed me the restrictions as well as the capabilities of Flash. I hope that the two techniques I'm going to introduce and explain here will help you in your Flash development

Yasuto Suga

The first of these is the Ray of Light effect. As the name implies, the site uses light effects extensively. In college, as a Fine Arts student, I studied the way light moves, reacts, looks, touches surfaces, and activates the things it touches. So in a sense, I was trying to recreate in Flash what I knew to be true in life. One of the great things about a creative medium is that it does allow you the freedom to exaggerate.

The second effect, or rather *feel*, that I'm going to talk about here is the one I get asked about the most, the animation of the girl, Anne. Although the explanation of this animation is extremely simple, the effect can be quite tough to execute. I painstakingly built Anne's dress frame by frame, using twenty-four hand drawn animations. I'll tell you how to put it together, but it's the tough step-by-step drawing work that really creates that effect, not any special Flash effects. Flash has four forms of animation: motion tween, shape

tween, ActionScript and frame by frame, and whether you find ActionScript or frame-by-frame animation simpler is very much a question of your own areas of expertise

Flash movies should be created as simply as possible, not only because it makes little sense to work hard for the sake of working hard, but, more importantly, because it makes changing them simpler. Although the simplest option for creating Anne's dress might at first appear to be to use a motion or shape tween, I think this approach would have been harder to make effective in the long run. Frame-by-frame animation in Flash isn't used widely, even less so recently, probably because it takes quite a bit of practice and an awful lot of patience. Traditional animation is, though, based entirely on frame-by-frame cells, and Flash allows you to use that approach on the same scale.

Rays

The Ray of Light Effect

The Ray of Light effect is created by tweening each letter individually. I'd recommend that you try it out with a smaller group of letters first, ideally between four and eight letters without spaces, as spaces can be tricky to work around. I'm going to use **lightray** as my example text.

The first step in any design process is to visualize what you want to create. Your job will be much easier if you visualize this as a real-life effect before you begin working in Flash, so visualize a light shining through a surface. The surface has some letters cut out of it and the light rotates from the viewer's left to her right, finally fading back into complete darkness.

Once you're ready, use the text tool to type your word. I used 18-pt Arial and put two spaces in between each letter. You'll find that extra spaces help to distinguish each light from the other later on.

Align the text to the center of the stage and then break it apart into fills. The letters are now ready to be turned into individual lights.

Insert each letter into its own layer. You need each letter on its own layer because Flash only lets you tween one object in a layer.

Each letter animation in fact involves two items: the letter itself and its light version, so you need to copy each layer you've just created and recreate it in a blank layer, remembering to rename it appropriately. So, for example, I used the names **Letter L**, and **Light L** for the two layers that, at the moment, contain the same thing.

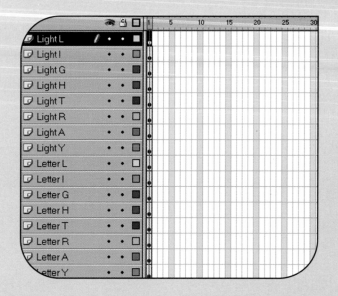

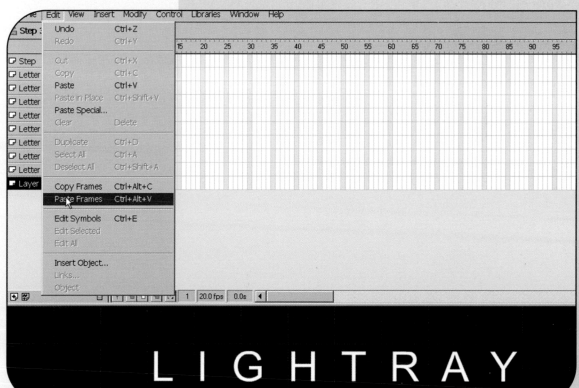

LIGHTRAY

Rays

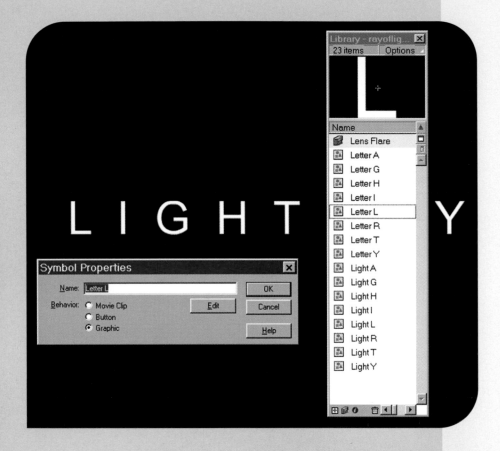

So now your layers contain the simple fill objects that you created by breaking apart a text object ready to be edited. Turn each object into a graphic symbol and give it the name of the layer that it is on. (A quick way to select all the information contained on a layer, and only that information, is to highlight the layer in the timeline while it is unlocked).

Your timeline and work area are now ready for animation. Open your library and make sure that you have a Letter and a Light symbol for each letter. Using the word *lightray*, I now have sixteen symbols in my Library.

This next step is the hardest part of the process. You need to draw the lights for each of the letters. You can do this by editing the Light symbols that you created for each letter. The best way to edit these is to use the Edit in Place command, by right-clicking on the object.

This will allow you to see the letter's place on the main stage while you edit the symbol version of the object. Select the Line tool and create a line extending from the top right of the letter you are editing out about 200 pixels to the left. (The red lines on these images indicate how I extended the lights from the letters.)

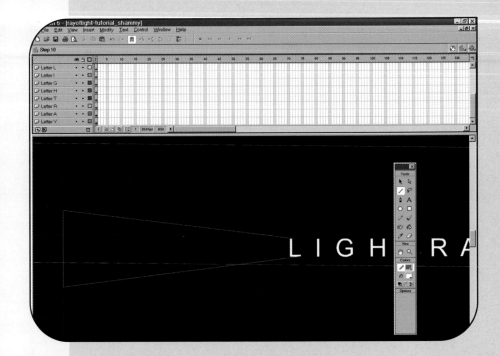

Draw a line from the bottom right edge of the letter to a point below the end of the first line. Next join the two lines with a vertical line. What you are creating is the outline of the light coming from the letter.

As letters from the left approach the center point, the length that the light stretches outward will decrease until it reaches the center. The amount that each light decreases in length is really your call, but you're likely to find the grid a very useful tool at this point.

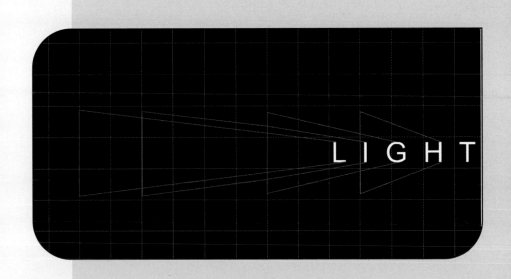

Rays

The center point is where the light shining through the text would be shining directly at you. You can determine this point, anywhere within the collection of letters that you are using.

LIGHTRAY

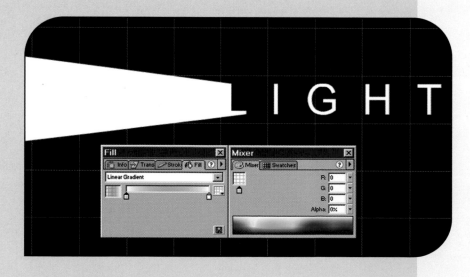

This center light effect is a different effect, and we'll cover this once we've dealt with the rest of the letters. The light shining through the letters past the center then moves to the right instead of to the left, (remember what it might look like in the real world). The example image I have created should help demonstrate what I mean.

The next step is to fill the outlines you have created with a gradient. Again, the Edit in Place action should give you the most control while you're opening and editing the symbols on the main stage. Begin with the leftmost light and edit it. Select the Fill tool and open up the palettes window. Go to the gradients palette and make a new gradient that begins with 100% opacity and ends with 0% opacity (I used white, but it's up to you).

Use this gradient to fill the space inbetween the lines of the shape you have created. The gradients should be at their whitest inside the letter, moving to 0% transparency at the outside. If the gradient is going in the wrong direction, you'll need to use the fill modifier tool to either rotate, scale or move it.

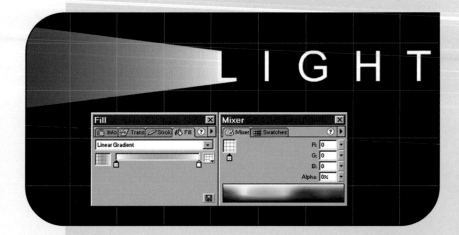

When you've finished creating your light symbols, erase the lines you used as guides, and you should have something similar to the example here. The shape and exact gradients you used for your text will probably be a bit different, but the overall sense should be the same.

Rays

The last step in this process is to edit the center point of the lights. Because of the motion of the tween, the center of the symbol should be more to the edge that the light is going away from. So for the first letter L, the center point must be moved all the way to the right of the symbol.

This will cause less distortion in the visible parts of the letter. This may seem unnecessary, but if you view this effect without editing the symbols, you will see what I'm talking about. For now, through, trust me and move the center of every symbol to the inside edge of the letters using the Modify>Transform>Edit Symbol command. Then drag the point to the inside edge, or just inside it.

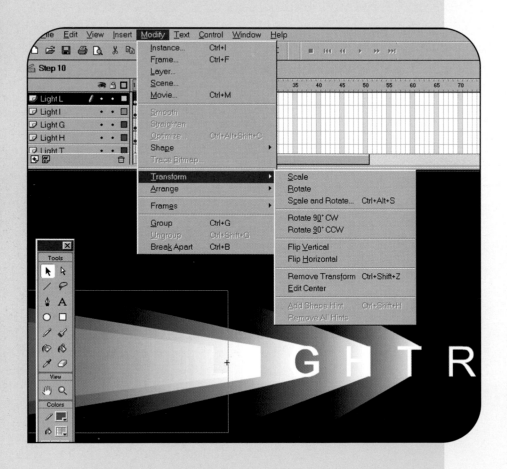

Now for the final step. The lights symbols are tweened individually, and timed so they begin with the first light on the left and travel to the final light on the right. Let's start with the leftmost letter. Add a keyframe nine frames after the first, and another one twelve frames on. Go back to first light keyframe and stretch the light out to the left, changing the opacity to 0%. At the third keyframe shrink the light in to the right, and change the opacity back to 0%.

There are no set percentages for how much the light should shrink in or stretch out Just go by feel. I generally stretch the light out twice as much as I shrink it in. Go through each of the lights using the same number keyframes, but decreasing the amount of stretching and shrinking as the lights reach the center point. In general, the longer the light, the more you should alter its size, and the shorter it is the subtler the change should be. If the light is tiny, it's better not to alter its size too much.

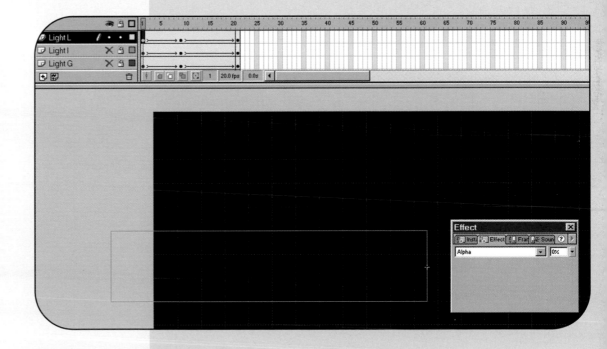

Rays

Now we can add in the motion tween between the keyframes. I used a +75 motion tween between the first and middle keyframe, and a –75 motion tween between the middle and last keyframes.

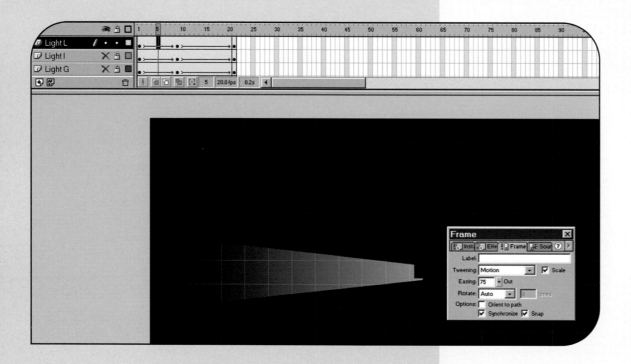

Now all the lights are animated you can move them to their respective letters on the timeline, so that they work from left to right. For this animation I left five frames between the beginnning of the first one tween and the beginning of the next. So in my example the Light L symbol begins to tween on frame 1, the next light, Light I, begins to tween on frame 6, the next on frame 11, and so on.

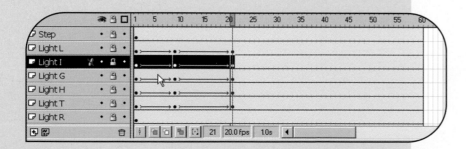

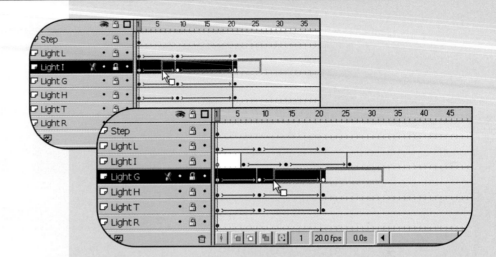

The second part to the letter animations is to leave behind the letters that the light has passed through. So once Light L is done tweening, the letter L should remain so that the viewer can read the text at the end. All you need to do is drag the letter keyframes you created earlier over to the point on the timeline that corresponds to the light's center keyframe.

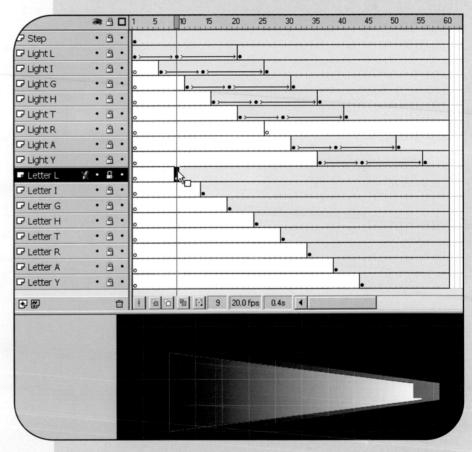

So, as the Light L symbol reaches its central keyframe (100% opacity, no scaling) at frame 9, I would insert the keyframe for Letter L at frame 9. Now as the light fades away, the letter that was showing through remains behind.

Rays

The final part of the animation concerns the center point of the light. In this instance the letter R was not animated, as it was the point at which the light shone directly at the viewer. For this effect, I used a lens flare that I had created in another piece of work, and adapted it for this effect. You can find the lens flare in the .fla. It is a series of radial gradients that are tweened to scale and alpha much like the light effects you have just created. This is placed on top of Letter R at the point where the normal light animation would begin.

That's all there is to the Ray of Light effect. It can get rather tedious and complicated at times, but it's really more a matter of practice and patience than anything else. You can add in other details - different gradients, or colors to create more elaborate animated lights. You could also change the details in each of the individual lights, so that they are made up of pieces, like the one on the Ray of Light Productions site.

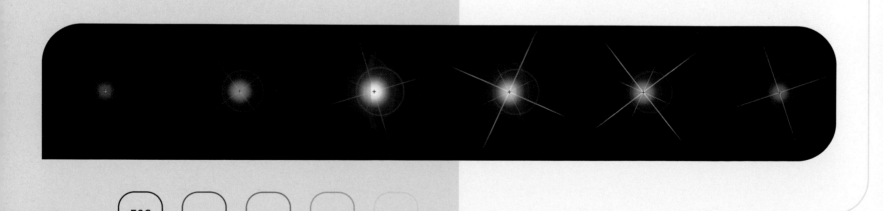

Anne's Dress

The basics of this effect and animation are rather simple. Anne's dress falls into the cartoon category of animation. The effect is created by redrawing the entire dress a split second after the frame that came before it, and then the next frame and the next, and so on until the entire animation loops. The last frame leads back into the very first frame. This process was pretty tedious and time consuming to build, and it requires more artistic skill than programming knowledge. You'll find it easier if you have tried this sort of animation before.

I drew the first frame of the animation by hand on a piece of paper, after many character sketches. I used pencils, and then traced over with a pen. I scanned in that image as a bitmap, and then imported it into Flash and traced it using the Trace Bitmap function. I broke the image down into four sections: Anne's head, her ponytail, her body, and her dress. The first and most difficult part of the animation was the dress, so I began with that.

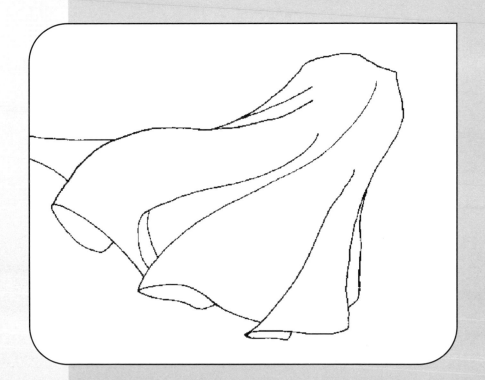

Rays

The first frame was simply the one that I'd just scanned and imported, but the others were rendered in Flash. I wanted to keep the animation to around twenty frames so I began by inserting keyframes every five frames until frame 20. This helped me to estimate where the animation would be at those points in time, and fill in the rest of the frames as those took shape. I used the Pen tool in Flash, and tried to keep the number of lines I used to a minimum in order to keep the file size low. The animation I ended up with was twenty frames long, but the transition from the last frame back to the first was not fluent enough, so I inserted a few more frames. The total animation for her dress finished at twenty-six frames, six more than I had anticipated.

The animation for Anne's head and shirt were very similar but didn't require nearly as many frames or as much animation.

I used four keyframes in addition to the initial keyframe, with a frame separating each of these to slow the transitions, although smoothness isn't necessary to complete the overall effect. The effect was created for was a piece called the *Allegory of the Seasons*, which I put together for the Infect World Flash Contest – it's on the CD. I hope you enjoy it as much as I enjoyed creating it.

If there's one thought I want to leave you with it is there is one thing that most of the excellent Flash work that you will see out there has in common: the best effects are time-consuming and can be pretty tedious to achieve. You have to put in a lot of hard work to make your effects really good.

And while ActionScripting can help alleviate the endurance test that tweening individual letters and elements can be, ActionScript is itself another delicate matter that requires a good deal of dedication. But, if you're able to use anything I've written about here in your own work, then I'll be glad in the knowledge that I have at least done my little bit to inspire another artist. Good Flash work isn't built so much on knowledge of the program or tool manipulation, but rather your imagination, and your approach to the tools made available to you. Don't let what others teach you, or how you learnt to use these tools, hinder the things your own imagination can bring to your work.

Boundaries don't hold us, don't let them hold you... the only boundary is your imagination

outro

"It is more rewarding to explore than to reach conclusions, more satisfying to wonder than to know, and more exciting to search than to stay put."

JOSHUA DAVIS
www.once-upon-a-forest.com

"Creating complexity from simplicity"

A look into Chaos Theory, nature, and applied interactive design in Flash.

by Joshua Davis

http://www.cyphen.com | http://www.praystation.com | http://www.once-upon-a-forest.com

Unite : Communicate : Explore | http://www.dreamless.org | http://www.antiweb-chaos.com

Kioken Incorporated : Senior Design Technologist | http://www.kioken.com

Scene : 01 / 13

Hi. My name is Joshua Davis and I'm a web developer here in New York City.

I would just like to extend a special thank you to friends of Ed for giving me the chance to stop working for a little bit and write down for you some of my thoughts and ideas. New Masters of Flash has collected together some of the finest web artists that I know, who've given you, I hope, more than a few "Aah.. that's how you do it" revelations. I want to round off this book with something a little different. I want to show you the way I think, not only the process but also the mentality of why I build the things that I build. I'd like to set you thinking in maybe a different way yourself so that you can turn what you've learnt here into something that you've never done before.

Get ready for a little science, some math, some models of CHAOS, a little bit on nature, fractals and, something that's important to me, UI. UI can be user interface, user interaction, or more interestingly, you and I – the relationship between two things that hardly know that the other exists.

I just first wanted to touch on a few misconceptions. Several people have come up to me at conferences and have e-mailed me personally saying that "you guys" are crazy or "your team" is very helpful. I just need to let everyone know that it's just me (though I have been known to team up with other developers to create new hybrid experiences). I think that it's important for you to know this.

Joshua Davis

Matt Owens from www.volumeone.com, who is my next door neighbor, sat with me one day and we talked about how we have all grown up in the 'Fugazi – do it yourself' mentality. For me, this means that you are your own most valuable resource. Sure, for commercial work, you may need a group of people to work on fairly large-scale projects and there is a structure for that. However, all of you can do what I'm doing. You don't need a team. If you have the passion and the motivation, you can do what I have done. And I'm nobody special; just a humble New York City Subway passenger amusing himself to death in Williamsburg Brooklyn.

Another misconception is that I fully understand the ins and outs of mathematics. I haven't a clue about any type of math whatsoever. In the late eighties I was a sponsored amateur skateboarder, and trust me, I wasn't going anywhere near a math class. This lack of math knowledge has led me to develop a habit of using what I call *Slam Mathematics*. Slam Mathematics is not understanding math. It's just a process of taking a movie clip and * it by 2 and / it by 1000 and + the difference of space between another object. What happens is that I get a whole load of messy accidents and it's in looking at these accidents that I uncover new techniques for doing things.

I recently spoke at a Flash conference here in New York City. There I tried to stress the importance of not understanding things. It's in the search to uncover new ideas that you find accidents. It's in those accidents that you observe new techniques.

So what does this mean?

In college I was studying to be a children's book illustrator and I was doing oil painting on paper. At one point I wanted to know what would happened if I set my paintings on fire. So I did just that. And in the process I observed an effect. What I found out was that if you mixed oil-based resins and placed your work in your oven at 450 degrees, the two resins would separate from each other and crack. So I rubbed the entire surface of the painting with black oil paint, took a dry cloth and very softly removed all of the black. This process removed the paint from the top surface, but most of the paint settled in between the cracks where the resins had separated. I had created these modern images but given them the feeling of being hundreds of years old. So, it was through not understanding something and experimenting with setting my artwork on fire that I uncovered something new.

I'll expand on this idea a little more. One day a few years ago, I walked into my mother's kitchen. I opened up a cabinet and found a bottle of red food coloring. I looked at the bottle, which said that it was non-toxic, so I tilted my head back and dropped a few drops of food coloring into my eyes. Now I don't suggest you all run out and try this, but I promise that result is pretty intense. For about twenty seconds, the whole world was tinted red.

Chaos

Now that I've given you pretty descriptive examples of how important exploration and discovery are to me, I hope that the rest of this chapter will inspire you to uncover new ideas. To be successful designers and technologists, we need the courage to let go of the old world, to relinquish most of what we have cherished and to abandon our interpretations about what does and doesn't work.

I'll use Einstein to back me up here:

"No problem can be solved from the same consciousness that created it."

While there are great resources and fantastic web sites on the net, we must look beyond the Web's boundaries for inspiration to bring to the table something never seen before. So where do I get mine from? Nature. Tons of science, physics in particular (even though the more I read the more confused I get). I love literature on Chaos Theory. I dislike the way that we have spent the better part of our lives trying to organize, classify, file, associate, identify, label and dissect everything that we see. So I sit down and I think about nature and chaos. I think about randomness, patterns, signals and the nature of living in this pulse.

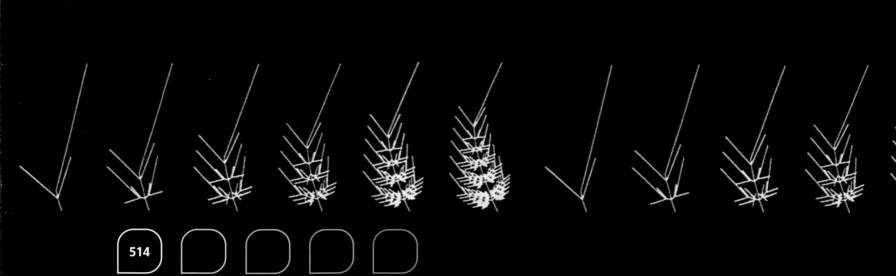

Joshua Davis

So how does this Chaos Theory, nature stuff relate to applied interactive design?

When I found this image of a fern, I thought it was the coolest thing I had ever seen. I used it for my conference presentation and I want to incorporate it into my writing here because I love the idea of deconstructing a plant as I talk about utilizing Flash in a whole new way.

"Strange as it seems, the basic shape of a fern can be captured in a simple stick drawing. To make a fern of curving, intricate complexity, all that is required is this simple shape, and a few basic rules. The only rules are that the stick shape is free to repeat itself at many different levels of scale, that it is placed in an upright direction, and that it connects with what is already on the page. From this combination of a few simple rules and high levels of autonomy – of order and chaos working in tandem - emerges the beautiful complexity of a fern."

(Margaret J. Wheatley, Leadership and the New Science, 1994, page 131)

Building a complex well-crafted piece doesn't just happen overnight. As you start out on a project, although you might have an idea of the total scope, I would encourage you not to think about the entire picture, but to start from a very stripped down foundation. Our work should reflect the nature of this fern and be comprised of tiny little objects that all talk to each other. The more we add these little objects, the more complex and intense the nature of our work becomes.

Chaos

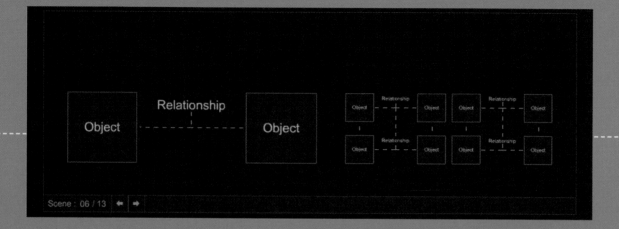

You can see here that we've started with two simple objects, with a relationship between them. The more of these little objects we add, the more dialog there is between them and, out of that, the site slowly grows into something dynamic and complex. But it's still built on the principles of simplicity.

So where does 'relationship' come from?

The quantum mechanical view of reality strikes against most of our notions of our own reality. It is a world where the word *relationship* is the key determiner of what is observed and how particles manifest themselves. Particles come into being and are observed only in terms of how they relate to something else. They do not exist as independent beings.

Now this doesn't translate into anything concrete in terms of my awareness of the universe and everything – but it does get me thinking. So I open up Flash to illustrate the quantum theory that I've just laid out. I create two movie clips, one called 01 and the other, 02. I then create a 100 pixel line, set at a 45 degree angle within a third movie clip. I tell that third movie clip to:

```
duplicateMovieClip ("line", "newLine1", 1);
setProperty ("newLine1", _x, getProperty("square", _x));
setProperty ("newLine1", _y, getProperty("square", _y));
setProperty ("newLine1", _xscale, getProperty("cross", _x)-getProperty("square", _x));
setProperty ("newLine1", _yscale, getProperty("cross", _y)-getProperty("square", _y));
```

Then I loop the action and it continues to re-draw a line between my two movie clips. The quantum theory that lies behind this is that clip 01 doesn't know that clip 02 even exists or vice versa and, while they don't change themselves, what does change is the line or 'relationship' between them.

Sometimes, even the most profound principles yield amazing results when taken out of context.

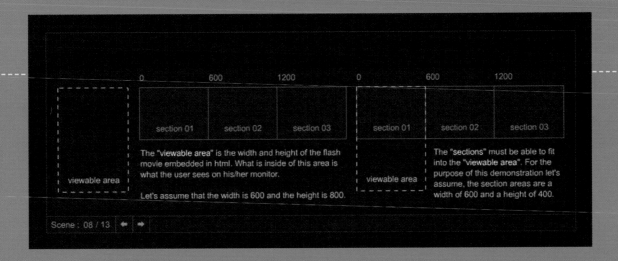

The "viewable area" is the width and height of the flash movie embedded in html. What is inside of this area is what the user sees on his/her monitor.

Let's assume that the width is 600 and the height is 800.

The "sections" must be able to fit into the "viewable area". For the purpose of this demonstration let's assume, the section areas are a width of 600 and a height of 400.

Scene : 08 / 13

Construction, Deconstruction and Reconstruction

OK, we have that idea as a good foundation and we're ready to start building. At the beginning of the design process, thoughts are flushed out, shifted around and cleaned up – there's a construction of what the final piece is going to look like. Then that finished art is put through a process of deconstruction, where the parts are separated into pieces that we will later reconstruct, in this case, using Flash. This is where we add our elements of interactivity and compound simple objects with simple properties to create complexity over time.

You've ripped your constructed layout apart into separate objects – you now must take on the role of the builder and define your environment for construction. Knowing where to buy bricks doesn't mean you know how to build a house, so take your time to think about the individual objects within your project, and how strong the links are between them to hold the project together soundly. Just as like the fern, our Flash project needs a firm foundation from which to grow and a set of parameters within which individual objects communicate and repeat themselves.

We now have two objects: the viewable area and the sections. At this point, we're going to introduce the 'relationship' between them, which is a third object, called the markers.

Chaos

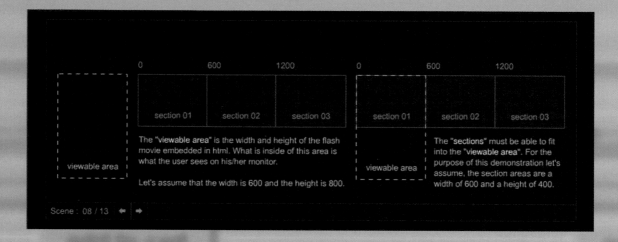

You can see that section 1 fits into the viewable area snugly. The viewable area, section 01 and the first marker all sit at 0 on the _x scale. All of the content is lined up at 0.

Now if we were to press the button which reads move to **section 02**, it would turn off the actions on marker # 1 and turn on the actions on marker # 2 – which is sitting at –600 on the _x scale.

Now the code sees that everything is not lined up at 0 anymore, that the marker has changed position:

```
marker = getProperty("/marker", _x);
sections = getProperty("/sections", _x);
difference = marker-sections;
move = difference/5;
setProperty ("/sections", _x, Number(sections)+Number(move));
```

Now this loop evaluates where the marker is on the _x scale, where the sections are on the _x scale and then calculates the difference between the two objects. A variable for movement is set up and then we use Set Property to move the sections _x position to the difference between the objects divided by an amount.

So every time the loop runs it evaluates "Where am I ?","Where do I need to go?" "Let's go (for the purpose of understanding) half the distance."

Essentially, your sections would make bigger jumps in the first initial runs of the loop and then would slowly decrease their movement as they get closer to their marker. As long as your markers are set up in the right place – by turning on and off the marker names – the sections will constantly be trying to line up with whatever marker has been turned on.

518

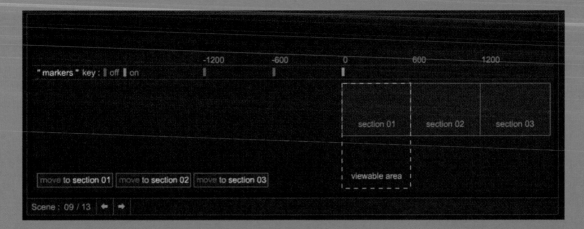

Now let's add a fourth object: menus. The menus are evaluating which marker has been turned on. They are also attracted to the marker, plus an offset number, so they appear to be floating within our sections.

Menu 1:

```
marker = getProperty("/marker", _x);
menu1 = getProperty("/menu1", _x);
difference = marker-menu1;
move = difference/4;
setProperty ("/menu1", _x, menu1, add (move))+4);
```

Menu 2:

```
marker = getProperty("/marker", _x);
menu2 = getProperty("/menu2", _x);
difference = marker-menu2;
move = difference/4;
setProperty ("/menu2", _x, menu2, add (move))+29);
```

Menu 3:

```
marker = getProperty("/marker", _x);
menu3 = getProperty("/menu3", _x);
difference = marker-menu3;
move = difference/4;
setProperty ("/menu3", _x, menu3, add (move))+54);
```

Using the same exact principal as the sections, the menus look for the marker and are attracted to the marker plus the offset number, so they kick back a bit into our sections: Menu1 +4 – Menu2 +29 – Menu3 +54.

Chaos

The menus now need properties that allow them to interact with their foundation, or viewable area. Establish the _y position of a menu. If the menu is within a specific _y position, it runs. If it's outside, it stops.

```
on (press) {
    gotoAndStop (5);
    startDrag ("", false, 0, 104, 767, 230);
}
on (release, releaseOutside) {
    posY = getProperty("/menu1", _y);
    if (Number(posY) >103 and Number(posY) <156) {
        gotoAndPlay (1);
    } else {
        gotoAndStop (5);
    }
    stopDrag ();
}
```

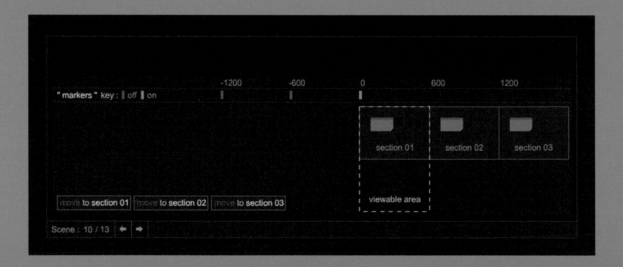

This sets up that invisible line and allows our objects to execute two separate instructions based on where they reside on the _y scale of our viewable area.

_y position = 103

goto 1 and play "play action "

_y position = 156

else

_y position = greater than 157 ?
goto 5 and stop " stop action "

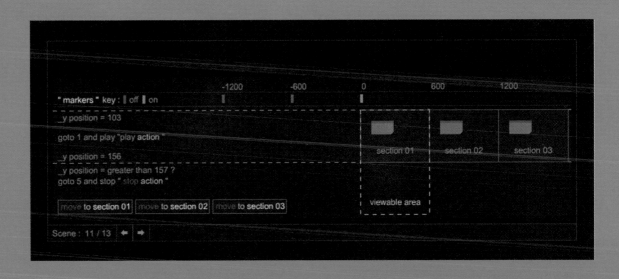

Chaos

Once Upon a Forest

What I've tried to get across here is how web design is about building forms of communication and relationships between separate objects that form the base of your web project's world.

Say you walk outside and find an enormous tree. The tree is old and its still standing rock solid to this earth. Why ? How did it withstand the forces of nature ?

A tree is an object. It exists in an environment, an environment based on rules.

Working in the web is no different - you're building objects, and they need to be designed into an environment - an environment based on the rules and boundaries of technology, and any additional rules you program. Any object, or button, or navbar, or menu you design should be fastened rock solid to your layout or environment that's just as strong as the roots that hold that tree to the ground.

Joshua Davis

once-upon-a-forest.com

Once upon a forest and many blades of grass ago, I was of the age of adventure and daydreaming. (Stardust and Twilight Ashes)

It's a digital black hole.

(Q.) What is "Once Upon A Forest" ?

(A.) Once upon a forest and several blades of grass ago... - It is the first four words of a children's book I wrote entitled "Stardust and Twilight Ashes".

(Q.) Who is Maruto ?

(A.) Maruto is a fictional character I have created to explore design, sound, and digital story telling.

(Q.) What is he doing ?

(A.) Maruto is attempting to define the surroundings and environment of his fictional world with motion and sound. In the beginning, the forest was static, but, little by little, Maruto is learning how to open up more portions of his reality to us through interactive installations.

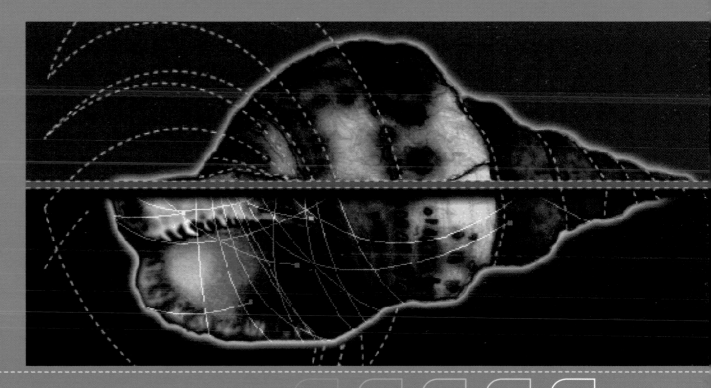

Chaos

As such an avid lover of children's books, I had been turned on to the work of an amazing artist and writer, Chris Van Alsburg. In one of his books, *The Mysteries of Harris Burdick*, he presents an amazing concept which was silently to become the foundation that I'd been looking for to start building my work upon.

The story is about a man named Harris Burdick who visits Alsburg to show him his illustrations. He also explains that he has written stories that accompany the drawings. Mr. Alsburg proceeds to explore Mr. Burdick's portfolio. He finds the most enchanting drawings and, at the bottom of each illustration, a quick block of copy that sets the scene of what the full story might be about.

Mr. Alsburg asks to see the rest of the stories. Mr. Burdick agrees to leave his portfolio and return the next day with the full stories that accompany the drawings. However, Mr. Burdick never returns. Days go by and still no word from the mysterious Mr. Burdick. Alsburg has no means of contacting him. Mr. Burdick has vanished without a trace.

A long time passes. Mr. Alsburg approaches his publisher, tells him the whole story of Mr. Burdick and shows him the portfolio that he left but never picked up.

They agree that it would be a shame not to let the world see the wonderful work of Mr. Burdick. So they publish the book, *The Mysteries of Harris Burdick*, a collection of single page illustrations accompanied with a quick tout about what the full story might have been.

You turn each page to see a wonderful set of imagery and some copy to set the tone. But it's your imagination that kicks in. You try desperately to search your mind for ideas of what the stories might have been about.

I heard that elementary teachers have given the book as homework assignments to help children with creative writing – pick a page and create the story. As an adult, though, you realize that there is no Harris Burdick. Mr. Alsburg has done all of the drawings and created the copy for each of the illustrations. It was the presentation of an idea and the fabrication of the character that had become a means to inspire a generation of children.

I felt at that moment that I had all the pieces I needed in order to create the online narrative and interactive net art experience that is once-upon-a-forest.com: a digital black hole where I could amuse myself to death.

In college, I had majored in illustration/communication design and minored in art history. I very much love the idea of incorporating history from the past, myths and folklore, mixed in juxtaposition with modern day movements and even touches of advances in science and philosophy.

For example on January 2000 – the current buzz was the issue of Y2K and the fear of Armageddon. We were so focused on time and the flaws of technology that some were rationing food and creating bunkers, let's call them the "obsessive doomsday fanatics". We know in history and myth that the Mayans too played an important role in mapping out time and had concluded that the world would end December 2012. So it made perfect sense to mark two positions in time, which would mark the apocalypse – giving them a sense of reassurance that if the world didn't end on January 2000 the next point of interest would be 2012 – ah, something to look forward to if you're obsessed with world destruction.

Joshua Davis

OK, we've established that my character Maruto has a sense of humor – but how many people actually picked up on the meaning of the two dates prior to me telling anyone just now? I think, to date, I have received 10 e-mails asking why I mention both dates of destruction. However, the bigger success was with the thousands of e-mails I received about "what does it all mean?"

Ah, the nature of confusion and CHAOS – what an amazing and powerful tool. If only for a few moments – visitors might take some time to imagine what might be going on – like a game or puzzle – trying desperately to accumulate the logic to understand why they are being presented with highlighted icons, background, and soundscape.

once-upon-a-forest is the nemesis of what we perceive the web to be. No easy, short domain name. No easy to use navigation. No instructions. No Faqs. No Ads, No Links, No Tech Support. No Help. No Answers.

The basic e-mail function is used to receive mail - but in the several months the work has been online - NO ONE has ever received a response or reply e-mail from Once-Upon-A-Forest.

 The work is meant to provoke questions not answer them.

No building can be built without a solid foundation.

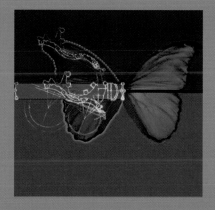
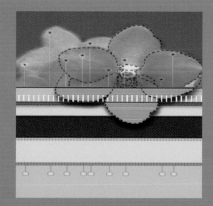
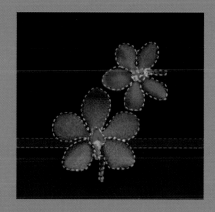

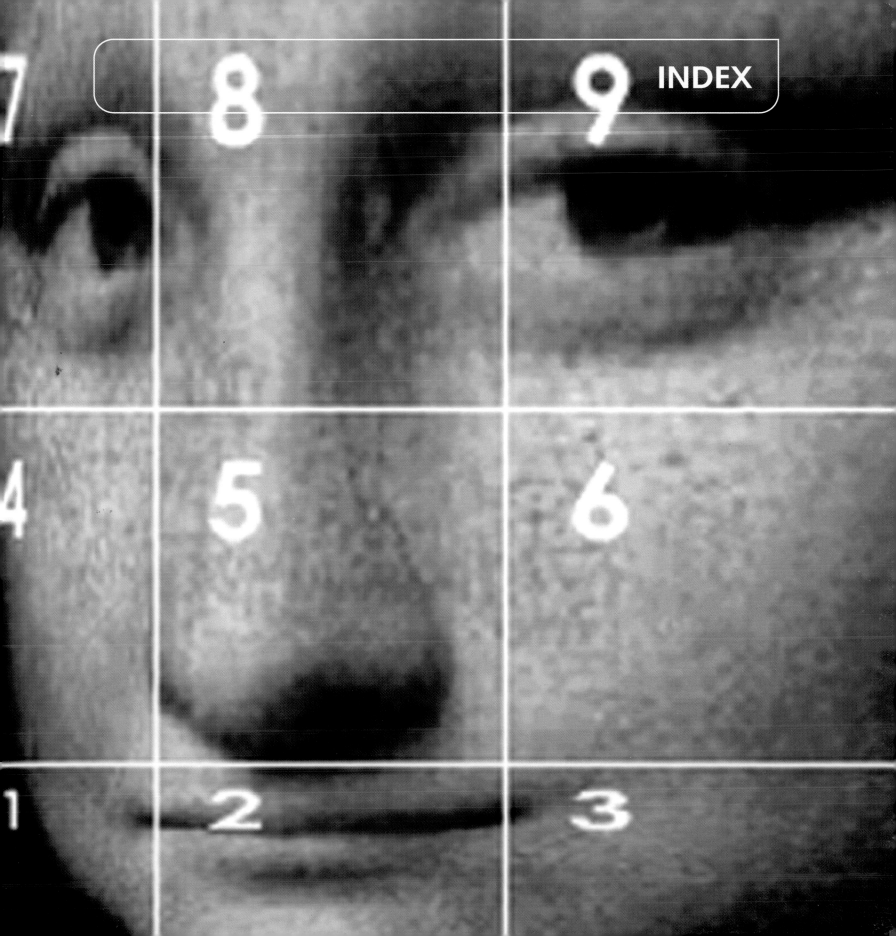

Symbols

A

B

C

S

We hope that you've enjoyed New Masters of Flash.

Whatever you think, please mail us at feedback@friendsofed.com to let us know.

We'll try to take everything you say on board, ready for the next New Masters.

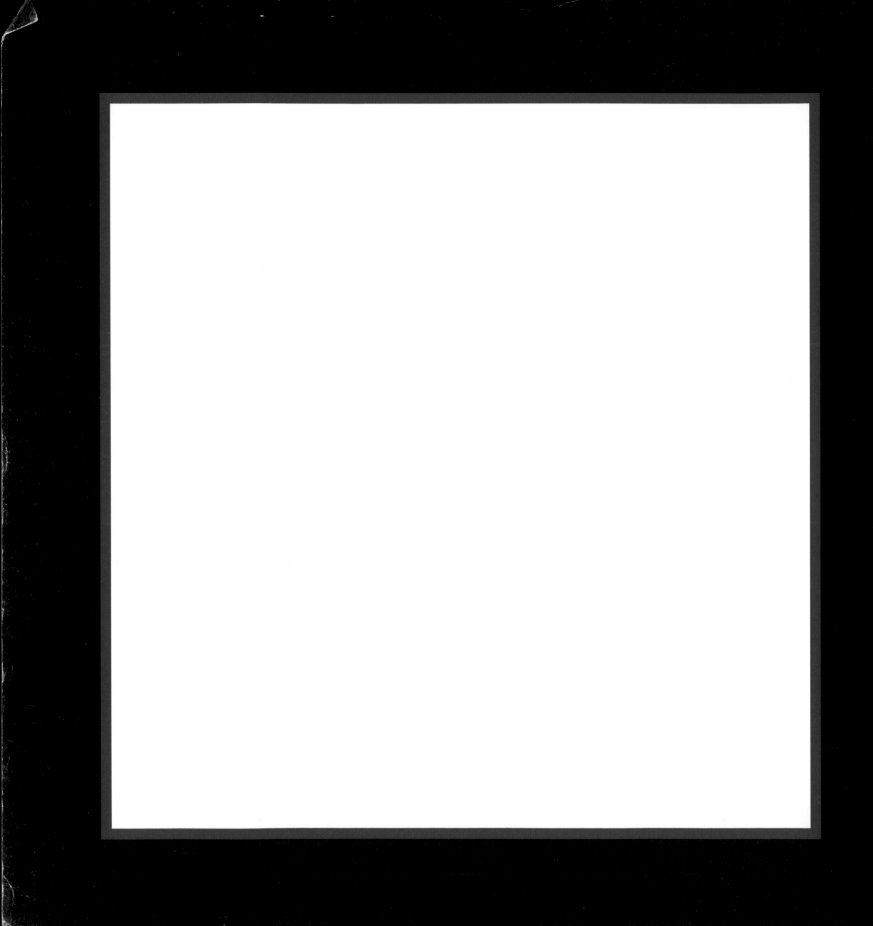

The CD-Rom was designed and built by

The New Media Works Ltd.
3rd Floor
Lupus House
11-13 Macklin Street
Covent Garden
London
WC2B 5NH

Tel: +44 207 8313391
Fax: +44 207 4044320
E-mail: info@newmediaworks.co.uk

Our thanks to Phil, Mark, Paul and all the guys for their great work.